St Martin's Island
An introductory history of forty-two Exeter buildings

St Martin's Island

An introductory history of forty-two Exeter buildings

Todd Gray & Sue Jackson

© The Mint Press & Todd Gray
& Sue Jackson 2017

No part of this publication may be reproduced, stored in a retrieval system or transmitted, in any form or by any means, electronic, mechanical, photocopying, recording or otherwise, without the prior permission in writing of the copyright holders, or as expressly permitted by law, or under terms agreed with the appropriate reprographics rights organisation.

Cover Illustration: detail of the Caleb Hedgeland model at the Royal Albert Memorial Museum.

ISBN 978 1 903356 71 5

The Mint Press,
Taddyforde House South,
Taddyforde Estate,
New North Road,
Exeter EX4 4AT.

Distribution through Stevensbooks:
www.stevensbooks.co.uk
sales@themintpress.co.uk
Telephone: 01392 459760.

Text and Cover designed by
Topics – The Creative Partnership
Exeter, Devon.
email: topics@eclipse.co.uk
www.topicsdesign.co.uk

Printed and bound in Great Britain by
Short Run Press Ltd, Exeter, Devon.

To the memory of

Ethel Lega-Weekes,

a campaigner for Exeter, whose research on

Cathedral Green has remained the

definitive work a century after it was written.

Contents

Acknowledgements		6
Introduction		7
	The parish of St Martin and its church	12
	The development of Exeter and changing perceptions of buildings	12
	The development of St Martin's Island	24
	The streets	27
	The buildings	28
	The residents	30
	The businesses	32
	The fires	36
1	High Street	39
2	Broadgate	106
3	Cathedral Yard	114
4	Martin's Lane	150
5	Lamb Alley	160
6	The Little or New Exchange	162
Conclusion		166
Abbreviations		172
References		173
Index		185
Sources of Illustrations		191

Acknowledgements

We have accumulated numerous debts of gratitude and would like to acknowledge the generous help given by Elly Babbedge, Sadhru Bhanji, Stuart Blaylock, Yvonne Cleave, Tony Collings, Professor Chris Dyer, Simon Hall, Yvonne Hensman, Susie Hewitt, Pete Jackson, Colin Laskey, Richard Lawrence, Darren Marsh, Hamish Marshall, Ian Maxted, Will Michelmore, Dr Lawrence Normand, Meriel O'Dowd, Dr Elizabeth Parkinson, Dr Robert Peberdy, Derek Portman, Andy Pye, Margaret Reed, Dr Alan Rosevear, Margery Rowe, Jennie Sampson, Dr Richard Stephens, Keith Stevens, Iris Sutton, John Thorp, Simon Timms, Deborah Tritton and Ed Williams-Hawkes. The staffs in the Island businesses have been welcoming and helpful in opening their buildings to examination. We are also grateful to the private collectors who have allowed the reproduction of their images.

John Allan and Richard Parker have been supportive throughout this project in sharing their knowledge and expertise and we are particularly indebted to them for the time and care with which they have read the text.

We would like to thank the staffs in the archives and libraries in which research has taken place as well as Sophie Clapp (Boots Archive), Peter Judge (Group Archives & Museums – Lloyds), Robin Richardson (J. Wippell & Co. Ltd), Maggie Goodall (Society for the Protection of Ancient Buildings), Anna Stone (Aviva PLC), Sally Cholewa (RBS Archives), Seth Michael James (Lilly Library), Max Clark (Kendal Archive Centre), Susannah Coster (The Postal Museum), Rory Lalwan (City of Westminster Archives Centre), Peter Monteith (King's College Archives), John Porter (Prudential PLC) and Customer Services (Office for National Statistics).

Finally, we would like to thank Devon Historic Buildings Trust for its financial support for the reproduction of images and Historic England for a publication grant which made this volume possible.

Exeter
September 2017

Introduction

1. The Royal Clarence Hotel on fire, 12.18pm, 28 October 2016.

In the early hours of 28 October 2016 fire broke out in Exeter's 18 Cathedral Yard. This Victorian building was soon consumed and over the course of that morning flames spread across the adjoining roofs of the Well House and then to those of the Royal Clarence Hotel. By the end of the day the hotel was also destroyed and a number of adjacent properties in Martin's Lane and High Street were damaged.

This sudden loss in the heart of Exeter, particularly of the hotel, was a great shock to local people. Extensive and prolonged national, and even international, media coverage seized upon the building's reputation as the country's oldest hotel and the fire had a public profile that no other incident in Exeter has had for many decades.

Hamish Marshall, East Devon Reporter for BBC Spotlight, recalled:

'I was called to Cathedral Green when the fire spread to the Royal Clarence. My colleague Harriet, who lived nearby, had been there since the fire first broke out in the adjoining

St Martin's Island: An introductory history of forty-two Exeter buildings

2. The interior of the Royal Clarence Hotel, 30 October 2016.
3. The ruins after the fire, with Martin's Lane to the left, 30 October 2016.
4. The demolition of the hotel's upper floors, 4.48pm, 2 November 2016.
5. The rear of 16 to 18 Cathedral Yard nearly ten months after the fire, 11 August 2017.

3.

4.

2.

8

Introduction

The Coat of Arms as it appeared on the top of the Hotel's facade prior to the fire.

5.

building. With it being a fire in an empty building and everyone accounted for she was dealing with the story. But then when a historic building became involved we knew this needed more than just a standard report. I rushed to the scene to join additional camera crews and our satellite truck to report events as they happened. For the next eight hours it was very busy. Reporting live for radio and television, filing the latest information and gathering reaction. We filmed the fire at the Royal Clarence and heard from experts like Todd Gray, got the latest information from the fire service, spoke to traders who had been forced to close their businesses and from members of the public who had come to see what was happening, many had personal memories of the Clarence. The operation continued through the afternoon and we prepared to have a large section of our television news programme devoted to the incident. I remember going down to the River Exe to see a special pump float on the water to bring water to the fire ground. The power of that and the volume of water it could shift was amazing. Then it was back to the site to do some live reports into BBC Radio Devon and prepare my introduction to the 6.30 television news programme. I had to set the scene and explain the significance of the day's events – the pictures we have gathered helped show the rest of the south west how serious this was. We had a colleague live on the High Street showing how the fire had affected the heart of Exeter. We heard live from Todd Gray to give the historical perspective and the Chief Fire Officer who explained how difficult the firefighting had been with the age of the buildings being a major factor. Our coverage continued through the evening and into Saturday. I was back on site at 5.30 on Sunday to bring the latest news to the national BBC Breakfast TV programme and the fire was still burning. That day services resumed at the cathedral. Eventually the fire was put out but the reporting would go on. Demolition, re-opening of the High Street in stages, impact on small traders on Cathedral Green, a service of thanks at the Cathedral and plans for the re-build. The impact of that day will live long in Exeter for years to come.'[1]

Richard Lawrence, Exeter Reporter for ITV Westcountry, recalled:

'I'd been called first thing in the morning to head to Cathedral Green where the former Michelmores building above the art gallery was well alight. That was sad enough. The former board room on the first floor was perhaps one of the most ornate in Exeter featuring floor to ceiling mirrors and ostentatious marble plaster work and chandeliers. The last time I was in it was when Occupy Exeter squatters took over the building but they were so in awe of the room they didn't let anyone in it. The fire crews were working hard tackling the flames above and below and by half past nine it was virtually extinguished. We were stood outside the west door of the Cathedral and could still see a small fire on the second or third floor towards the rear of the former Michelmores building on the right hand side and alerted fire crews. At that time some firefighters were heading back to their muster points and there was a general feeling the operation was being wound down. We were waiting to interview the fire commander and around ten thirty, just before we started, I asked him how it all was and he said 'yes, fingers crossed!' Another firefighter had just reassured him that everything was pretty much out but there was just a couple of spots they were still watching over. The interview focused on how they'd overcome the intense fire and whether they would be able to reopen the high street soon to traffic and pedestrians. We soon finished the interview but probably less than thirty seconds later, as we were walking away, we were alarmed to see a menacing barrel of smoke that appeared to roll right along the top of the frontage of the Royal Clarence Hotel from left to right. At that point I have to admit I thought the battle was lost. We were all deeply shocked to see the thick plumes of dark cloud of smoke grow. It was clear that the fire had made its way right through the roof voids. Earlier I had called the news desk to let them know everything looked under control. But now I called them to tell them this was likely to be a major story – the building known as England's oldest hotel was on fire. I felt it would only be a matter of time before parts of the building would be destroyed. We started to show a live feed of the scene on social media using the periscope app on our mobile phones and soon were attracting thousands of viewers from all over the world. I knew Todd Gray, who was standing with us, knew the layout of the surrounding medieval buildings and I introduced him to the fire commanders to advise them. The ITV Westcountry news desk agreed to send another reporter and presenter to ensure the story got the comprehensive coverage it merited from the efforts of the firefighters to its historic significance'.[2]

Simon Hall, Home Affairs Correspondent for BBC Spotlight, reflected on the impact of the fire. He recalled:

'It took a week after flames devoured the Royal Clarence to truly understand why the loss of the historic hotel caused such shock and sadness. The magnificent facade was left standing after the fire, and only knocked down days later for recovery work to begin. I was there with three BBC camera crews, broadcasting live, to witness the poignant moment. Millions around the world saw the facade fall, and thousands made the journey to see it in person. After the facade had been demolished, we had to interview spectators about what they had seen. Often, it can take a while for a television reporter to persuade people to go on camera. But not this time. This time, everyone wanted to speak out, because everyone had a story about the Royal Clarence. I met a couple who spent their wedding night there, another who celebrated the birth of their first child there, and a young woman who marked her graduation there. There were countless other such stories. That was what the Royal Clarence meant to the area, the story behind the headline images of the destruction. It was a place where the seminal moments of life were marked. That was why the loss of the hotel caused such shock'.[3]

The fire of 2016 is uncannily reminiscent of another generation's fire in this same block of buildings. It was concluded of a fire in 1881 that it was 'on so large a scale that at one time it seemed to threaten destruction of the whole block of buildings between the Broadgate on the one side and Martin's Lane on the other. Had there been any wind to fan the flames, this in all probability would have been the result, for unfortunately by far the greater portion of the premises in the main street of the city appear to be built of material specially adapted for feeding a fire'.[4] One hundred and thirty five years later Exeter once again had a near miss.

The recent fire has been the catalyst for unprecedented public interest in Exeter for its ancient buildings: a sense of loss has been accompanied by a reawakened appreciation of surviving historic buildings. This volume is a response to this. It incorporates existing detailed research conducted by building specialists in recent decades but its core is the result of only a

Introduction

year's investigation into original sources. It provides 'biographies' of the four dozen buildings which make up *St Martin's Island*, the near rectangular block of properties in the parish of St Martin which is bounded by High Street, Broadgate, Cathedral Yard and Martin's Lane. The term was coined shortly after the fire but 'island' had been used to described this block of buildings as far back as 1881. Each of the four thoroughfares outlining the island have had an evolution in their names and the recent creation of other place names can be seen in Exeter in such places as Princesshay (1949), Guildhall Shopping Centre (early 1970s) and the Corn Exchange of just a few years ago.[5]

This block is unusual for Exeter in the number of ancient buildings. Three buildings were destroyed in the great fire of 1881 but not one was destroyed during the Baedeker raids of 1942 which otherwise decimated the city centre. Instead, it was during the post-war years that buildings were lost. Five were in High Street. In 1963 several properties were demolished in order to erect a new store for Lillywhites (now occupied by Burger King). A second set lies at the west end: 61 to 63 High Street were destroyed by an arson attack in 1975 (now Trailfinders). Another group of buildings were demolished in the early 1960s in Cathedral Yard.

There are also highly significant buildings in the Island. The row from 39 to 47 High Street is one of the most important in the city[6] and ranks alongside other groups such as 192 to 203 High Street, Three Gables (3–5 Little Stile, Cathedral Yard), 1 to 13 Cathedral Close, 58 to 68 South Street, and 118 to 125 as well as 150 to 154a Fore Street.

The Island's buildings also have an unusually high survival rate of ancient documents. The parish register was heavily damaged during the city's Blitz in 1942[7] but there is a long series of nineteenth-century rates.[8] Most important of all are the high number of deeds and leases, extending back to the 1200s, which survive in the city and cathedral archives. Many of the latter were sent in 1862 to the Ecclesiastical Commissioners in London but nearly all were returned to the cathedral archive from the 1970s to the 1990s. Some of these missing documents have recently been located.[9]

The deeds and leases are supplemented by an important, and hitherto unused, collection of Tothill family papers which are now held by the Somerset Heritage Centre. This Exeter family came to live at Peamore, a country house three miles from the city in Exminster parish, which they acquired in 1554 upon the execution of Henry Grey, Duke of Suffolk and father of Lady Jane Grey.[10] The family held a number of buildings in the Island at the Reformation: on 27 March 1545 William Tothill (Mayor in 1552) and his son Geoffrey (later Recorder and M.P. for Exeter in 1563, 1571 and 1572), purchased four properties which had belonged to St John's Hospital in Exeter. These tenements were described as being near the Guildhall and in the parish

6. Numbers 43 – 47 High Street, 8 September 2017.

11

of St Martin.[11] The family had also acquired at least two Exeter properties before the Dissolution[12] and leased others from the Dean & Chapter. Thus, in High Street they held Numbers 53, 54, 57, 58 and 59.

The family's land holdings passed in the early 1600s on the marriage of a Tothill heiress with a member of the Northleigh family. The properties subsequently passed in 1739 through the marriage of a later co-heiress with a member of the Hippisley-Coxe family of Ston Easton in Somerset. The other co-heiress was Miss Margaret Northleigh who in 1773 owned three properties in the Island (53, 54 & 59 High Street). She was declared in law a lunatic, her affairs were managed by her brother-in-law John Hippisley-Coxe and each Exeter property was sold within a generation.[13]

The parish papers are supplemented by an extensive amount of illustrative material which is in both public and private ownership. Other documentary material has been used from a wide range of archives most notably legal papers at the National Archives and insurance documents at the London Metropolitan Archives. There has been extensive use of newspapers with the most notable that of a previously unused bound volume of eighteenth-century editions of Exeter newspapers. This has been particularly relevant in understanding the early years of the Royal Clarence Hotel.

The parish of St Martin's and its church

Exeter has sixteen parishes within the mile and a half extent of ancient walls which encircle the city (Allhallows Goldsmith Street, Allhallows on the Walls, St George, Holy Trinity, St John, St Kerrian, St Lawrence, St Martin, St Mary Arches, St Mary Major, St Mary Steps, St Olave, St Pancras, St Paul, St Petrock and St Stephen). Two churches were built in the walls: these were Allhallows on the Walls and Holy Trinity. There were also four extra-parochial places (Bedford, Bradninch, Exeter Castle, Exeter Cathedral including the Close) and St David, St Edmund and St Sidwell are situated outside the walls. St Leonard was not incorporated into the city until 1877, St Thomas in 1900 and Heavitree[14] in 1913. Only seven parish churches survive within the city walls, one of which is St Martin, whereas five of the six of those outside the centre still exist.

The parish is Exeter's third smallest at 1.751 acres. Only St Petrock (at 1.687 acres) and St Pancras (at 1.744 acres) were smaller. Altogether there are some 93 acres within the city walls.[15] The parish boundaries are confusing as they are with many Exeter parishes. The Island makes up the entirety of the parish with the exception of two outliers. Firstly, there are two detached properties, 197 & 198 High Street, which are located directly across from the Island. Jigsaw and Ann Summers are the current occupiers. Secondly, the church itself is also detached and is situated across from the Island in Cathedral Close. It was argued in 1864 that the church was within the precincts of the Close and therefore outside of the bounds of its own parish.[16] There was once a building which adjoined the church tower on what may be empty land today. In 1741 it was described as 'under' the tower while another lease, in 1768, noted it was 'over' the tower. This latter building comprised a shop and a chamber 'commonly called the Cockpit'. In about 1630 an earlier lease noted two rooms, neither of which were in good repair. These were situated above a storeroom which measured 10 feet square and was six feet in height. The staircase 'ready to fall down' led to 'a personal room for lodging with a cockloft wherein no man can stand upright and another chamber open to the roof… the timber being old and rotten and the tile ready to fall down.'[17] The parish was combined with St Stephen in 1864 and its rector lived outside the parish of St Martin.[18]

The church is typical of the several dozen that were in and around Exeter: these were nearly all small structures built of the local red (or purple) stone and attached to surrounding properties. The tower is unusual for Devon in that it is placed on the north side of the church; some ninety per cent of the county's church towers are at the west end.[19] The dead of the parish were buried either in the church or in the cathedral churchyard (or later in the graveyard at Bartholomew Street).

The development of Exeter and changing perceptions of buildings

Exeter grew in prosperity through the late medieval period and remained one of England's leading commercial centres until the eighteenth century. The woollen cloth industry was the main economic stimulus but the city also benefited from being the centre of the diocese of Exeter and the region's retail hub. As with all English county towns, it was the focus for society and politics. This was aided by the county law courts being held in Rougemont Castle: Exeter swelled in population during the quarter sessions and the assizes. Devon's cloth trade reached

Introduction

7. Samples of Exeter cloth, 16 April 1764. Woollen cloth was the city's principal commodity.

St Martin's Island: An introductory history of forty-two Exeter buildings

8. Cloth samples from Henry Stocker & Company, tailors of 46 High Street, 1913–1933.

its economic peak in the early 1700s and had dissipated by the start of the nineteenth century. There was low population and economic growth in the Victorian period while other parts of Devon, notably Devonport, Plymouth and the coastal resorts, rapidly expanded.

The city's building fabric had two early periods of disruption. In the 1530s the Reformation effected a change of ownership, and subsequent use, of land held by the priories of St Nicholas and Polsloe as well as of the Franciscan Friary outside South Gate and the Dominican Friary in what is now Princesshay. It also reduced the need for diocesan and cathedral ancillary buildings which resulted in the conversion of canons' dwellings, including the later Royal Clarence Hotel, into secular uses. Then, a century later, the 1640s brought great destruction to buildings outside the city walls: the battles of the Civil War did not cause as much damage within the centre as it did to the surrounding suburbs although there was damage by soldiers and drastic alterations to such buildings as the Cloisters and the Bishop's Palace.[20]

Visitors' views of Exeter changed with the rise and fall of the economy. Their accounts also chronicled changing fashions in architecture. Early travellers praised the city. In 1694 Edmund Spoure visited from Cornwall and found Exeter to be 'a very sweet and a fine city, and except London or one or two cities more, perhaps the pleasantest and the most comfortable place to live in, without vanity I think in England'.[21] Other visitors wrote with similar enthusiasm and continued to do so until the mid 1700s. The walls, first erected by the Romans nearly two thousand years ago, encased most of the city with

9. Peter Berlon's trade card, 1768 – 1774.

the exceptions of some prominent communities outside; the parishes of St Thomas to the west and St Sidwell to the east were particularly populous and economically active. Gradually Exeter expanded outside its walls: the five gates were removed and Georgian developers built grand homes in and around Southernhay and throughout the parishes of St David, St Leonard and Heavitree.

The Georgian decline in commercial vitality was the cause for a slower redevelopment or upgrading of the city's architecture in the renewed Classical style. Far more fashionable than Exeter's existing building stock were the new buildings of Devonport or those being erected in the growing coastal resorts of Torquay, Sidmouth, Exmouth and Teignmouth. Hence, one visitor in 1760 was greatly disappointed with the 'London of the West'. Miss Girle thought the buildings were of 'an ancient model' of which she 'saw not any that can be called good'.[22] That same year an Italian was even less impressed. He wrote Exeter 'is one of the ugliest I have seen in England. The houses are so stupidly built that Vitrario and Palladio would have hanged themselves in vexation if they could have seen them. The streets are narrow, badly paved and full of filth and bad smells, and the inhabitants (of whom I saw a great number in two churches this morning and afternoon) are for the most part meagre and ill-dressed'.[23] Even so, a generation later another traveller admired Exeter's level of commerce and noted 'was it not for the vile manner in which it is paved, few cities would rival it.'[24] Robert Southey was more damning in 1802: he thought Exeter had 'the unsavoury odour of Lisbon'. He elaborated that it reminded him of the Portuguese city because of the 'beastly slovenliness or sluttishness or swinosity of its pork-people'. A few years earlier Southey had been even more abrupt: 'Exeter is ancient and it stinks'. He added 'the corporation used to compel people to keep their doors clean. Twelvemonths since it was discovered that they had no authority to do this, and now the people will not clean away the dirt, because they *can't force us to*'.[25]

It was at this time that one of Exeter's earliest historians commented on civic enhancement. Alexander Jenkins wrote in 1808 'the city had been greatly improved of late years by new buildings'. He thought that it was the year 1768 that Exeter's spirit of improvement 'now began to manifest itself'. He praised William Mackworth Praed for considering 'the lack of a commodious room for holding public baths, assemblies, concerts etc. being much complained of, the same gentleman built the [Royal Clarence] Hotel, in St Peter's Churchyard, in which he erected a large and elegant room for those purposes'.[26] Jenkins disregarded the destruction of the city's gates as ancient structures in his approval of civic improvement.

The formation of the Improvement Commission in 1806 was another sign of a growing awareness, and perhaps eventual consensus, that Exeter needed to update its sanitation, transport and housing. It came to lead the upgrading of the city albeit with the interference of the antiquated ruling elite.[27] The streets were described in the early 1800s as having pavements 'except for the great thoroughfares [which] consisted of rounded pebbles, locally known as pitching, so arranged as to secure a fall from the sides towards the centre of the road, which thus formed the gutter; this, in very nearly all the streets, was the only means whereby the sewage and nuisances of the city were removed'.[28] The Commission's work was given an added stimulus when cholera came to Exeter in 1832: buildings were demolished or reconstructed in order to allow light, air and water to reach the city's streets.[29] St Martin's parish had no cholera deaths although 402 individuals died across the city. The parish immediately to the west, St Petrock, also had no deaths but the highest number were only a few hundred yards away in the West Quarter.[30]

The working class increasingly dominated the residential character of the centre, within the ancient walls, as wealthier citizens moved into new suburban houses. In effect, owners abandoned their large sixteenth and seventeenth century townhouses, in which they had lived on the upper floors while the ground floor was reserved for workshops and retail. This was noted by John Cooke, a prominent Exonian in the early 1800s, who wrote 'you want both new houses for strangers… to come to Exeter and old houses and streets for the lower class'.[31]

By the middle of the nineteenth century there was another change: Exeter, like elsewhere, developed an appreciation of early buildings. In 1859 one traveller wrote the city had 'a great variety of all shops, it appears a very old town, the houses most remarkably built, very irregular, all gable ends and windows of all sorts'.[32] Eight years earlier Charles Knight more comprehensively summarised the buildings. He wrote 'the city hardly retains so much of the character of antiquity as might be expected. You may pass from end to end of the long High-street and Fore-street, and hardly have the attention attracted by any very remarkable feature; and equally so, from one extremity to the other of North and South Streets. Still there are appearances

10.

10 – 12. Three nineteenth-century views of 46 High Street. These arose from the Victorian appreciation of these buildings and, although sometimes unreliable, are nevertheless fundamental in chronicling changes in building fabric.

of antiquity, and if it had not been necessary, from time to time, to alter and improve the houses, it is easy to see that the city would be a picturesque one. When the gables of the houses, which are set towards the streets, were ornamented, and the upper storeys hung forwards, it must have been eminently so. But the narrowness of the streets of course made it advisable to remove the projecting storeys where the old houses remain; and in the *smartening* process which all have more or less undergone, nearly all the rich decorations of the old gables have been removed or hidden, and they have been made as smooth, and

11.

12.

plain, and mean, as the modern houses on either side of them. Still, if it be not remarkably picturesque, the city is pleasant and apparently prosperous; and there yet remains enough relics of antiquity within it, even apart from its noble cathedral, to amuse the vacant hours and reward the researches of the visitor who is of an antiquarian turn.'[33] Knight was perceptive in that some ancient buildings in the Island had modern facades but these had been re-fronted to disguise their older characters.

This appreciation for early buildings was not repeated by two town planners of the first half of the twentieth century. In 1914 Thomas H. Mawson & Sons, an internationally renowned town planning firm, authored *Exeter of the Future: A Policy of Improvement within a period of 100 years*, a development plan for the 'beautification of the city of Exeter'. It had been commissioned by the city council and Thomas Mawson wrote his intention was to 'blend the new with the old that the point of departure from one to another shall not be obvious but that the two shall merge into one harmonious composition'. His main idea focused on creating a cultural centre on the west side of Queen Street (a new library where the Higher Market now stands and municipal offices and a town hall on the site of what is now the Harlequin's Shopping Centre) but the plan also included what he regarded as the 'inevitable' widening of Martin's Lane. Mawson proposed that it should have 'an architectural screen… through the archway most inviting peeps of the east end of the cathedral would

13. Depiction of a medieval joiner carving a bench end, inserted into the fabric of Wippell's new building in High Street and Cathedral Yard, 1884.

14.

15.

16.

14 – 17. Four grotesques, carved by Harry Hems & Sons, 1907, on the first floor exterior of 53 High Street.

Introduction

be obtained and at the same time the somewhat cul-de-sac appearance of this end of Queen Street would be relieved'. The screen would be turreted to act as an eye-trap 'and prevent a barren appearance'. This would have destroyed a considerable number of buildings in Martin's Lane and High Street.

Mawson also suggested carving out a new thoroughfare across from the guildhall into Cathedral Yard. The guildhall itself would be cleared of its surrounding buildings, including the Turk's Head, partly for the practical aim of reducing the fire risk but Mawson also intended to have the aesthetic benefit of open views of both the cathedral and guildhall. He proposed that the surrounding buildings in the Island should have new facades that were not 'crude or bizarre' but quiet and subdued.[34] His plan envisioned the demolition of three High Street buildings (Numbers 56 to 58) and at least one more (Number 23) in Cathedral Yard. The following year the president of the Devon & Exeter Architectural Society commented that the plan had merit for a modern town but 'to embark upon such an idea would detract from all the beauty of our present High Street'.[35] Given the losses which occurred in 1942, it is perhaps fortunate that Mawson's suggestions were not followed in 1914 nor in the interwar years that followed.

During the Victorian and Edwardian years there had been a great suburban expansion of housing which continued after the Great War: in the 1930s the West Quarter was cleared of its slums and the residents were rehoused mainly in new council estates created in the suburbs. A generation earlier one commentator had stressed that West Quarter people were 'herded together like swine, grovelled in filth, led profligate lives and lived in houses and in situations which were overcrowded and unhealthy'. Buildings in Bartholomew Street were pulled down: one resident, in 1914,

19. Thomas Mawson's new thoroughfare from High Street into Cathedral Yard, 1914, which would have involved demolishing 56 to 58 High Street and 23 Cathedral Yard.

17.

18. Thomas Mawson's architectural screen, intended to be built at the High Street entrance to a wider Martin's Lane, 1914.

20. The view of the Guildhall from Cathedral Yard through Thomas Mawson's planned thoroughfare, 1914.

refused to leave his home even as the front was dismantled.[36] Other parts of the city, including Paul Street, were also cleared of ancient buildings which had become sub-standard housing. In 1916 there was anguish expressed by one newspaper columnist about an antique ceiling discovered in a West Quarter building at the corner of King and Preston Streets. The building faced demolition. The journalist asked 'why don't the council learn to be consistent and adhere to a policy of preservation which will be more beneficial to the city and less expensive than the mad cap schemes of modernising which now and then seem to captivate a section of the council?' However, in committee one councillor said this was 'a case of restoration or preservation of old buildings gone mad'.[37]

The Exeter Pictorial Record Society chronicled change. It had been formed in 1911 'with the idea of collecting photographs and drawings of life in the city at the present time and also to secure any old drawings and photographs of the doings of citizens and of buildings in bygone days'. The society provided a photographic record of some buildings which had demolition orders. The Great War interrupted its work and it became less active.[38] Nevertheless, its collection demonstrates the usefulness of recording the fabric of buildings before their destruction.[39] There were earlier instances which happened on an occasional basis: in 1785 the council commissioned two engravings of the East Gate before its demolition in order that future generations would appreciate the structure and George Townsend later drew one High Street building with a man outside carrying a sign which proclaimed 'Ancient House High Street Exeter formerly the Rose & Crown pulled down AD 1836 by Mr Coffin proprietor'.[40]

In about 1930 Charles S. Brooks, an American visitor, was told by 'a man in a shabby coat with the listless bearing that goes with want of work' that the city council had rejected the replacement of a High Street ancient building with a chain store 'emporium of steel and glass'. Brooks' informer was disgusted by what he saw as a general lack of civic progress and yearned for Manhattan's tall buildings.[41] Another American visitor at this time commented upon High Street. She thought it was 'narrow, swarming with traffic, and lined with hunched-up buildings three or four storeys high. Occasionally the round-shouldered ranks of commercial architecture are interrupted by an old Tudor façade, slanting, insecure and quaint, with projecting upper floors'.[42]

The small plots of property in the city centre were mostly owned by private individuals and it was not until after the Second World War, with the Blitz of 1942, that the council was able to clear great stretches of High, Sidwell, Paris, South and Fore Streets of the ruins of these buildings and purchase the land. It coincided with a ruthless policy of removing sound ancient buildings. The demolition of a building in South Street in 1942 prompted B. H. St John O'Neill, Chief Inspector of Ancient Monuments in the Ministry of Works, to write 'in my experience this is the worst case of vandalism which I have known to be perpetuated after a raid anywhere in England under the aegis of a local authority'.[43]

> '... in my experience this is the worst case of vandalism which I have known to be perpetuated after a raid anywhere in England ...'

Some 37 acres in the centre had been devastated in 1942 and two years later Thomas Sharp, a town planner, was appointed to prepare a reconstruction plan. This was a generation after Mawson's plan. Sharp theorized there were three solutions. The first was reconstruction which he thought would result in turning the city into a dead or fake museum but he concluded 'perhaps it can be assumed that no one in his senses will suggest that it should be'. He thought it more likely, and despaired, that 'the well-known English capacity for compromise will triumph'. This was his second option and he felt it would result in the erection of modern buildings which would be disguised with frontages of medieval or later styles. He regarded this as meaningless and incongruous and suggested it would look contemptible. Sharp's third, and preferred option, was to build in a modern style ('sympathetic not ruthless') and in scale similar to those buildings which had been destroyed.[44]

Some suggestions were taken up. Like Mawson, he proposed creating a new thoroughfare, of some fifteen feet in width, which would cut through the Island between High Street and Cathedral

Introduction

21. The most heavily bombed areas of Exeter in 1942, as drawn for Thomas Sharp in 1947. St Martin's parish is highlighted in red.

22. Aerial view of Exeter, 1947, showing bombed parts of the city and the untouched character of St Martin's parish (outlined in red).

St Martin's Island: An introductory history of forty-two Exeter buildings

23. Thomas Sharp's vision of Exeter, 1947, showing his thoroughfare from High Street to Cathedral Yard.

Introduction

24. Sharp's view of the Cathedral from Goldsmith's Street looking through the planned thoroughfare into Cathedral Yard, 1947.

Yard. This would lay further east than Mawson's scheme: Sharp wanted an extension from Goldsmith Street.[45] He does not appear to have known that his plan was a reinstatement of the Little or New Exchange which had been there in the mid 1700s. Nevertheless, this was rejected and the Island remained largely untouched by the second world war and the reconstruction schemes which were implemented in its aftermath.

Much of the destroyed centre was rebuilt from the late 1940s into the early 1970s. The clearance of undamaged buildings of architectural interest caused Professor W. G. Hoskins to write in 1960 that the city's greatest enemies were the motor car and the speculative builder.[46] The demolitions prompted Hoskins to form the Exeter Civic Society in 1961; he was its first chairman. Three years later Exeter's single skyscraper was built: a 140 foot concrete building (now John Lewis) was constructed immediately outside the old East Gate in Sidwell Street. At this time the bus station, the crematorium, the university's Great Hall and the Tower Block of Exeter College were among the prominent buildings being erected. It was also during these years that 50 to 52 High Street (now Burger King) and 21 to 22 Cathedral Yard were demolished. The Deputy Town Clerk was at the opening meeting of the Civic Society and responded to

23

what he thought were 'cheap and unkind jibes' about the city council:

'It is easy to say that the 68 members of the council are iconoclasts, trying to destroy the city and that they have no feelings for Exeter. But it is wrong. I suggest that some of the critics here tonight would do very much greater service to the city by coming on to the council and give the benefit of their views from within'.

Two years later Hoskins was elected a Liberal City Councillor and joined the Planning Committee. He was then employed by the University of Oxford and commuted during term time.

A year later, in 1964, Hoskins resigned his position as a councillor and left Exeter shortly afterwards for a post in Leicester 'after making too many potentially slanderous remarks about other politicians'. His comments have been described as 'incautious'.[47] In 1964 two aldermen and several members of the council's planning committee had issued a writ against him for alleged libel regarding redevelopment. Hoskins settled out of court and withdrew any imputation of dishonesty.[48] In 1966 he reminisced about Exeter and wrote it 'has been busily engaged in destroying most of the evidence of its rich past, and there is little left to study. What the Germans failed to destroy in May 1942, the city council have been systematically demolishing ever since. Most of what remains is under constant threat'. Hoskins concluded 'the bigotry of modern Exeter is still unbelievable to civilised people. As for their politics, they are savage'.[49] Hoskins' view of Exeter in the 1960s is reminiscent of the charges against it during the Reform years of the early 1800s. He wrote privately 'As a Liberal in this rotten Tory borough, unreformed and unregenerate, it is a terrible uphill battle... twelve unbroken years of the stinking Tories and their 'Affluent Society', which seems to breed whores chiefly'.[50] Hoskins' own term for his former fellow councilors was 'The Destructives'.[51]

It remains commonplace today to blame the Nazi bombing of 1942 for the loss of ancient Exeter but less remembered is that the imprudent redevelopment removed additional buildings. While the 'House that Moved' is a heartening tale of saving an ancient building in 1961 with it being placed on another plot of land, it should be remembered that a building of equal merit had recently been destroyed on that same site. The creation of the Guildhall Shopping Centre (the 'Golden Heart' project) in the 1960s and 1970s and the Harlequin's Shopping Centre in the 1980s was achieved only with the loss of significant buildings: it is particularly hard to forgive the destruction of superb medieval townhouses in North Street.[52] Roman Exeter was dramatically revealed in Cathedral Yard in the early 1970s but this was made possible by first destroying the Victorian church of St Mary Major. It is against this background, of uncompromising redevelopment at the expense of our ancient built heritage, that the consequences of the Cathedral Yard fire need to be considered.

The development of St Martin's island

The block of buildings that make up the Island has had varying phases of development. Part of the line of High Street originated with King Alfred in the 890s and a long section (from East Gate to St Stephen's Church) survives from the Roman street plan nearly two thousand years ago.[53] It appears that High Street has had a continuous series of buildings in the Island as far back as documentary records survive with the exception of Number 45 (which in the later 1500s was constructed in the entrance to Lamb Alley). Several deeds for the early 1200s note that some High Street properties extended to the churchyard without separate buildings facing the cathedral.[54]

The buildings situated in Cathedral Yard have a more complicated development process than those in High Street. The eastern and western ends developed earlier than the middle. The corner building with Martin's Lane has recently been discovered to have been built by the thirteenth or early fourteenth centuries, the site of the Royal Clarence Hotel also has building fabric of this date and the Well House has reused early sixteenth-century building materials. Properties further to the west may have been built in the sixteenth or seventeenth centuries and gradually evolved into more substantial structures. Archaeological finds have suggested a much earlier history. The Cathedral Yard structures were erected upon the sites of earlier graves (from the cathedral churchyard) and a dispute in the later 1600s notes the wall which still separated the High Street properties from the churchyard.[55] Underneath these medieval remains is evidence of the Roman occupation of nearly two thousand years ago. The two gates, Broadgate and Martin's Gate, were erected in 1285 but there may have been earlier gates as well as buildings adjoining Martin's Lane and Broadgate.

The model of eighteenth-century Exeter, constructed by Caleb Hedgeland, shows the congested nature of the city in general and St Martin's parish in particular. Hedgeland, who

Introduction

25. Numbers 40, 41–2, 43 & 44 High Street, September 2017.

lived in Bartholomew Street, was both an architect and builder and his intention was that the model, 2.5m by 1.5m, would depict the city around 1769 when he was nine years old. His son recalled the inspiration was a model of Paris which had been on show in Exeter. It was not completed until 1824. Hedgeland based it on the most accurate map he could find.[56] The model provides an extraordinary vision of Georgian Exeter but cannot be relied upon in regards to individual buildings. It is disappointing to compare the features of ancient buildings which have survived, such as 39 to 47 High Street or the Well House in Cathedral Yard, with the manner with which Hedgeland depicted them.

The model offers an aerial view of the city which can be supplemented with drawings, sketches, paintings, engravings, trade cards, advertisements and photographs and these provide particular further, and often alternative, details of building frontages. Also, a series of building plans of the late eighteenth

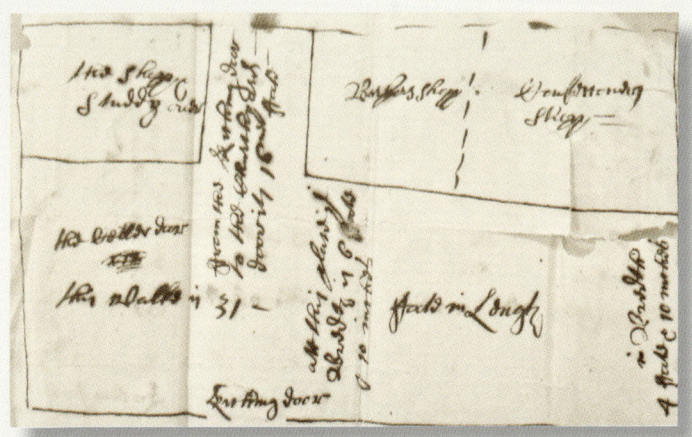

26. Ground plan, c1670, of ramshackle buildings in the western end of Cathedral Yard, for a baker and confectioner.

and early nineteenth centuries by John Tothill, who was appointed the Dean & Chapter's land surveyor,[57] detail interior layouts of individual buildings. At least 11 plans, many by Tothill, have survived for buildings in the Island.

27 – 29. Three plans of 18 Cathedral Yard made in 1770, 1790 and 1829 plotting the development of the building.

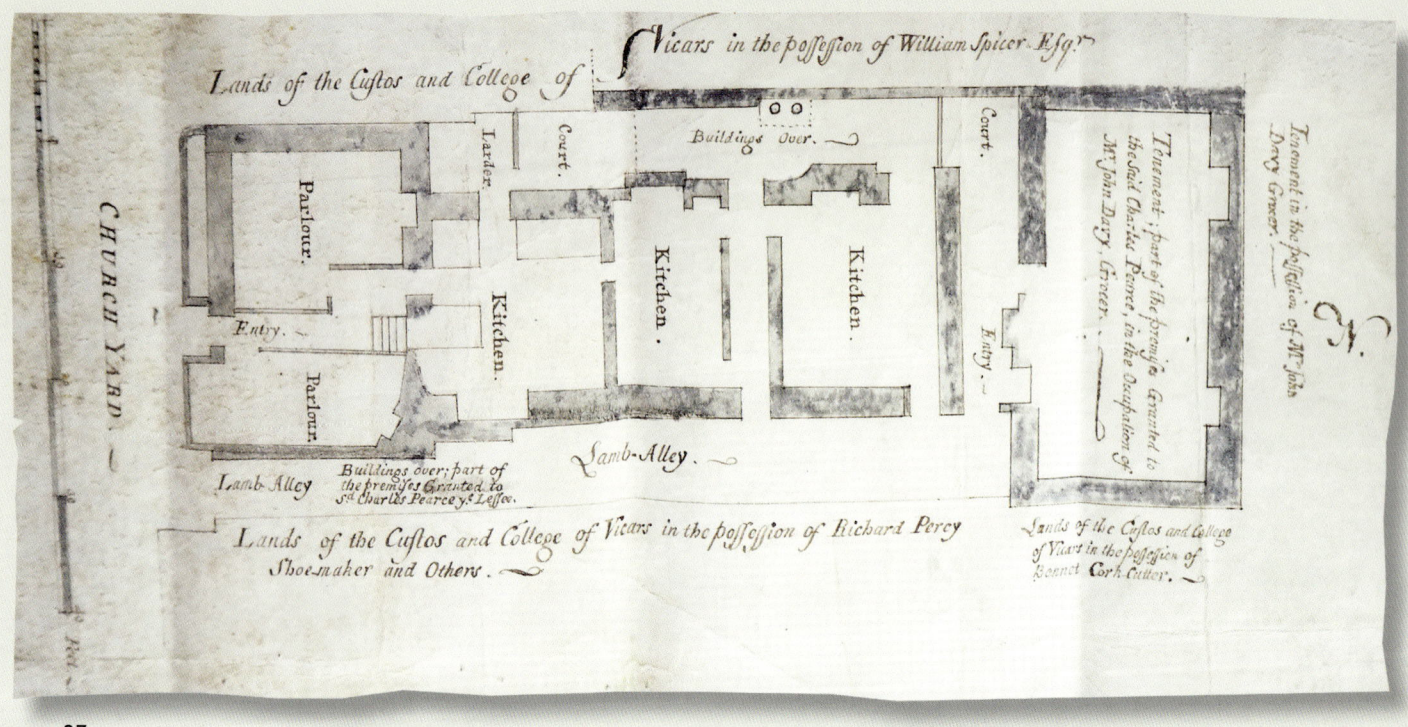

27.

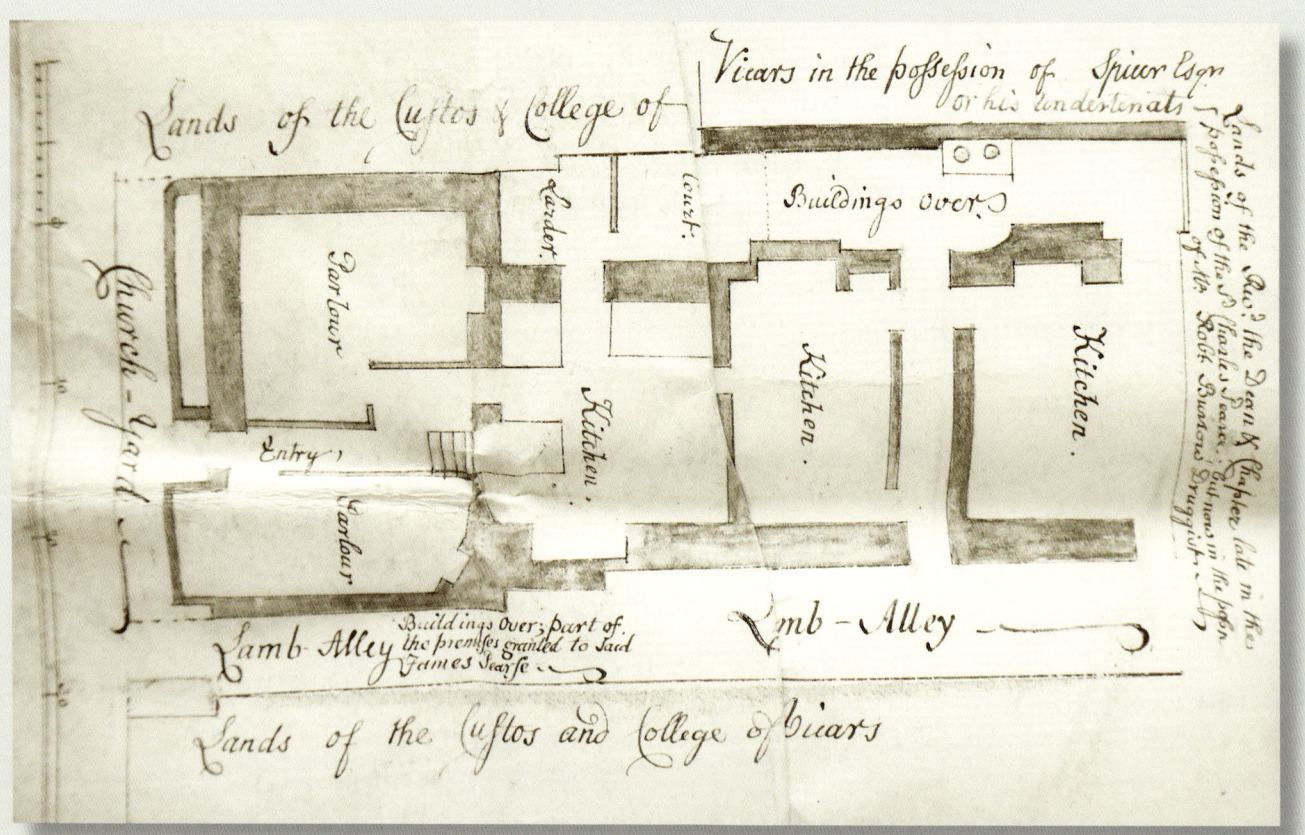

28.

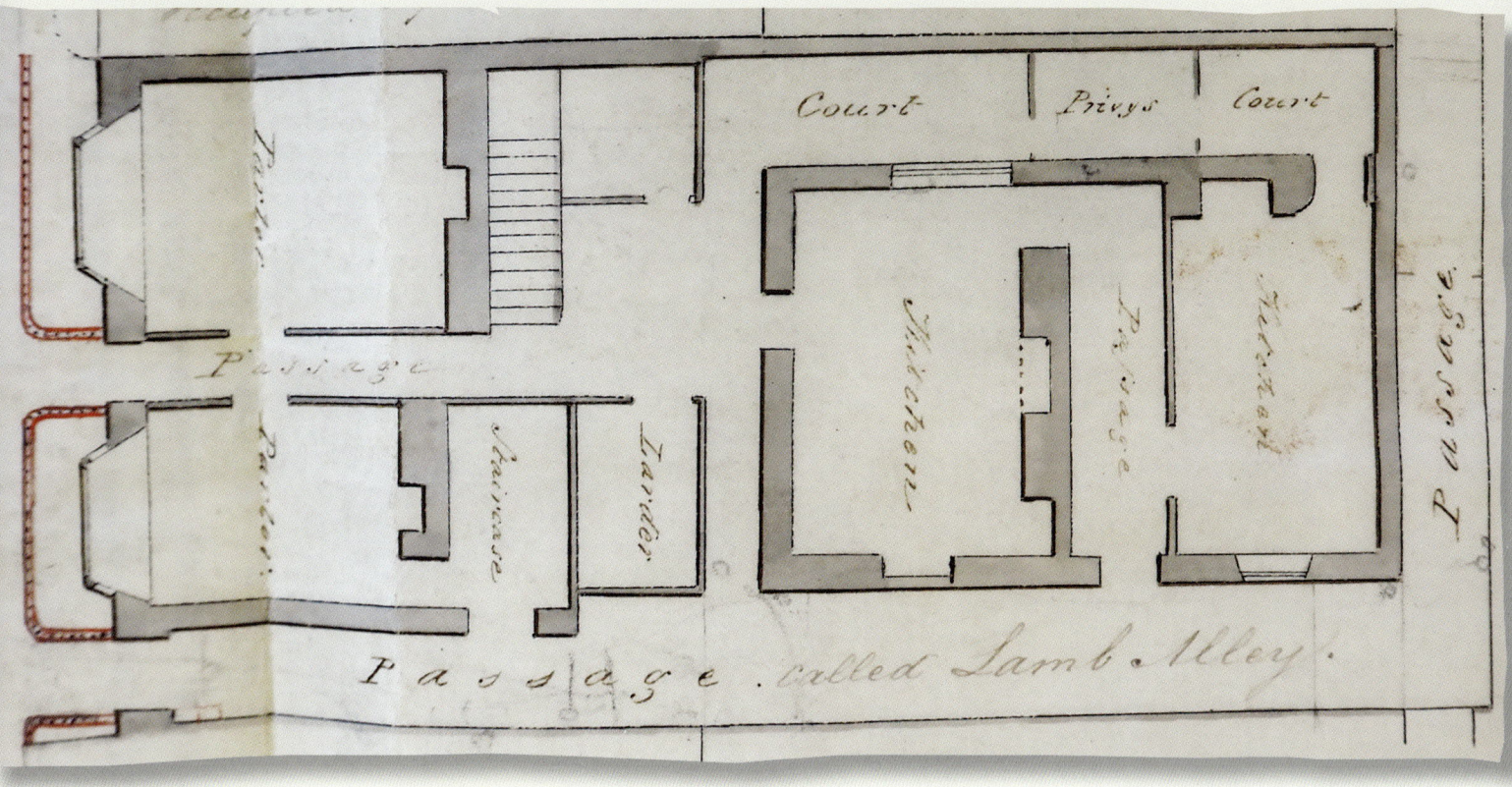

29.

The streets

The Island's four rows of buildings have had distinctly different characters. Those in Martin's Lane were unique in the parish for the sale of provisions in the late 1800s and early 1900s: high-quality game, fish and cheese were notable commodities. More substantial tradesmen dominated the High Street and they used their buildings as retail outlets. These were not necessarily the great merchants who were found elsewhere in the city but the location was advantageous for trade. In contrast, some buildings in Cathedral Yard continued to be residences long after many of those on the opposite side of the Island in High Street were confined to retail use. Here too were Devon lace sellers.

Street names were not as fixed as they are today. High Street, for instance, was not given a name in one lease in 1606 but merely described as 'the king's highway or street leading from the East Gate to the West Gate'.[58] Fore Street was intermittently noted as extending into what is now called High Street as far as Queen Street. Martin's Lane was sometimes termed Martin's Street and it occasionally was called St Martin's Lane or St Martin's Street. In the 1500s it was even called Fish Street.[59] Cathedral Close and Cathedral Yard are clearly demarcated today but this is a modern practice. Both terms have been used interchangeably as well as 'St Peter's Churchyard' or 'the church yard'. The term 'Cathedral Green' has also been used since at least 1853.[60] Broadgate was called Broadgate Place in the 1820s and later, for a short while, it was known as Broad Street.

There were at least two passageways, or drangs, which crossed between High Street and Cathedral Yard. One, Lamb Alley, survives in part. As a place name it dates back to at least the early seventeenth century.[61] One entrance was between 17 and 18 Cathedral Yard and the other between 44 and 46 High Street. A second alley, the Little or New Exchange, was created in the eighteenth century but it disappeared after redevelopment in the early 1960s. It had entries between 49 and 51 High Street and 20 and 21 Cathedral Yard.

St Martin's Island: An introductory history of forty-two Exeter buildings

The buildings

Those of Exeter's ancient buildings which have survived long enough to be studied by historians were most likely those built for wealthy occupants and thus among the best of their time. Little is known about the vast majority of other buildings (those which housed the working class) and it could be assumed that they have not survived because of their poorer construction and that they were of little use to succeeding generations. The Island's houses, at least those located on the four main streets, were mainly substantial buildings.

Exeter's houses visually conformed to certain types during the period 1400 to 1550. These included those with side passages, those with an open hall and ones built around a central courtyard which needed wider plots of land than could be found in the High Street section of St Martin's parish. A more typical Exeter house for the wealthier inhabitants comprised a rectangular building built at a right angle to the street and with a prominent gable. These suited the narrow frontages of the High Street building sites in the Island which were also long in depth.

These had two or three storeys with either one or two rooms on each floor. A shop (more usefully thought of as a workplace) occupied the ground floor. These were open at the front and enclosed at night with shutters (rather than glass windows). The relatively open nature of these windows was revealed in the details of a court case in 1620: an Exeter woman testified that she had often dined at the window with her family when a belligerent neighbour would arrive and urinate through that open window onto the table. These buildings sometimes had a cellar; this was particularly the case with the High Street buildings in the Island. Many still retain their cellar steps; this can be seen in the basement of the Well House and in most of the High Street properties. Fireplaces were served by chimneystacks situated in a rear or side wall.[62]

There were two main types of houses in the subsequent 150 years from 1550 to 1700. Both can still be found in the Island. The first was a continuation of the prevalent type in the earlier period which in some instances was only one room deep from front to back and these were from one to four storeys high. During the early sixteenth century a new house emerged: there

30. Ownership of property in the early 1500s.

were two rooms to each floor and some of these buildings had a side through-entry on the ground floor. Secondly, there were also buildings in which the roof ran parallel to the street. Some were only one room deep from front to back and one or two rooms wide on the ground floor.[63] Back block houses were in some cases connected to the main building with a gallery (as remains at 47 High Street).

In around 1450 the Island's buildings were nearly all owned by one of seven religious institutions (the Dean & Chapter, Hospital of St Mary Magdalene, St James' Priory, Vicars Choral, St John's Hospital, Plympton Priory or Polsloe Priory). The exceptions may have been properties owned by the City of Exeter. The Reformation brought some changes.[64] The structures with known early fabric include that on the corner of Martin's Lane with Cathedral Yard: the recent fire has uncovered a party wall of the thirteenth century. Tinley's Café, now Pizza Express, at the corner of Broadgate and Cathedral Yard, incorporates part of a sixteenth-century townhouse and it has been suggested that there was earlier fabric in adjoining basements.[65]

The most intriguing set of buildings lies at the eastern end of the High Street range: these date to the sixteenth and seventeenth centuries. There is a handsome brick 'Queen Anne' building within this row and there are several others of that period in the western end of High Street and in Cathedral Yard. The most notable Victorian buildings were the work of Best & Commin (built for Wippell) and lie in High Street and Cathedral Yard. Fourteen other buildings were demolished in the twentieth century and replaced by new structures.

TABLE ONE: REDEVELOPMENT, 1900–2000

61– 63 High Street	1905	new front
53 High Street	1907	new front
59 – 60 High Street	1912	new building
48 – 49 High Street	1922 – 1923	new building
22 Cathedral Yard	c1947 – 1953	new building
50 – 52 High Street	1962 – 1963	new building
19, 20 – 21 Cathedral Yard	1965	new building
61– 63 High Street	1975 – 1979	new building

The numbering of buildings makes it possible to identify individual structures but the allocation of numbers in Exeter was later than London and even Plymouth: it did not begin until the early 1800s. In 1819 John Cooke, the prominent but controversial Exonian, wrote that 'about twelve years since, I rose one morning before the people were up, and numbered every house in the Fore Street with chalk, which made the people stare. I was told I had not begun at the right end, with the sun. I went over the ground again. My house being a corner one, I got it properly numbered, and the street labelled, which soon led to be general. I paid for seven label boards at the street. Who would have done it beside?'[66] Advertisements in Exeter's newspapers show that numbers were given in various streets in 1805.[67] Two generations later, in 1874, the city's postmaster singled out Cathedral Close, by which he also meant Cathedral Yard, as having confusing building numbers. There was, he wrote, irregular numbering and inconsistent designations. The council's street committee decided not to renumber High Street, Fore Street, Gandy Street and Goldsmith Street and agreed that all other streets were to be given new numbers. Those buildings on the right side were to have odd numbers while those on the left were to be even. The guildhall was to be considered 'the centre of divergence'.[68]

In addition to numbers, some buildings in the Victorian period were named. For instance, two different High Street buildings were once called Victoria House. One had previously been known as Nottingham House. The Mansion House was a name given to 18 Cathedral Yard in 1870 and one behind it from the 1500s through to the late 1700s was known as The Three Chambers. It is easy to misunderstand building names. In 1770 a property in Lamb Alley was known as Belfields but this was the surname of the previous leaseholder, John Belfield, who was one of the city's MPs in 1728 and was the civic official who had presented the Prince of Wales with the city's freedom. The building had been his in the first years of the eighteenth century.[69] First- or second-floor offices were known variously as Central Chambers (50 High Street & 20 Cathedral Yard), Prudential Chambers (19 Cathedral Yard) and Guildhall Chambers (59½ High Street). Elsewhere in the city there was also Post Office Chambers (Queen Street), Castle Chambers (Castle Street), Queen Street Chambers (Queen Street), City Chambers (Gandy Street), Commercial Chambers (Gandy Street), Bedford Chambers (Bampfylde Street) and Custom House Chambers (the Quay).

Few properties have not been rebuilt; some have had new facades which obscure the older structures lurking behind them. A few buildings were combined during rebuilding while others were divided to create separate tenements. Rebuilding in some cases enlarged buildings beyond their plots but some, with a view to street improvements, were rebuilt on sites of reduced footage.

The residents

The population of St Martin's parish has historically been low.[70] In 1623, when Exeter had some 10,000 residents, the population of St Martin was probably between 300 and 350.[71] Table Two shows that there was little change two centuries later. In 1801 the parish had 310 occupants and the number vacillated for the next fifty years until it gradually declined. In 1881 the new census revealed 'the noticeable feature of the return is that in the majority of the parishes in the heart of the city the population has decreased; this is highly satisfactory, because there can be but little doubt that in times past there was much overcrowding in these localities and they have of late years been relieved of their surplus population by the erection of large numbers of houses in the suburbs'.[72] This loss accelerated and from 1973[73] the only residents in the parish have been the guests and staff of the Royal Clarence Hotel; the year 2017, following the destruction of the hotel, was the first for presumably more than a thousand years when there have been no residents.

32. Graffiti by Ernest Allen, in upper floor of 47 High Street, 1900, who noted he 'left in 1903', the year the building was auctioned.

TABLE TWO: ST MARTIN'S POPULATION, 1801–1891[74]

City	Parish	Males	Females	Houses	
1801:	17,398	310	149	161	45 (5 void)
1811:	18,896	295	111	184	41 (1 void)
1821:	23,479	329	126	203	45 (1 void)
1831:	28,241	298	113	185	45 (3 void)
1841:	31,333	254	93	161	40 (3 void)
1851:	32,810	285	101	181	41 (5 void)
1861:	33,738	207	69	138	37 (0 void)
1871:	34,650	228	80	148	34 (10 void)
1881:	36,974	188	65	123	28 (14 void)
1891:	37,580	115	34	81	26 (18 void)

31. Victorian wallpaper in the back room on the upper floor of 46 High Street. According to the census, the building was last lived in during the 1870s.

Exeter's population doubled during the nineteenth century but by 1801 Plymouth was a comparable size (16,378) and Devonport had become greater (27,154). By the twentieth century Devon's two cities had greatly different population sizes. In 1931 Plymouth had 208,182 residents while in Exeter there were 66,029.[75] Plymouth remains roughly three times the size of Exeter.

As noted earlier, fewer of the Island's buildings were occupied as the nineteenth century progressed. The census returns also reveal that only a minority of the heads of the households were born in Exeter.

TABLE THREE: **BUILDINGS WITH RESIDENTS, 1841–1911**[76]

	High Street	Broad Gate	Martin's Lane	Cathedral Yard	Total	Head born In Exeter
1841	20	2	2	13	37	N/A*
1851	22	2	2	10	36	9
1861	20	1	4	7	32	13
1871	21	1	4	9	35	17
1881	13	0	3	8	24	11
1891	15	1	0	8	24	4
1901	12	1	0	8	21	4
1911	10	1	0	5	16	4

*The 1841 census recorded whether born in the County (Y), or not (N), or Foreign Parts (FP including Scotland or Ireland)

These businessmen lived across the city at the beginning of the twentieth century. An examination of those who were engaged in retail in the High Street shows how disparate their residences were in 1902.[77]

39 High Street	29 New North Road
40 High Street	Pennsylvania Road
43 High Street	14 Lyndhurst Road
44 High Street	5 Grosvenor Place
46 High Street	Black Boy Road
48 High Street	18 Prospect Park
50 High Street	22 Magdalen Road
52 High Street	3 Old Tiverton Road
54 High Street	26 Powderham Crescent
55–6 High Street	6 Haldon Road
57–8 High Street	40 Prospect Park
59 High Street	Pennsylvania Park
62 High Street	Red Hills

A handful of illustrious individuals have lived in the Island. John White Abbot, the landscape painter, is perhaps one of the best known. The view from an upstairs window of his home (41 High Street) or one further along provided the perspective for

33. The effigy of Philip Hooper, who lived at 41 High Street, in St Martin's Church, 1715.

his well-known painting of Exeter. Another celebrated individual was Gilbert Dyer, a nationally renowned bookseller who lived at 56 High Street. He is one of the few Islanders to have merited inclusion in the *Oxford Dictionary of National Biography*. Another was William Holwell Carr who was born and raised also at Number 41. Carr's father, an apothecary, had been succeeded by Abbot who would know Carr as a nationally-renowned art collector and benefactor of the National Gallery.[78]

Peter King, 1st Baron King, who became Lord Chancellor of England, may have resided in the Island. He was born about 1670 and died in 1734. It was claimed that he lived in a house across from St Petrock's Church, situated near Broadgate and in the High Street. A Victorian described it as having 'one of those old picturesque fronts'. His father Jerome was a seventeenth-century grocer and dry salter who 'though carrying on a wholesale and retail trade, is said to have been of a genteel family… The sensible and worthy tradesman intended that his son should increase *his store* by likewise dealing in figs and hams, and having given him a school education suitable to this mode of life, placed him while still a lad behind the counter. For some years the future Chancellor continued to serve customers in the shop or to go on errands about the city of Exeter.' In other accounts the elder King was noted as 'a reputable grocer in the High Street of this city' and as being 'prosperous'. On his son's own monument Jerome King and his wife were described as 'worthy and substantial parents'.[79] The family home may have been 192 High Street but King also had the lease of the building which later became the Royal Clarence Hotel. It is possible the future Lord Chancellor lived in Cathedral Yard instead of above his father's High Street shop.[80]

From 1769 Andrew Brice, Exeter's leading printer, had his press at 54 High Street and his newspapers ran from 1714 until after his death in 1773. He was one of the city's best-known Georgians and his fame was partly due to his books including 'Bricisims'; his writing style was punctuated with his own newly-coined words. Brice was also unusual in the number of women he employed as printers.[81]

James Veitch, a member of the famous family who were internationally known nurserymen, opened his seed shop across from the guildhall at 54 High Street in 1838. Veitch lived at Buckerell Villa where he died in 1863. His son Robert then managed the Exeter business[82] including the shop which moved in 1930 to Cathedral Yard.

The final luminary was Charles Elkin Mathews who is discussed in the following pages.

The businesses

Four particularly significant Exeter firms were occupants in the Island for considerable periods of time although most of their owners resided in more affluent parts of the city.

By 1930 the Royal Clarence Hotel was considered, at least by one visitor, as being 'of respectable antiquity and fame'.[83] It had been rebranded a 'hotel' shortly after it was built in the 1760s and renamed the Royal Clarence Hotel following a visit by the Duchess of Clarence in 1827. Its main appeal lay with its location directly across from the cathedral. A visitor in 1930 was surprised to find his room had no key and the porter told him that in 50 years no other guest had asked for one. He further explained that 'no person of Devon would ever think of stealing and that hardened thieves turned honest when they came across the border'. The stranger to Exeter insisted upon a key and was finally given one.[84] The hotel is the Island's longest occupant.

J. Wippell & Company was formed in the early 1800s and based in the Island in 1883. 55 & 56 High Street had been destroyed by fire two years earlier and the firm rebuilt on the site and at 23 Cathedral Yard. It was there for nearly a century and remains the leading clerical outfitters and church furnishers in Exeter. Curiously, three decades earlier, the firm had been at 42 High Street for a year.

Veitch's seed shop was in two different buildings in the Island. From 1838 to 1930 it was at 54 High Street and then it moved to 17 Cathedral Yard where it remained until 1982. The firm had begun in the late 1700s with John Veitch's arrival from Scotland. He was employed at Killerton and subsequently established a nursery nearby at Budlake. His family later established others in Exeter (including at Mount Radford and New North Road) and in London. The firm became known for sending plant collectors across the globe and through them it imported more than a

34. Andrew Brice, Exeter's illustrious printer, whose *Old Exeter Journal* was printed at 54 High Street in 1766.

Introduction

37. Undated catalogue for Robert Veitch & Son, Ltd, of 17 Cathedral Close.

35 – 36. Fine food at 48 High Street: in the occupation of Shapley, confectioner (1878–1919) and Deller's Café (1923–62).

thousand unknown plants into England. However, it was only one of several businesses to sell seeds in Exeter albeit the best remembered.[85]

Deller's Café was one of Exeter's most illustrious businesses of the twentieth century and it began in 1906 at the corner of Cathedral Yard and Martin's Lane, having purchased the Exeter Bank building. In 1919 it moved to a new building on High Street near Bedford Circus but four years later a branch was opened at 48 High Street and continued there until 1963. The firm had been established in 1844 by Edwin Deller, a grocer, in Paignton and it was his grandson, William Lambshead, who opened the Exeter business as well as branches in Paignton and Taunton.[86]

There were other well-known businesses. One, Tinley's Café, was located for two generations at Broadgate. It is still remembered partly because its name remains at the top of the building which was a confectionery shop in the late 1700s. This business was developed by Sarah Murch née Mardon in the 1820s, passed through the family to become Goff's Restaurant and then, after several other endeavours, emerged as Tinley's Café. Another was Pinder & Tuckwell which was located in the Island from 1933 to 1988 at 43 High Street. It was already a long-established firm and later moved from the Island to Fore Street.

The most common trade in the High Street row of buildings was selling clothing. Two of Exeter's clothing retailers with the longest histories, Pinder & Tuckwell and Luget, were once occupants of the Island but both have recently closed (2011, 2015). One of the most common outfitters for women were the milliners: single ladies predominated in selling hats, generally on the first floor, in the High Street buildings in the Island.

The Island has been home to a number of banks and building societies including at 57 High Street (Fox Brothers, Fowler & Company and later Lloyds Bank, Alliance & Leicester Building Society), 59–60 High Street (West of England and South Wales District Bank, Devon County Bank, National Provincial Bank of England, National Westminster Bank), 62 High Street (Charing Cross Bank), 19 Cathedral Yard (Devon & Cornwall Bank), 26 Cathedral Yard (National Provincial Bank of England, National Westminster Bank) and 14 Cathedral Yard (Exeter Bank). Two remain in the Island.

The most significant use of a building by apothecaries, who were otherwise called chemists or druggists, was that over three centuries at 41–2 High Street but others were at Numbers 47, 53, 58, 60 and 63. Jewellers, known earlier as goldsmiths or silversmiths, were also commonly seen in the Island in High Street (at Numbers 39, 41, 43, 48–9, 58 and 61).

The Island was a centre for bookselling with half of the row of buildings in High Street having housed booksellers at some period. There were also other buildings in Cathedral Yard which were in the book trade. The most notable was that from 1884 to 1887 of Charles Elkin Mathews at Number 16, now part of

38. Women's clothing items sold by Mrs Charles Adams at 53 High Street, mid nineteenth century.

Introduction

39. Broadgate, Cathedral Yard and Martin's Lane, 1841.

40. Properties in the Island as depicted on a Dean & Chapter map of 1810.

35

the Well House. Mathews sold books and 'dabbled' in publishing including Maria Susannah Gibbons' *We Donkeys on the Devon Coast*. He then moved to London and founded The Bodley Head, in partnership with John Lane of West Putford in North Devon. The firm's name was taken from Sir Thomas Bodley, the Exeter man who several centuries earlier had founded the Bodleian Library partly with books he acquired from the cathedral which he viewed from his shop window.[87] Waterstones is the Island's last bookseller.

Perhaps the most surprising business venture was John Chaplin's museum. This was, in 1824, the city's first public museum. There were many similar travelling exhibitions or temporary shows but Chaplin offered a permanent display of unusual items at 44 High Street. It only lasted two years but was a milestone for the city. Nearby, in Cathedral Close, the Devon & Exeter Institution had similar exotica but these were accessible to its members whereas Chaplin offered admission to the general public.

Most businesses occupied these buildings for short periods but two have been established for generations (the Royal Clarence Hotel from 1766 and the National Westminster Bank's banking predecessor in 1835) and more recently Laura Ashley (1984) and Burger King as well as Edinburgh Woollen Mill (both 1990).

The fires

Fires occasionally broke out in the city such as those in 1669 in Gandy Street and in 1670 at West Gate.[88] There were fires in 1836,[89] 1837,[90] 1853[91] and 1876[92] as well as many others. The most destructive in the Island took place in 1881. On the 9th of October fire broke out and destroyed 55 to 58 High Street. Smoke was discovered at three in the morning but within hours the four buildings were gutted and half a dozen others damaged. Three policemen smelled fire and they were searching for it in High Street when a window or door opened at Number 57: a woman inside raised the alarm. The occupants were Davis & Davis, haberdashers, and the policemen managed to rescue Mr Davis, an invalid, who was in his bedroom on the second floor. They used a small fire escape which was kept at the Guildhall. Number 56 had some two dozen inhabitants. This building ran through to Cathedral Yard. Mr W. G. Davies and five family members slept in a smaller building which overlooked Cathedral Yard and which was separated from the High Street building by a courtyard. In Number 58 were twelve employees, a housekeeper and two children. All managed to flee down the stairs except for Miss Welsh who had to be rescued through a second floor window. Between four and five o'clock the roofs of Numbers 56 to 58 fell in and at ten o'clock Number 55 collapsed. Readers of the *Western Times* were reminded

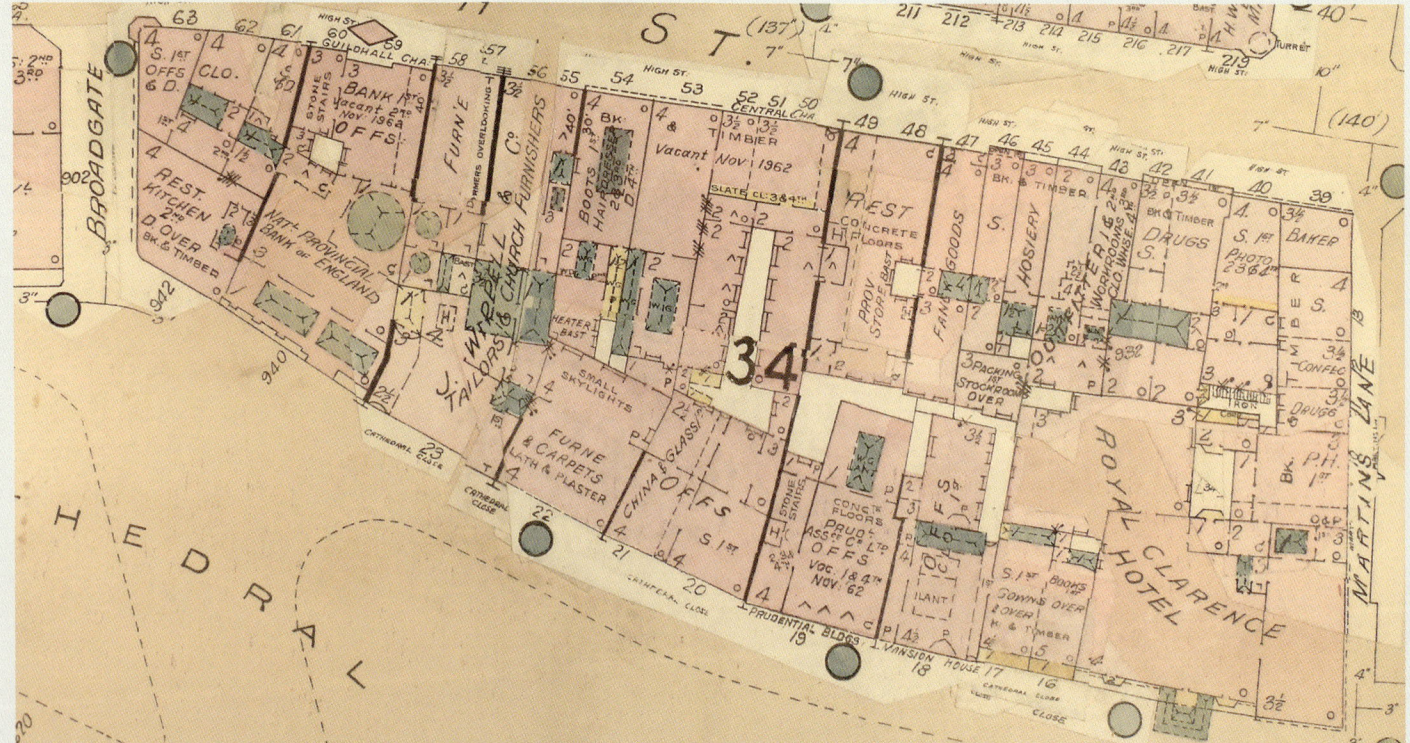

41. The Island as portrayed on the Goad Insurance Map of 1889.

that the buildings were part of a block that extended from Martin's Lane to Broadgate and that these were then 'two lines of houses back to back, one line having its front in High Street and the frontage of the other line being in Cathedral Yard'. The journalist described the building as made of 'very flimsy materials' which burnt 'like a lot of match wood'. He concluded 'recent events have directed attention to the structure of business premises, and no more practical lesson of the necessity of stability in new buildings could be given than that afforded by this fire. In this particular case the fire was unchecked until it was met by brick walls, the lath and plaster partitions that existed between several of the houses supplying food to the flames rather than proving any obstacle to their progress. Further than this, the flimsy character of the buildings was a source of danger to those who were endeavouring to extinguish the flames, for the structures collapsed in such an unexpected manner that some of the firemen were precipitated into the flames and others escaped by little short of a miracle'.[93] On 9 May 1882 the building sites were sold. The first lot was Numbers 55 to 58. Their combined frontage was 50 feet 3 inches. The depth was 49 feet 4 inches for Numbers 57 & 58, while there was 103 feet 6 inches for Numbers 55 & 56. The second lot was 23 to 25 Cathedral Yard. They had a frontage of 50 feet 6 inches and a depth of 23 feet 6 inches. Wippell & Company purchased the first lot for £4,000 and the second for £1,620.[94] After the fire a journalist observed there had been six disastrous fires within the last year and noted that the buildings were 'old, slight and of the most inflammable character possible'.[95]

Chronology of Improvement, 1769–1844

1769	North Gate demolished
1771	conduit in High Street demolished
1773	Bedford Circus started
1774	county court house built
1784	East Gate demolished
1787	new theatre built in the circus
1792	Barnfield Crescent started
1796	Southernhay started
1799	conduit moved to South Street
1802	Colleton Crescent built
1804	new theatre built
1815	West Gate and Quay Gate demolished
1817	gas light in Fore & High Streets
1818	laying of city prison foundation stone
1819	South Gate (with prisons) taken down
1820	Martin's Gate demolished
1821	Public Baths & new theatre opened
1823	four houses of Pennsylvania Park finished
1824	Broadgate demolished
1825	Bedford Circus begun to be completed
1830	widening of South Street begins
1830	the Basin opened
1833	houses at Broadgate begun to be taken down
1835	Great Conduit moved to George Street
1835	the Iron Bridge begun
1836	the Western Market opened
1837	new cemetery consecrated
1838	the Eastern market opened
1841	the Dispensary opened
1844	railway reached Exeter

Explanatory Note

Each property has a list of occupants mostly from 1800 onwards. In most cases they were leaseholders but in some instances they also owned the properties. The lists have been compiled from a variety of sources (notably newspapers, telephone books, parish tax accounts and street directories) but the patchy nature of the survival of these records has resulted in some imperfect lists. These should also not be viewed as definitive given some sources may not in themselves have been accurate. It has not been attempted to list the medieval occupants or the background in that period to these properties. There are a substantial number of documents, held principally at the Exeter Cathedral Library & Archives and the Devon Heritage Centre, from which it would be possible to provide, to some degree, an outline of the leaseholders and sub-tenants from the thirteenth to fifteenth centuries. The descriptions of the buildings follow an order which would allow a reader to walk from 39 High Street to Broadgate, into the Cathedral Yard and then through Martin's Lane.

42. The High Street buildings, notably occupied by Hinton Lake and Pinder & Tuckwell, 1940s.

1
High Street
also known as Fore Street

Early visitors consistently praised the High Street. One such enthusiast was John Leland who in 1542 wrote 'there be divers fair streets in Exeter but the High Street, which goeth from the west to the east gate, is the fairest' while nearly a century later an East Anglian traveller commented 'the buildings and streets are fair especially her High Street from East to West Gate'.

He was followed a generation later, in 1669, by an Italian visitor who thought 'the city is intersected almost in the middle by a very large and straight street, full of very rich shops, which is its best and most considerable part'. Travellers invariably repeated similar remarks: in 1694 one commented Exeter had 'very good streets but especially the High Street is most commendable', in 1700 another recorded that it 'is very large and very good and has something of everything in it that is accounted great in the nation' and in 1724 yet one more wrote 'the beauty of the place consists mainly of one long street, running the length of the parallelogram, called High Street, broad and straight: the houses are of a very old but good model, spacious, commodious and not inelegant. This street is full of shops well-furnished and all sorts of trades look brisk'. By the mid 1700s the praise had turned to criticism. In 1760 one visitor wrote that Exeter 'principally consists of one very long street, tolerably broad, but not very straight, the houses every one of which are shops of a most ancient model. Indeed, we saw not any that can be called good in this grand city'. It was during these years that Exeter was becoming poorer as its cloth industry diminished and its buildings appeared antiquated.

By the late 1800s tastes had changed: in 1884 one Victorian wrote that High Street 'still wears in some parts an aspect of antiquity, a seeming anachronism amid its newer surroundings. The projecting front of the Guildhall and the square-headed double windows and quaint projecting stories and gables of some of the Elizabethan houses along this avenue of a thousand years offer many a picturesque bit for the artist and the antiquary'.[96] It was at this time that a guidebook urged its readers to stand in front of the guildhall and 'look right and left at the old street, tortuous and picturesque, diversified by old house fronts, of many ages, among them some fine examples of the timbered fronts of the 14th and 15th centuries, whose carved brackets, grotesque heads and overhung stories remind the spectator of what are called the good old times when men built and manufactured as if for eternity.' The writer particularly noticed the buildings to the west of Martin's Lane.[97]

The High Street buildings between Martin's Lane and Broadgate were in a prime position. Their footfall was increased by the proximity to the Cathedral, the Guildhall and, from 1783, the Fish and Potato Markets. The demolition of the latter buildings in the 1830s created the entrance to Queen Street which was also advantageous as was the subsequent building of Higher Market.

Pedestrians had two additional thoroughfares which ran from High Street into Cathedral Yard; these were Lamb Alley and the New (or Little) Exchange. The former was a medieval lane which had one end at what is now 45 High Street and the other between 17 and 18 Cathedral Yard. The latter was an alley which ran between 20 and 21 Cathedral Yard to a gap between 49 and 51 High Street. Sections of Lamb Alley survive whereas the New Exchange was destroyed in the early 1960s.

Until the early 1800s many if not all High Street occupiers were also residents: the upper floors were reserved for domestic use and the ground floor for retail. By the early 1800s some buildings were no longer residential and, as noted earlier, by the turn of the twenty-first century only ten of these High Street buildings were dwellings. The last buildings to have residents were Number 61 in 1971 and Number 60 in 1972.[98]

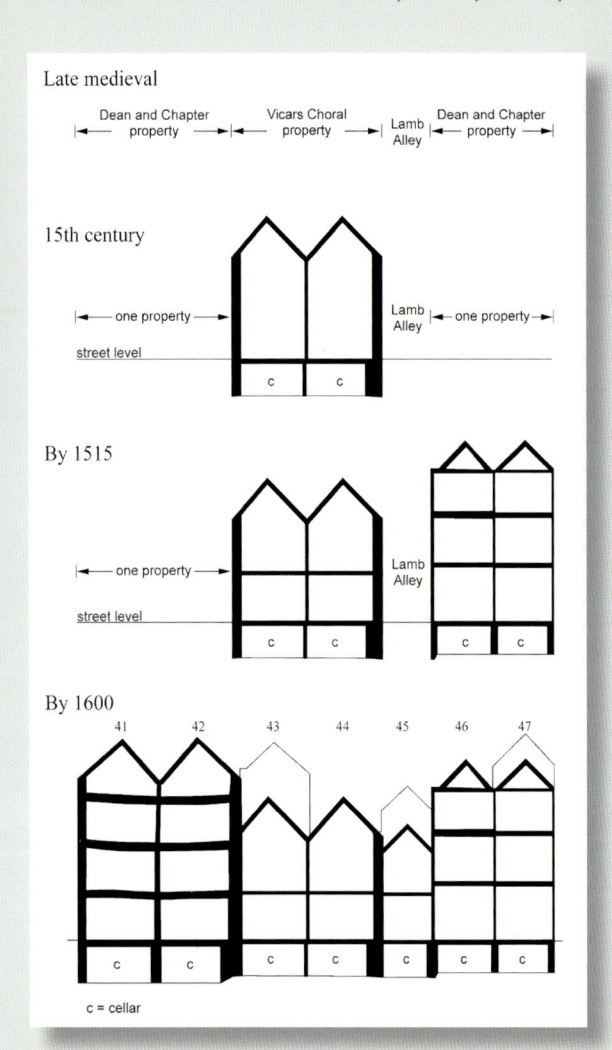

Rebuilding has been a continual feature. There are now seventeen distinct structures although their numbering indicates there are twenty-four. The discrepancy is due to the retaining of all the building numbers after fourteen structures were rebuilt as six buildings: thus, for example, the single building which now houses Trailfinders is known as 61 to 63 High Street. This is made more complicated by firms using adjoining premises: nine properties are currently being used by four businesses.

Rebuilding and remodelling makes it difficult to determine the appearance of the buildings. Caleb Hedgeland's model of late eighteenth-century Exeter would appear to be the best indicator of their general layout. It shows thirteen separate buildings, each with their own front door, and eight were built as pairs which indicates there were 21 distinct properties at that time. However, the buildings which today comprise Numbers 39 to 47, whose outlines have survived intact, would have been known to Hedgeland but their architectural features do not correspond with those depicted in his model. It suggests that few Island buildings in High Street were accurately modelled. More useful indicators are photographs, drawings and plans.

In 1943 it was recalled that Exonians had long used High Street for evening promenading, particularly on Saturdays. One resident wrote that

43. A reconstruction drawing by T. Ives of the development of 41 to 47 High Street.

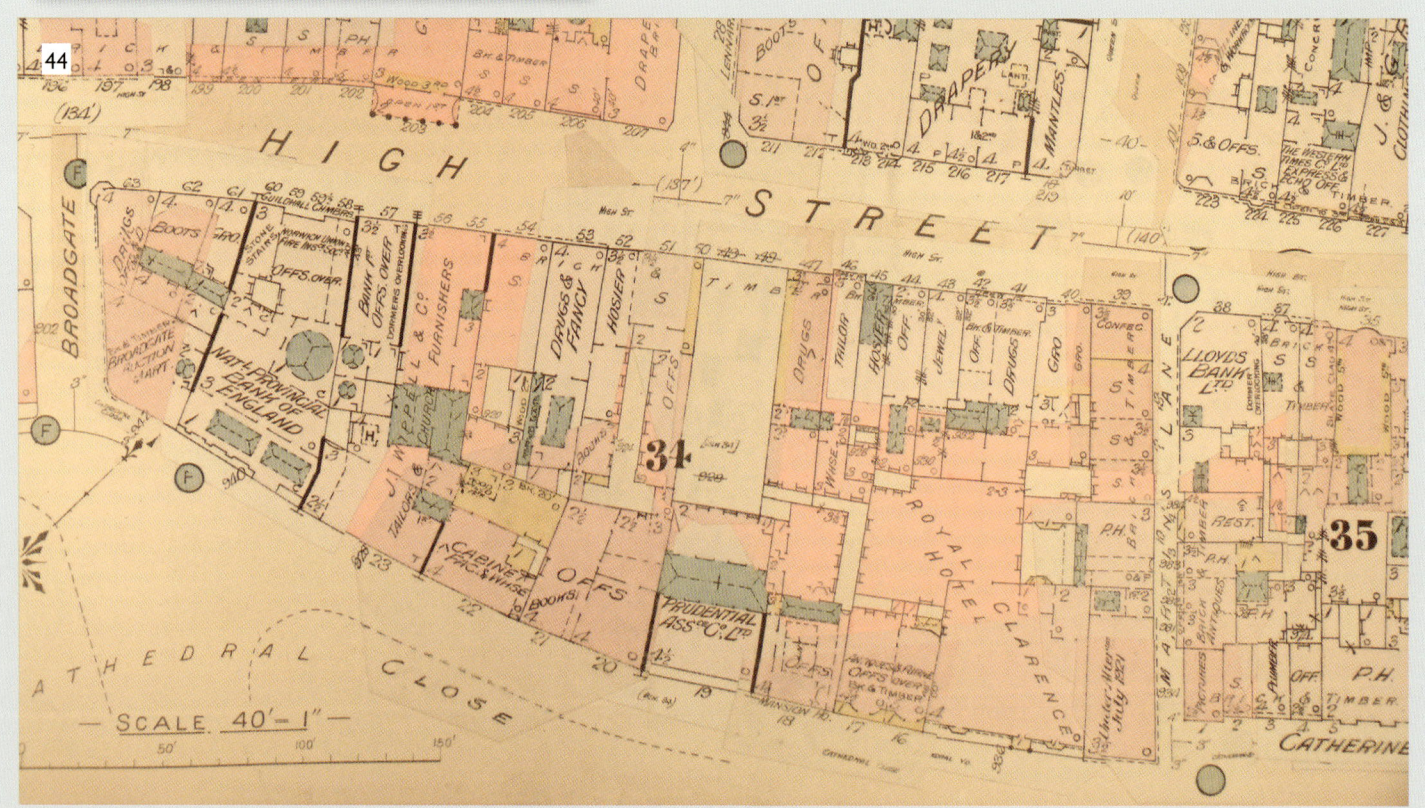

High Street also known as Fore Street

motorists made 'half-amused comments on finding a stream of pedestrians in the road, all cheerful and orderly. Those whose memories go back to a distant childhood recall the old practice, a roadway filled with townsfolk of a compact community, proud of their city'. Thirty years before a stranger to Exeter was puzzled by the city's version of Rotten Row, the London thoroughfare for public promenading. He commented:

'that portion of your High Street, during certain hours, is made a meeting place of both sexes to such an extent as to make one wonder what the attraction is. Surely there must be something to cause so many people to while away their hours in such a way. Is there any solution to this problem?' A local man responded by informing him that all English cities of a comparable size had similar meeting places and that it only occurred when 'the workaday folk are free'. He added 'High Street on a Sunday night and on a Tuesday or Friday afternoon are socially two very different places'.[99] Partial pedestrianisation was introduced in the late 1900s.

44 – 45. The Goad insurance maps of 1921 and 1962.

NUMBER 39

In 1974 this timber-framed and rendered building was listed Grade 2 and recorded as 'probably late seventeenth century' with a 'gabled front with later rendering and windows, 4 storeys, 3 windows, sashes, no glazing bars except in the attic. Rusticated quoins. Modern shop front shared with Number 40. Slate roof. The frontage onto Martin's Lane is similar, but has sashes with glazing bars.' The frontage is 23 feet.

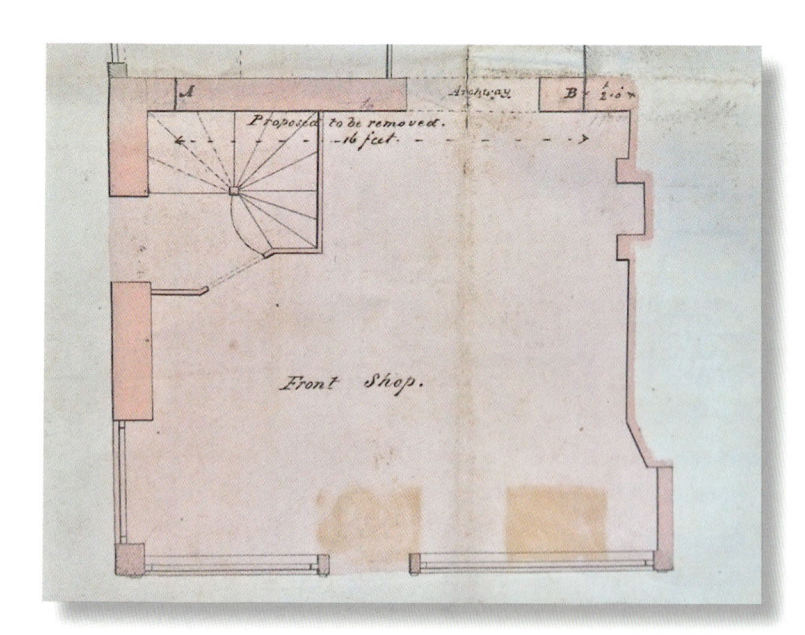

46. Plan of 39 High Street (in pink).

39 High Street, at the corner of Martin's Lane, was held by St James' Priory until 1444, acquired by a Cambridge college, served as a goldsmith's shop through most of the 1700s, housed a circulating library in the early 1800s and became a bakery in 1890.

St James' Priory owned Number 39 by the late thirteenth century but Henry VI dissolved the priory and in 1444 gave it to King's College, Cambridge, which retained ownership until 1937.[100] The priory was said to have had 'shops' in the building.[101] In 1472 Thomas Molle, once suggested to be the inspiration in the naming of Mol's Coffee House, held a lease.[102]

Details are sketchy for the next two centuries although in 1597 the frontage was specified as being 20 feet and the length was 14 feet.[103] The manorial court was held here but in 1674 it was derided as being 'the little pitiful house'.[104] It was probably built not long afterwards. Caleb Hedgeland's Georgian model is similar to that which survives today and in 1789 it was noted as built of brick with a slate roof.[105] There is no image of the earlier building.

In the eighteenth century[106] goldsmiths were the main occupiers and included John Burden, a warden of the guild.[107] Number 39 was too small for the last Georgian goldsmith who relocated across Martin's Lane because he had been 'under the necessity of showing his goods in an inner room'.[108] Over the following generation linen, boots and shoes were sold. The first business was Thomas Drew's 'Cheap Linen-Drapery, Mercery and Hosiery Warehouse'[109] and Number 39 was then 'a dwelling house… consisting of a shop only on the ground floor and staircase – a kitchen and offices under and three floors above'. In 1812 an opening or archway was made in the wall between it and the adjoining property in Martin's Lane. Fifteen years later the college authorities consented to it being enlarged.[110] It was probably on the first floor that 'Mesdames Bowchers and Gove' had their 'genteel and fashionable assortment of millinery, dresses, etc.'[111] Drew rebranded himself as the Irish

NUMBER 39 High Street

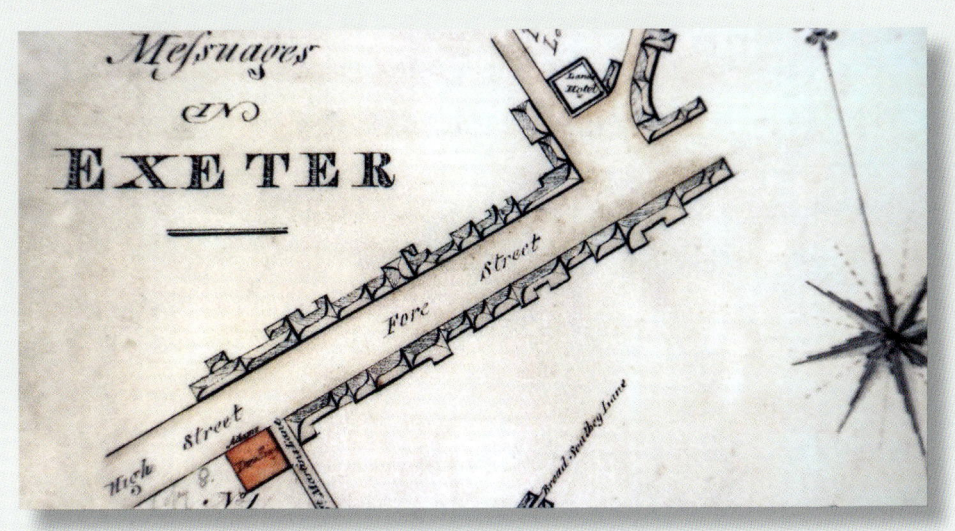

47. The location of 39 High Street shown on a map of 1827.

Linen, Print and Muslin Warehouse[112] and Mrs Pinwill's Ladies and Gentlemen Boot and Shoe Warehouse succeeded him.[113] Men in the same trade followed her.[114]

For nearly a generation Number 39 housed the Cornish-born Fitze family's 'circulating library, reading room, book selling and stationery business'.[115] It is likely that the first floor was used for the library whereas the ground floor was dedicated to retailing books and stationery. Number 39 was then described as a 'messuage and spacious shop most advantageously situated, fronting High Street and at the corner of St Martin's Lane'.[116] Until this time the Fish & Potato Markets were located directly across High Street but both were about to be demolished to make way for Queen Street. In 1835 there were eight libraries in Exeter, including that at Number 39, and there were six other reading rooms.[117] When Maria Fitze died[118] her brother James[119] moved into Number 39 with his daughter who later continued the business but sold the books 'at an immense sacrifice in order to open with an entire new stock'.[120]

A chronometer, watch and clock maker, whose business had been established in the mid 1600s, took over[121] but he died, aged 59, in 1866 and twelve months later his widow married James Edward Michie, a 24 year old watchmaker of London. The business continued but eight years later Mrs Michie was once again a widow.[122] She offered for rent the first floor and 'upper part', which then comprised five rooms along with a kitchen and other 'conveniences', and another watchmaker and jeweller took over the business.[123]

A new phase began in 1890 when J. P. Hoskins, who produced machine-baked bread, opened a branch to his principal shop in Sidwell Street.[124] He was the only Exeter baker to produce Eurissa, 'a new bread, a white bread and best bread on earth', which had been developed by W. A. Wrenn of Exeter. The loaf differed in weight and size from ordinary bread.[125] In the early 1900s Number 39 also housed St Martin's Restaurant[126] or St Martin's Café (a different establishment to Martin's Café, a Victorian coffee house in Market Street which catered for teenage boys who played bagatelle).[127] In 1939 'two of Exeter's biggest and oldest established bakery establishments' were amalgamated and took over the building.[128] It offered loaves of bread that could be sliced and wrapped for an extra farthing which cost would 'be amply repaid by the time and labour saved'.[129]

A fire in 1918 caused little damage although it was noted that it could have destroyed 'some of Exeter's finest old properties'.[130] Nearly a century later the building again narrowly escaped destruction.

OCCUPANTS OF THE PROPERTY

1731–1743	John Burden, *Goldsmith*
1751	Lewis Courtall, *Goldsmith*
1766 – 1769	Matthew Skinner, *Jeweller*
1783 – 1800	John Adams, *Goldsmith, Jeweller & Engraver*
1800 – 1829	Drew & Company, *Linen Drapers*
1821	Bowcher & Gove, *Milliners*
1829 – 1830	Mrs Pinwill, *Boot & Shoe Maker*
1831 – 1833	John Davey and William Frederick Wescomb, *Boot & Shoe Makers*
1833 – 1843	Miss Maria Fitze, *Bookseller & Library*
1843 – 1860	James & Ellen Fitze, *Bookseller & Stationer*
1855 – 1877	Robert Upjohn, *Watch Maker* (later Upjohn & Michie)
1878 – 1888	Samuel Anthony Aviolet, *Watchmaker and Jeweller*
1889	Charles Wood, *Hatter*
1890 – 1892	J. P. Hoskins *Exeter Machine Bread & Cake Baker*
1892 – 1939	Hoskins & Son (including from 1902 to 1920 St Martin's Restaurant or St Martin's Café)
1940 – 1965	Hill, Palmer & Edwards, *Bakers & Confectioners*
1950 – 1955	Daniel Maher & Co., *Auctioneers, Estate Agents & Business Transfer Agents* (upstairs)
1966 – 1995	Dorothy Perkins, *Ladies' Wear* (& 40)
1968 – 1987	Tact-Contact, *Employment Agency* (upstairs)
1996 – 2015	Clinton Cards, *Gift cards*
2016	Vacant
2017 –	Skechers, *Casual shoe retailer*

NUMBER 40

In 1953 this seventeenth/eighteenth-century building was listed Grade 2* and recorded as a 'very interesting late seventeenth century, 3 storey, 3 windows, red brick front showing Dutch influence. Stone quoins and cornice, the latter with heavy ovolo moulding. Short lengths of cornice above windows, and semicircular pediment above central 2nd floor window. Brickwork panels, late eighteenth-century sash windows. Shop-front is modern, shared with Number 39. Hipped slate roof.' The provisional listing of 1947 noted wrongly 'shop front is early nineteenth century with coved fascia'. The frontage is 18 feet.

48. 40 to 42 High Street, first half of the twentieth century.

40 High Street, anciently owned by the City of Exeter, the late seventeenth-century brick front disguises an earlier building. This was a jeweller's shop at the turn of the eighteenth century and subsequently used as a grocery and Italian delicatessen for nearly 150 years.

This timber-framed seventeenth-century building of three storeys, with a cockloft, has a brick façade of about 1700. There is a cellar, or cellars, which run to the rear of the later building. The walls are of Heavitree rubble.[131] There was a building on this site as early as 1294.[132] It may have later been divided into two parts and, unusually for the Island, was then probably privately owned. Number 40 later came into the possession of Exeter's council.[133] There were several goldsmiths who occupied the building in the late 1600s and early 1700s at the time it was rebuilt and when it would have looked distinct from the other buildings along this part of High Street.

By 1731 it was occupied by Daniel Pring, a bookseller who had earlier married a colleague's widow,[134] and later that century he was succeeded by a leather breeches maker, dealer and chapman. The building was described as a brick-built dwelling house which had 'a basement story and two good cellars, likewise a shop, a good parlour, kitchen and court, with a well of water, and lead pump in the same, with every convenient office, also a water closet. On the first floor a handsome drawing room, a good dining room, and two good bed rooms. On the second floor four good bedrooms and three good garrets over the same'.[135]

Compared to its neighbours the building offered modern retail facilities.

NUMBER 40 High Street

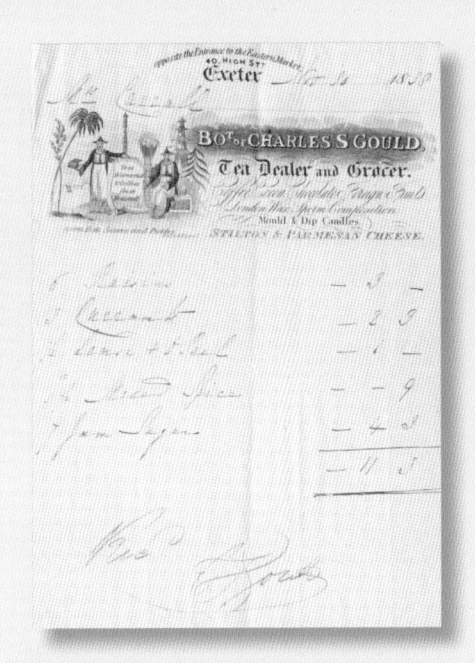

house, in 1851, not only Gould but his Exeter-born wife Sarah and a domestic servant named Elizabeth Rouse.

On Gould's death in 1859 his widow Sarah held the shop, counting house, kitchen, cellar and water closet and leased it to George Goodwin Gould of Broadclyst. She also sold to him the remaining stock[139] and the firm was renamed by its new proprietors, Gould and Allen.[140] Seven years later Gould died and the premises, described as slated and 'substantially built of brick', were put up for sale. It then comprised 'a spacious shop and room (fitting for a counting house) with cellars underneath, an excellent drawing room and parlour, with five good bed and other rooms and two servants' bedrooms, with the other and necessary offices'.[141] In 1886 a local architect wrote 'the bold and characteristic Queen Anne front to the house occupied for business purposes by Messrs. Gould & Allen has long been the most striking feature in entering the city through Queen Street'.[142] The firm remained until 1948. In 1969 the building had considerable repairs to its roof.[143]

49. Bill of Charles Gould, tea dealer & grocer, of 40 High Street, 1838.

This may have been the reason for its long grocery history with the Gould family. From 1803 it was occupied by William Gould, grocer and tea dealer, and his London-born nephew, Charles Spry Gould, succeeded him.[136] By 1841 the business specialized in Italian food and was known as the Italian Warehouse. The following year there was 'rich Stilton, Parmesan and Chapzugar cheese, Westphalia and York hams, Russian ox, Reindeer and pickled tongues'.[137] Two years later Gould offered German sparkling Champagne.[138] The building had sufficient upstairs accommodation to

50. Repair work on 40 High Street, 1969.

51. James Crocker's drawing of 40 to 43 High Street, 1884, only the ground floor differs with today.

OCCUPANTS OF THE PROPERTY		
1689–1708	Daniel Slade,	*Goldsmith*
1715	William Slade,	*Goldsmith*
1731–1742	Daniel Pring,	*Bookseller*
1751	Joseph Rowe,	*Fuller*
1796–1802	George Hancock,	*Leather Breeches Maker*
1803–1835	William Gould,	*Grocer and Tea Dealer*
1835–1859	Charles Spry Gould,	*Grocery and Italian Warehouse*
1859–1948	Gould & Allen,	*Italian Warehousemen and Family Grocers*
1949–1995	Dorothy Perkins	(& 39 from 1966)
1996–2015	Clinton Cards,	*Gift cards*
2016	Vacant	
2017–	Skechers,	*Casual shoe retailer*

NUMBER 41

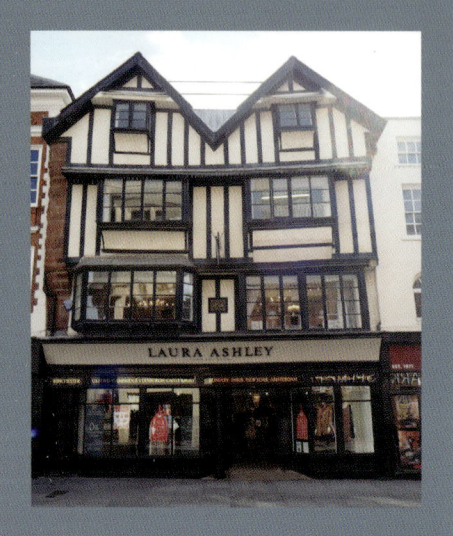

In 1953 this sixteenth-century building was listed Grade 2* and recorded as a 'timber-framed 4 storey front with 2 gables dated 1564. Each storey oversails with moulded beam at 1st floor level. One stone sidewall corbelled forward. 1st floor has two 6-light square oriels with moulded timbers, one with carved brackets. 4-light and 2-light oriels to 2nd and 3rd floors respectively. Front has been roughcast and some timbers applied. Modern shop front. Slate roof. Interior: carved oak board dated 1564. Parts of the house may be more ancient and there are remains of the Close wall in the basement. Some other original features, staircases, chamfered beams, etc.' The frontage of the two buildings is 29 feet 10 inches.

52. Photograph of the shop front of John Hinton Lake, chemist, at 41 High Street, early twentieth century.

41– 42 High Street, a pair of houses with the only plaque erected to show the date (1564) when they were built. Each has two storeys above the ground floor, an attic, cellar and are two rooms deep. The front rooms have oriel windows of six lights on the first floor, four lights on the second floor and two lights in the attic. The rear rooms are lit by windows overlooking a narrow courtyard. Heavitree stone can be seen on the eastern side of the front of Number 41.

Number 41 High Street, a property anciently held of the Dean & Chapter, rebuilt in 1564 (along with Number 42) and occupied by a series of apothecaries, most notably Hinton Lake, nearly continuously from 1660 to 1974. Laura Ashley has occupied the building since 1984. The date 1564 on the facade in Arabic numbers is commonly misread as 1164. In the nineteenth century it was in Roman numerals and an interior plaque was placed on the second floor. A carved door head, now in the Royal Albert Memorial Museum, also has the date which has been confirmed by recent dendrochronological analysis. An archaeological excavation in the basement in 1980 revealed Roman foundations including stone walling which was thought to have been the footing of the aqueduct which supplied water to the legionary bath-house in what is now Cathedral Yard.[144]

A considerable amount of internal painted decoration (on timber and plaster walls) was revealed in 1976. It has been suggested that these date to the period from 1570 to 1600. The colour schemes

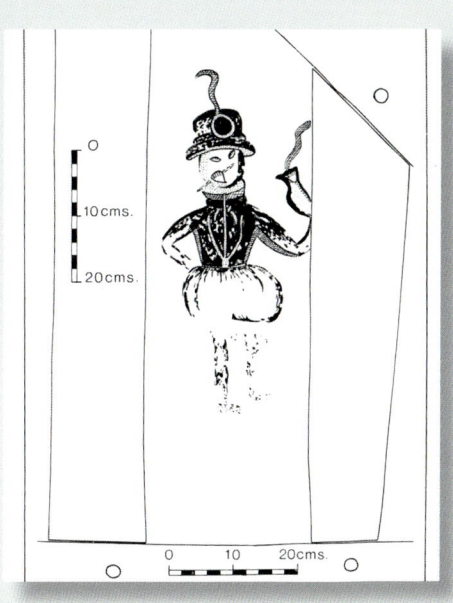

NUMBER 41 High Street

53 – 54. Wall painting of an Elizabethan man, possibly holding a hawk, at 41 High Street, with a drawing by John Thorp.

vary and include decoration to suggest oak screens, strapwork cartouches, a male figure with a hawk, and St George with his dragon. A fragment of French Elbeuf tapestry, of the 1660s or 1670s, was found in the first-floor rear room.[145]

Philip Hooper is the first apothecary known to have occupied Number 41. He took residence in 1660 and others followed, almost without interruption, for the next three centuries. After Hooper's death[146] the property passed through his family to an apprentice and his son-in-law, Charles Yeo, was at Number 42.[147] A rare survey, taken in 1701, shows that a successor also occupied the ground floor shop of Number 42. The property then had a cellar and the ground floor comprised an entry, shop and kitchen, behind which was a curtilage. On the floor above were a dining room and lodging room, above which were two lodging chambers, with two cocklofts above them. Both properties were 'ancient but strong built'.[148] The building continued in the apprentice's family into the eighteenth century.[149]

In 1926 Ethel Lega Weekes examined the remains of a fireplace in the east wall of the first floor front room and noted that it was thought to have been refurbished in about 1742. She concluded that other features, including panelling and a cupboard, were probably inserted at this time.[150] The occupant's tax account in 1768 showed the building then had 21 windows[151] and that year he was appointed apothecary to the cathedral choristers, possibly because

55. Drawing of 41 to 42 High Street, with Numbers 40 and 43 seen on the sides, nineteenth century.

St Martin's Island: An introductory history of forty-two Exeter buildings

56. Drawing of 41 to 42 High Street, without visible timberwork on the façade, but with 1564 in Roman numerals on the façade, c1910.

his grandfather was Bishop Offspring Blackall.[152] By 1788 he was succeeded by John White Abbott[153] whose insurance policy noted the slated building was built of brick, stone and plaster.[154] Abbott is remembered chiefly as a landscape painter but like his predecessor he served as the cathedral choristers' apothecary.[155] A visitor in 1810 wrote that Abbott 'is an apothecary and now practises as such, but will be heir to a very good fortune at the death of a gentleman, his near relation'. A local cleric told him that Abbott suffered from living in Exeter: he 'had been so admired and extolled that he was content with copying himself'.[156] Abbott probably gave up Number 41 when he inherited from his uncle in 1825.[157]

For the next 13 years there was an interruption in the apothecaries including Signora Maria C. Rovedino who held singing and language lessons at her home, probably upstairs, at Number 41.[158] A jeweller[159] was followed by a boot and shoemaker[160] who was described as 'a respectable tradesman… a zealous and indefatigable commissioner under the Poor Law'.[161] That year a man found guilty of stealing shoes from his shop was transported overseas.[162] There were 84 other boot and shoemakers in Exeter.[163] Number 41 also housed 'Blunden's Wholesale Warehouse for Tuscan, straw and fancy bonnets, French and English Flowers'.[164] Mrs Blunden was

NUMBER 41 High Street

one of twenty-one straw-hat makers in Exeter but her bonnet making skills were questioned in court.[165] A 'working jeweller' also moved to Number 41 and invited 'inspection of the various styles of his workmanship recently executed'. He had 'pebbles and stones cut as specimens for the cabinet, dealer in shells, fossils, minerals, etc., jewellery and plate repaired, also spectacles' and later offered 'spectacles of every approved description at greatly reduced prices'.[166]

In 1838 the building revived its apothecary tradition. It was then a 'dwelling house with front shop, extensive formerly three premises' and occupied by Thomas Knott. The following year an assistant, two apprentices and a servant lived on the premises. Knott later recalled that he had had an 'interruption to business for some time past, consequent upon his uncertain position with the town council'. His former premises were demolished to create Queen Street and this prompted his move. Knott sold, amongst other items, inhalers. From 1845 his 'Exeter and West of England Soda Water and Lemonade Manufactory' was also at Number 41.[167]

Later chemists[168] included John Hinton Lake. A neighbour noted 'the Lakes are abundant in this parish in the present day, but yet not related, for we have Mr Lake, silversmith, carrying on a highly respectable business (at Number 43)' as well as his 'young pharmaceutical friend Mr John Lake and Miss Lake, milliner'.[169] In 1886 a local architect wrote 'it has been humorously remarked of Numbers 41 to 42 that these, and houses of a like character, were designed before the age of umbrellas, so that people might run along the pavement fully protected by the overhanging storeys! But this by the way. In this, as in most instances, the old medieval builders did not begrudge either the quantity or the quality of British oak, and with what results we may see after a lapse of more than three centuries'.[170] Lake continued until 1974 and Laura Ashley has been the occupier since 1984.[171] There was fire and water damage to the rear of the buildings in 2016.

57. Engraving of the shop front of Thomas Knott, chemist, at 41 High Street, mid nineteenth century.

OCCUPANTS OF THE PROPERTY

1660 – 1693	Philip Hooper,	Apothecary
1693	Jane Hooper,	Widow
1694 – 1706	Samuel Sampson,	Apothecary
1707 – 1751	Samuel Sampson the Younger,	Apothecary & Mr Chute
1768 – 1788	Edward Howell,	Apothecary
1788 – 1825	John White Abbot,	Apothecary
1825	Signora Rovedino,	Musician (upstairs)
1827 – 1831	Samuel Maunder,	Boot & Shoe Maker
1828 – 1831	Walter Tucker,	Watch and Clock Maker, Jeweller, Silversmith
1832 – 1836	Mrs Ann Blunden,	Straw Hat Maker
1836 – 1837	George Carter,	Working Jeweller
1838 – 1862	Thomas Knott,	Chemist & Druggist
1862 – 1868	Charles Ham,	Chemist
1869 – 1974	John Hinton Lake,	Chemist (later Hinton Lake & Son) (& 42)
1976 – 1981	Star Jeans (& 42)	
1982 – 1983	Vacant	
1984 – 2017	Laura Ashley (& 42)	

NUMBER 42

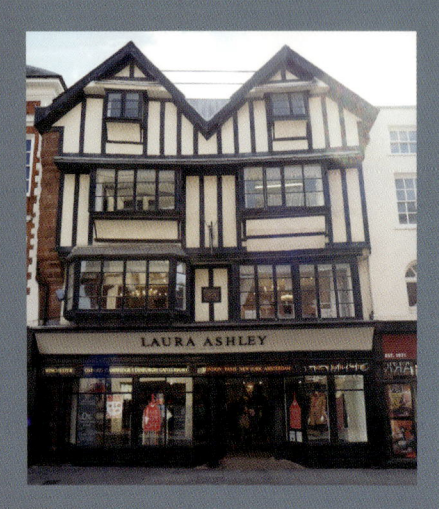

In 1953 this sixteenth-century building was listed Grade 2* and recorded as a 'timber-framed 4 storey front with 2 gables dated 1564. Each storey oversails with moulded beam at 1st floor level. One stone sidewall corbelled forward. 1st floor has two 6-light square oriels with moulded timbers, one with carved brackets. 4-light and 2-light oriels to 2nd and 3rd floors respectively. Front has been roughcast and some timbers applied. Modern shop front. Slate roof. Interior: carved oak board dated 1564. Parts of the house may be more ancient and there are remains of the Close wall in the basement. Some other original features, staircases, chamfered beams, etc.' The frontage of the two buildings is 29 feet 10 inches.

58. 41 to 42 High Street, early nineteenth century, with Number 43 seen on the right.

42 High Street, a property which, like Number 41, was anciently held of the Dean & Chapter and rebuilt in 1564. A number of apothecaries occupied the building, as with Number 41, but there was a much more varied type of retailer.

The occupiers were more varied than those at Number 41. Two booksellers were there in the late 1600s but in 1701[172] most of the ground floor was occupied by their neighbour at Number 41 leaving the booksellers with the cellar, the entry and kitchen on the ground floor, the dining room and lodging room on the first floor, two lodging chambers over them, and two cocklofts above these.[173] At the end of the century it was

NUMBER 42 High Street

59. Drawing of High Street, with on the left, Number 41, 1836–7.

60. Detail of wall painting of c1600, 42 High Street.

61. Fireplace, constructed of local stone, 42 High Street.

noted that there was a shop, curtilage, dining room, three lodging chambers and two cock lofts.[174] In the early 1800s there were milliners and dressmakers,[175] an engraver who shortly afterwards died 'after a lingering illness' aged 30[176] and W. L. Ponsford who may have been an auctioneer: he sold not only glass but dried fruit.[177] Miss Quantrell had her Dancing Academy upstairs but also rented a room in South Street for her dances.[178] Two generations of wine importers followed[179] and in 1840 Thomas Knott, who occupied Number 41 as a chemist, ran his Soda Water Factory at Number 42.[180] He shared the building: in 1839 Mrs Higgs opened her *Magasin des Modes* (Store Fashions) in the 'commodious show rooms' which had French and English millinery, dresses, mantillas, straw & chip bonnets, corsets and other items. She also sold her newly invented French and English corsets and was joined by Mrs Elizabeth Bailey, a Londoner 'renowned for her taste and skill in the fashionable world'. After Higgs retired Bailey travelled to Paris for her stock[181] and held the 'commodious millinery rooms and house'.[182] In 1845 'the shop had been newly fitted up, with a glass plate front' and was taken on by a Scottish hairdresser and perfumer. A few years later an assistant was fined for cutting an errand boy's hair expressly to be laughed at: the boy's head was covered with grease and rouge 'having the appearance of being painted with red paint'.[183] The Scot lived upstairs with his wife, their seven children (most of whom had been born in Exeter) and two servants.[184]

In 1852 Joseph Wippell extended his business which lay immediately opposite (now Marks & Spencers). He

NUMBER 42 High Street

offered tailor, habit and robe making but a year later returned to 219 High Street.[185] For a generation his successors were women: this included a furrier from Martin's Lane[186] who also lasted only a year,[187] and several milliners[188] including Charlotte Chamberlain who allowed Miss Roston Johnson to use her shop for consultations on rheumatism.[189] There were also female 'Hosiers, Haberdashers and Trimming Sellers' who were followed by Heyman Wreford's Gospel Depot,[190] Bradley's bicycle shop,[191] Heywood's coal and building materials[192] and the Western Times. By 1906 it was the premises of Brown & Sons, who sold choice fruit, flowers and wedding bouquets and continued for forty years.[193]

62. An early wooden toilet seat.

63. Colouring of the wall painting, 42 High Street.

OCCUPANTS OF THE PROPERTY

1660	Philip Hooper, *Apothecary*
1676	Edward Portbury, *Bookseller*
1689 – 1708	Charles Yeo, *Bookseller & Stationer*
1701	Samuel Sampson, *Apothecary* (ground floor)
1769 – 1788	Edward Howell, *Apothecary*
1788 – 1798	John White Abbot, *Apothecary*
1807	S. & E. Rudall, *Milliners & Dressmakers*
1798 – 1814	William Maunder, *Cordwainer*
1814 – 1816	James Rickard, *Engraver*
1814 – 1818	W. L. Ponsford, *Merchant*
1818 – 1819	(Miss Quantrell) *Dancing Academy*
1825 – 1827	W. Maunder, *Importer of Foreign Wines*
1827 – 1829	W. Maunder, Junior, *Importer of Foreign Wines*
1830 – 1839	John Sharland, *Tea Dealer & Grocer* (& 43)
1839 – 1844	Magasin des Modes, *Mrs Higgs & Mrs Bailey*
1845 – 1851	Robert Hopekirk, *Hair Dresser and Perfumer*
1852 – 1853	Joseph Wippell, *Tailor, Habit and Robe Maker*
1853 – 1854	Mrs W. H. Brown Hill, *Furrier*
1855 – 1878	Misses Bessie & A. H. Lake, *Milliners*
1878 – 1886	Charlotte Chamberlain, *Milliner*
1888 – 1890	Misses Anna & Emma Scudder, *Fancy Drapers*
1891 – 1897	Gospel Depot
1898 – 1900	R. Bradley, *Cycles*
1900	G. Heywood, *Building Material and Coal Merchant*
1901 – 1903	The Western Times
1906 – 1946	Brown & Sons, *Fruiterers & Florists*
1942 – 1946	R. H. Cummings, *Umbrella Specialists*
1947 – 1974	Hinton Lake & Son, *Chemists, Photo Dealers & Opticians* (& 41)
1976 – 1981	Star Jeans (& 41)
1982 – 1983	Vacant
1984 – 2017	Laura Ashley (& 41)

NUMBER 43

64. View of 43 to 46 High Street, showing the gabled roofs of 43 & 44 High Street hidden behind the later flat-roofed façades, 8 September 2017.

In 1974 this building was listed Grade 2 and it was recorded as a 'nineteenth-century stucco front on a probably older timber-framed building. 4 storeys, 2 windows, sashes with glazing bars, round headed on the first floor. Modern shop front shared with No 44. County insurance plaque. Parapet, roof not visible. Included for group value'. The frontage is 15 feet.

43 High Street, anciently a property of the Vicars Choral which was used by number of traders including booksellers, grocers and, most notably, jewellers.

This four storey building is older than its appearance suggests: it was built in the fifteenth century as a pair to Number 44. An extra storey was added in either the later seventeenth or early eighteenth century. The flat roofline of the façade disguises the pitched roof behind it.[194] Number 43 was occupied by a range of merchants selling various goods with jewellery being the trade having the longest use.

Glovers and booksellers predominated in the eighteenth century; one of them was John March who traded under the name of The Bible.[195] In the early 1800s Number 43 housed a grocery business and it comprised 'a spacious shop, a parlour, court and kitchen, with cellars underneath, a drawing room, five bedrooms and attic'.[196] During the early Victorian period four merchants in quick succession used Number 43 to sell various types of clothing. For five years John Toms ran his 'ready-ware linen warehouse'[197] but he announced plans to leave England, sell his household furniture and offered the shop and house for letting. By then Number 43 comprised various bedrooms, a dining room, drawing room and breakfast parlour.[198] That year the Improvement Commissioners granted Toms permission to 'form an oven at the house, No. 43 High Street, but not to excavate beyond the kerb'.[199] Mr Salaman, a tailor and breeches maker,

NUMBER 43 High Street

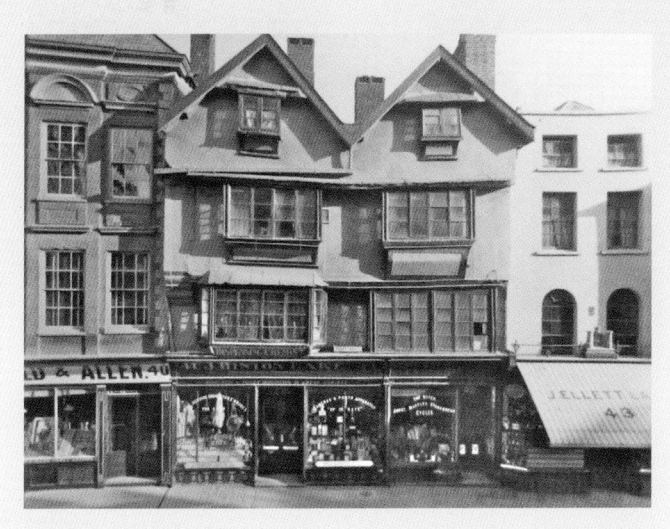

65. 40 to 43 High Street, c1900.

succeeded Toms but within a year he left Exeter because of an accident.[200] A draper and hosier succeeded him but only lasted two years[201] and he was followed by a London bookseller, stationer, bookbinder and account book manufacturer who lived in Number 43 with his wife, one son and three servants.[202] After seven years he also left.

The fortunes of the building changed in 1856 when Henry Lake, a jeweller, watchmaker and silversmith took residency. He and his family continued until 1930 when William Bruford & Son took over the firm and three years later J. E. Lake closed.[203] Pinder & Tuckwell then moved from 191 High Street and announced that they would be erecting an 'imposing new front' for Numbers 43–4. The ground floor was a shop, the first floor housed the tailoring department and the 'upper part of the building is used by the staff themselves, who work under the supervision of the firm's own cutters'. By then the building had been 'rebuilt on up-to-date lines and have added an attractive modern front to the street and pleasant and convenient accommodation for the staff as well as the customers'. One commentator noted the building was 'reconstructed'.[204] It was at this time or afterwards that the first floor windows were altered: these were shortened and the bars of the panes removed. Pinder & Tuckwell continued for more than 50 years at Number 43.

66. The shop window of John Ellett Lake & Son at 43 High Street, with the city's coat of arms above the door, c1910.

OCCUPANTS OF THE PROPERTY

1661 – 1679	Christopher Trehane,	*Glover*
1684 – 1689	Mary Trehane,	*Widow*
1708	Thomas Whitty,	*Glover*
1705 – 1713	Abraham Gandy,	*Glover*
1713 – 1726	John March,	*Bookseller*
1731 – 1740	Aaron Tozer,	*Bookseller*
1746 – 1762	Benjamin Wood,	*Hosier*
1768	John Saunders,	*Glover*
1799	William Hussey,	*Linen Draper*
1808 – 1814	Benjamin Cramp,	*Grocer (& 44)*
1815 – 1838	John Sharland,	*Tea Dealer & Grocer (& 42)*
1839 – 1843	Outfitting Warehouse	*(J. Toms)*
1844 – 1845	S. Salaman,	*Tailor and Breeches Maker*
1845 – 1847	William Couch,	*Linen & Woollen Draper, Hosier*
1848 – 1855	David Thomson,	*Stationer & Bookbinder*
1856 – 1874	Henry Lake,	*Jeweller, Watchmaker & Silversmith*
1874 – 1930	John Ellett Lake,	*Jeweller*
1930 – 1933	William Bruford & Son,	*Jeweller*
1933 – 1988	Pinder & Tuckwell,	*Ladies & Gentlemen's Tailors (& 44)*
1989 – 2000	Principles,	*Ladies Wear (& 44 – 5)*
2001 – 2004	First Sports	*(& 44 – 5)*
2005 – 2007	Portman Building Society	*(& 44 – 5)*
2008 – 2017	Costa Coffee	*(& 44 – 5)*

NUMBER 44

In 1953 this building was listed Grade 2 and recorded as 'probably sixteenth century but very altered eighteenth/nineteenth centuries. Timber-framed, rendered, overhang at 1st floor level. 2 storeys, one window above modern sash in flush frame. Modern shop front with No. 43. Cornice, roof not visible. Included for group value.' In 1947 the provisional listing had noted 'Numbers 44 & 45 adjoining [Number 43] may also be old houses, but the fronts are of no interest'. The frontage is 13 feet 4 inches.

67. 44 to 47 High Street, c1899 to 1909.

44 High Street, anciently a property of the Vicars Choral, this unassuming building had no clear retail identity but is distinguished by having at one time the name Cheviot House, for housing Exeter's first permanent museum and, most significantly, for being the only known building outside Cathedral Close that is characteristic of a medieval open hall.

This is perhaps the plainest and least imposing building in the Island. The frontage is barely thirteen feet. The first floor has a single window and slightly jetties out over High Street. Sometime between 1893 and 1911 it retained a (triangular) pediment which may have been erected in the eighteenth or early nineteenth centuries. The building has recently been assessed as having kept 'the arch-braced and smoke-blackened roof of a medieval open hall, set behind a former chamber on the street front. [Along with Number 43] they offer a good example of the manner in which progressive portioning and flooring of the interior of a medieval townhouse provided more space: in the

NUMBER 44 High Street

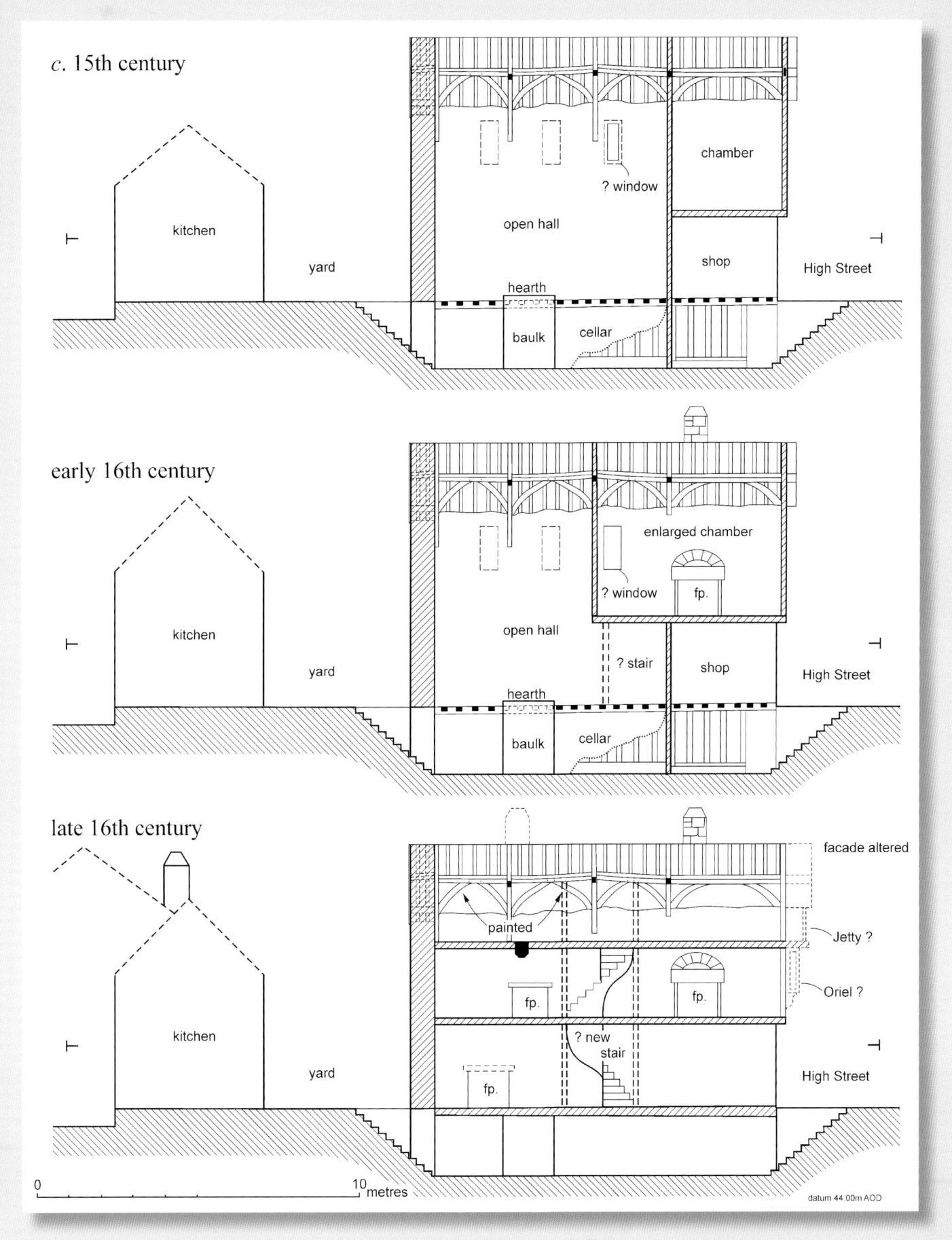

c. 15th century

early 16th century

late 16th century

68. The development of 44 High Street from the 1400s through to the late 1500s, drawn by T. Ives.

St Martin's Island: An introductory history of forty-two Exeter buildings

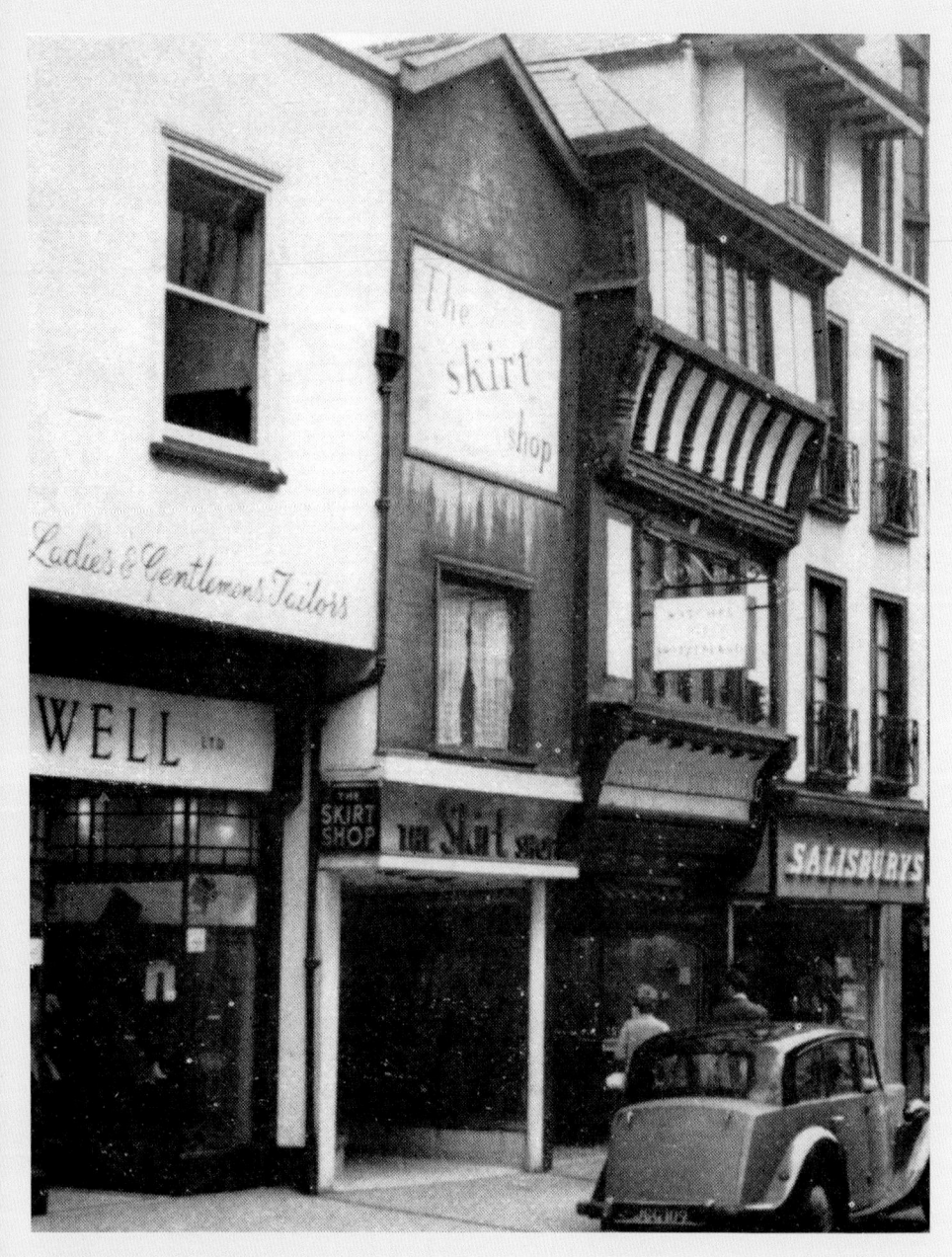

69. 44 to 47 High Street, c1962–5.

sixteenth century the hall was subdivided into ground and first floor rooms (the latter with painted decoration on the roof timbers) and the space itself was later pressed into use as a separate room, lit by dormers'.[205]

Although it was conveniently situated in High Street and had Lamb Alley to its rear, the building was too small for many merchants. Therefore it had a multitude of merchants and trades, including a cork cutter in the 1760s,[206] and was probably empty when used for a book sale in 1809.[207] The building was then for sale[208] and was 'a house in complete repair containing a spacious shop, a parlour, court and kitchen, a lead pipe, and communication to the common sewer; with five bedrooms and attics'.[209] In 1816 it was noted as a dwelling house with 'several cellars, counting houses, a ware house, stable and loft in Lamb Alley behind the dwelling house, and lately in the possession of Mr Pearce, wine merchant'.[210]

In 1824 Number 44 housed 'Chaplin's Museum'. This was an enterprise of John Chaplin, an auctioneer and assessor who held public sales such as a consignment of cut glass as well as 'superb antique china'. He also exhibited curiosities such as an Egyptian mummy which had been purchased for £435 at Plymouth's Custom House. Chaplin's museum differed in that it was not temporary and his museum included 'rare articles of taste and magnificence comprising a cabinet of pictures by esteemed masters, an assortment of oriental, Dresden and Sevres porcelain, Bughl, ebony and pearl cabinets, marble statues, bas relief and antique busts, beautiful India ivory carvings'. Chaplin also had 'a rare and precious collection of Italian mosaics, intaglios, cameos and antiques. A series of exquisite anatomical figures etc. in wax, calculated for public lectures, and now forming a lucrative exhibition. Forty-six models in wax by the celebrated Percy, of the most distinguished characters of their day. A magnificent plateau in Florentine alabaster, 45 feet in length, illustrating the principal characters and events in the siege of Troy; this combination of talent is allowed to be the finest specimen of modern Italian genius in Europe. A rare assortment of Etruscan vases, warranted genuine, many of which were the property of the late Lord Bristol. A great variety of Volcanic specimens, from Etna, Vesuvius and Stromboli; Egyptian idols, minerals, petrifications, fossils, etc.'[211] The museum was anticipated to be a popular destination during the Assizes. His alabaster plateau was allegedly commissioned by Napoleon and Chaplin also had specimens of Oriental and Dresden china, Indian carvings of ivory and rare foreign shells.[212]

NUMBER 44 High Street

However, the museum closed in 1826 and was replaced by The City Tea Warehouse. Two Londoners announced their business was on an extensive scale and 'adapted in all respects to meet the views of the higher classes of society, as well as all large consumers who wish to purchase *strong rich-flavoured teas* on economical terms'. Mr Philpot purchased tea in London and Mr Davies handled the Exeter business; he lived locally and in 1831 was married in St Paul's church. The firm had unusual visitors in 1829: a swarm of bees lodged themselves in a large gilt canister. The firm sold sugar & coffee which was made without slave labour and in 1863 two other men took over the business.[213] Four years later that partnership was dissolved and the shop fittings were sold. These included mahogany top counters with drawers, nest of drawers and shelves, 'superior tea mills and mixers', coffee mills, sugar chopper, beams, scales and weights, 54 'handsome-fronted' 12 pound tea canisters and sugar & currant sieves.[214] The tea trade had lasted 43 years at Number 44.

Occupancy rapidly changed over the following two generations: initially it was an ironmonger (who renamed the building Cheviot House),[215] male clothing was then sold by two different firms[216] and they were followed in quick succession by a general draper, milliner & dressmaker,[217] a printer[218] and another draper.[219] The Western Morning News lasted five years and during the Great War it was the Red Cross Depot. In 1931 the building, along with Number 43, was 'reconstructed'.[220] A period of stability came two years later when Pinder & Tuckwell moved from 191 High Street, used both Numbers 43 & 44 and continued until 1988.[221]

70. Medieval roof at 44 High Street, c1920s – 1930s.

OCCUPANTS OF THE PROPERTY

1715	Robert Bradford, *Ironmonger*
1723 – 1762	William Moore, *Druggist*
1762 – 1768	James Bennett, *Cork Cutter*
1801 – 1807	James Pearce, *Wine Merchant*
1808 – 1809	Benjamin Cramp, *Grocer* (& 43)
1814 – 1823	W. Smallridge, *Hosier*
1824 – 1825	Chaplin's Museum
1826 – 1863	Samuel Davies and Mr Philpot, *Wholesale Tea Dealers*
1863 – 1869	William Henry Cole & William Luxmoore, *Tea Dealers*
1869 – 1880	Edwin Lancey & Company, *Furnishing Ironmongers*
1881 – 1882	J. T. Cowey, *Tailor, Hosier and Hatter*
1883 – 1888	Daw Brothers, *Fabrics*
1889 – 1891	F. W. Haydon, *General Draper, Milliner & Dressmaker*
1892	William Pollard & Company, *Printers*
1893 – 1911	Miss S. J. Knowling, *Draper*
1911 – 1916	Western Morning News
1917 – 1918	Red Cross Depot, *Exeter Food Control Campaign Committee*
1919 – 1930	Brooking & Company, *Electrical Engineers*
1931 – 1933	R. J. Woodley, *Boot & Shoe Warehouseman*
1933 – 1988	Pinder & Tuckwell, *Tailors & Outfitters* (& 43 & 45)
1989 – 2000	Principles, *Ladies Wear* (& 43 & 45)
2001 – 2004	First Sports (& 43 & 45)
2005 – 2007	Portman Building Society (& 43 & 45)
2008 – 2017	Costa Coffee (& 43 & 45)

NUMBER 45

In 1974 this timber-framed and rendered building was listed Grade 2 and recorded as being 'probably sixteenth century but very altered on the frontage eighteenth/nineteenth centuries. Timber-framed behind, rendered and painted. 3 storeys, modern shop front, window above only on the 1st floor. Slight overhang. Gable to street, roof not visible. Moulded 1st floor beams. Included for group value.' In 1947 the provisional listing had noted 'Numbers 44 and 45 adjoining [Number 43] may also be old houses, but the fronts are of no interest'. The frontage is 10 feet 6 inches.

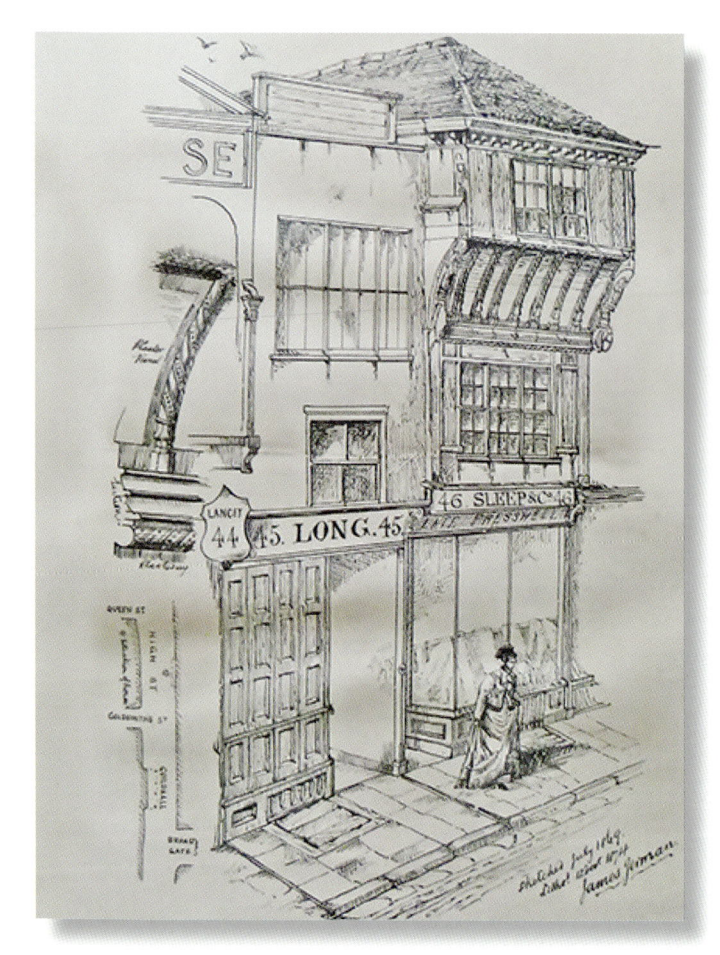

71. Drawing by James Jerman of 44 to 46 High Street, July 1869.

45 High Street, a property probably built in the mid 1500s on the High Street entrance to Lamb Alley. It was owned by the Dean & Chapter and mostly occupied by clothing retailers. Its frontage is the narrowest of any building in High Street.

The entrance to Lamb Alley was narrow, not even eleven feet, and it has been suggested that Number 45 was erected on that site in the late sixteenth century. The timber-framed building has three storeys, a noticeable gable, and a cellar lined with Heavitree stone. There were originally front and rear rooms on each floor.[222] A rectangular pediment existed in the nineteenth century but has since been removed. In 1769 the building had nine windows[223] but by the mid 1800s one on the second floor had more than doubled its size only to be removed altogether in the 1900s.

Aaron Tozer, a haberdasher, was an occupant in the late 1600s[224] and for much of the nineteenth and twentieth century Number 45 continued to be used for selling clothing, particularly hats. No fewer than 16 such different businesses (including haberdashers, drapers, milliners, hatters, hosiers and tailors) dominated the use of the building. There were some exceptions including an accountant, a fishing tackle manufacturer[225] and three photographers[226] in the Victorian period.

NUMBER 45 High Street

In the early 1800s a draper specialised in Irish cloth[227] and he was succeeded by two maiden ladies who sold millinery. They advertised their association with the Princess of Wales and the Duchess of York.[228] The building then comprised eight rooms and an underground cellar.[229] Other firms that followed[230] included The Silk Mercery, Urling, Thread Lace and Glove Warehouse[231] and The London Straw Hat Warehouse. In 1850 Number 45 comprised a 'shop and parlour behind, kitchen, curtilage, etc., drawing room, five bedrooms, an attic, closets, etc., with a cellar under the shop'. It was noted that it had been 'papered and painted throughout'.[232] Two other clothing retailers followed in quick succession[233] including John Beedell who had 'the cheapest house in the city for hats and caps, carpet bags, umbrellas, water-proof coats, & etc.'.[234] George William Fox, a hatter, glover and shirt maker, was the occupier from 1910 until his death in 1919 at the age of only 30 years. He was described as having been of a 'pleasant, cheery disposition' and markedly popular among a wide circle of friends. The 1911 census shows there was no one then resident in the building; Fox had then lived at College Road with his mother.[235]

In 1946 the building was renovated, including the insertion of a new shop front, and workers found 'oak carvings beneath three layers of plaster. The carvings, in quatrefoils and other designs, apparently formed part of the exterior decoration of the adjoining house on the west side'.[236] Sixty years later the medieval carvings were rediscovered during renovation work.[237]

73. Late medieval carved panels of Gothic tracery with shields, on west wall of 45 High Street. These would have been seen on the exterior of 44 High Street from Lamb Alley.

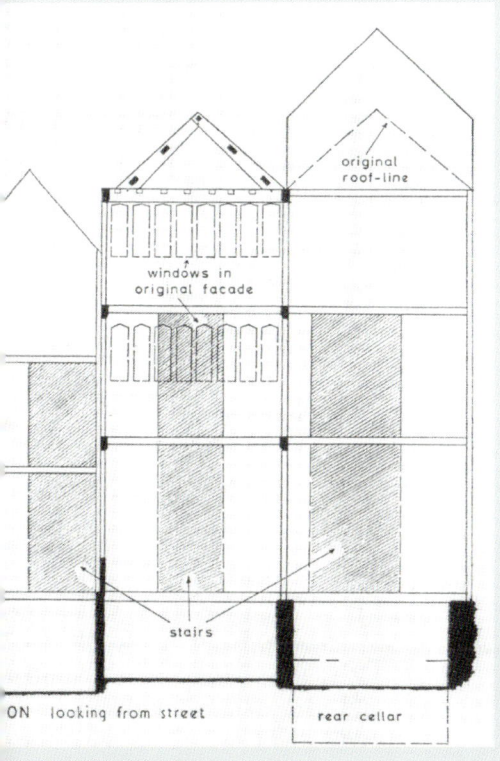

72. 45 to 47 High Street.

OCCUPANTS OF THE PROPERTY

1660	Edward Portbury,	Bookseller
1673 – 1676	Aaron Tozer,	Haberdasher
1689	John Ash,	Grocer
1708 – 1746	Robert Mudge,	Druggist
1747 – 1751	Agnes Maddock	
1768	Michael Jennings,	Sadler
1772 – 1801	William Strong,	Tinman
1801	William Floyde,	China-man
1806 – 1813	J. Jenkins,	Linen Draper
1814 – 1819	Misses F. & E. Snell,	Milliners
1821 – 1822	J. D. Shephard,	Haberdasher & Draper
1823 – 1825	R. Hillier,	Silk Mercery, Urling, Thread Lace and Glove Warehouse
1826 – 1829	Elias Butland,	Haberdasher and Laceman
1829 – 1834	D. Westaway & Sons,	Tailors
1834 – 1850	Millinery Rooms, later Millinery,	Straw Bonnet and Artificial Flower Warehouse, Mrs Eliza Mayne, & Robert Mayne, Accountant
1850 – 1852	George Haines,	Haberdasher
1852 – 1854	Samuel B. Watts,	Hat & Cap Manufacturer
1854 – 1855	Frederick Wood,	Whip and Fishing Tackle Manufacturer
1855 – 1856	John Beedell,	Hatter
1857 – 1859	London Photographic Company	
1861	Groom & Company,	Photographers
1861 – 1897	James Frederick Long,	Artist and Photographer
1899 – 1909	Robert Henry Baker,	Hats & Caps
1910 – 1919	George William Fox,	Hosier & Outfitter
1923 – 1953	Frederick William Anstice,	Hosier
1954	Empty	
1955 – 1968	Skirt Shop	
1969 – 1988	Pinder & Tuckwell,	Ladies Wear
1989 – 2000	Principles,	Ladies Wear (& 43-4)
2001 – 2004	First Sports (& 43-4)	
2005 – 2007	Portman Building Society (& 43-4)	
2008 – 2017	Costa Coffee (& 43-4)	

NUMBER 46

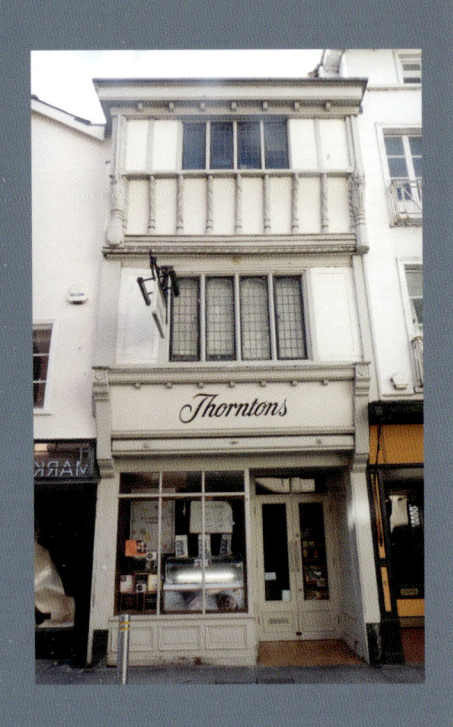

In 1953 this building was listed Grade 2* and recorded as 'sixteenth-century or earlier, 3 storeys, timber-framed front. Eighteenth-century modillion cornice. Windows and timbers generally much restored. Above first floor is unusual coved framing with carved upright members, on left hand side carved figure forms angle bracket. 4-light lattice windows. Modern shop front. Modillion cornice, hipped slate roof. Some internal features.' The frontage is 13 feet 2 inches.

74. Drawing of 46 High Street, c1829–40. Notice the bonnets placed against the first floor window panes. The chimney pots have since been removed.

46 High Street, a property anciently held of the Dean & Chapter, was notable for nearly a century having been used to retail clothing and most particularly for being one of the most impressive early buildings to survive in High Street.

In 2009 an analysis of the woodwork suggested the timber was probably cut between 1492 and 1515.[238] This establishes Number 46 as one of the oldest known buildings in High Street. It has recently been celebrated for the retention of the old fabric and for having been well-built and richly carved. It was pointed out that 'the impressive run of primary arched windows on the frontage, which formerly extended onto the sides of the house, is an early example of the extensive use of window glass and must have given a lantern-like quality to the properties.'[239]

The eighteenth-century occupants included a saddler, a haberdasher of small wares, a druggist, a bookseller

NUMBER 46 High Street

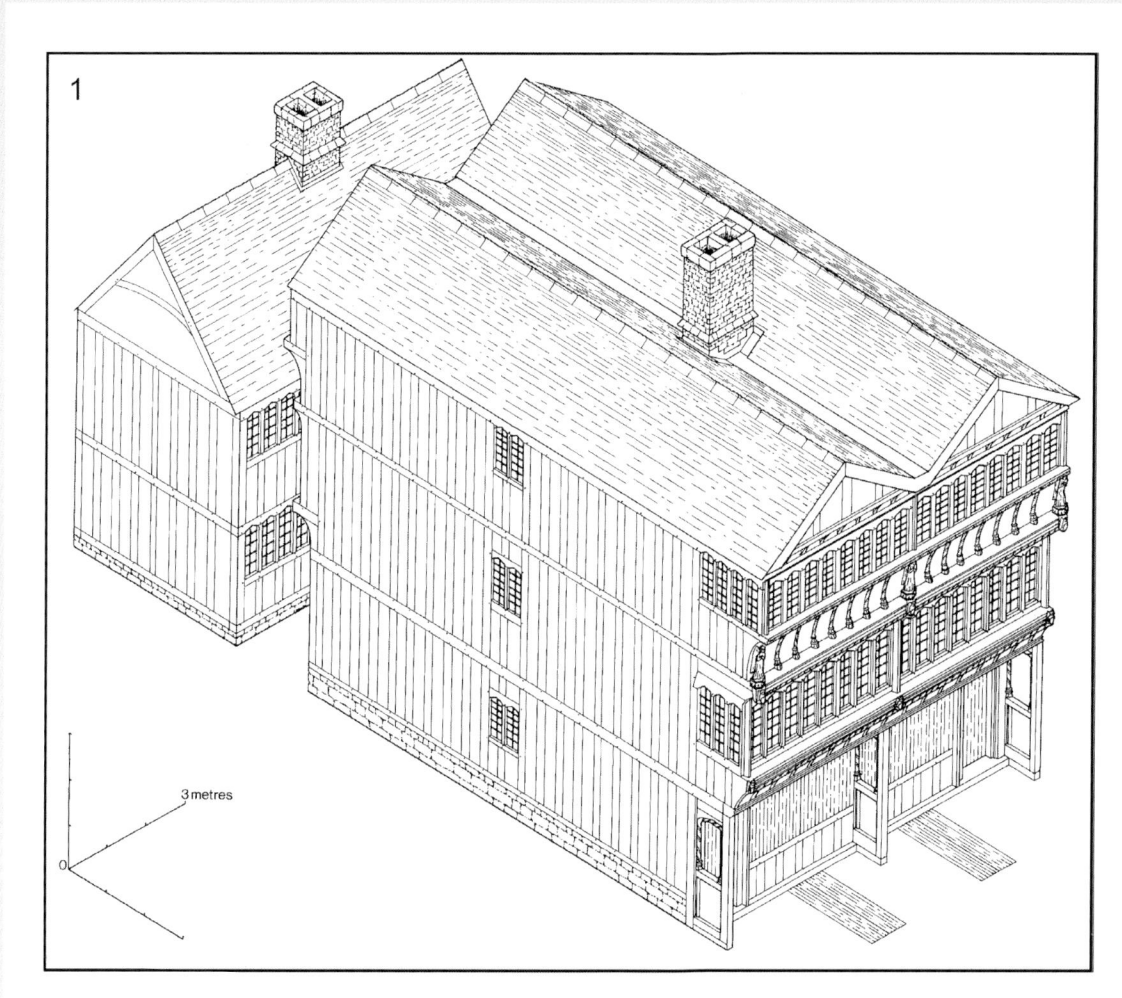

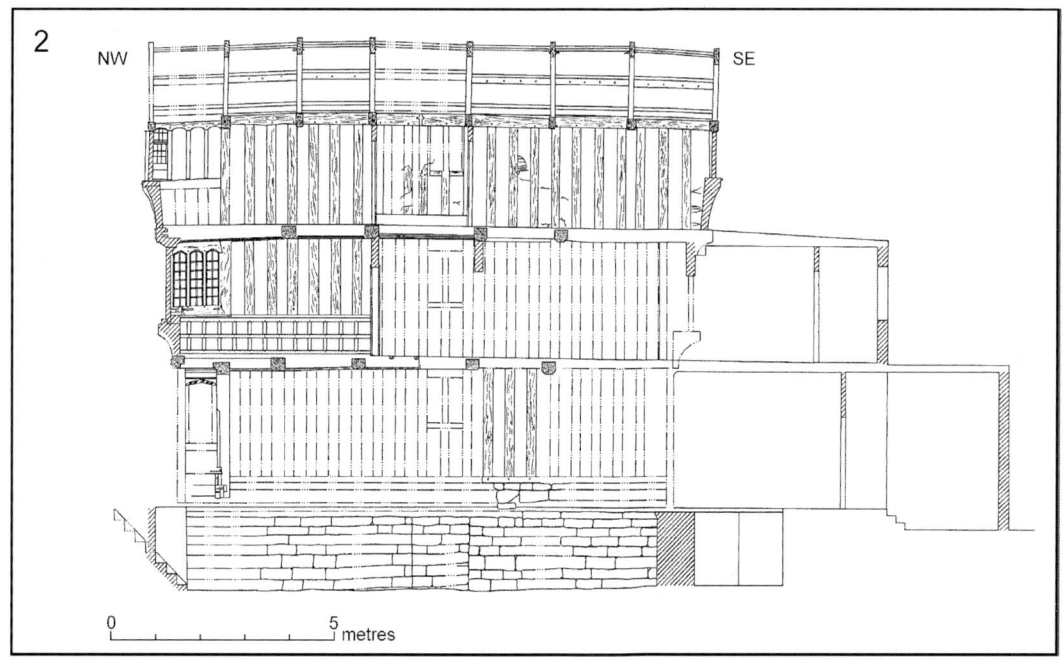

75. 46 to 47 High Street drawn by K. Westcott of (1), appearance of the newly-constructed building and (2), eastern appearance along Lamb Alley.

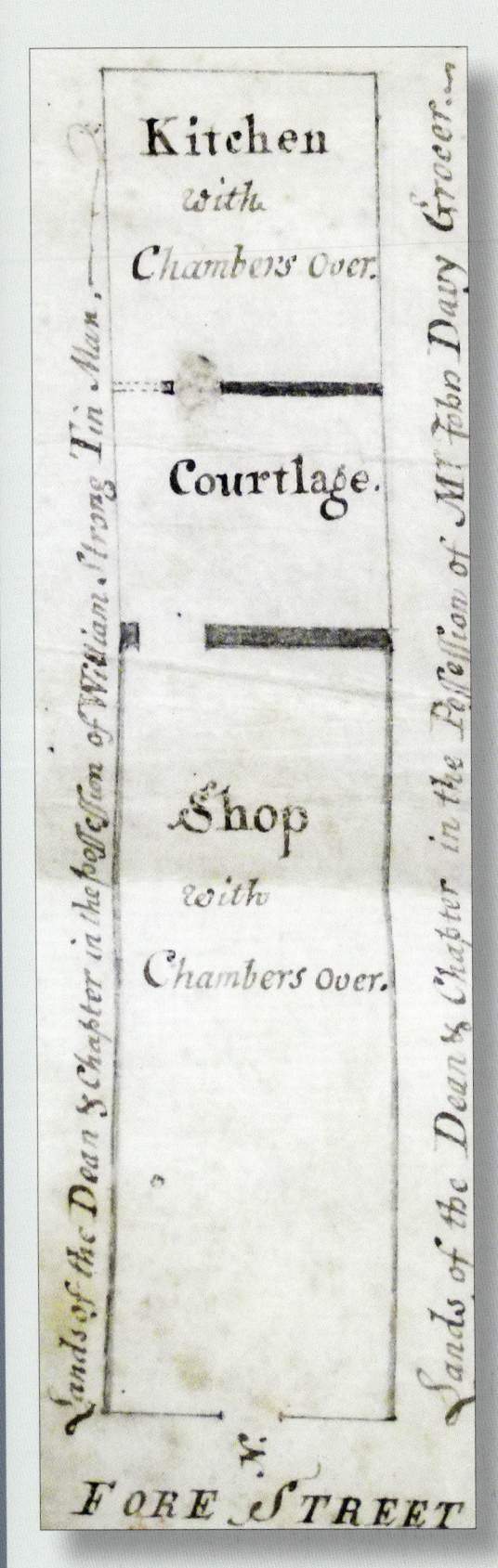

St Martin's Island: An introductory history of forty-two Exeter buildings

77. The courtyard at 46 High Street featuring a gallery to the back building.

and a grocer who was also the occupier of 18 Cathedral Yard.[240] A plan made in 1772 shows the entrance led into a shop with chambers overhead. Behind lay a courtyard beyond which was a kitchen with additional rooms overhead.[241]

In 1800 an ironmonger occupied the building[242] but for nearly the rest of that century, and continuing until 1925, merchants selling clothing dominated Number 46. On two separate occasions two pairs of maiden sisters sold hats. For three years E. and A Stamp, Milliners & Fancy Dress Makers, were occupants but closed their shop upon the engagement of one sister to a London baker.[243] Ten years later Elizabeth and Charlotte Tapley opened their 'millinery, chip, straw and Leghorn, ribbon and trimming warehouse' and sold 'ostrich plumes mounted in the newest style' as well as 'black and white pressed Italian chips'.[244] A decade later Elias Butland purchased their haberdashery and fancy trade business but continued the 'London Straw and Leghorn Establishment' upstairs.[245] During the 1800s Number

76. Plan by John Tothill of 46 High Street, 1772, with High Street noted as Fore Street at the bottom. The outline remains the same nearly 250 years later.

78. The Sun Insurance mark, 46 High Street.

NUMBER 46 High Street

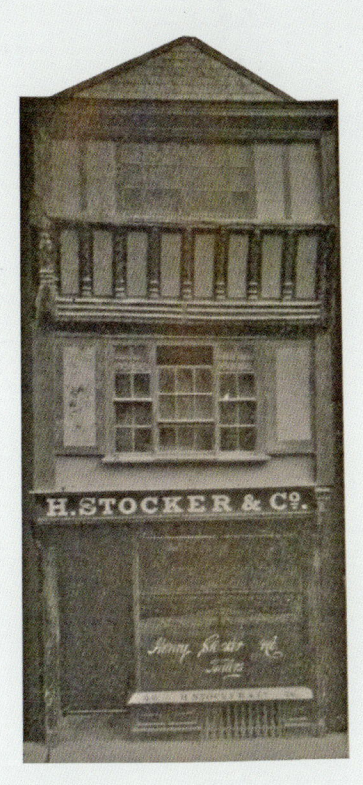

79. 46 High Street, c1908.

80. Glass panes in a covered window frame in the front room of the upper floor of 46 High Street facing north.

46 had eight businesses run by male clothing retailers and these were also short-lived.[246] It was not until 1877, with Henry Stocker & Company, that a firm lasted a considerable length of years;[247] it continued to 1925.[248]

In 1926, when Freeth's Tofferies became the occupant, concerns were voiced about renovations. A journalist wrote 'it is hoped that the alterations will not interfere with the preservation of the fine old front, which is one of the most interesting features of High Street. It is a splendid opportunity for sympathetic treatment, and, with a window in keeping with the age of the front, the new owner, whoever he may be, would earn the gratitude of all lovers of the old city, and it might not turn out an unwise move from the point of view of business either'.[249] In 1932 minor damage was caused by fire from a gas leak[250] and it was presumably at this time that the windows on the upper floors were altered.

OCCUPANTS OF THE PROPERTY

1660 – 1676	Edward Painter,	Skinner (& family members)
1708 – 1731	James Horswell,	Saddler
1740	Samuel Tozer,	Haberdasher of Small Wares
1769	Robert Burrow,	Druggist
1772	John Davy,	Grocer
1782	Richard Tucker,	Bookseller
1800 – 1804	Thomas Hill,	Ironmonger
1806 – 1809	E. & A. Stamp,	Milliners and Fancy Dress Makers
1811 – 1812	William Coplestone,	Linen Draper (& 47)
1813 – 1820	M. Comerford,	Bookseller
1814 – 1819	William Maunder (Junior),	Woollen Draper & Mercer
1819 – 1830	Misses Elizabeth & Charlotte Tapley,	Milliners & Haberdashers
1829 – 1840	Elias Butland,	Haberdasher & Laceman
1840 – 1841	John Burgess,	Ladies' and Gentlemen's Boot & Shoemaker
1841	J. R. Beer & Company,	Coal, Porter & Ale Merchants
1842 – 1853	George Elworthy,	Woollen Draper, Hatter & Tailor
1854 – 1869	Charles Benjamin Presswell,	Tailor & Draper
1869 – 1877	Samuel Colin Sleep & Company (John Evans),	Tailors & Drapers
1877 – 1925	Henry Stocker & Co. (John Evans),	Tailors and Outfitters
1926 – 1956	Freeth's Tofferies	
1957 – 1959	House of Bewlay,	Tobacconists
1960 – 1961	Etam Ltd,	Ladies' Outfitters
1962 – 1983	Watches of Switzerland Ltd	
1984	Telefusion	
1985	Connect	(TV electrical)
1986	Vacant	
1987 – 2017	Thorntons,	Confectioner

65

NUMBER 47

In 1953 this building was listed Grade 2 and recorded as 'early nineteenth century. 4 storeys stucco front on an older, probably sixteenth-century, building. Top storey is set back and has wide eaves with brackets. Incised lines to quoins. French casements to 1st and 2nd floors. Iron balconies with Greek ornament. 2 windows on each floor. Modern shop front. Roof not visible, Some internal features. Originally a pair with No 46. An important feature is the first floor open gallery to seventeenth-century rear block, original balusters.' The frontage is 14 feet.

81. 46 and 47 High Street drawn by James Crocker, 1884.

47 High Street, a property which was anciently held of the Dean & Chapter, was occupied by a series of chemists for 110 years.

Number 47 has a narrow frontage but has four floors. The large size of the building, in comparison to some of its neighbours, made the upstairs rooms suitable for residential use through to at least 1911 when there was one male and two females living there.

In the seventeenth and eighteenth centuries Number 47 was occupied by a silkweaver, a tailor, a barber, three grocers and by John Hill who described himself as a chemist and druggist. Hill had been an occupant by 1796 and when he left there followed a fifteen year interruption in the use by chemists: first two linen drapers occupied the building[251] and they were followed by the India Tea House for two years.[252] However, from 1822 two men in the pharmaceutical trade occupied the building and another eight followed them until 1932. One business was called the Exeter Genuine Drug Establishment and another The Pharmaceutical Hall.[253] One of the chemists kept a bust of Galen, the Greek physician of the second century, over the door.[254]

In 1932, for the first time in more than 100 years, the building was not occupied by a chemist but by A. L. Salisbury,

NUMBER 47 High Street

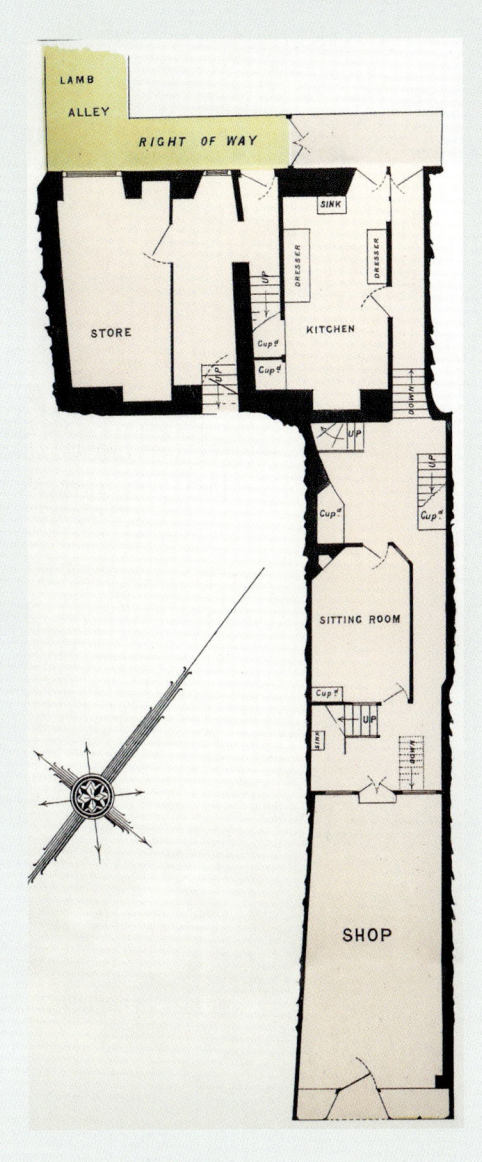

specialists in leather. It continued through to 1965 when the firm moved next door to Number 48. In 1966 Visionhire, a television rental business, was the next occupier and it was not until 1990 that it was replaced (by a newer technology firm).

In 1903 Number 47 comprised on a ground floor a double fronted shop, sitting room with cupboard and kitchen, on the first floor was a dining room with casement windows and four store rooms, on the second floor were three bedrooms and two storerooms and the top floor had two bedrooms, one with French casement windows.[255] In 1800 John Hill also possessed a dwelling house behind Number 47 which had an entrance into Lamb Alley. Subsequent occupiers continued to hold this building through into the early twentieth century (see Lamb Alley, pages 161).

82. Ground floor of 47 High Street, as offered for sale, 1903.

83. Gallery walkway from 47 High Street to rear building, 29 August 2017.

84. Sixteenth-century chimney stack now encased by the adding of a higher roof at the rear of 47 High Street, 29 August 2017.

OCCUPANTS OF THE PROPERTY

1660	Joan Acland,	*Widow*
1668 – 1686	James Acland,	*Silkweaver*
1689 – 1699	Thomas Clarke,	*Tailor*
1708	John Hooker,	*Grocer*
1715	Thomas Collibear,	*Barber*
1731	John Stephens,	*Grocer*
1740	Richard Densham	
1751 – 1773	John Davey,	*Grocer*
1796 – 1807	John Hill,	*Chemist & Druggist (from 1802 Hill & Williams)*
1807 – 1809	Robert Sowden,	*Linen Draper (later Sowden & Children)*
1811 – 1816	William Coplestone,	*Linen Draper (& 46)*
1820 – 1822	India Tea House, S. Cornish,	*Grocer*
1822 – 1826	Salter & Beedle,	*Druggist*
1827 – 1833	Exeter Genuine Drug Establishment, Thomas George Beedle,	*Druggist*
1833 – 1853	John Croome,	*Chemist & Druggist*
1853 – 1874	Pharmaceutical Hall, John Knapman,	*Family & Dispensing Chemist*
1874 – 1879	John Fegan,	*Chemist*
1880	David Jones,	*Pharmaceutical Chemist*
1880 – 1883	Walter Wright,	*Chemist*
1883 – 1921	Eric Lemmon,	*Chemist*
1920 – 1929	Harold Densem,	*Chemist*
1930 – 1932	W. Hosegood Clarke,	*Chemist*
1932 – 1965	A. L. Salisbury Ltd.,	*Leather Specialists*
1966 – 1993	Visionhire,	*Television Rental*
1994 – 1996	Granada	
1997	Vacant	
1998 – 2008	The Orange Shop,	*Mobile Telephones*
2009 – 2017	L'Occitaine,	*Perfumiers*

NUMBER 48

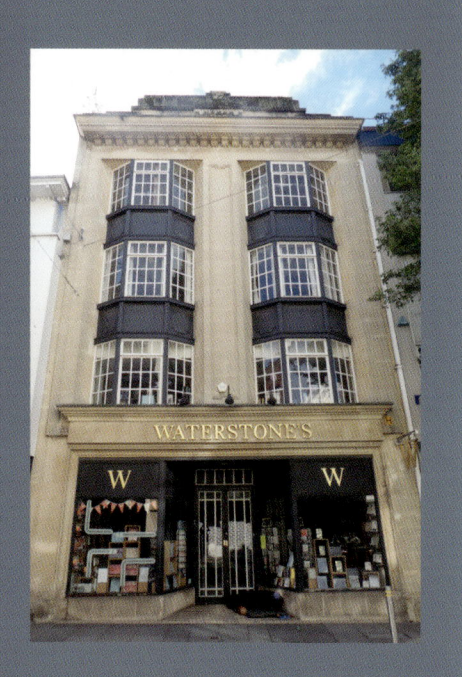

The building is not listed. The frontage, with Number 49, is 30 feet 8 inches.

48 High Street, anciently owned by the City of Exeter, comprised the eastern half of an early nineteenth-century building which was demolished, along with Number 49, in 1921 and had a new building on the site two years later.

By the late 1800s this was one of the two buildings in the Island to have five floors. Above the ground floor there were a pair of casement windows on each upper storey. One occupant in 1916 was Miss Kernick, a dress and costumier, who had been there for at least three years when the building was damaged by fire. The ground floor was occupied by a confectioner, the first floor was rented to an architect and Miss Kernick had the two top floors for her clothing business. The fire started in an upper floor possibly by Miss Kernick's candle having ignited rubbish. The rear staircase suffered considerable fire damage but it was suggested that greater damage had been caused by water.[256]

The Prudential Assurance Company purchased the building and in 1921 Numbers 48 and 49 were demolished. The architect of the replacement building was J. Henry Pitt and the local supervising architect was J. Archibald Lucas, a former resident.[257] The first occupant was Deller's Café. The firm had begun in 1906 at the corner of Martin's Lane and Cathedral Yard and thirteen years later it moved its

NUMBER 48 High Street

The older building also had a great number and diversity of nineteenth-century occupants: these included The London Fur Manufactory and Huckvale's T Warehouse. Robert Nesbitt Gollop had his ironmongery business at Number 48 in the early 1800s and in 1874 it was recalled that the building during his time comprised 'two humble shops with small panes of glass'. It was then said that Gollop's character 'was truly just and correct and his memory will long be revered by his numerous friends and relations'. There were fourteen other ironmongers then working in Exeter.[259]

Five short-lived businesses followed including the 'Hat, Hosiery, Glove and Ladies Boot and Shoe Warehouse' but from 1845 the firm only sold hats[260] and went out of business the next year. A linen draper moved in but that same year he too was bankrupt.[261] He was followed by a furrier whose two principles in business were to operate honourably and to

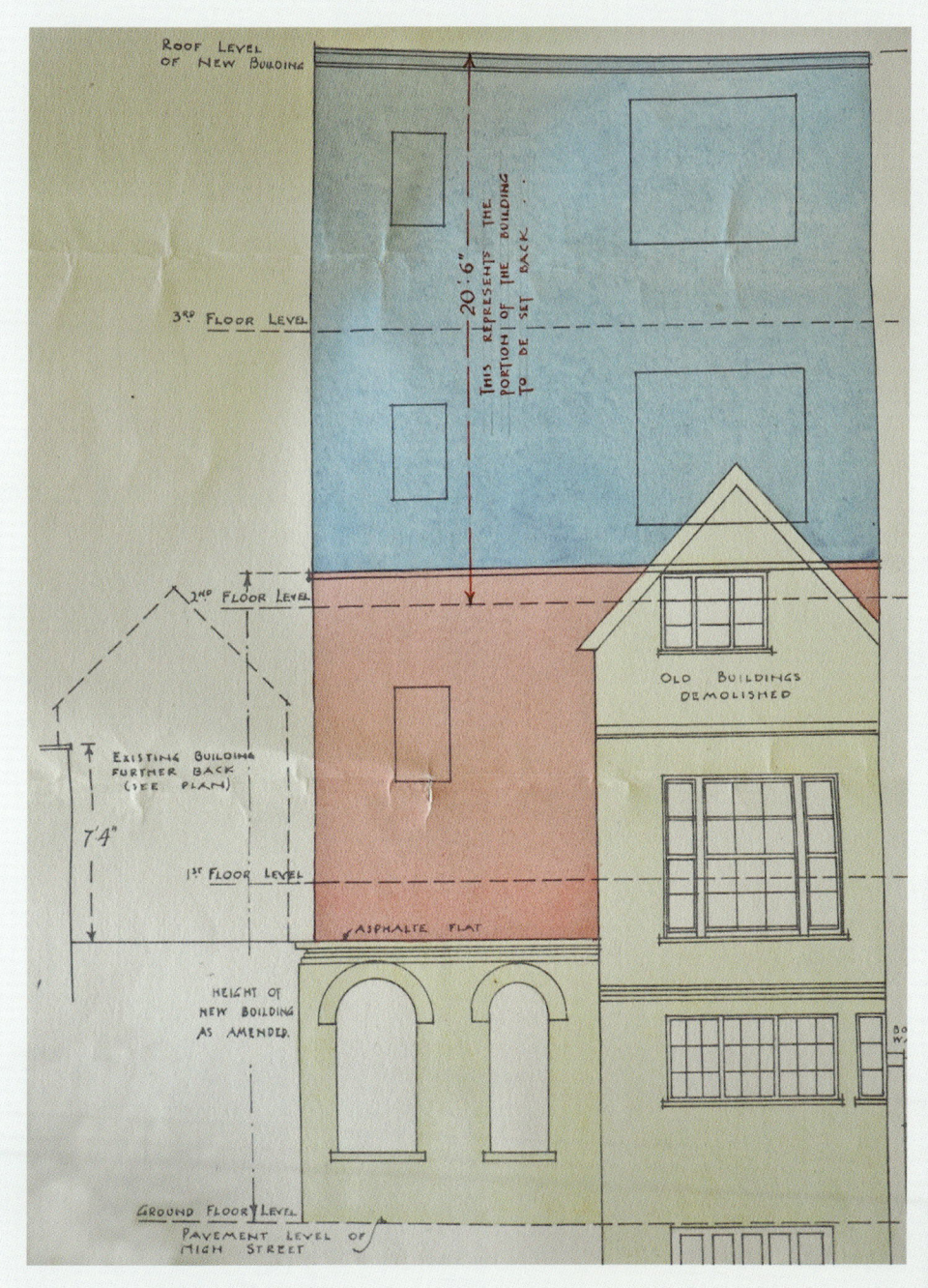

85. The High Street featuring 48–52 High Street, early 1900s.

operations near Bedford Street. Numbers 48 & 49 was a branch operation: it had a shop on the ground floor with a soda-water fountain for cold drinks at the rear, on the first floor there was a lunch café, the second floor had two smaller tea rooms as well as a rest room for ladies and a smoke room for gentlemen. The top floor was the bakery. The lunch and tea rooms overlooked High Street. These rooms had light wicker lounge chairs and rich carpets. Rubber flooring was supplied by W. Brock & Company.[258] The café closed in 1962 and since then there has been a considerable number of occupants including Waterstones, the last bookseller in the Island.

86. Undated plan of proposed reconstruction of 48–9 High Street, by W. H. Woodroffe & Son.

NUMBER 48 High Street

St Martin's Island: An introductory history of forty-two Exeter buildings

87. Front room overlooking High Street into Goldsmith Street, Deller's Café.

88. First floor of Deller's Cafe at 48–9 High Street.

89. Ground floor of Deller's Café, 48–9 High Street.

NUMBER 48 High Street

please his customers. He claimed to have 'every novelty that has yet appeared in the Metropolitan or Parisian circles in every kind of fur, in every shape and in every quality' but was bankrupt two years later.[262] That year the 'New Tea Establishment' opened[263] but two years later it was taken over.

The next business lasted longer: J. C. Lake, hair dresser and perfumer, claimed that his salons were fitted with elegance and comfort and had 'a first-class Parisian artiste' who had come from 'the establishment of Monsieur Felix, hair dresser to the Empress Eugenie'.[264] The building was then in multiple-use. Later Miss Trump, a milliner and dressmaker, shared the building with the City Tea Supply.[265] Trump had the eleven rooms, kitchen and 'other offices' which Lake had occupied. The following year the Special Agency moved in. It supplied specialities such as greenhouses, conservatories, cork and iron pillars.[266] In 1879 the building comprised 'a large and well lighted shop, together with thirteen show, bed and other rooms, cellars, etc.'[267] It was taken on by Frederick Shapley who had 'the best and cheapest house in the city for all kinds of sweets'. He was the 'Confectioner to the Queen' and his sweets were manufactured in Catherine Street.[268] The firm lasted nearly a generation and was the 'original and only maker of sugar fruit and vegetables'.[269] Christmas shoppers in 1889 saw 'sweetmeats formed into curious shapes, bon-bons are most numerous and chocolates, comfits etc. are to be seen in any variety. No wonder the children crowd outside with longing eyes for few shops make a more attractive display'.[270] By 1894 it had won a gold medal for its Mitchim Mints, 'a splendid remedy for influenza'.[271]

OCCUPANTS OF THE PROPERTY

1674	David Robinson, *Grocer*
1689 – 1699	Jane Tripe, *widow of Nicholas*, Goldsmith
1718 – 1731	Anthony Tripe, *Goldsmith*
1740 – 1751	Thomas Blake, *Goldsmith*
1803 – 1827	R. N. Gollop, *Ironmonger*
1827 – 1837	Thomas Russell Baker, *Ironmonger*
1837 – 1845	William Veysey, *Hat, Hosiery, Glove & Ladies Boot & Shoe Warehouse*
1846	W. H. Trew, *Draper*
1846 – 1847	Henry Prince, *The London Fur Manufactory*
1847 – 1849	Mead, Ash & Company, *The New Tea Establishment*
1849 – 1856	William Huckvale, *Huckvale's T Warehouse*
1857 – 1872	J. C. Lake, *Hair Dresser & Perfumer (afterwards* Mrs Lake, *Dressmaker)*
1872 – 1875	Miss Trump, *Milliner & Dress Maker (upstairs)*
1872 – 1879	J. H. Newman, *City Tea Supply (& 49)*
1873	John H. Howard, *Special Agency*
1878 – 1919	Frederick Shapley, *Confectioner (& 49)*
1889	Mrs Annie Mugford, *Dressmaker*
1889	Ernest Linwood Brothers, *Artificial Teeth Maker*
1893	J. W. Melhuish, *Hardware Dealer*
1897	Liverpool Victoria Legal Friendly Society
1902 – 1903	Mrs Wayborn's Registry
1906 – 1910	Henry Stafford Moss, *Music Teacher*
1910	Western Morning News
1919	General Accident Insurance Co. Ltd
1913 – 1916	Miss Kernick, *Dress & Costumier*
1920 – 1922	Vacant, demolition and rebuilding
1923 – 1963	Deller's Café
1964 – 1965	Vacant
1966 – 1975	Salisbury's, Leather Goods
1966 – 1967	Ricky, *Ladies' Hairdresser (upstairs)*
1969 – 1973	Gerardo, *Ladies' Hairdresser (upstairs)*
1969 – 1970	Audrey Clare, *Costumiers (upstairs)*
1972 – 1985	Manpower, *Employment Agency (& 49 upstairs)*
1973 – 1974	BOCM Silcock Ltd, *Animal Food Manufacturers (upstairs)*
1976 – 1985	Collingwood, *Jewellers (& 49)*
1981	Property Seekers Ltd, *Auctioneers, Estate Agents, Surveyors & Valuers (& 49 upstairs)*
1983	Robin Hills (systems) Ltd, *computer services (& 49 upstairs)*
1983 – 1985	Bambridge Moyse & Co., *Auctioneers, Estate Agents, Surveyors & Valuers (& 49 upstairs)*
1981 – 1985	Overdrive Ltd, *Driving Staff Agency (& 49 upstairs)*
1983	Teffont Business Systems Ltd *(& 49 upstairs)*
1985	Chiro Podia Services, *Chiropodists (& 49 upstairs)*
1986	Vacant
1987 – 1990	Sherratt & Hughes, *Booksellers*
1991 – 2017	Waterstones, *Booksellers*

NUMBER 49

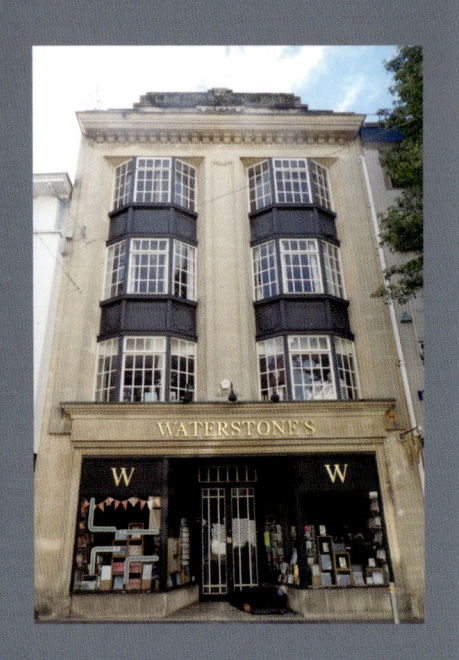

The building is not listed. The frontage, with Number 48, is 30 feet 8 inches

90. 49 & 51 High Street photographed by Edward Pocknell, as seen through the remains of Allhallows Goldsmith Church, 7 June 1906.

49 High Street, a property which was held by the Dean & Chapter but anciently owned by the City of Exeter. Number 49 comprised the western side of a nineteenth-century building which was demolished, along with Number 48, in 1921 and rebuilt over the following two years. The frontage, with Number 48, is 30 feet 8 inches.

Architectural plans for the new building in 1922 reveal an earlier building that had been demolished in the nineteenth century: it had two storeys with an attic and the gable was presented to the street.[272] By 1756 Exeter's council owned the building and leased it to the Dean and Chapter.[273] A silk weaver and a trunk maker were occupiers in the late 1600s and early 1700s while from the 1760s until 1860 the building housed a series of clothing merchants including linen[274] and woollen drapers, a mercer,[275] hatters, a glover, a milliner and a stocking manufacturer. Several generations of hatters were in Number 49 from 1813 to 1856.[276]

NUMBER 49 High Street

with a room over the kitchen, a large cellar underneath the shop and parlour, a very good drawing room, four best bedrooms and three servants' rooms'.[278] Its size allowed the building to become multi-occupational and serve a range of businesses.

In 1839, and through to at least the following year, E. Mayne ran her millinery business from both Numbers 45 and 49. In the latter she had rooms upstairs; these were described as 'the spacious apartments over Veysey's.[279] A Tewkesbury stocking manufacturer followed in 1856 but moved to Peamore Terrace four years later.[280]

A great number of firms rented rooms upstairs in the 1800s including the Electric & International Telegraph Company,[281] the South Western Railway[282] and the City Coal Offices.[283] In 1873 J. Bodley Browning, lay vicar at the cathedral, announced he was opening his Pianoforte & Music Warehouse[284] and that year the City Tea Supply was also an occupant.[285] They were followed by the Western Daily Mercury as well as the Western Morning News.[286] Others that shared the building included a confectioner,[287] railway carriers,[288] a hairdresser,[289] and Exeter City Council's architect and surveyor.[290] In 1913 he advertised Number 49 as having a shop with 9 rooms and 'every convenience' including a side entrance.[291]

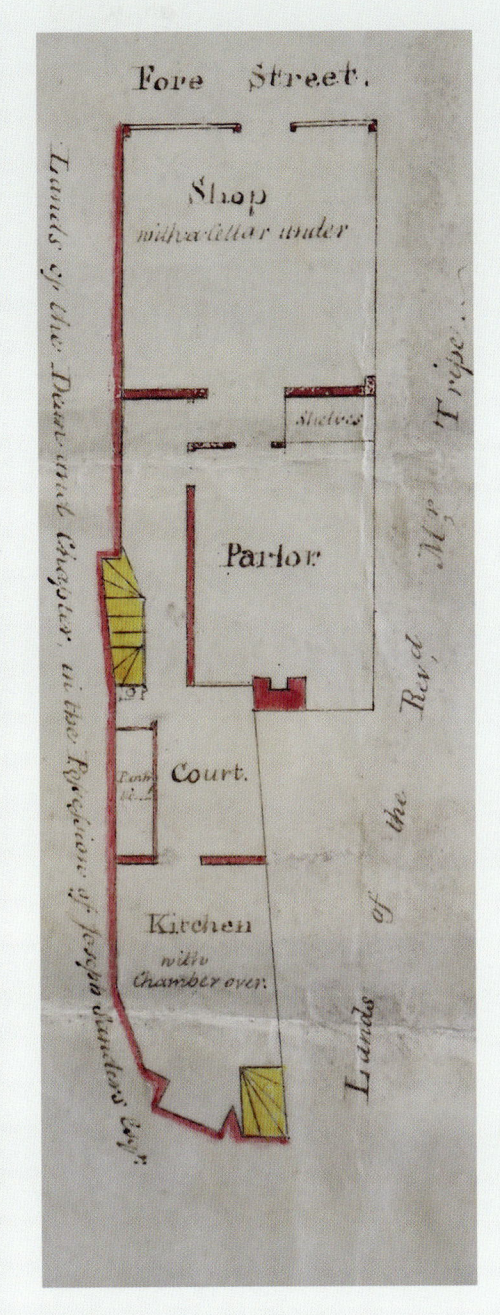

91. Ground plan by Robert Cornish of 49 High Street, 1805.

A plan made in 1804 shows the entrance led into a shop behind which was a parlour and courtyard leading to a kitchen which had a room above.[277] The size of the building is shown by a description made in 1813. The building then had 'a spacious and lofty shop, good parlour behind, a court, with a never failing supply of excellent pump water, and a good kitchen on the ground floor,

OCCUPANTS OF THE PROPERTY

1674 – 1682	John Barons,	Silkweaver
1691 – 1702	Henry Rogers,	Trunkmaker
1804 – 1812	Robert Cross,	Junior, Mercer and Woollen Draper
1813 – 1820	Ann Veysey,	Hatter
1821 – 1827	Ann & William Veysey,	Hatter
1827 – 1856	William Veysey,	Hosier, Hatter & Glover
1839 – 1840	E. Mayne,	Millinery (upstairs)
1856 – 1860	Joseph Hooke,	Stocking Manufacturer
1861 – 1870	Electric & International Telegraph Company	
1863 – 1878	South Western Railway	
1870 – 1872	City Coal Offices	
1873	Piano & Music Warehouse (J. Bodley Browning)	
1873 – 1876	City Tea Supply (J. H. Newman) (& 48)	
1877 – 1878	District Office, Western Daily Mercury	
1878 – 1881	Frederick Shapley, Confectioner (& 48)	
1869 – 1903	Chaplin & Company (also known as Chaplin & Horne)	
1902 – 1910	Sidney Albert Smith, Hairdresser	
1912	J. Archibald Lucas, Architect & Surveyor	
1914 – 1927	Prudential Assurance Company	
1920 – 1922	Vacant, Demolition & Rebuilding	
1923 – 1963	Deller's Café	
1964 – 1965	Vacant	
1966 – 1975	Salisbury, Leather Goods (& 48)	
1966 – 1967	Ricky, Ladies' Hairdresser (upstairs)	
1969 – 1973	Gerardo, Ladies' Hairdresser (upstairs)	
1969 – 1970	Audrey Clare, Costumiers (upstairs)	
1972 – 1985	Manpower, Employment Agency (& 48 upstairs)	
1973 – 1974	BOCM Silcock Ltd, Animal Food Manufacturers (upstairs)	
1981 – 1983	Robin Hills (Systems) Ltd, Computer Services (& 48 upstairs)	
1976 – 1985	Collingwood, Jewellers (& 48)	
1981	Property Seekers Ltd, Auctioneers, Estate Agents, Surveyors & Valuers (& 48 upstairs)	
1976 – 1985	Overdrive Ltd, Driving Staff Agency (& 48 upstairs)	
1986	Vacant	
1987 – 1990	Sherratt & Hughes, Booksellers	
1991 – 2017	Waterstones, Booksellers	

NUMBER 51

The building is not listed and has a frontage of 39 feet 3 inches.

92. Ground plan by John Tothill of 51 High Street, 1765.

50 High Street, this building lay behind the street. In 1852 Thomas Lee, who was accused of being a swindler, unwisely referred to having a shop at this address and it was later pointed out in court that 'there is no shop at 50 High Street',[292] see the New Exchange.

51 High Street, a property anciently held of the Dean & Chapter but owned by the City of Exeter. The late Georgian building was renamed Union House in 1821, demolished in 1962 and rebuilt the following year on the site of both 51 & 52 High Street.

Numbers 51 & 52 High Street were often held as one property. By 1695 two tenements were converted into making one building[293] and it was used by ironmongers during nearly all of the next century.[294] By this time it was a council property leased to the Dean & Chapter.[295] A building plan made in 1763 shows that a single room was on the ground floor. The frontage was then approximately 22 feet and the New Exchange ran along its eastern side.[296] Number 51 was rebuilt in about 1799 for, or by, a tea dealer and grocer.

In 1802 he auctioned the leases of Numbers 51 & 52 which were described as 'newly built dwelling houses with shops etc. eligibly situated nearly opposite the guildhall'. Number 51 had on the ground floor 'a spacious shop and parlour, a cellar underneath the whole, on the second story a dining room, wareroom and kitchen, with a lead pump and five good lodging rooms over'. It was noted that the buildings 'have not been built above three years and are neatly fitted up'.[297] This probably survived until 1962. In the 1930s it had three storeys and an attic. The first floor had three windows placed

NUMBER 51 High Street

93. Partial view of 51 High Street with Numbers 48–9 somewhat obscured by Rodney, 2 September 1941.

94. High Street with Numbers 49 to 51 in view, post 1922.

symmetrically in contrast to the three smaller ones on the second floor. The attic had two dormer windows.

Afterwards Number 51 had a mixed history of retail use including linen drapers[298] and a bookseller and general agent for the sale of literary property who had been at Number 46.[299] In 1821 the building was renamed Union House and used partly for linen drapery but largely given over to the selling of hats.[300] Subsequent firms included The Ready-Made and Baby Linen Warehouse, The Artificial Flower Warehouse, The Flower & Feather Warehouse and The Millinery & Fancy Show Room.[301] The New Hat & Cap Warehouse followed and succeeding merchants sold hats or boots and shoes.[302]

In 1882 a period of stability began with John Webber & Sons, the sports outfitter.[303] In 1945 the city's redevelopment plan advocated demolition to create a walkway through to Cathedral Yard but it was not until the early 1960s that building was taken down, along with Number 52, in order to build new retail premises. The architects were Drury, Gundry & Dyer of Exeter. Webber amalgamated with Lillywhites and in 1963 the new building was erected.[304] In 1984 Wimpy took occupancy[305] and in 1990 was succeeded by Burger King, now one of the longest established businesses in the Island.

OCCUPANTS OF THE PROPERTY

1699 – 1708	James Ross, Watchmaker, & John Cove, Grocer
1715 – 1751	Thomas Bale, Ironmonger
1768	Robert Reynolds, Ironmonger
1796 – 1804	Thomas Luke, Tea Dealer & Grocer
1805 – 1809	William & John Mildrum, Linen Drapers
1809	John Mildrum & Mr Proctor, Linen Drapers
1810 – 1817	Copp, Alford & Copp, Linen Drapers
1817 – 1819	W. & A. Copp, Linen Drapers, Silk Mercers, Hosiers & Carpet Dealers
1820	M. Comerford, Bookseller
1821 – 1834	Union House (H. & J. Veysey, Hatters)
1834 – 1837	Francis Veyse, Hatter, Hat, Cap and Umbrella Warehouse
1837 – 1844	James Blunden, Artificial Flower Warehouse
1843 – 1844	Mrs Sarah Stockham (later Lendon) Ready-Made and Baby Linen Warehouse (upstairs)
1845 – 1853	William Bond, Flower & Feather Warehouse
1854 – 1856	Mrs Haycock, Millinery & Fancy Show Room
1857 – 1877	Charles Bisney, Bisney's New Hat & Cap Warehouse
1878	Mrs S. A. Brailey, Milliner
1879 – 1881	W. H. Seaton, Boot and Shoe Warehouse
1882 – 1962	John Webber, Ironmonger, and Sports Outfitter (from 1902 John Webber & Sons) (& 50)
1962 – 1963	Demolished & redeveloped
1963 – 1964	Lillywhites, Sports Outfitters
1965 – 1973	Peter Robinson, Ladies' Outfitters (& 51 & 52)
1974 – 1975	Brown's, Ladies Fashion
1976 – 1977	Vacant
1978 – 1983	Bambers, Ladies' & Children's Wear
1984 – 1989	Wimpy, Fast Food Restaurant
1990 – 2017	Burger King, Fast Food Restaurant (also 50 & 52)

NUMBER 52

The building is not listed and has a frontage of 39 feet 3 inches.

52 High Street, a property built in about 1799, rebuilt in the early 1960s and which was anciently held of the Dean & Chapter. From 1842 to 1844 it was known as Nottingham House and from 1883 to 1894 as Victoria House (with Number 53).

Numbers 51 & 52 High Street were often held as one property. By 1695 two tenements were converted into making one building[306] and it was used by ironmongers during nearly all of the next century.[307] Number 52 was rebuilt in about 1799 and comprised 'a good shop and parlour, with cellar underneath the whole, on the second story a dining room, kitchen and lead pump, four good lodging rooms over'.[308] The building was less than half the size of its neighbour Number 51: it had three

NUMBER 52 High Street

96. The new Lillywhites building at 51–2 High Street, 1963.

97. The new show rooms at Lillywhites, 1963.

95. 51 to 53 High Street, c1931.

storeys and a single window on both the first and second floors which faced High Street. There was also an attic.

In 1833 the first business of its kind opened in the Island: Joseph Baker came from London to sell 'patterns of paper hangings and borders'. The following year he died in Number 52; Baker was aged 29 and described as 'a man of most kind and obliging manners, and possessing great taste and ingenuity in his business'. His widow continued the business, which comprised both a dwelling house and shop, until 1836. In the Exeter Pocket Journal in 1834 he was described not only as having a paper hanging establishment but was listed as a carver and gilder.[309] Baker's successors ran businesses similar to those in Number 51. The Artificial Flower Warehouse moved from Number 41 to Number 52 in 1836.[310] A new shop front was put in at this time.[311] A milliner took occupancy for only a few years[312] and then the New Hosiery, Glove and Stock Warehouse opened. The building was renamed 'Nottingham House'.[313] A laceman, mercer, hosier and glover[314] was followed by several fancy trimming retailers[315] and a milliner who renamed the building Victoria House.[316] From the 1890s through to 1983 the building continued to be used to sell women's clothing.[317]

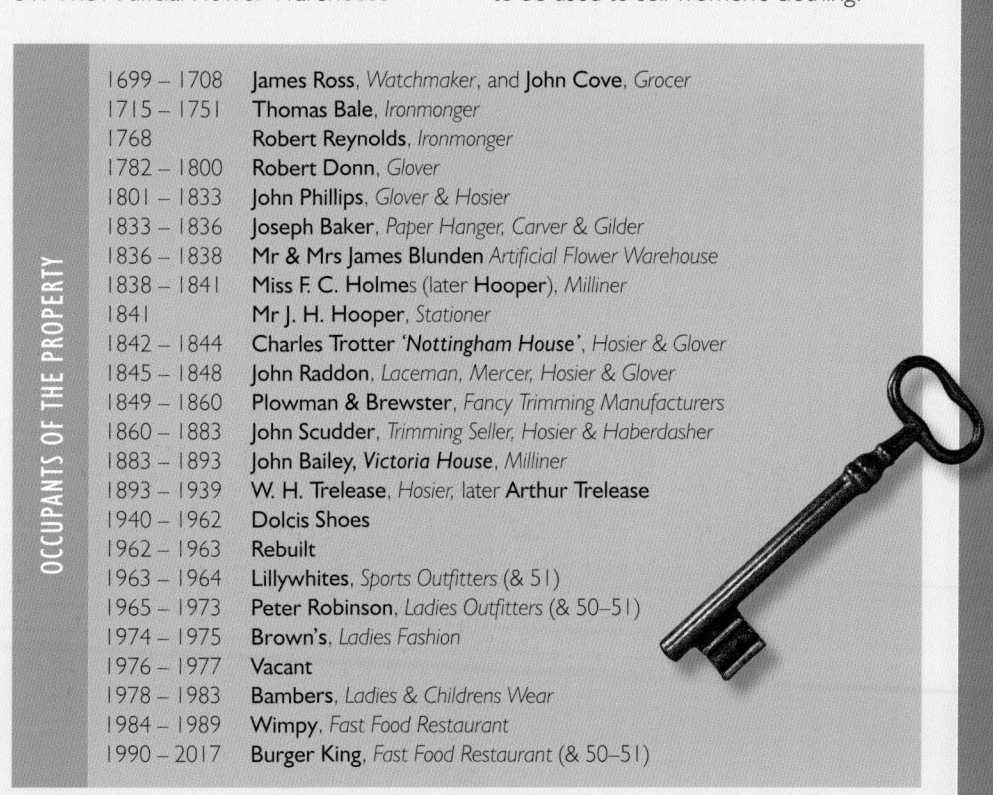

OCCUPANTS OF THE PROPERTY

1699 – 1708	James Ross, *Watchmaker*, and John Cove, *Grocer*	
1715 – 1751	Thomas Bale, *Ironmonger*	
1768	Robert Reynolds, *Ironmonger*	
1782 – 1800	Robert Donn, *Glover*	
1801 – 1833	John Phillips, *Glover & Hosier*	
1833 – 1836	Joseph Baker, *Paper Hanger, Carver & Gilder*	
1836 – 1838	Mr & Mrs James Blunden *Artificial Flower Warehouse*	
1838 – 1841	Miss F. C. Holmes (later Hooper), *Milliner*	
1841	Mr J. H. Hooper, *Stationer*	
1842 – 1844	Charles Trotter *'Nottingham House'*, *Hosier & Glover*	
1845 – 1848	John Raddon, *Laceman, Mercer, Hosier & Glover*	
1849 – 1860	Plowman & Brewster, *Fancy Trimming Manufacturers*	
1860 – 1883	John Scudder, *Trimming Seller, Hosier & Haberdasher*	
1883 – 1893	John Bailey, *Victoria House*, *Milliner*	
1893 – 1939	W. H. Trelease, *Hosier*, later Arthur Trelease	
1940 – 1962	Dolcis Shoes	
1962 – 1963	Rebuilt	
1963 – 1964	Lillywhites, *Sports Outfitters (& 51)*	
1965 – 1973	Peter Robinson, *Ladies Outfitters (& 50–51)*	
1974 – 1975	Brown's, *Ladies Fashion*	
1976 – 1977	Vacant	
1978 – 1983	Bambers, *Ladies & Childrens Wear*	
1984 – 1989	Wimpy, *Fast Food Restaurant*	
1990 – 2017	Burger King, *Fast Food Restaurant (& 50–51)*	

77

NUMBER 53

98. Mr Boot's new branch store at 53 High Street, 1907.

53 High Street, anciently owned by St John's Hospital and then by the Tothill family of Peamore, rebuilt in the late 1760s, renamed in 1879 Victoria House (with Number 52) and rebuilt in 1907 with carvings by Harry Hems' firm.

In 1974 the building was listed Grade 2 and recorded as 'late nineteenth/early twentieth century front on a possibly earlier building. 4 storeys, 2 windows. Richly carved half-timbered frontage in the Elizabethan manner. Modern shop front. Central niche on the 2nd floor with a statue of Leofric, 1059. Cornice and barge-boarded gable with carved finial. Tiled roof.' The frontage is 22 feet.

99. Bishop Leofric holding his minster, carved by Harry Hems & Sons, 1907, at 53 High Street.

In 1907 this Georgian four-storey building was given a Neo Elizabethan façade. Five years before it had a 'handsome new shop front' but Boots refaced it in its own in-house style.[318] Its gable is presented to High Street and there are rich carved embellishments, notably a statue of Bishop Leofric with the date 1050, foliage running along the roofline, four heads below the third floor window and there are four grotesques.

In 1766 Richard Coffin, a haberdasher of small wares, arranged with the owner to 'to erect and build or cause to be erected and built at his and their own proper cost and charge in and upon the plot or piece of ground and premises hereinafter mentioned to be demised and granted a good and sufficient dwelling house with proper offices and conveniences thereto belonging three stories high at the least and to completely finish the same in good workmanlike manner and with good materials within the space of two years next ensuing hereof the same length and breadth and agreeable as near as can be to the plan, drawn and marked out in the margin hereof'. The building was one-room wide; the main entrance led into a shop and then to a warehouse at the rear of which was a parlour. Behind the building lay a courtyard with a brewhouse and back kitchen. The front of the building had a second entrance on the western side and extended eighty-six feet.[319]

The subsequent occupiers were members of the Hedgeland family; each was a bookseller. Philip Hedgeland was the first and described himself as a bookseller, stationer and bookbinder but he also published books including Alexander Jenkins' history of Exeter.[320] His son and grandson continued to trade in Number 53.[321] In 1819 the building comprised 'a commodious shop with a parlour behind the same, a cellar underneath, on the first floor a drawing room 21 ft by 19ft, a dining room 18ft 6 inches by 15 ft 6 inches, a housekeepers' room, on the second floor four bedrooms and four ditto in the attic'. It also had a curtilage with a lead pump, two detached kitchens 'with a printing office over the same'.[322]

The booksellers were succeeded by a pair of milliners,[323] an ironmonger[324] and more milliners: in 1855 the first of five firms of milliners and drapers occupied the building.[325] In 1863 there was a minor fire but it was not serious enough to warrant rebuilding.[326] A few years later one of the milliners named the building, along with Number 52, Victoria House.[327]

In 1907 Boots, the chemists, renovated Number 53 as part of a corporate policy of 'drawing on the past to boost prestige'. Michael Vyne Treleaven, the Cornish architect, designed buildings for the company across the country which celebrated local historical figures. The stained glass may have been the work of Alexander Gascoyne: there are

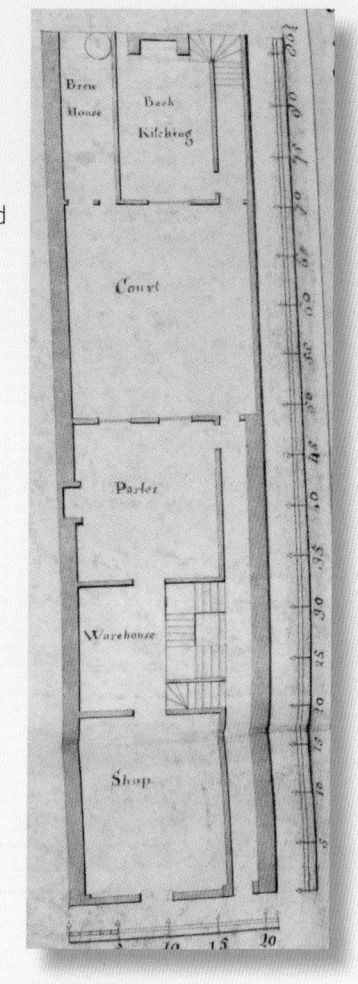

101. Ground plan of the proposed building, 1766.

panels representing the city's coat of arms, Princess Henriette Anne and William of Orange. Harry Hems' firm was the carver. At the time it was noted that the shop 'will be built entirely of well-seasoned wainscot oak – not planed, mitred, sandpapered and varnished in modern style, but following the tried old practice of being left just as it comes from the adze, the saw, and the chisel of the handicraftsman; and all will be held together with oak pins. The edifice will consist of three floors, the whole surmounted by a richly-carved gable, with apex crowned by a tall, tapering and effectively crocketed finial'.[328]

Its successor[329] was Frederick William Sellick who held the lease of the upper portion of Number 53 and spent 'considerable sums in alterations and fittings for a café'. When the city council asked for improvements Sellick purchased the lease for the upper floors of Number 54, obtained a music and dance licence and called his new venture The Cathedral Café.[330]

100. Architectural drawing of a proposed rebuilding of 53 High Street, 1766.

OCCUPANTS OF THE PROPERTY

1765	Richard & Lucretia Wish	
1766 – 1768	Richard Coffin,	*Haberdasher*
1796 – 1817	Philip Hedgeland,	*Printer & Bookseller*
1817 – 1819	Philip Hedgeland,	*Bookseller*
1819 – 1825	Samuel Hedgeland,	*Bookseller*
1820 – 1823	S. & M. Gard,	*Milliner (upstairs)*
1827 – 1854	John Somers Gard,	*Ironmonger*
1855 – 1868	Mr & Mrs Charles Adams,	*Drapers & Milliners*
1868 – 1874	John Stanbury & Company,	*Drapers*
1874 – 1878	T. G. Wheeler (from 1877 Wheeler & Bailey),	*Drapers*
1879 – 1896	James Bailey, *Victoria House*	*Milliners*
1896 – 1906	Stuart Hunt,	*Draper*
1907	Rebuilt	
1907 – 1929	Boots, Cash Chemists, including Boots Library (1911 to 1931)	
1929 – 1962	Dolcis Shoes	
1931 – 1932	The Cathedral Café (upstairs)	
1962 – 1968	Vacant	
1969 – 2009	Abbey National Building Society (& as Abbey National Bank at 54 from 1994 – 2009)	
2002 – 2006	Costa Coffee	
2010 – 2017	Santander UK (& 54 from 2010 – 2011, 54 – 6 from 2012 to 2017)	

NUMBER 54

In 1974 this building was listed Grade 2 and recorded as 'eighteenth-century front on a possibly older structure. Timber-framed, rendered and painted, quoins, bands at 2nd and 3rd floor cill levels. 4 storeys, 2 windows. Modern shop front. The 1st floor has 2 arched windows joined together making a 5-light casement. The 2nd floor has 2 sashes with architrave surrounds, the 3rd also. Bracketted eaves cornice, hipped slate roof'. The frontage is 21 feet.

102. Elevation of 54 High Street, 1756.

54 High Street, a property anciently owned by St John's Hospital and then purchased by the Tothill family at the Dissolution, part of the site was owned by the City of Exeter, it was rebuilt in the mid 1700s and among its later occupants was the Veitch firm.

By 1758 a building which occupied what is now Numbers 53 and 54 was divided by a partition wall. This created two separate tenements and shortly afterwards a replacement building was erected. It comprised four storeys, with a pair of sashed windows on each floor. Quoins ran along the western end. There were two doors on the ground floor with one nearly centrally placed and the other situated on the eastern end. The building was twenty-one feet in width and only one room wide. At the High Street end was a shop behind which lay two parlours. A courtyard lay between this building and a kitchen and coal house at the far end. For insurance purposes the building was described in 1786 as built of stone and timber. In 1931 the building was 'rebuilt' including excavating the foundations for party walls.[331]

The building had three main phases of occupiers in newspapers, drapers and seedsmen until 1930. The first occupant was Barnabas Thorn, a bookseller, who in 1766 went into partnership with Andrew Brice, the renowned newspaper proprietor: *Brice and Thorn's Old Exeter Journal or Weekly Advertiser* was printed at 'the said Thorn's house, nearly opposite the Guildhall, in the Fore Street'.[332] Thorn had a shop where he sold 'books in all arts and sciences, memorandum books of all sorts, account books, letter cases, writing paper of all sorts, magazines, warrants of all sorts, viz the land tax, window tax and highway, etc. All sort of paper hangings of the newest patterns, with every other article in the bookselling and stationery way; likewise, all sorts of patent medicines'.[333] Thorn's son continued printing the newspaper until his own death two years later. The newspaper was for sale in 1788 and the advertisement offered 'the purchaser could have the house opposite the guildhall where the business was carried on'.[334]

Drapers used the building for the next fifty years. The last of them was John Bending who in 1837 announced 'in consequence of the great increase in business, he is obliged to make extensive alterations which cannot be done without the whole of the interior of the premises [being] pulled down'. When it reopened he renamed the building 'Victoria House' but was out of business the next year.[335]

That year James Veitch & Son moved its seed business to Number 54 despite seven other seedsmen being in Exeter.[336] Shortly afterwards several specimens of 'Allen's Early Frame Cucumber' were exhibited: they measured 18 inches in length.[337] Upstairs Mrs James Welch ran her corset, dress & millinery rooms[338] but later, in 1851, the Veitch staff lived in the upper floors; these were William Coker, an Exeter-born man aged 32 who was described as a seedsman, his family which included his brother Richard, another seedsman, and one domestic servant. Only employees, and their families, were resident from 1841 to 1871 and from 1881 the building was only used for business. Upon James Veitch's death in 1863 the business was known as Robert Veitch & Sons. In 1874 one neighbour referred to Robert Veitch as 'that enterprising horticulturist… to whom we owe so much for our splendid displays at the meetings of our Devon & Exeter Botanical society and for his liberality in the loan of his plants for our festive gatherings in Exeter and the county'.[339] In 1857 James Veitch & Son advertised that they were 'the only persons of the name of Veitch now carrying on the seed trade in Exeter and that they have no connection whatever with any other seed house in Exeter'. It was also noted that Thomas Veitch had lately retired from his seed shop at 195 High Street.[340] Veitch's shop continued until 1930 although the building was unroofed and flooded during the fire of 1881.[341]

Frederick William Sellick ran the Cathedral Café in 1931 and 1932. He extended the café from Number 53 when he purchased the lease for the upper floors of Number 54 but went bankrupt the following year.[342] The building has since been used by a great number of firms.

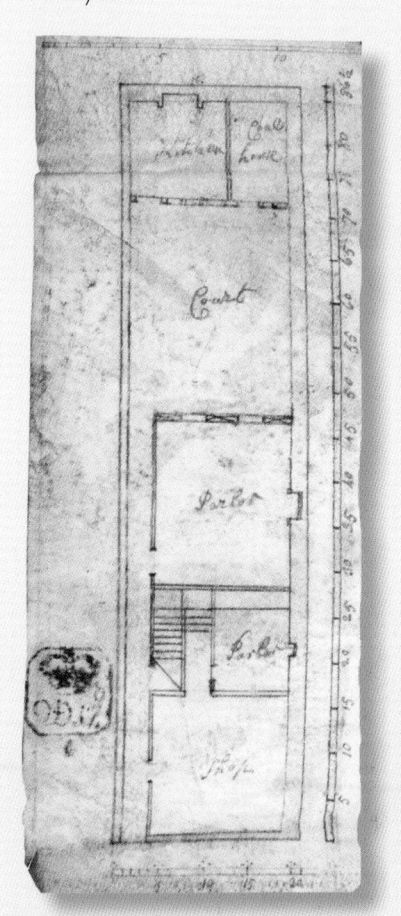

103. Ground plan of 54 High Street, 1756.

OCCUPANTS OF THE PROPERTY

1758 – 1785	**Barnabas Thorn**, Bookseller
1785 – 1787	**Richard Thorn**, Bookseller
1789 – 1814	**Benjamin Mardon**, Mercer & Woollen Draper
1815 – 1821	**Elizabeth Mardon**, Widow
1822 – 1829	**Tory, Copp & Company**, Linen Drapers
1829 – 1836	**George Tory**, Linen Draper
1836 – 1838	**John Bending**, Linen Draper
1838 – 1864	**James Veitch & Son**
1841 – 1844	**Marianne Welch**, Corset & Stay Maker (upstairs)
1864 – 1930	**Robert Veitch & Sons**, Seed Warehouse
1931 – 1940	**The Cathedral Café** (upstairs)
1931 – 1935	**J. V. Hutton**, Costumiers
1936 – 1960	**L. Whitbread & Company, Ltd**, Ladies' Wear Specialists
1936 – 1940	**Devonia Billiards Club** (upstairs)
1937 – 1939	**Marcina School of Dancing** (upstairs)
1943 – 1953	**Rowland's Fabrics & Fashions**, Hosiery & Underwear Specialists (upstairs)
1954 – 1964	**A. H. Shooter Ltd**, Ladies' & Gentlemen's Hairdressers (upstairs)
1961 – 1976	**John Farmer Ltd**, Shoe Makers
1966 – 1973	**M. Charles**, Hairdresser (upstairs)
1977 – 1978	Vacant
1979 – 1981	**Golden Egg, Restaurant** (**Philomena's Restaurant**, 1980)
1981 – 1988	**Fox & Sons, Auctioneers**, etc. (upstairs)
1981	**Focus**, Photography
1981	**Thomas Acland & Denis Lambeth**, Chartered Architects (upstairs)
1982 – 1986	**Poppins**, restaurant
1987 – 1991	**Kate Karneys**, restaurant
1992	Vacant
1993 – 2009	**Abbey National** (& 53 from 1993–2009)
2010 – 2017	**Santander UK** (& 53 from 2010–2011, 53 & 55–6 from 2012 to 2017)

NUMBER 55

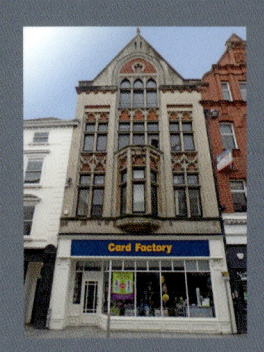

In 2000 55 – 6 High Street was listed Grade 2 and recorded as Gothic Revival, having four storeys, built c.1880s 'possibility of earlier core. Bath stone ashlar with red brick dressings and slate roof with spikey ridge tiles... Symmetrical 3-bay front with a steep, coped gable to the front with kneelers and a finial at the apex; stone mullioned windows… The centre bay rises to a moulded arched head in the gable. Outer windows are set in recesses to left and right', first floor 'central bay contains a canted oriel with a modillion frieze, glazed with one-light high-transomed windows with blind trefoiled heads. To right and left similar flush windows have panels of flamboyant tracery above the lintels; similar windows above, 3-light to the centre bay and 2-light to the flanking bays with modillion frieze above panels of decorated style blind tracery...' The frontage is 28 feet.

104. 55 High Street (left), with adjoining buildings, drawn by James Crocker, 1879. Two years later the building, of two parts under one roof, was destroyed by fire.

55 High Street, on the site of the Eagle (along with Number 56), destroyed by fire in 1881 and rebuilt in 1883 by and for Wippell, the ecclesiastical outfitters.

On this site was the late medieval home of Robert Wilford, a wealthy merchant, which was given in 1437 to the city. It was known as the Eagle and was Exeter's hospitium, a building which offered accommodation to pilgrims and other travellers. In 1912 Ethel Lega-Weekes thought that it was built along the site of the Chapel of St Peter the Less which had become deserted by 1285, the year in which the Close was walled. A grant shows it faced both High Street and the churchyard and referred to 'the place where was formerly situated the chapel of St Peter, near the High Street of Exeter, which was formerly called the chapel of St Peter the Less, late and for a long time back deserted, together with an entrance and exit towards the High Street, pertaining to the said place'. In 1472 the building became the city's cloth hall (where all cloth was sold).[343]

Number 55 had two particular uses in the 1800s. One involved surgical instruments made by Richard Dunsford, a cutler. In 1835 there were three other Exeter men in the same profession but Dunsford, like his son Richard, was the Devon & Exeter Hospital's cutler, surgical instrument and truss maker.[344] He was resident in 1834 when a maid servant, attempting to clean windows, fell 36 feet. Her fall gives an indication of the building: she first hit the lead work on the second

NUMBER 55 High Street

105. Drawing by Maurice Bingham Adams of front elevations of 55–6 High Street, as designed by Best & Commin, 22 February 1884.

floor, then onto two open casement windows, through a latticed sky light and finally into a courtyard. No bones were broken 'nor were the bruises of any great importance'.[345]

The Exeter Chess Club may have operated upstairs[346] but Number 55's main subsequent use was in tailoring and drapery.[347] There were two disruptions to this. The first was when a furnishing ironmonger sold 'a choice new stock of Sheffield Electro Silver Plated tea and coffee pots, cruets, biscuit boxes, spoons, forks'.[348] A drawing of 1879 shows that Number 55 was a four storey building, with an attic, which it shared with Number 56. Number 55 was approximately one third of the building and must have been one room wide.

The main disruption was caused by fire on the 9th of October 1881. It was reported 'the lath and plaster structure was so saturated [with water] that it was unable to sustain its own weight, and after one or two premonitory cracks the house slowly heeled over and plunged into the burning ruins of those premises which had for so many years stood alongside it. As the houses fell the cathedral [clock] struck ten'.[349] A newspaper noted 'an extraordinary escape' for 'A cat was among the members of the household. When all the others ran from the burning building the cat still remained behind, and when the house fell Puss went down with it. Three days later after the fire, the men were removing the debris and heard a cat crying. Eventually they discovered the owner of the voice and pussy was released, apparently not much the worse for her imprisonment'.[350]

Wippell, the ecclesiastical furnishers, purchased the building sites of Numbers 55 to 58 and 23 to 25 Cathedral Yard.[351] A year later a journalist reported that a 'semi-ecclesiastical looking structure' had a Gothic frontage. The ground floor had two shops and offices, the first floor had two showrooms and on the third floor were workshops. The architects were Best and Commin. *The Builder* pronounced 'there seems to have been a praiseworthy desire to make something suitable to the character of the locality'. Its reporter noted the character was 'entirely modern but Gothic forms are employed in the way of pointed windows and tracery, part of the wall space being decorated by white stone tracery on a red brick backing, with not quite satisfactory effect, as the stone appears as if merely placed in front of the brickwork with no bond, and this gives an appearance at least of weakness'.

The earlier building was noted as being 'of some antiquity and possessed architectural features which were lacking in the adjoining premises'. In 1883 the council was unhappy with the window projection but the architect contended 'we have not exceeded the two feet beyond the street line more than a quarter of an inch and when the stonework is cleaned down this quarter of an inch will cease to exist'. They also stressed that the new building had been set back 5¼ inches further than the previous building.[352]

When the building was completed 'the woollen drapery and clerical outfitting department occupies the front shop… the first floor is set apart for church furniture and school fittings. The rooms are large and well-lighted, and the windows looking towards High Street, consisting of a centre bay and two sides, making altogether seven lights, are filled in the upper part with stained glass, in which appear figures at work in the various departments of the business. These have been specially executed, and the figures include draughtsman, carpenter, church furniture maker, engraver, tapestry worker, sculpture and metalworker'.[353] The upper floors are being converted for domestic use.

OCCUPANTS OF THE PROPERTY

1826 – 1845	**Richard Dunsford**, *Cutler*
1845 – 1851	**Richard Dunsford, the Younger**, *Cutler*
1850	**Exeter Chess Club** (upstairs)
1852 – 1872	**Warren & Son, Tailors**, *Drapers & Habit Makers* (later **W. H. Warren**, *tailor*)
1872 – 1877	**John J. Norris**, *Woollen Draper, Tailor, Habit & Breeches Maker*
1877 – 1881	**John Webber**, *Furnishing Ironmonger*
1881 – 1882	**Fire and development**
1883 – 1981	**J. Wippell & Co. Ltd**, *Ecclesiastical Furnishers* (& 56)
1964 – 1968	**Henri Fashions**, *Gowns*
1965 – 1985	**Leicester Permanent Building Society** (& 56)
1986 – 2010	**Alliance & Leicester Building Society** (& 56)
2011 – 2015	**Santander** (& 53–4, 56)
2016 – 2017	**Card Factory**, *Greeting Card retailer*

NUMBER 56

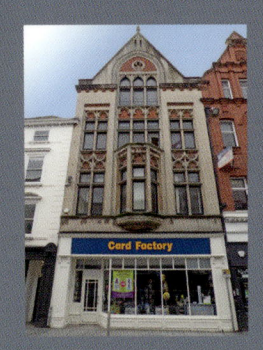

In 2000 55 – 6 High Street was listed Grade 2 and recorded as Gothic Revival, having four storeys, built c.1880s 'possibility of earlier core. Bath stone ashlar with red brick dressings and slate roof with spikey ridge tiles... Symmetrical 3-bay front with a steep, coped gable to the front with kneelers and a finial at the apex; stone mullioned windows… The centre bay rises to a moulded arched head in the gable. Outer windows are set in recesses to left and right', first floor 'central bay contains a canted oriel with a modillion frieze, glazed with one-light high-transomed windows with blind trefoiled heads. To right and left similar flush windows have panels of flamboyant tracery above the lintels; similar windows above, 3-light to the centre bay and 2-light to the flanking bays with modillion frieze above panels of decorated style blind tracery...' The frontage is 28 feet.

106. 55 to 63 High Street, 1863–6.

56 High Street, on the site of the Eagle (along with Number 55) and home to the noted Georgian bookseller Gilbert Dyer. The building was destroyed by fire in 1881 and rebuilt over the following two years.

The building has had several transformations. It was possibly an Elizabethan bookshop, with succeeding members of the Dight family, but Number 56, along with Number 55, before then was part of the Eagle, the medieval mansion (see 55 High Street) which was destroyed by fire and rebuilt in the early 1880s.

By the late 1800s it had a brick front[354] of four storeys; substantial oriel windows were on the three upper floors and a dormer window in the attic. It may have retained medieval fabric. It was noted as a 'fine old house' with literary associations: for nearly a century it was a bookshop among whose proprietors was Gilbert Dyer,[355] 'a respectable and eminent bookseller of this city; he was possessed of great natural talents, general knowledge and reading, and was the author of several ingenious works'. This 'distinguished veteran in the book trade'[356] and 'most extraordinary, very ingenious and eccentric man'[357] was remembered later as the erudite 'collector of a circulating library, the choicest, and perhaps the most extensive of any in the whole kingdom except in the metropolis'. A former neighbour recalled the 'old gentleman' had several thousand books while a visitor noted the 'collection of theology was astonishing; it was stacked on manifold shelves to the angle point of the gable of their huge

NUMBER 56 High Street

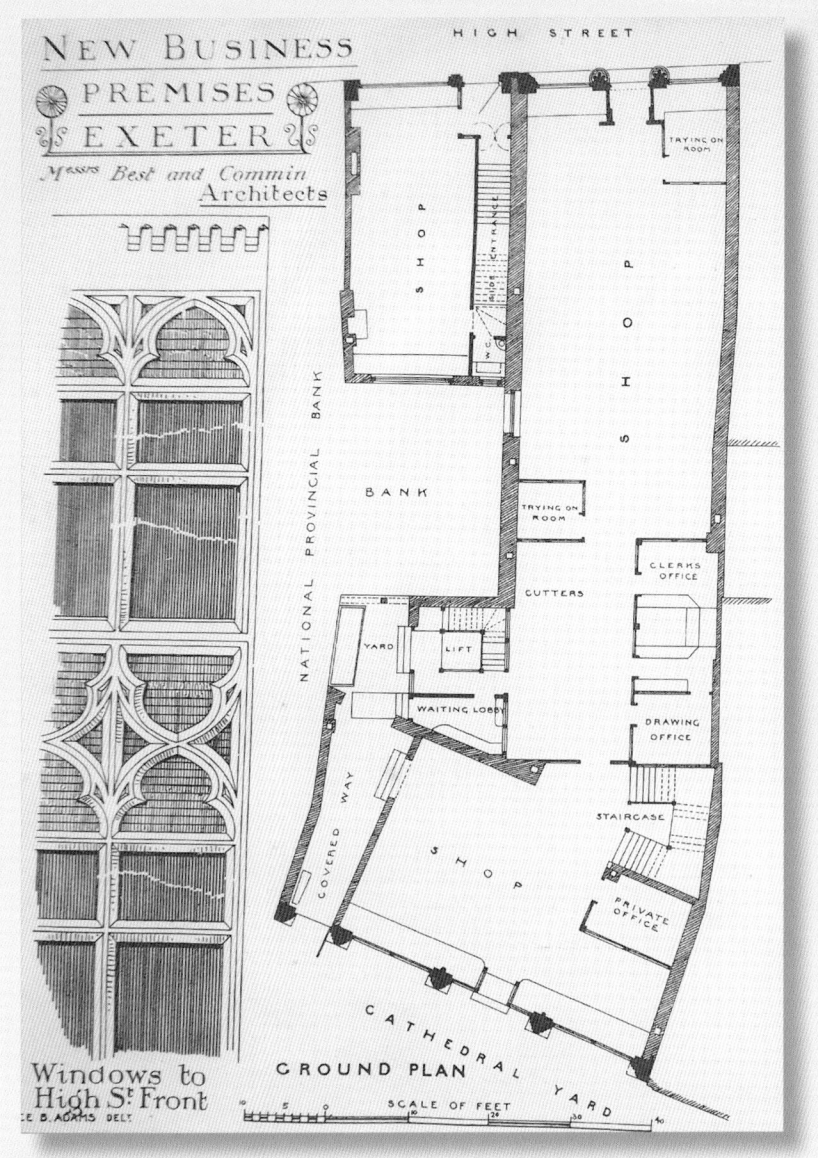

proprietors.[360] In the 1840s Number 56 was held by clothing retailers[361] but returned to selling books in 1850 when there were 30 rooms 'two of which are of very considerable size, a shop 58 feet long, with a handsome modern plate-glass front, over an extensive cellarage'.[362] Number 56 had a printing, book and stationery business, the Exeter Reading Rooms and the Public Select Library which had more than 6,000 volumes but excluded 'works on controversial divinity, party politics, novels and dramatic productions'.[363] The proprietor lived upstairs with his sister and two servants, one of whom worked in the shop. Two more booksellers followed.[364]

A draper was the occupant[365] when fire broke out in 1881: About a dozen shop assistants slept over the shop while the family were domiciled 'in the portion which overlooked the Cathedral Yard.'[366] Shortly afterwards it was lamented 'the loss of the old house is to be regretted because of its picturesque old frontage, which made it one of the show buildings of the High Street. Its large bay windows, which extended to the gable, projected boldly, and formed a fine feature in street architecture'.[367] Wippell's new building was erected the next year.[368]

107. Ground plan by Maurice Bingham Adams of 55–6 High Street extending into Cathedral Yard, 1882, with detail of windows, 22 February 1884.

upper warehouse and their love of books so great that the thought of parting with them was as iron entering into the soul'.

Intriguingly, a journalist noted 'there is a story current that in this house there was a room which was always kept locked, and in order to ensure its secrecy a special proviso as to the room was inserted in the leases to the tenants. A daughter of a former occupier was once asked if she knew of such a secret apartment. She replied that she did, but that before long the mystery, if any, would be disclosed, as time was wearing away the door, and making an opening'.[358]

Maria Fitze moved the circulation library to Number 39[359] and the bookshop passed through various

OCCUPANTS OF THE PROPERTY

1667	Walter Dight, *Bookseller*
1785 – 1820	Gilbert Dyer the Elder, *Bookseller*
1820 – 1829	Gilbert Dyer the Younger, *Bookseller*
1829 – 1837	William Strong, *Bookseller*
1837 – 1841	Edwin Jeanes, *Bookseller*
1841 – 1844	Nash & Company (later Nash & Gardiner), *Linen and Woollen Drapers*
1845 – 1847	Henry Farrant, Draper, *Haberdasher & Hosier*
1848 – 1849	Vacant
1850 – 1855	William Balle: the Public Select Library, the Exeter Reading Rooms and printing, (& until 1853) *Bookseller and Stationer*
1853 – 1855	John Evans, *Bookseller and Stationer*
1855 – 1870	Henry Hodge & Company, *Stationer*
1870 – 1881	Davies & Davies, *Haberdashers & Drapers*
1881	Fire
1882	Redevelopment
1883 – 1968	J. Wippell & Co. Ltd (& 55) *Ecclesiastical Furnishers*
1969 – 1981	Wippell Mowbray Church Furnishing Ltd
1982 – 1985	Leicester Building Society (& 55)
1986 – 2010	Alliance & Leicester Building Society (& 55)
2011 – 2015	Santander (& 53–5)
2016 – 2017	Card Factory

85

NUMBER 57

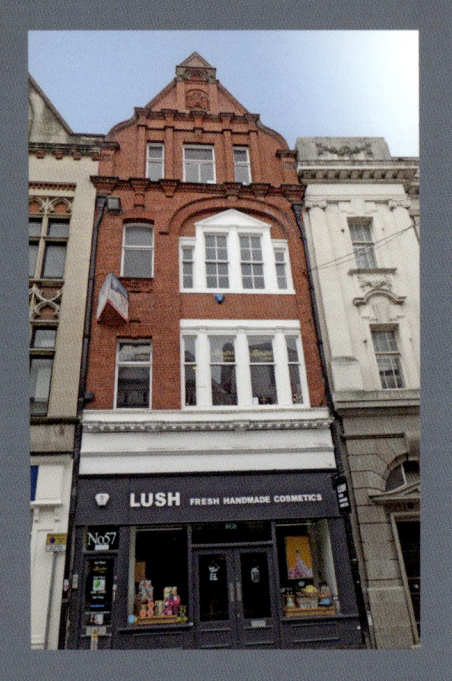

The building is not listed. The frontage is 21 feet 10 inches.

108. Drawing of 57 & 58 High Street, c.1850–1852.

57 High Street, destroyed by fire in 1881 and rebuilt in 1883, once known as Guildhall Chambers and as Alliance House, with Number 56, by 1985.

Until 1881 Numbers 57 & 58 were a pair of possibly seventeenth-century buildings with three storeys over a ground floor shop. The buildings were one room wide and they had pitched roofs with the gables presented to the street. Number 57 had its only front door on the left-hand side and large centrally placed windows on the first and second floors. The top floor had a sashed window.

NUMBER 57 High Street

In 1766 Mathew Blackamore used a room, most likely upstairs, to teach a variety of subjects.[369] By 1789 John Hitchcock, a shopkeeper, had a wareroom in what was described as a house built of stone and timber. In 1800 he occupied the third-floor front room which was eighteen feet and five inches in length and fourteen feet and nine inches in width. The room's height was seven feet and nine inches. For nearly one hundred years, through the 1800s, the building housed a series of merchants, including maiden ladies,[370] involved in the clothing trade.[371] Davies & Davies, haberdashers, became the occupants in 1877 and continued until the fire of 1881 destroyed the building.[372]

In 1883 a journalist with *The Builder* wrote 'a piece of pronounced Queen Anne brickwork is getting up. The elegant details of the upper portion of the old Town Hall opposite might have inspired something better than this'.[373] It was noted that Wippells had 'become the purchasers of the spot of land in High Street between their new premises [Number 55 & 56] and the National Provident Bank and on this Messrs Howell are erecting for them a shop and offices to be known as Guildhall Chambers. This site has a frontage of 22 feet and extends back to a depth of 40 feet. This building will be in the Queen Anne style, in red brick, with the exception of the bay windows on the first and second floor, which will be of Bath Stone.' The ground floor was intended to be a shop, the first and second floors were to be offices and the top floor was intended to be the caretaker's private rooms.[374] When the building reopened it served a multitude of occupiers, many were in banking including Fox Brothers, Fowler & Company which opened a branch of their Wellington bank at Numbers 57 and 58 High Street.[375] Another occupier was Charles Ltd, home furnishers, and Burton was an occupier after the Blitz in 1942.[376] Number 57 is now the upstairs address for Number 58.

109. 57 High Street: with the original oriel window, between 1894 and 1906

OCCUPANTS OF THE PROPERTY

1789 – 1812	John Hitchcock, *Shopkeeper* (upstairs)
1802	Edward Wills, *China Merchant*
1812 – 1834	Mrs Elizabeth Dinneford, *Linen Draper, Silk Mercer & Fancy Haberdasher* (& 58)
1827 – 1829	Gilbert & Pickard (Miss C. Pickard & Miss M. A. Gilbert), *Milliners*
1829 – 1830	Miss M. A. Gilbert, *Millinery & Dress Rooms*
1834 – 1840	Robert Nightingale, *Haberdasher, 'Berlin, Embroidery Wool and London Shoe Warehouse* (& 58)
1841 – 1847	Abraham Cleeve, *Linen Draper*
1848 – 1851	Vacant
1852 – 1861	Jane Cole, *Corsets, Hosiery & Haberdashery*
1862 – 1863	Mr & Mrs R. R. Chubb, *Women's Clothing*
1863 – 1866	S. Pyne & Sons, *Brush Manufactory*
1866 – 1868	Albert Sully, *Draper*
1869 – 1877	Henry J. Whitton, *Draper*
1877 – 1881	Davies & Davies, *Haberdashers*
1881 – 1884	Destruction & rebuilding
1885 – 1922	Fox Brothers, Fowler & Company, *Bankers* (& 58)
1885 – 1904	Sun Life Assurance Society (& 58)
1895 – 1897	Lewis Braund, *Woollen Draper & Hatter*
1906	Charles J. Tait, *Architect*
1909 – 1919	Territorial Force Association
1919 – 1931	British Red Cross Society
1923 – 1932	Lloyds Bank Ltd
1926 – 1934	Employers' Liability Insurance Corporation, Ltd
1931 – 1934	Clerical Medical & General Life Assurance Company
1934 – 1940	Charles Ltd., *Artistic House Furnishers* (& 58)
1942 – 1954	Montague Burton, *Men's Outfitters* (& 58)
1955	Vacant
1956 – 1960	Boyds of Bond Street, *Piano Dealers* (& 58)
1961 – 1969	David Greig, *Grocers* (& 58)
1970	Vacant (& 58)
1971 – 1985	Alliance Building Society (& 58)
1986	Alliance & Leicester Building Society (& 55–6)
1987	Vacant (& 58)
1988 – 2002	Jaeger Ladies' Wear (& 58)
2003 – 2017	Lush (& 58)

NUMBER 58

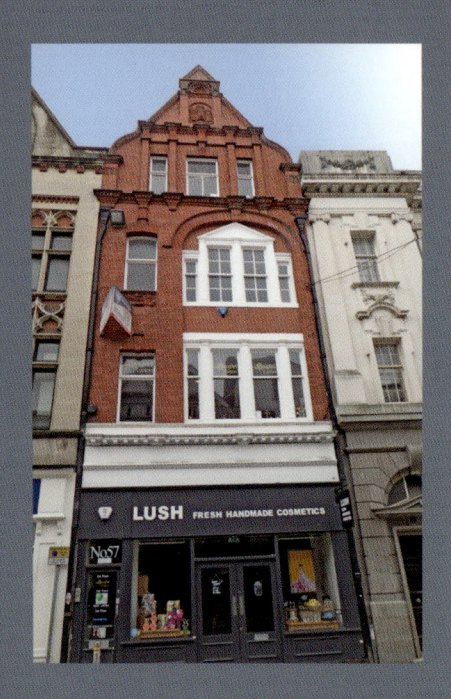

The building is not listed. The frontage is 21 feet 10 inches.

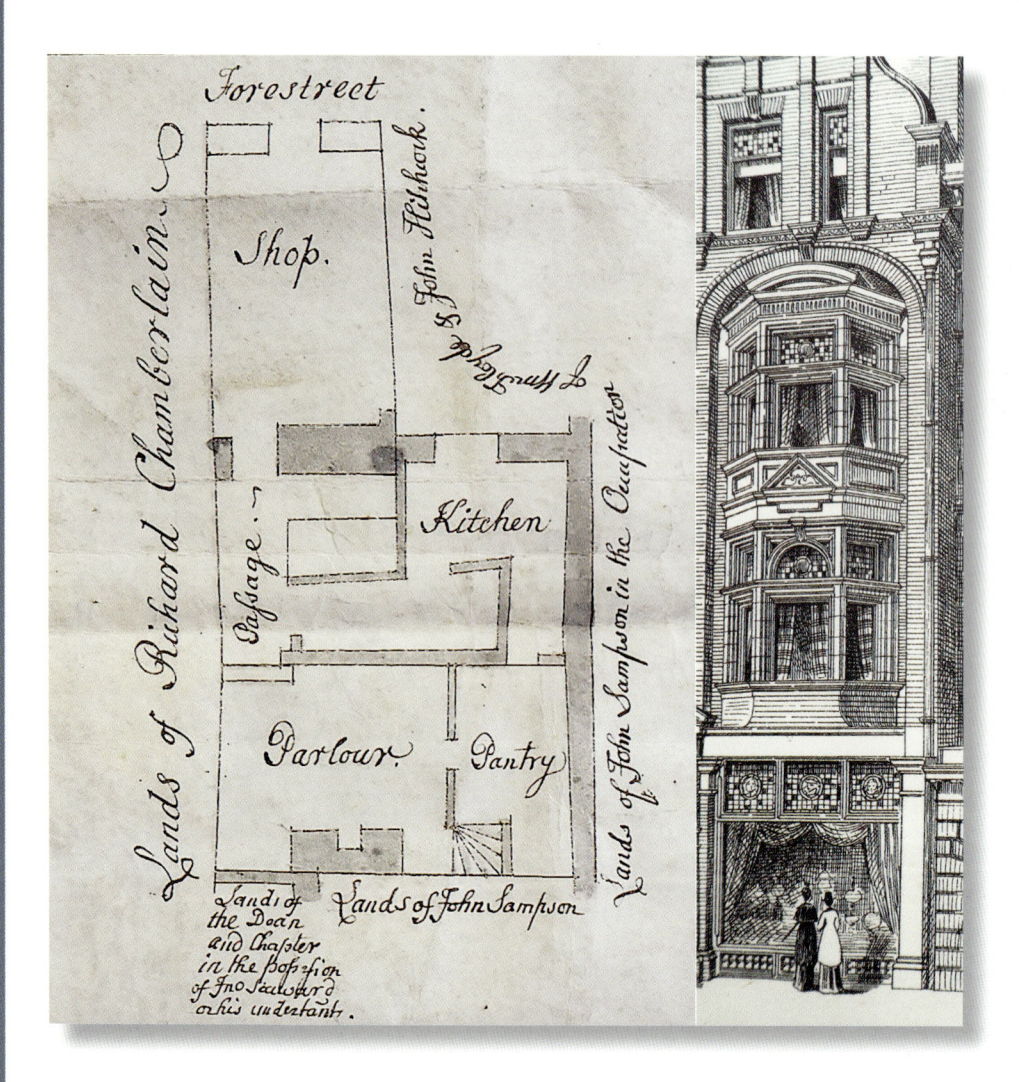

58 High Street, a property which was anciently held by the Dean & Chapter, on long lease to the Tothill family, occupied by the Parr family from the mid 1500s through to the early 1700s, destroyed by fire in 1881 and rebuilt in 1882.

Until 1881 Numbers 57 & 58 were a pair of possibly seventeenth-century buildings with three storeys with pitched roofs and were one room wide. In 1770 number 58 had its door on the right side and by 1850 two sash windows on the first and second floors. The top floor had a single sashed window.

Several generations of the Parr family were resident from at least the 1570s through to the late 1600s.[377] In 1666 the property comprised 'one shop, one cellar under the shop, one entry besides the shop and chamber over the said shop and entry, one garret over the said chamber, one hall, one gallery in the side of the said hall, one buttery within the said hall, one woodhouse within the said buttery, one chamber or kitchen over the said buttery and woodhouse and within that one kitchen where is a chimney and one oven, and within the kitchen one parlour and within the parlour one buttery, and over the parlour one great chamber and three little chambers and a loft or room over the said chambers and two little studies over some part of the said curtilage. And the said premises extend in breadth in the said hall one and

NUMBER 58 High Street

Left:
110. Ground floor plan by John Tothill of 58 High Street, 1770.
111. Engraving of front elevation, 1881.

twenty feet or thereabouts and in the parlour fifteen feet or thereabouts'. A plan made in 1770 shows the same plan: the front door led into a shop from which there was a passage to a parlour, pantry and kitchen around all of which was a courtyard. It was claimed in 1727 that the building was built of brick.

In 1666 the courtyard at the back was enclosed by a wall in which Sibley Parr's father in law had made a door into Cathedral Green without the permission of the Dean & Chapter. She promised to remove the door and reinstate the wall.[378] Nine years later John Parr was permitted to reinstate the door on condition that the porter was given a key in order to lock it at 9pm each night. Parr's two unmarried daughters subsequently took out a lease[379] and may have been the last of the Parr family to occupy the building because in 1717 the next occupants were Margaret Hagedott, a spinster, and Edmund Richards, a goldsmith.[380]

Numbers 57 & 58 were used as one building from at least the 1820s and from the mid eighteenth-century through to the fire of 1881 was used for the retailing of clothing.[381] In 1838 the second floor comprised 'two sitting rooms, a light closet and a water closet, with three bed rooms over them and an underground floor consisting of an excellent kitchen, scullery, larder, large wine, coal and beer cellars, with hard and soft water on each floor, grates, kitchen grange, etc. complete'.[382] Hats, lace, gloves, boots and shoes were among the goods sold by subsequent traders.[383] One was George Burrington who moved his business from Fore Street to Number 58. He advertised to 'his agricultural friends that in order to meet the present prices, he will sell them a good hat for a good bushel of wheat'. He had been born in Crediton and in 1851 lived at 58 High Street with his wife, who was a milliner, and two daughters.[384]

George Herbert sold shoes and boots at Number 58 when the fire destroyed the building in 1881. During that morning the fire had 'undermined the fronts of Mr Herbert's house and the houses above and about six o'clock [am]… the front gave way. There was hardly any warning – the whole frontages of the burning houses seemed to shiver, incline at first towards the road and then they fell back on the fiery mass inside'.[385]

Upon being rebuilt the new building housed various firms such as Fox Brothers, Fowler & Company which opened a branch of their Wellington bank at both 57 & 58 High Street.[386] In 1911 three males and five females lived upstairs. Charles Ltd, a Bristol firm of home furnishers, was an occupier just before the second world war and the opening day was announced as 'a new era' 'for all those intending furnishing or refurnishing, as always every article is sold under our fearless guarantee.'[387]

OCCUPANTS OF THE PROPERTY

pre 1574	Robert & Sabine Parr
1574	John Parr, Merchant
1646	John Parr, Merchant
1666 – 1673	Sibley Parr, Widow
1673 – 1682	John Parr, Merchant
1683	Elizabeth Parr, Widow
1690	Judith and Sarah Parr
1717	Margaret Hagedott (Spinster) and Edmund Richards, Goldsmith
1725 – 53	Samuel Stephens, Apothecary, & others
1759 – 1770	Sarah & Mary Spry, Thomas Wigginton the Younger, Mercer & others
1770 – 1808	Enoch Francis, Minister
1809	Mrs Francis, Milliner
1813 – 1823	Thomas Sparkes, Junior, General Haberdashery
1823 – 1834	Mrs Elizabeth Dinneford, Linen Draper, Silk Mercer & Fancy Haberdasher (& 57)
1834 – 1840	Mr R. Nightingale. Berlin, Embroidery Wool and London Shoe Warehouse, (& 57)
1850 – 1852	George Burrington, Hat Manufacturer
1853 – 1857	Charles Adams, Laceman and Glover, & Mrs Adams, Milliner
1855 – 1868	Mr C. Cambridge, Boots and Shoes
1868 – 1881	Harriet & George Herbert, Boot and Shoe Makers
1881– 1883	Destroyed & Rebuilt
1885 – 1922	Fox Brothers, Fowler & Company, Bankers (& 57)
1885 – 1904	Sun Life Assurance Company (& 57)
1934 – 1942	Charles Ltd., Artistic House Furnishers (& 57)
1943 – 1954	Montague Burton, Gents' Tailor (& 57)
1955	Vacant
1956 – 60	Boyds of Bond Street, Piano Dealers (& 57)
1961 – 1969	David Grieg Ltd, Grocers (& 57)
1970	Vacant (& 57)
1971 – 1986	Alliance Building Society (& 57)
1981 – 1990	Life Association of Scotland Ltd
1981	Exeter & Torbay Districts Training Group
1987	Vacant (& 57)
1988 – 2002	Jaeger (& 57)
2003 – 2017	Lush (& 57)
2016 – 2017	Songbird Tattoo

NUMBER 59

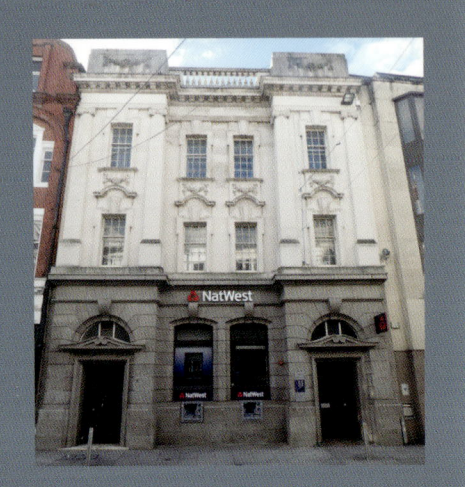

In 1973 59– 60 High Street was provisionally listed by Historic England as Grade 2 and recorded it as 'elaborate early twentieth-century frontage. Three storeys, four bays, the outer ones set forward. Continuous ground floor is granite, Portland stone above. Sash windows with glazing bars, architrave surrounds. Giant Ionic pilasters. Swags, cornice, balustraded parapet, roof not visible'. The frontages of Numbers 59 & 60 are 39 feet 5 inches.

112 and 113. Front elevation and plan of 59 High Street, 1768.

59 High Street, owned by the City of Exeter but on long lease to the Tothill family and their descendants after the Reformation, rebuilt in 1912. The building has served as a bank for more than a hundred years.

The current building is the second one on the site since the late 1700s. In 1768 a drawing was made of the façade of the building then standing. It shows the ground floor was two rooms wide, the first and second floors had two sash windows each and there was an attic with two dormer windows. Number 59 has been involved in banking, insurance and other financial services since the 1830s. Before then it was occupied by a series of linen drapers including members of the Chamberlain family from the late 1700s through to the 1820s. When Richard Chamberlain died in 1807 he was noted as 'a very respectable linen draper, and one of the chamber of this city; a gentleman so much respected and beloved by his friends and the public, and so well known for his excellent character and amiable manners, that it would be difficult to pass an eulogium on his equal to his worth'.[388] Successors in 1827 boasted that their firm has excelled expectations and suggested one reason was 'the extraordinary attraction of the windows'.[389] The *Exeter Flying Post* enthused 'the fashionables have long noticed the very great attraction which the windows at 59 High Street in this city have caused during

NUMBER 59 High Street

the period that establishment has been conducted by the present proprietors, by their being decorated with such a superb and splendid variety of fancy articles comprising some of the most elegant evening, ball, dinner and promenade dresses.'[390] A series of milliners had rooms upstairs[391] as did Tycho Pilbrow for his Music Repository.[392]

The Norwich Union Fire Insurance occupied the building from at least 1839 through to 1912. It rented the ground floor (consisting of a front office, a bank office and a water closet, a coal cellar underneath the stairs leading to the underground offices and apartments).[393] The upper floors were rented out for offices[394] including to George Townsend, who described himself as an 'artist, lithographer and drawing master' and a 'lithographic draughtsman and writer for the trade', from at least 1844 to 1848. Upon his death in 1894 he was noted as being 'a good and gentle soul' who was 'singularly modest and unassuming'. He had been the local artist for the *Illustrated London News*. Many of his drawings and paintings of Exeter were collected by Thomas Shapter and given to Exeter City Library. Another journalist noted 'old buildings and antique glimpses found in him a methodical recorder, and he was always proud to exhibit his sketches of ancient houses and scenes which have disappeared in the advance of the improver and the destroyer. His collections will, it is hoped, come into the possession of the Albert Museum authorities. They will be useful to all who try to realise what Exeter once was, and to the future historian of the city will supply precious glimpses'. In 1844 Townsend was one of a number of artists in Exeter including those who

114. 56–60 High Street, between 1894 and 1906.

OCCUPANTS OF THE PROPERTY

1745 – 1753	Henry Wilcocks, *Druggist*
1759	William Walker, *Druggist*
1759 – 1762	Nathaniel Spry, *Mercer & Woollen Draper*
1768 – 1780	Grace Chamberlain, *Widow, & Nathaniel Spry*
1781 – 1807	Richard Chamberlain, *Linen Draper*
1808 – 1812	Elizabeth Chamberlain, Son & James Pittman, *Linen Drapers*
1812 – 1817	Elizabeth Chamberlain & James Pittman, *Linen Drapers*
1817 – 1826	James Pittman, *Linen Draper*
1826 – 1828	Snell, Pinwill & Please, *Drapers & Mercers*
1828 – 1829	Pinwill & Please, *Linen Drapers, Silk Mercers, Hosiers & Glovers*
1826 – 1827	Mesdames Snell & Darke (upstairs)
1830 – 1831	Twose & Baker
1830 – 1836	Tycho Pilbrow's Music Repository (upstairs)
1832 – 1834	E. & J. Nash, *Linen Drapers*
1839 – 1911	Norwich Union Assurance Company
1839 – 1855	Western Annuity Office
1840 – 1842	William Norris, *Surveyor*
1842 – 1843	A. P. Prowse, *Public Accountant*
1844	William Pim, *Engraver*
1844 – 1848	George Townsend, *Lithographer & Drawing Master* (upstairs)
1854 – 1860	John H. Baker
1865	S. Pyne & Sons, *Brush Manufactory*
1868	Town Clerk's Office (upstairs)
1842 – 1970	National Provincial Bank of England Limited
1875 – 1877	I. J. Kennaway (upstairs)
1875 – 1880	W. Cotton (upstairs)
1878	Edward H. Houlditch (upstairs)
1912	Rebuilt (& 60)
1970 – 2017	National Westminster Bank (& 60)

St Martin's Island: An introductory history of forty-two Exeter buildings

115. Elizabethan wall painting found during rebuilding of 59–60 High Street, October 1911.

NUMBER 59 High Street

specialised in portraits (Theodore Garland, Henry Haiusselin, Frederick Havill, James Leakey, William Spreat and Edward Tucker) and landscapes (Benjamin Abraham, Henry Melville Ball and William Traies).[395] William Pim, another engraver, was also an occupant in 1844.[396]

There were also residents such as, in 1851, Thomas Fouraker (sometimes Fouracre), then an inspector of police, his wife and a cousin. He was later a mace sergeant and city sword bearer. Fouraker died at Number 59 at the age of 79 having served 47 years in the city's employ.[397] The entrance was flooded with water during the great fire in 1881 but had little other damage.[398] In 1911 the building was demolished along with Number 60 and rebuilt the following year. When it was an empty site one journalist pondered 'one cannot gaze into the at present empty square without thinking of the wonderful tale which the uncovered stones could tell if they could speak'.[399] Shortly afterwards a colleague wrote 'there are few archaeological regrets over the new structure, as the premises which it supersedes contained no features of particular age or interest'.[400]

59½ High Street Guildhall Chambers

From January 1893 Lucas & Lucas, Auctioneers, were at the newly-named Guildhall Chambers (upstairs of Number 59) and the following year they were joined by Archibald John Lucas, an architect.[401]

OCCUPANTS OF THE PROPERTY

1893 – 1895	Lucas & Lucas, *Auctioneers*
1894 – 1906	Archibald John Lucas, *architect*
1913 – 1934	Norwich Union Fire Insurance
1926 – 1939	Bishop, Fleming & Co., *Accountants & Auditors*
1928 – 1931	Devon Insurance Committee
1928 – 1931	Provident Accident & White Cross Insurance Co. Ltd.
1931 – 1935	John Archibald Lucas, *Chartered Architect & Chartered Surveyor*
1931	Douglas C. Langford
1933	Harris & Co. (Assessors Ltd.), *loss assessors, insurance experts & valuers*
1933 – 1934	The Anglian Insurance Co. Ltd
1934 – 1935	The African Life Assurance Society Ltd.
1936 – 1939	Devon County Association for the Blind
1938 – 1944	Exeter Greyhound Racing Co. Ltd. *Registered Office*
1938 – 1942	Smith & Marshall, *Chartered Surveyors*
1939	Forestry Commission
1939 – 1946	Ministry of Agriculture & Fisheries
1940 – 1942	Women's Land Army
1940 – 1942	Devon County Committee
1940 – 1951	Fleming & Co., *Accountants & Auditors*
1943 – 1945	Board of Education
1943 – 1944	Songhurst & Richard, *Valuers, Surveyors & Assessors*
1946 – 1948	The Road Haulage Association Ltd.
1946 – 1960	Caledonian Insurance Co.
1946	Ashley Courtenay
1948 – 1949	Ministry of Agriculture & Fisheries
1950 – 1962	Employers Liability Assurance Corporation Ltd
1950 – 1956	King & Kearey Ltd., *Removers & Warehousemen*
1950 – 1973	Clerical, Medical & General Life Assurance Society
1952 – 1960	Portley & Lethbridge, *Accountants*
1953 – 1955	Drive Yourself Cars
1958 – 1960	Guardian Assurance Co. Ltd
1965 – 1966	National Society for Handicapped Children
1968 – 1973	Haroll Chorley & Irlam, *Licensed Property Valuers*

NUMBER 60

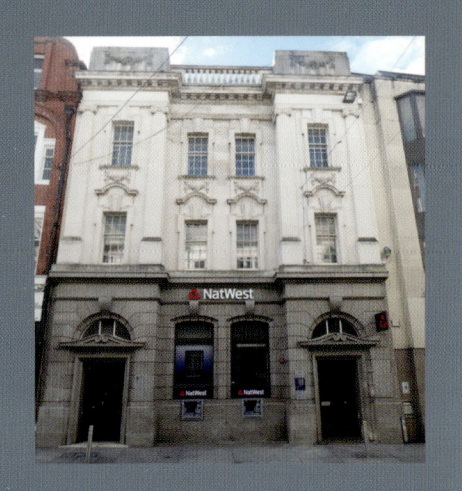

In 1973 59-60 High Street was provisionally listed by Historic England as Grade 2 and recorded it as 'elaborate early twentieth-century frontage. Three storeys, four bays, the outer ones set forward. Continuous ground floor is granite, Portland stone above. Sash windows with glazing bars, architrave surrounds. Giant Ionic pilasters. Swags, cornice, balustraded parapet, roof not visible'. The frontages of Numbers 59 & 60 are 39 feet 5 inches.

116. Lithograph, c1830, based on an unknown drawing, showing the entrance to Broadgate with the last houses of St Martin's parish in High Street.

60 High Street, demolished in 1911 and rebuilt the next year. It has been a bank for more than a century.

Number 60 had during the first decades of the nineteenth century an undistinguished history. One occupant was Richard Paul, a grocer[402] and cork manufacturer, who left in 1826 when Number 60 was described as 'a dwelling house with the shop and warehouse'. The *Exeter & Plymouth Gazette* later noted 'our attention has been called to a sad case of the distress of a very respectable decayed old tradesman of this city, Mr Richard Paul, formerly cork-cutter, and latterly a grocer. He is in his 79th year and so totally helpless that he has not left his room for more than seven years; he has been for ten years past maintained by his children but death has bereaved him of two out of three, particularly his only son, his principal support, who having died within the last week, he is now entirely destitute; every article of furniture must be sold to meet the rent'.[403]

In later years women's clothing and books were sold.[404] In the 1830s the building was twice offered for sale and noted as 'recently put in complete repair at a considerable expense'. Furthermore, it had 'the advantage of a passage or side entrance to the house unconnected with and distinct from the shop'.[405] The New London Hat Warehouse was the first new occupant: William Pinwill acted as the Exeter agent to 'Moore, the Hatters to the King and the Royal Family'. The firm specialised in beaver hats as well as Brazilian grass hats but within a year the business was bankrupt.[406]

1835 proved to be the year of profound change as it began a history of banking that has continued through to today. In 1835 an Exeter branch of the West of England and South Wales District Bank opened[407] although a year later it was rented to the National Provincial Bank[408] and within a few years Number 60 was let to other businesses. In 1843

NUMBER 60 High Street

would have been more effective had the frontage been more extensive. As it is, the design seems almost too bold for the available space. The upper stories are graceful except for the straight line of the cornice, which appears to me to look too hard – as if the building had had its top cut off at some time.'[416] The building has served as a bank since.

117. Painting by Joseph C. Yelland, 1885, based on W. H. Bartlett's view of 1829.

118. Steel line engraving by LePetit after drawing by W. H. Bartlett, 1829.

Adam Holden opened his bookshop and he was followed by another firm, only for a year.[409] For sixteen years Number 60 was used by an optician[410] who was succeeded by a hatter who moved from a shop two doors away and who shared the building with S. F. Luget, tailor.[411] Another hatter subsequently moved in[412] and then in 1896 a 'refreshment house' (temperance hotel and restaurant) was opened by Thomas Parsons Wilson but closed two years later.[413] It was replaced by The Guildhall Drug Store which was run by a Yeovil chemist and druggist. His business continued to at least 1907[414] during which time, in 1881, the building was damaged by the great fire: the next morning it was discovered that the building was unroofed and flooded with water. Number 60 was subsequently used as offices of the Norwich Union Fire Insurance, the Chief Constable of Exeter City Council, the Exeter Improved Dwellings Company and Mr Payne, a solicitor.[415] Number 60, along with Number 59, was demolished in 1911 and redeveloped. The architect was J. H. Brewerton. At the time it was commented upon by a journalist who thought it was one of the 'handsomest' buildings in Exeter. He wrote 'the polished granite of which all the lower portion is composed, is very striking and attracts general attention. Really it

OCCUPANTS OF THE PROPERTY

1807 – 1826	Richard Paul, *Cork Cutter & Grocer*
1826 – 1828	Lee & Wescombe, *Milliners, Dress Makers & Haberdashers*
1828	Thomas Neale, *Haberdashery, Hosier, Glover & Laceman*
1828 – 1832	John Risdon, *Bookseller & Stationer*
1833 – 1834	William Pinwill, *New London Hat Warehouse*
1835 – 1836	West of England and South Wales District Bank
1836 – 1970	National Provincial Bank
1843 – 1856	Adam Holden, *Bookseller*
1856 – 1857	S. Drayton & Sons, *Bookseller*
1857 – 1874	Myers Solomon, *Optician*
1874 – 1880	Charles Wood, *Hatter*
1875 – 1880	Samuel F. Luget, *Tailor*
1880 – 1895	Fulford & Caseley, *Hatters*
1896 – 1898	Thomas Parsons Wilson's Refreshment House
1899 – 1906	The Guildhall Drug Stores
1906 – 1910	Weston Aplin, *Chemist*
1911 – 1912	Demolished and redeveloped (& 59)
1913 – 1934	Norwich Union Fire Insurance
1970 – 2017	National Westminster Bank

95

NUMBER 61

The building is not listed.

119 and 120. Map of 61 High Street, 1905, and photograph taken between 1894 and 1905.

61 High Street, at the start of the eighteenth century one property was rebuilt and divided into two properties, it was re-fronted in 1905, heavily damaged by fire in 1975 and rebuilt four years later.

In about 1700 a woollen draper rebuilt one property and turned it into two dwelling houses. Subsequent occupiers included a druggist and bookseller[417] and they were followed in the early nineteenth century by an ironmonger, silversmith and cheesemonger.[418] Perhaps it was the shop theft in 1830 by a 17 year-old Cornish runaway or another a few months before[419] that caused the cheesemonger to last a short period, but few nineteenth-century tradesmen had long tenures. A grocer was the occupant in 1833 when Number 61 was rebuilt and he described it as 'consisting of a good warehouse, shop, convenient sitting and bed rooms, together with requisite offices'.[420] He was the occupant when the roof was damaged when a chimney collapsed during a storm in 1836 and left the next year.[421] The following occupant only lasted a year and Number 61 was offered at auction. It was described as a 'newly built dwelling house… consisting of a handsome shop, spacious warerooms, cellars and every possible convenience for trade and as a residence. The situation is considered the most desirable for business in the city; the house has been newly and substantially built, no expense was spared in its erection or fitting up and it is in a complete state of repair'. The bankrupt merchant sold his stock to the next occupant who also left a year later.[422] It was next the turn of the shop manager to take occupancy. He also purchased the existing stock and continued to

NUMBER 61 High Street

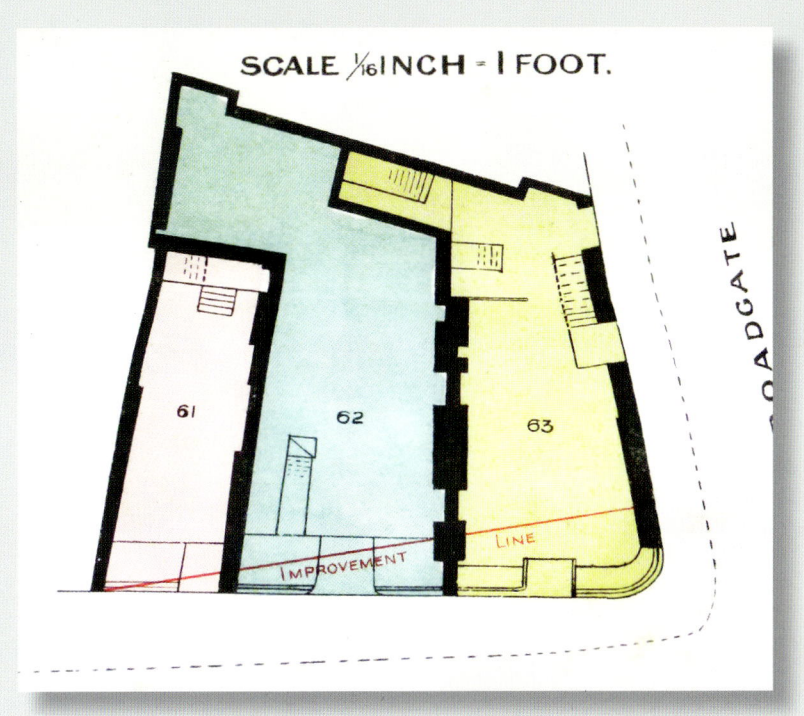

121. Map of 61 to 63 High Street showing the portion of the buildings to be cut back, 1905.

range and trough and recess cupboards. 2nd floor: front room with 2 windows, W.C., small room at back. 3rd floor: front room with 2 windows and recess cupboards, small room at back and cupboard at top of landing stairs'. The frontage on High Street was approximately 56 feet.[428] Five years later, in 1910, the owner, J. Archibald Lucas, the architect and surveyor at Number 59½ sold them to a South African. In 1905 Lucas had overseen 'the necessary alterations to set back to the new street line including the present elevations to High Street'.[429] The Maypole Dairy was a later occupant as was ABC Tobacconists.

In 1971 it was proposed to demolish Numbers 59 to 63 and the latter three buildings were described by Lady Aileen Fox, chairman of the Exeter Civic Society, as being 'late Victorian or Edwardian buildings in red brick with Bath stone dressings, unpleasing in texture and design'. She concluded 'the Society would welcome its replacement'.[430] In 1975 the building was set alight by an arsonist and rebuilt four years later.

trade, principally in hats and caps, until 1857 when he moved to Number 51. That year Number 61 was once again auctioned and noted as being 'entirely and substantially rebuilt a few years since, under the superintendence of an able architect; and is now in repair, both materially and ornamentally'.[423] The second half of the 1800s saw Number 61 occupied by a watch & clock maker, a maker of mops and clogs,[424] a stationer[425] and the Berlin & Fancy Business.[426]

In 1905 Numbers 61 to 63, along with 1 Broadgate, were purchased to widen High Street.[427] They had 'the fronts back to the Street Improvement Line, the new frontages to be constructed of brick or stone'. Number 61 was described as being a shop and dwelling house. The auction catalogue noted it as 'for many years in the occupation of Miss Coxwell as a fancy Wool Depository, consisting of Shop. 1st floor: showroom with 2 windows and marble mantel, kitchen with

OCCUPANTS OF THE PROPERTY

1724 – 1744	Edward Score,	*Bookseller*
1815 – 1817	George Strong,	*Ironmonger*
1822 – 1826	Joseph Trist,	*Silversmith & Jeweller*
1827 – 1837	Joseph Coplestone,	*Grocer & Tea Dealer*
1830	Messrs Edwin Dunn & Company,	*Cheesemongers*
1837 – 1838	James Brookman,	*Woollen Draper & Hatter*
1838 – 1845	Charles Thornley,	*Hat Manufacturer*
1846 – 1857	Charles Bisney,	*Charles Bisney's New Hat & Cap Warehouse*
1857 – 1861	Abel Uglow,	*Watch and Clock Maker*
1862	John Mortimore,	*Brush, Mop & Clog Maker*
1863 – 1881	Henry Welsford,	*Wholesale & Retail Stationer & Account Book Manufacturer (& later Auctioneer)*
1881 – 1886	W. Densham,	*Berlin & Fancy Business*
1887 – 1904	Caroline A. Coxwell,	*Berlin Wool Warehouse*
1905	Mr W. A. Gardner,	*Novelties*
1905	Refronted	
1906 – 1926	Maypole Dairy Company,	*Provision Dealers*
1928	Vacant	
1929 – 1933	Brooking & Son,	*Jewellers*
1933 – 1973	A. B. C. Tobacconists	
1939	J. Webber & Sons,	*Radio (upstairs)*
1962 – 1964	Walter & Mrs Gatrill	
1974	(unknown)	*charity shop*
1975 –1979	Arson and reconstruction	
1980 – 1990	Dunn & Company,	*Tailors (& 62–3)*
1991 – 1992	Vacant (& 62–3)	
1993	Original Levis Store (& 62–3)	
1994	Vacant (& 62–3)	
1995	Picture Zone Computer Games (& 62–3)	
1996 – 2001	Electronics Boutique Computer Games (& 62–3)	
2002 – 2009	Game Computer Games (& 62–3)	
2010 – 2017	Trailfinders (& 62–3)	

NUMBER 62

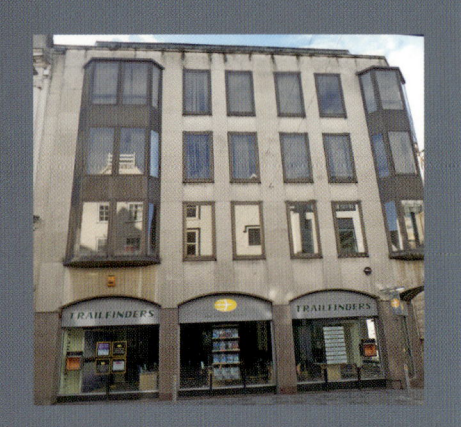

The building is not listed.

122. Exeter High Street, with Numbers 61 & 62, 1900.

62 High Street, for most of two centuries it was used to sell clothing, was rebuilt in 1833, combined in 1836 with Number 63 to form one retail building, renamed Broadgate House in the 1850s and rebuilt in 1905 and 1979.

In 1661 Ralph Herman, an alderman, lived at Number 62 which he had purchased from the bishop of Chester. Herman later bequeathed the sum of one pound to be paid annually from the rental of the building to maintain a poor boy and in addition 'one shilling's worth of penny loaves is provided weekly, in respect of this gift, at the expense of Mr Charles Upham, as the owner of a tenement in St Martin's parish, on the south side of Fore Street, a little above the passage leading to Broadgate'.[431] Nearly 100 years later it was still owned by Herman's family.[432] The subsequent occupation history is complicated by the local dominance of the Upham family: they occupied not only Number 62 but Number 63, 1 and 2 Broadgate, and 195 High Street (which was situated directly opposite Broadgate). It may have been the upper floors of Number 62 that Charles Upham offered in 1809: he described this as 'a good house near the Guildhall in the High Street'. He was a hatter, hosier and laceman and his billhead proclaimed that he also furnished funerals. In 1831 Mrs Swain opened her new Millinery & Dress Rooms in what was probably the first floor. The entrance was 'at the private door of Mr Upham, Hatter'.[433] Two years later Number 62 was rebuilt and Swain moved. By this time Upham's business was run by another hatter[434] who in 1833 conducted business nearby until the rebuild was completed. The building materials were auctioned 'of all those three spacious dwelling houses and shops... consisting of slating and woodwork to roofs, lead, floors, joists and beams, skirtings, partitions and boarding, doors, staircases,

123 – 4. Two photographs of the corner of Broadgate with High Street before and after street improvements, 1905–6.

125. Detail of painting by Emmanuel Jeffery, first half of the nineteenth century, showing the corner of Broadgate with High Street, providing architectural details of 61 to 63 High Street.

NUMBER 62 High Street

sash frames and sashes, marble chimney pieces and hearth stones, shop front sashes and shutters, water closets, lead pump, etc.'.[435] The new building comprised 'an extensive and lofty shop, a drawing room and parlour, on the first floor; seven good bed rooms and water closet over; a spacious kitchen, scullery and convenient offices on the basement'.[436] In 1834 the occupant offered 'a spacious drawing room with parlour' for a professional gentleman.[437]

A linen draper became the occupant of both Numbers 62 & 63[438] and a series of short-term clothing retailers followed including the Fur, Cloak, Shawl and Family Linen Warehouse.[439] A successor[440] named the building Broadgate House.[441] In 1868 'The People's Draper' became the occupier[442] and he was succeeded by the Japanese Curtain, Bed Furniture, Blind, Tapestry and Paper Hanging Depot.[443] Household appliances were subsequently sold and later Goff & Gully, Cabinet Makers, Art Decorators and Upholsterers, occupied the building.[444]

In 1905 Numbers 61 to 63, along with 1 Broad Street, were purchased by Exeter City Council for street widening;[445] Number 62 was a 'double-fronted shop with showrooms and dwelling accommodation adjoining' which comprised 'on ground floor: large double fronted shop with well-lighted showroom at the back extending behind Number 61 High Street. On the 1st floor, approached by staircase in shop are 2 good showrooms, and a recess room under staircase. 2nd floor: front room with 2 windows and cupboards in corner; room at back. 3rd floor: 3 rooms, w.c., trough and water supply. 4th floor: 2 attics. The shop front is mahogany with plate-glass front and embossed door of recent construction'. The frontage was approximately 21 feet. The four buildings were sold on condition the frontages were rebuilt in brick or stone and would be set further back.[446]

Subsequent occupiers included the Charing Cross Bank,[447] the Britannic Assurance Company[448] and a chocolate specialist.[449] Chalk's Stores returned to retailing clothing and Dunn & Company later continued that tradition. The building was heavily damaged by fire in 1975 and rebuilt shortly afterwards.

OCCUPANTS OF THE PROPERTY

1759 – 1803	Charles Upham (father & son), *Haberdasher*
1804	John Upham, *Haberdasher*
1804 – 1828	Charles Upham, *Hatter, Hosier & Lace Man*
1828 – 1833	John Upham, *Hatter & Hosier*
1831 – 1832	Mrs Swain (upstairs)
1833	Rebuilt
1833 – 1835	Joseph Vinnicombe, *Hatter*
1836 – 1845	James Windeat, *Linen Draper* (& 63)
1837 – 1838	Miss Gould, *Baby Linen Establishment*
1840	M. A. Saunders
1845 – 1852	Edger & Harris, *Drapers* (& 63)
1853 – 1855	James Windeat & John Taylor, *Drapers* (& 63)
1855 – 1864	James Windeat, *Draper* (& 63)
1857 – 1862	Mrs Hake (upstairs)
1864 – 1867	Brewer Howell, *Draper* (& 63)
1867 – 1868	R. B. Ling & Company, *General Drapery*
1868 – 1873	Albert Sully, *Draper*
1874	C. Wood, *Hatter*
1874 – 1875	Henry Welsford
1876	William Monkhouse & Company, *Household Appliances*
1877	Henry Gadd (upstairs)
1877 – 1878	Goff & Gully, *Cabinet Makers, Art Decorators and Upholsterers*
1879 – 1882	W. Dymond (cellar)
1880 – 1902	Saunders & Mumford, *Drapers*
1891	Miss Chastey, *Dressmaker*
1905	Refronted
1906	Mazawattee Tea Company
1907	Public Benefit Boot Company
1908 – 1910	Charing Cross Bank
1911 – 1912	Possibly vacant
1913 – 1919	Britannic Assurance Co. Ltd
1919 – 1926	J. L. Tannar Ltd., *Boot & Shoe Makers*
1923	Guildhall Art Studios
1928 – 1933	F. H. Seymour, *Confectioner*
1933 – 1975	Chalk's Stores, *Clothing*
1946 – 1957	Neville, Hovey, Smith & Co., *Chartered Accountants* (upstairs)
1946 – 1951	Friends' Provident and Century Insurance Offices (upstairs)
1946 – 1949	Zoe Hutchings, *Postage Stamp Dealer* (upstairs)
1963	Reginald Howard Publications (upstairs)
1965 – 1967	Godfrey & Brand, *Accountants* (upstairs)
1975 – 1979	Arson & reconstruction
1980 – 1990	Dunn & Company, *Tailors* (& 61 & 63)
1991 – 1992	Vacant (& 62–3)
1993	Original Levis Store (& 61 & 63)
1994	Vacant (& 61 & 63)
1995	Picture Zone Computer Games (& 61 & 63)
1996 – 2001	Electronics Boutique Computer Games (& 61 & 63)
2002 – 2009	Game Computer Games (& 61 & 63)
2010 – 2017	Trailfinders (& 61 & 63)

NUMBER 63

The building is not listed.

126. The corner of Broadgate with High Street, c1919–1926.

63 High Street, a property which has been known for Roman artefacts and which had its rent used by the City of Exeter for charitable purposes from 1596, combined with Number 62 in 1836 as one building, renamed Broadgate House in the 1860s, rebuilt in 1904 and 1979.

This property, at the corner with Broadgate, was posthumously given in 1596 by Joan Tuckfield to the City of Exeter on condition that it would be used for charity. In the late eighteenth century it comprised 'a shop, parlour, passage, little curtilage, and kitchen, with chambers over the same'.[450] In the 1750s it comprised a shop, parlour, passage, curtilage and kitchen on the ground floor and 'chambers' above.[451] In 1833 it, like Number 62, was rebuilt. Three years later a Heavitree man was given 'a parcel of coins found near Broadgate by workmen digging for laying on water pipes'.[452] These were reputedly found near Number 63 where five Roman bronze statues had been discovered in 1777: the latter 'were discovered last July in digging a cellar under the house of Mr Upham, situated in the High Street at Exeter, at the corner of Broadgate which leads from that street to the Close of the cathedral church. They were found within a very narrow space and not more than three or four feet below the present pavement of the street'. The figures were 'with or rather surrounded by a considerable quantity of oyster shells' along with bones, glass, metal and broken pottery. It was thought that the breaking of the pottery had occurred previous to the workmen's labours and it was stressed 'Mr Upham, the owner of the house, was too attentive to their work after the first appearance of the statues, to suffer them to proceed without a constant inspection: he caused them to continue their search, and discovering a large Roman tile, expected to find it the covering of a Roman urn, but to his great disappointment found it lay only on the natural earth; which certainly was not its

NUMBER 63 High Street

127. Procession in honour of the marriage of the Prince of Wales passing 63 High Street, 1863.

St Martin's Island: An introductory history of forty-two Exeter buildings

original position; but it must have been thrown there together with these broken urns; which then lay included within a space too narrow to have contained them if they had been entire'. Other discoveries were made nearby.[453] In the mid 1800s a relation, Edward Upham, 'a man of varied attainments and gifted with a spirit of inquiry into whatever was either curious or useful', sold the Roman *penates* along with a bronze cock.[454] These are now owned by the Ashmolean Museum, Oxford.

For more than a century Number 63 housed haberdashers, milliners, tailors and drapers.[455] Several were female milliners including Mrs Clark in the 1820s[456] and in 1836 it was Mrs Higgs who occupied the building when a stack of chimneys crashed into her workroom

128. Shop windows of Dunn & Company, at the corner of Broadgate, 1934.

129 The corner of Broadgate with High Street, c1906.

NUMBER 63 High Street

the upper floors 'suitable for offices, millinery and dress rooms' were offered for let.[461] Some of the firms that rented offices include Beer & Driffield (formerly Alfred Beer), artists in stained glass and medieval decorations,[462] and the Cooperative Dental Supply Association.[463]

In 1902 the council agreed a compulsory purchase order for Numbers 61 to 62.[464] They were sold in 1905 and Number 63 was described as 'all that prominent valuable corner shop, dental surgery, dwelling house and premises' which comprised a 'double-fronted shop with side entrance from Broadgate, good cellars in the basement; and on the 1st floor 2 rooms and on the 2nd floor 2 rooms.' The purchaser was required to rebuild the fronts in brick and stone and set the building back.[465]

The first occupant was a chemist[466] but the building subsequently returned to the sale of clothing. Melvilles, 'a new fashion centre for ladies wear'[467] was followed by May, Dunn & Company.[468] In 1975 an arsonist destroyed the building and four years later a new structure, designed by Sir Hugh Wilson, was erected in its place. A council planning officer told the firm 'this is probably the most critical site you will deal with for some time to come and the design is of great importance'. The initial design was withdrawn and another plan substituted.[469]

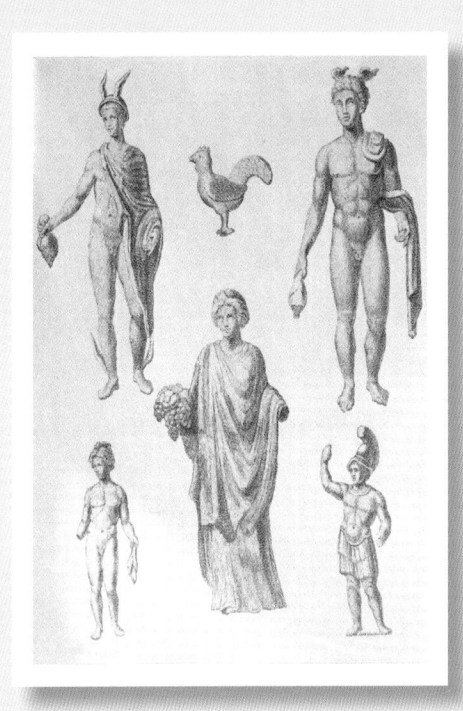

130. Roman *penates* found at 63 High Street in 1777.

'spreading the greatest alarm among the females who were industriously labouring in their vocation'. In 1833 the occupier moved because Number 63 was 'about to be pulled down by the commissioners'.[457] The new building comprised 'the dwelling house and shop, fronting Broad Gate… comprising a shop, with a parlour behind it, a drawing room, five bed rooms, and water closet, with a kitchen and wash house on the basement'.[458] The building reopened with a new occupant: J. Windeat, a draper, had both Numbers 62 and 63 and his business was called The Shawl Warehouse, The Silk & Shawl Warehouse or the The Silk, Shawl & General Drapery Warehouse. The subsequent occupier renamed the building 'Broadgate House'.[459]

The year 1869 heralded a change in use. Wine, spirits and beer replaced the sale of clothing and Number 63 stopped being used in conjunction with Number 62.[460] In 1874 and 1875

OCCUPANTS OF THE PROPERTY

1820 – 1828	Mrs Clark, *Milliner*
1828 – 1829	Mesdames Snell & Company
1828 – 1832	J. W. Snell & Co., *Draper & Tailor*
1832 – 1833	Thomas Hourston, *Tailor & Draper*
1834 – 1845	James Windeat, *Linen Draper (& 62 from 1836)*
1845 – 1852	Edger & Harris, *Drapers (& 63)*
1852 – 1855	James Windeat & John Taylor, *Drapers (& 62)*
1855 – 1864	James Windeat, *Draper (& 62)*
1864 – 1867	Brewer Howell, *Draper (& 62)*
1867 – 1868	R. B. Ling & Company, *General Drapery (& 62)*
1869 – 1871	William Opie & William Dymond, *Wine and Brandy Importers*
1872 – 1884	William Dymond, *Wine, Spirit & Hop Merchant*
1877 – 1878	Beer & Driffield, *Artists in Stained Glass & Medieval Decorators*
1884 – 1896	Frederick Townsend, *Wine, Spirit & Ale Merchant*
1885 – 1889	The Cooperative Dental Supply Association
1896 – 1902	Messrs Richard Southwood & Co., *Wine & Spirit Merchants*
1900 – 1903	William Lloyd Jones, *Ye Olde Broadgate Wine & Spirit Stores*
1905	Refronted
1905 – 1925	Timothy White, *Cash Chemists*
1923 – 1927	Car & General Insurance Corp. Ltd
1923	Royal Exchange Assurance Corp.
1928	Sellicks, *Furniture & Antique Dealers*
1928 – 1934	Melville, *Ladies Outfitters*
1934 – 1975	G. A. Dunn & Co., *Men's Tailors*
1975 – 1979	Arson & reconstruction
1980 – 1990	G. A. Dunn & Co., *Men's Tailors (& 61-2)*
1958 – 1962	Nevill, Hovey, Smith & Co., *chartered accountants* (upstairs)
1961 – 1962	Institute of Chartered Accountants, Exeter and District Branch of The Bristol and West of England Society (upstairs)
1991 – 1992	Vacant (& 61-2)
1993	Original Levis Store (& 61-2)
1994	Vacant (& 61-2)
1995	Future Zone Computer Games (& 61-2)
1996 – 2001	Electronics Boutique Computer Games (& 61-2)
2002 – 2009	Game Computer Games (& 61-2)
2010 – 2017	Trailfinders (& 61-2)

131. The south front of Broadgate, probably by and after John Gendall, 1835.

2
Broadgate

Broadgate is the name applied to the thoroughfare which runs along the western end of the Island from High Street into Cathedral Yard. The name has continued for nearly two hundred years since the gate itself was demolished although for a short while, in the 1820s and 1830s, the area was known as Broadgate Place and from 1850 to the 1870s it was called Broad Street.[470]

The gate was built in 1286 following the murder of a cathedral official in the Close three years before. Longstanding rivalry between the dean and bishop culminated in the arrest of the mayor, a trial before Edward I at Rougemont Castle and the mayor's execution. Shortly afterwards permission was granted to the cathedral authorities to enclose the precinct with a security wall. In 1915 Ethel Lega-Weekes believed (probably wrongly) that portions of it remained. She wrote 'in the cellars of nearly all the premises from Broadgate to St Martin's [Church] I have found remains of very massive walling, ranging from 6 to 15 feet in thickness, which lie roughly speaking, in a median line between the High Street and the Close frontages, and are neatly constructed, being faced with large ashlars in some parts and exhibiting in some places round-headed arches'. Lega-Weekes also suggested that much if not all of the Close had been walled before the 1280s.

There were seven gates. Broadgate was so named because it was constructed to allow the passage of a cart. In 1286 it was referred to as apud le fissand. This term has been interpreted as having meant a fissure in an ancient wall but Lega-Weekes suggested that it was a combination of fish with the Teutonic word *handeln*, to sell, or it correlates with the fourteenth-century Exeter place name fishshamlis (combining the words fish with shambles, a market place) which was in High Street. There is also documentary evidence from the 1340s for Broadgate having been called Fishfoldsgate.[471]

The gate was constructed of several types of stone with limestone on the ground floor and a darker one on the two upper storeys. In 1825 a journalist reported that 'some specimens, which we have seen, taken from the upper part, appear to abound in marine productions'.[472] In a niche on the first floor of the south face stood a statue of St Michael. In 1806 Alexander Jenkins explained 'the principal gate is now called the Broad Gate, anciently St Michael's, from its having the statue of that archangel overcoming Satan, placed in the interior front; this embellishment is much mutilated. In the vaulting of this gate is displayed elegant tracery. St Martin's Gate appears formerly to have been ornamented with tracery; a small part now remains'.[473]

Broadgate's position at the heart of the city centre has led to it being the scene of various incidents such as that of 1881 when there was a fatal accident at the High Street entrance when a procession of circus camels frightened a horse: the animal bolted and killed a pedestrian.[474] It has also served as the main entrance to the cathedral. Through it processed the city's mayors, fellow councillors and retinue in their civic finery and it was here that cathedral officials introduced their new bishops to the Close. In 1921 the Prince of Wales walked from the guildhall through Broadgate to unveil the county's war memorial.[475] It was also the site for disputes between the city and cathedral officials. Adjoining the gate was the Beavis Tavern which the mayor claimed in the 1440s attracted 'night walkers and rioters' who came through a wicket into the hostelry and there caused mayhem at night.[476] In 1554 an enquiry was held into the jurisdiction boundaries in the Close between the city and Dean & Chapter. The passageways were considered the king's highways and therefore in the city's control but ancient trees, which had marked the edges, had been felled. Malefactors, it was said, had even hidden in the trees

St Martin's Island: An introductory history of forty-two Exeter buildings

132 –135. Four views of Broadgate. One or more of these may have been created by artists after the gate had been demolished.

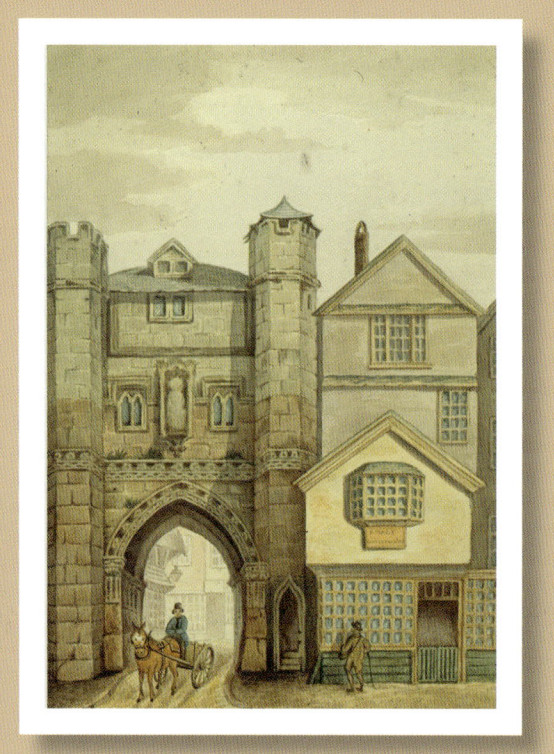

133.

134.

108

to escape prosecution. Disputes continued through the sixteenth century[477] and in 1638 a riot ensued following the porter of Broadgate swearing at city officials. The mayor fined Richard Commins and ordered his arrest after he refused to pay. The incident developed into a public spectacle and involved more than a hundred observers who watched the bailiffs enter the porter's lodge but were then locked inside by the porter's wife. No window was large enough to allow the men to escape. Four years later, in 1642, at the start of the civil war, the mayor wrote to the Dean & Chapter requesting that Broadgate be kept open all night. This was agreed on the condition that a watch was kept to prohibit entry into the Close of 'loose and disorderly people'.[478]

Discussions took place as early as 1822 on the gate's demolition. That year the Improvement Commissioners agreed in a vote of 16 to 6 that it should be pulled down along with two adjoining buildings and began discussions with the Dean & Chapter that lasted until 1824. The proprietor of the Royal Clarence Hotel petitioned the Commissioners to remove the gate on safety grounds. He cited an accident in which a coach driver and guard were thrown from their places, the horses and pole raced off to the hotel and the coach with its passengers were left behind at the gate.[479]

There was some notable opposition. In 1823 Reverend Pitman Jones, one of Devon's earliest advocates for antiquities, urged Bishop Carey to retain Broadgate in writing 'this beautiful Gate is almost the last remaining vestige of the antiquity of the City: its other monuments of former taste and grandeur have been rapidly disappearing under the hands of innovation.' He mentioned the high status visitors who were conducted from the gate to the cathedral and added 'As to the Gate itself, it is allowed by competent judges to be elegant in design and of superior workmanship. Whilst most of our Closes retain an ancient entrance gate, as a suitable accompaniment to the Cathedral Church, and as a fit preparation of the mind for the religious service, would it not be a subject of future regret if St Peter's Close were deprived of this advantage?' Pitman felt the Close was already 'disfigured by Inns and Coffee Houses' and urged that only the adjoining buildings should be removed. He suggested 'Your Lordship is aware, that the arch of the Gateway is sufficiently high to admit of any coach passing under it, however loaded.'[480] According to one neighbour, Henry Ellis, it had been suggested that the gate could be taken down and re-erected in Northernhay.[481]

The gate was demolished in 1824 and the passageway reopened on 28 February 1825. The gate's stone was reused to repair the cathedral. A stone was inscribed 'Here stood Broadgate, removed 1825' and set into the nearby wall as a reminder for future generations.[482] One of those displaced was an old woman by the name of Bondon who stood under the arch and served sassafras tea to workmen early in the morning. A colleague had the pitch at St Martin's Church.[483]

The gate, as with St Martin's Gate, Bear Gate and St Katherine's Gate, had accommodation. In Broadgate were rooms on the first and second floors. The porter lived in what was described as the lodge and in a room within the gate there occasionally was housed the cathedral's dog whipper or the scavenger. The latter not only kept the streets and passageways clean but he also lit the street lamps.[484] The porter was responsible for locking the gates each evening.[485] The gate's demolition in 1825 made the dog whipper and scavenger homeless and the Dean & Chapter had to find other accommodation.[486] In January 1826 a few lines of poetry were written about the gate.[487]

Broadgate now yields to Gothic sway,
　Despoil'd of every feature;
Saint Michael driven thus away,
　The Lord defend St Peter!

There are only two properties on the east side of Broadgate. Their shared four-storey frontage obscures a complex medieval history and subsequent development. 1 Broadgate has ceased to be a separate address.

NUMBER 1

Historic England has listed the building as part of 2 Broadgate. The frontage is 19½ feet.

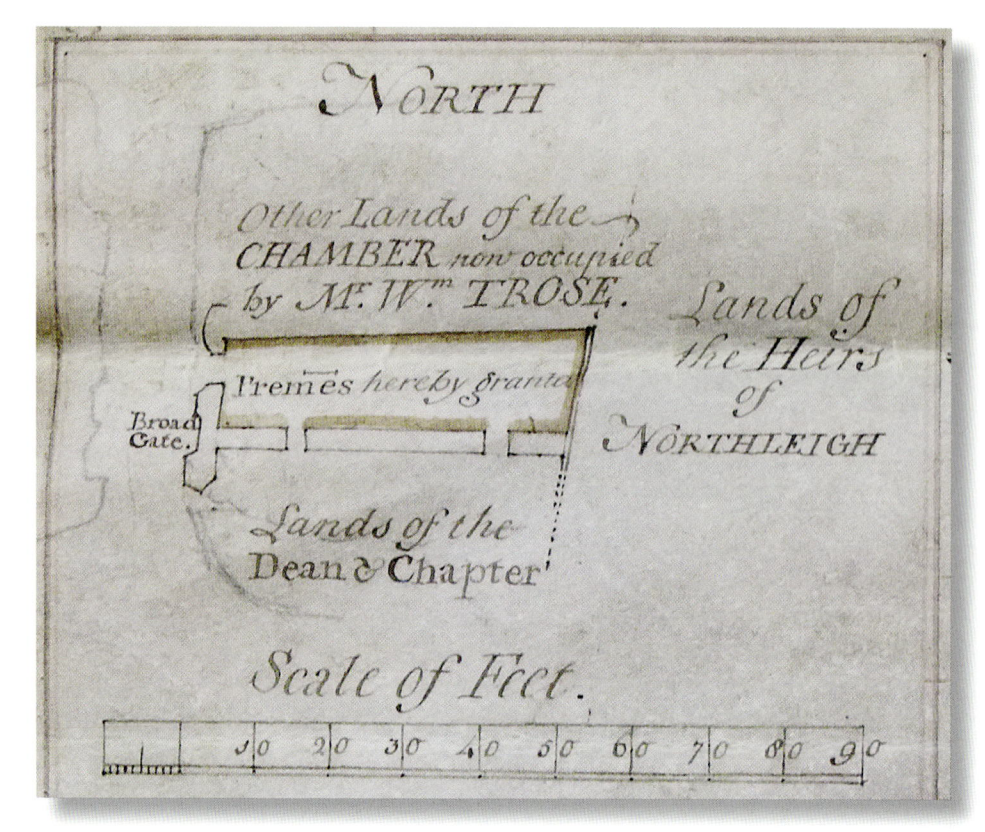

136. Map with 1 Broadgate in brown, 1754.

1 Broadgate, an anonymous building whose medieval fabric is effectively disguised by an early nineteenth-century frontage.

By 1355 a large tenement occupied the eastern boundary of Broadgate from High Street to Cathedral Yard. It may have included the site of the disused chapel of St Simon and St Jude. The property was rebuilt by the Wilford family as their home in the early sixteenth century and then sold in 1554. It was, as explained for 63 High Street, given in 1596 to the City of Exeter. Nearly two hundred years later, in 1789, 1 Broadgate was noted for insurance purposes as built of stone, lath and plaster with a slate roof. By 1603 the building had been subdivided to create two properties and in 1825 the western half was demolished when Broadgate was pulled down.[488]

From 1838 through to 1867 the occupiers also held 62–3 High Street.[489]

The next occupant was Samuel H. Hutchinson, 'a church and house decorator, painter, glazier, etc.', who used 1 Broadgate as his residence while his warehouse and workshops were in nearby Bear Street. Hutchinson's speciality was 'paper hangings, in every design direct from the manufacturers'. 1 Broadgate also housed his wife's fur and lace warehouse.[490] Another occupier appears to be another lace manufacturer.[491]

Cornish & Company, Gents and Boys Outfitters, occupied the building in 1903 when there were archaeological finds. These included one end of the Roman basilica whose other end was exposed by excavation from 1970 to 1975. A journalist wrote 'through the courtesy of Mr Cornish, outfitter (who has removed from Broadgate to Fore Street, to make room for the City Bank extension), we have been able to inspect some Early English arches in the cellars of his old premises. These arches appear to have formed a portion of a crypt, and Mr Harbottle thinks they belong to a building formerly connected with the cathedral. Mr Cornish suggested whether they might not have some relation to Broadgate (removed in 1823) but they extend a considerable way beyond the site of the Broadgate to High Street. The arches are, of course, older than any portion of the Cathedral excepting the Norman towers. They are close to St Petrock's but they cannot be connected with that church on account of the dissimilarity of styles'. Shortly afterwards the journalist noted these two arches were 'laid bare showing that they supported a massive wall'.[492]

In 1904 the council completed the statutory purchase of 1 Broadgate.[493] It was re-sold and the buildings were 'set back to the new street line including the present elevations to High Street'.[494] 1 Broadgate was then 'a dental surgery, with separate entrance… comprising on the 1st Floor: large room with 3 windows; another room used as surgery. Spacious landing (formerly a room with fireplace). 2nd floor: sitting room with 2 windows, kitchen, etc. 3rd floor: 2 rooms. 4th floor: attic and box room'. It was sold on condition that it was rebuilt in brick or stone.[495] In 1917 there was a minor fire when match boarding caught light.[496]

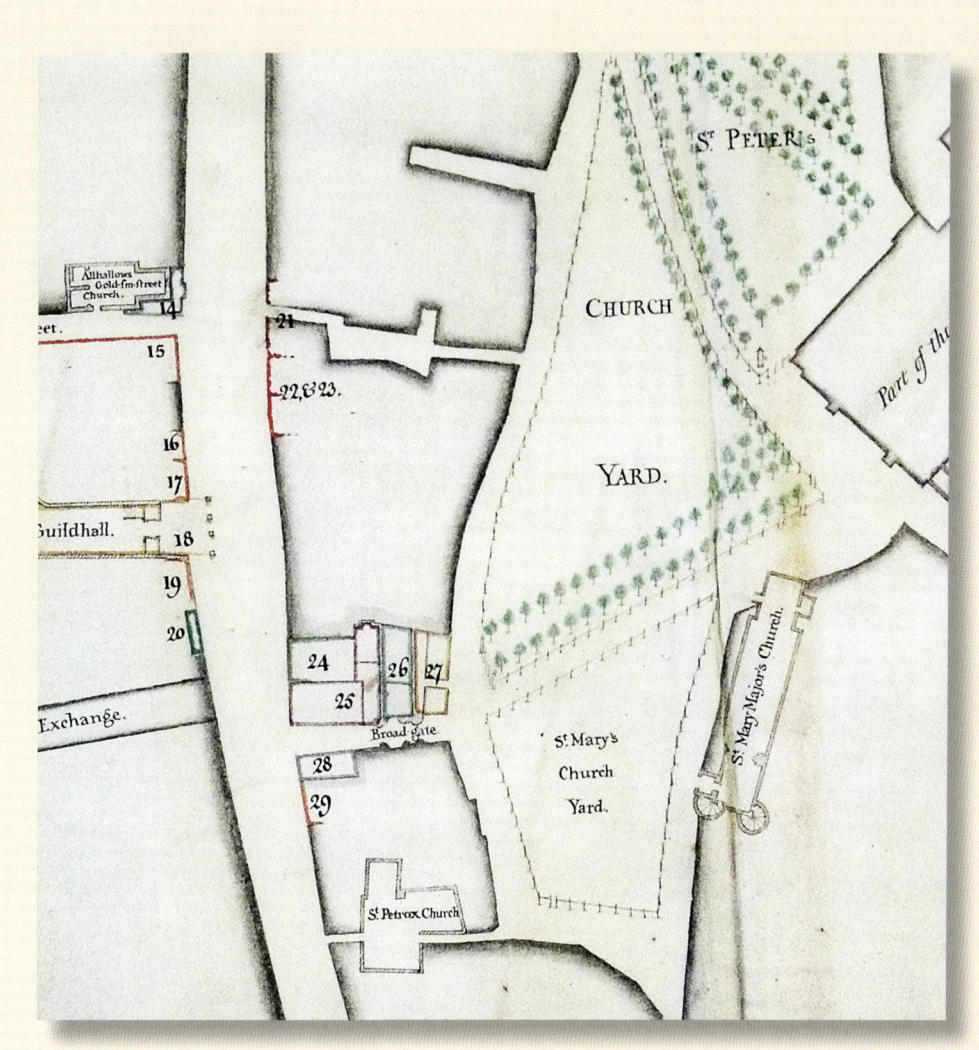

138. St Martin's Island as depicted in the Exeter Map Book, 1756, with 63 High Street and Broadgate outlined.

137. Drawing by John Harris of the north side of Broadgate, 23 July 1823.

OCCUPANTS OF THE PROPERTY

1838 – 1864	James Windeat (& 62 – 3 High Street)
1864 – 1867	Brewer Howell (& 62 – 3 High Street)
1867 – 1872	Samuel H. Hutchinson, *Church and House Decorator*
1867 – 1877	Mrs S. H. Hutchinson, *Furrier & Honiton Lace Manufacturer*
1875 – 1878	Miss C. B. Cossins, *Honiton Lace Manufacturer*
1889 – 1903	Cornish & Company, *Outfitters and Clothiers*
1904 – 1917	G. F. Passmore, *Dentist*

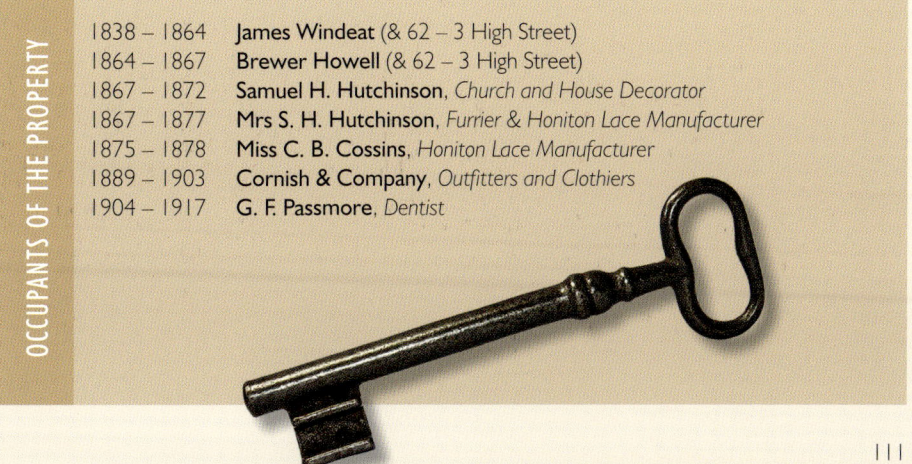

NUMBER 1 Broadgate

111

NUMBER 2

In 1953 this deceptive building was listed Grade 2 and recorded 'Tinley's Café & No. 2 Broadgate. Front built 1825 when Broadgate was demolished, but the back part of the building is still partly the seventeenth-century timber-framed house which stood there previously. The front is rendered, four storeys, six windows, on a curved line. Bands at each level. Good nineteenth-century curved shop frontage, sashes some with glazing bars and casements. Parapet roof not visible. Remains of the Close wall are exposed internally on the ground and first floors; two medieval arches are included'. The frontage on Cathedral Yard is 26 feet 23 inches and that along Broadgate is 22 feet.

139. Copper line engraving by F. Nash after Joseph Farington, 1822, of Broadgate with the most western building then in Cathedral Yard.

2 The Broadgate, a medieval building with a much later frontage that cloaks a history of piecemeal rebuilding. Its dominant use has been as a confectioner's shop and restaurant.

As with 1 Broadgate, this building has a shared history of rebuilding and its boundaries have had considerable changes. The back portion comprises the remains of the Wilford family's rebuilding. There was a considerable area of open land between the front of the building and the boundary of the churchyard which in the 1600s and 1700s was, from Broadgate to a mid point in Cathedral Yard, gradually filled in with temporary buildings which became permanent. By the 1750s there were at least two ramshackle structures in front of 2 Broadgate and by 1772 there were three which were more substantial. The westernmost of these buildings was removed during the rebuilding of 1825 and a new frontage was erected to tie the remaining two buildings together as one.[497]

By the mid 1750s the building was in length from east to west 39 feet and in width 14 feet.[498] In 1767 it was occupied by Richard Upjohn, a member of the illustrious family of clockmakers. One hundred years later a descendant occupied 39 High Street.[499] At the end of the eighteenth century Upjohn was succeeded by a series of confectioners including one who sold ice cream throughout the year and by the Smale family who were occupiers when the front building was demolished in 1825. It was this building which was in the midst of being demolished when the Dean obtained an injunction which delayed the proceedings for a short period.[500]

The next prominent confectioner was Sarah Mardon who lived above her shop.[501] In 1833 she married James

NUMBER 2 Broadgate

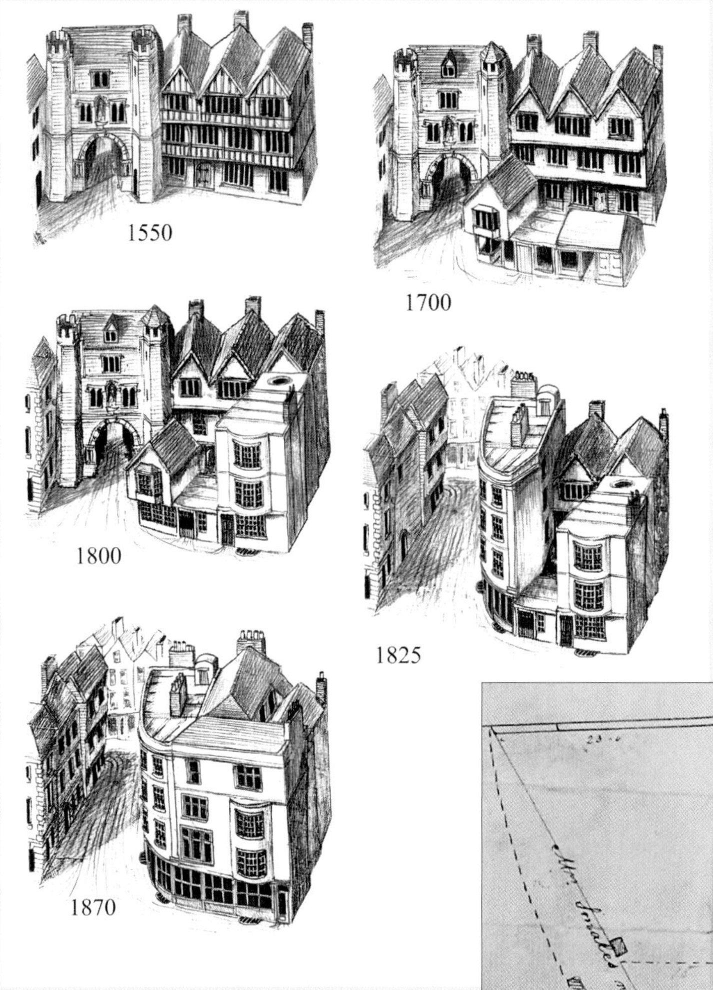

140. Sketch reconstruction by Richard Parker of the development of 2 Broadgate from 1550 to 1870.

Murch, a Honiton-born accountant/wine merchant. She did not restrict herself to selling sweets but also sold turtle soup. At this time there were eighteen other confectioners in Exeter.[502] Her son James took over the business in 1868, at the age of 31, but died five years later.[503] Three years later his widow married J. C. Goff.[504] Goff had come to Exeter to be a cabinet maker but left that occupation upon his marriage to Ann Murch and had a management role until his own sudden death, of pleurisy, in 1894.[505] In 1877 Mrs Sarah Murch was remembered as having been for 50 years a 'genial and well-known proprietoress'. The firm continued until 1917 when Mrs Ann Goff and her son sold the Cathedral Restaurant & Café, under which name the business had run since at least the early 1870s.

In 1920 Mark Rowe & Sons purchased the building with the intention of transforming the premises 'lately known as Goff's Restaurant' into 'high class auction rooms' to be known as The Broadgate Mart. It continued until 1924[506] when the Women's Institute acquired 2 Broadgate. It was then known as Glebelands and run as a Craft Workers Club.[507] A club for ladies was also opened. It comprised a lounge, drawing room, a writing room, two small tea rooms, a rest room and two dressing rooms. Its motto was thought, culture and quietude.[508] In 1924 Miss Dyson was a third occupier. She offered face massage, manicures and the removal of superfluous hair.[509] In 1930 Tinley's Café returned 2 Broadgate to selling food and continued until 1992. In 1965 Exeter City Council granted permission for 2 Broadgate to be demolished (along with 61–3 High Street) with the condition that medieval walling and a turret were retained. The scheme was not followed through.[510]

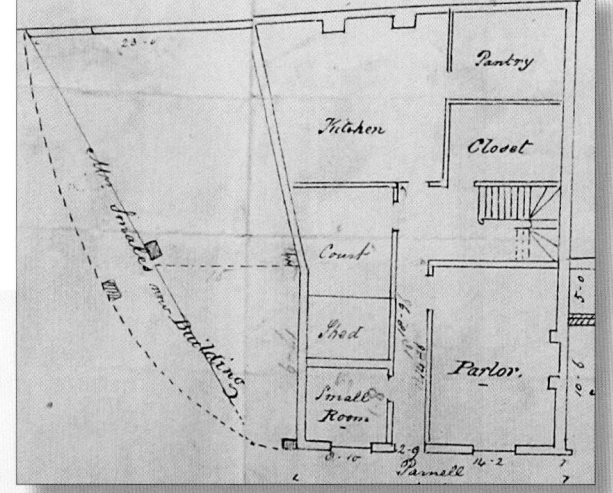

141. Map showing line for cutting back western end of 2 Broadgate, along with Mary Parnell's tenement, 1825.

142. Drawing of Tinleys, c.1970.

OCCUPANTS OF THE PROPERTY

1767 – 1778	Richard Upjohn, *Watch Maker*
1778 – 1789	James Upjohn, *Watch Maker*
1795 – 1797	John Drewe, *Confectioner*
1797 – 1801	William Huxham, *Confectioner*
1813 – 1824	John & Eliza Smale, *Confectioners*
1824 – 1827	Mary Parnell, *Confectioner*
1829 – 1868	Sarah Mardon (from 1833 Murch)
1833 – 1868	Sarah Murch, *Confectioner*
1868 – 1873	James Murch, *Confectioner & Cook*
1873 – 1920	Murch, Goff & Company, including Murch's Cathedral Restaurant & Café from at least 1885 to 1918
1920 – 1924	The Broadgate Mart (Mark Rowe & Sons)
1924 – 1937	Glebelands, Art Repository
1924	Miss Dyson
1930 – 1992	Tinley's
1993 – 1994	French Stix
1995 – 2017	Pizza Express

143. Undated procession through Broadgate from the Guildhall to the Cathedral.

144. Second view of a similar procession with varying details of the Cathedral Yard buildings.

3
Cathedral Yard
previously also called Cathedral Close

The precinct of the Cathedral is often referred to today as Cathedral Green and the section running along the north side, from the Royal Clarence to Broadgate, is now known as Cathedral Yard. It was also until recently occasionally called Cathedral Close but through into the nineteenth century it was more commonly called Cathedral Churchyard, Peter's Churchyard or simply the churchyard.

Nearly two thousand years ago this was the heart of Roman Exeter and it has since remained the city's centre. It served as the city's main graveyard until 1637. Reverend George Oliver wrote in 1821:
'we cannot leave the close without reminding the reader that this area was once the general burying place of the citizens for nearly the space of a thousand years... this interesting spot is a melancholy proof of the instability and vanity of all human things; and awfully reminds us all, that we must soon be inevitably forgotten. The memory of the tens of thousands that here lie entombed in their kindred mould has passed away. In this plain of bones not one monument remains to record the profession, character, fortune, rank, talents, beauty or age of the unnumbered dead of Exeter'.[511]

By the mid 1600s it had become a favourite place for promenading. In 1669 an Italian visitor commented that 'in the square of the cathedral is a most beautiful summer walk, under the shade of trees, into several rows of which it is distributed, like those which are customary in Holland'.[512] Nearly a generation later, in 1694, a Cornishman thought 'the Close, or the Church Yard, is the very pleasure or jewel of the place.'[513]

The Green also served another purpose. In 1698 Celia Fiennes observed 'there is also a very large space railed in just by the cathedral with walks round it, which is called the Exchange for merchants, that constantly meet twice a day, just as they do in London'.[514] This was linked to a building in High Street, called The Exchange, by a lane called the New or Little Exchange.

The Green has also been the city's location for public events and demonstrations. Mayors have processed from the guildhall through the precinct to the cathedral for hundreds of years. In the nineteenth century it was infamous for the disturbances caused by 'Young Exeter' celebrating the 5th of November. Typical was that of 1849 when there were rockets, fireworks and the burning of effigies. Bishop Philpotts was a favoured target but in 1849 it was the turn of a local cleric who was suspected of fathering an illegitimate child. Reverend Rook was paraded through the precinct in the guise of his avian namesake and there were effigies of the unfortunate young mother and her child. Each was thrown onto the bonfire. In other years towering grotesque figures promenaded and bowed at the windows of the houses in Cathedral Yard as their guests watched the proceedings. In 1892 Beatrix Potter stayed at the Clarence and recalled the infamy of those nights.[515] Several generations before an earlier proprietor of the hotel was worried about the effects on her guests. Mrs Sarah Street and some of her neighbours petitioned the Dean & Chapter to control the disorder. Mrs Street explained that she had fitted up the Hotel 'at a considerable expense' but was now worried about trade. She wrote that 'in consequence of the number of fireworks which have of late nightly been let off in the Cathedral Yard, and some of them thrown into her house, added to the great noises that nightly occur some Ladies who were staying at her House, which is a family Hotel, have from alarm withdrawn themselves to another

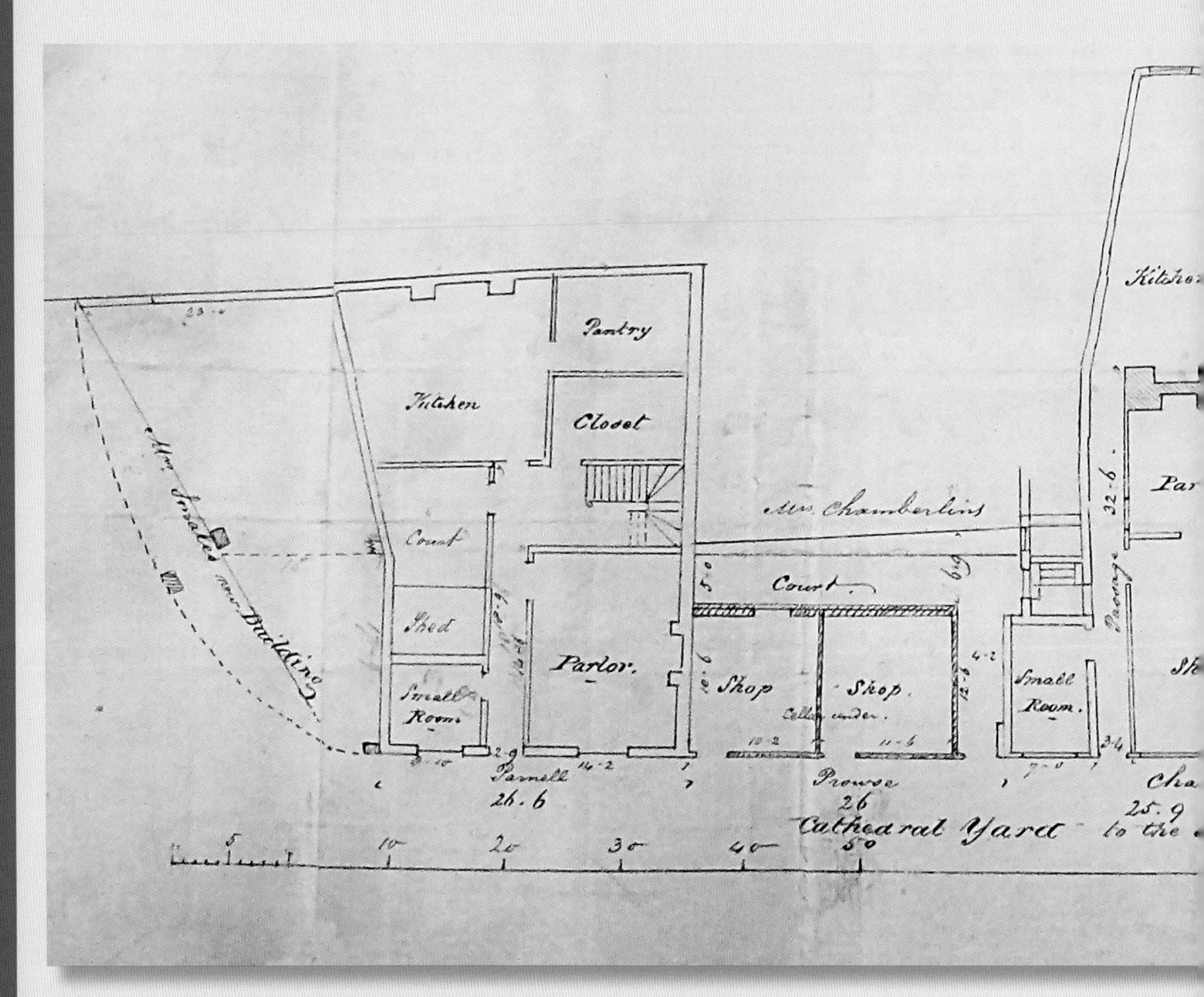

St Martin's Island: An introductory history of forty-two Exeter buildings

145. Cathedral Yard from Broadgate to Number 22 (now Michael Spiers), 1825.

Inn.' The inhabitants, led by Thomas Tierney, complained about 'the nightly disturbed state of the Cathedral Yard where, in the absence of all police, fireworks are constantly let off not only dangerous in themselves but to the great annoyance of passengers as well as the inhabitants in general, and where a number of disorderly persons assemble who continue to a late hour making noises and using language the most disgusting and last night only murder was repeatedly cried.'[516] Typical of the chaos was an incident in 1846 when 'a very serious outrage' was committed to 18 Cathedral Yard. A journalist castigated 'the growing spirit of outrage on these occasions, young men going about in masquerade and giving vent to the wildest spirits and indulging in practical jokes'. The windows were broken between midnight and one o'clock in the morning.[517] In 1879 a rocket or a 'rip rap' caused further damage when it passed through a second-floor window. In many other years windows in the Close were boarded up in order to stop fireworks from entering the buildings.[518]

Redevelopment schemes in 1971 prompted the Society for the Protection of Ancient Buildings to take an interest in Exeter. The secretary of the society then commented 'Exeter Close is one of the most important townscapes in the whole of England. It may not be near-perfect as Salisbury Close but personally I prefer it, because of the happy accident of its scale, shape, topography, disposition of buildings and relationship to the cathedral, and the

Cathedral Yard

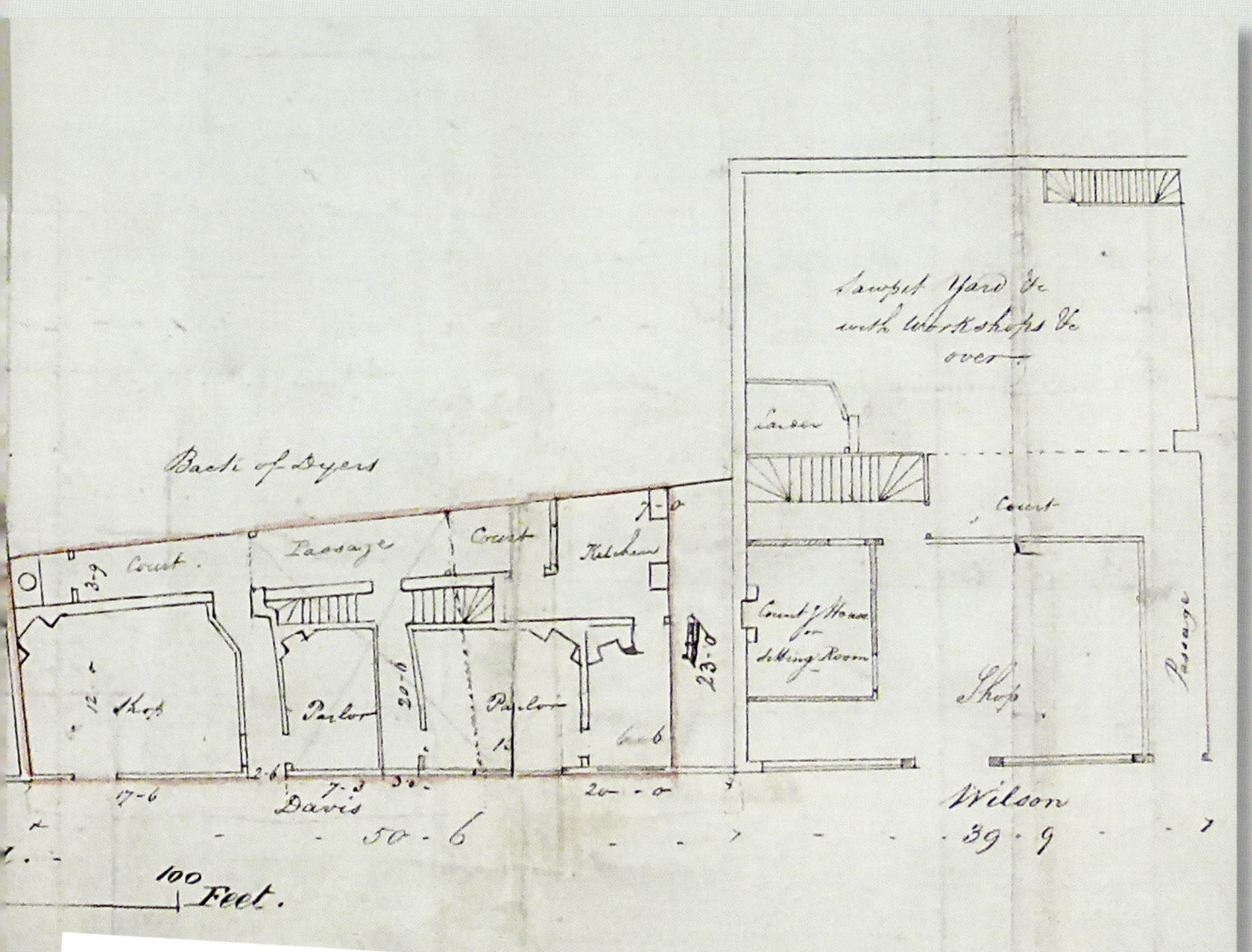

146. View of the west end of Cathedral Yard by Jean Rocque, 1744.

fact that within it the life and commerce of the city graphically withdraws, the closer one gets to the cathedral – in contrast to Salisbury where there is a sudden break at the gate. And anyway <u>everything</u> worthwhile in Exeter ought to be kept'.[519]

Historic England has determined that 'all the listed buildings of Cathedral Yard and Numbers 1 and 2 Deanery Place form a group'. The last residents of Cathedral Yard (besides those of the hotel) were at Number 18 in 1968.[520]

NUMBER 24

In 1974 this building was listed Grade 2 and recorded 'set back behind a later screen. Eighteenth century. Rendered. Three storeys, six windows, sashes with glazing bars. The first floor windows have dentilled heads and sliding shutters. Slate roof with dentil and modillion parapet. The ground floor projects with a mid nineteenth-century five bay arcade of engaged rusticated columns with arched windows and door between. Parapet over with ball finials. All the listed buildings of Cathedral Yard and Nos 1 and 2 Deanery Place form a group.' The footage is 51 ft.

147. Victorian imagining of the early nineteenth-century Cathedral Yard buildings including that (on far right) now occupied by the National Westminster Bank.

24 Cathedral Yard, a ramshackle property which was divided into parts by 1825 until 1879 when it was demolished and a new building was erected in its place for use as a bank.

The site on Cathedral Yard occupied by the National Westminster Bank held two properties in 1825. A central entry led into the eighteenth-century building which remains on the site. The two small shops were consolidated in 1836 when the two buildings were demolished and a single structure erected in their place. In July 1836 it was noted in the *Exeter Flying Post* that 'Messeurs Cole, Holroyd & Company have commenced taking down the premises in the cathedral yard, at the back of Pilbrow's musical repository, Fore Street, the whole of which, we understand, will be rebuilt in a splendid style by this firm, and where the business will afterwards be carried on'. This would become the new premises of the Devon County Bank.[521] It was also reported that in early November archaeological discoveries were made while digging the foundations of the new building. This included red Samian ware, large flat Roman tiles and some fifteen copper coins. There were also potters' marks, a 'coarse Roman vase of baked clay', a skeleton and 'some curious pieces of bottles with escutcheons probably from the Vine Tavern near this spot'. W. P. Shortt of Heavitree reported a month later that 'a low arched chamber was discovered at a great depth, containing bones of men and animals; the stones were of tufa or refrigerated lava like the

NUMBER 24 Cathedral Yard

castle walls of Rougemont'.[522] This may have been a stone-lined garderobe.

In 1879 the building was acquired by the National Provincial Bank and the council approved the plans which were by Hayward and Son.[523] Numbers 26 & 27 were then absorbed into the use of the bank and ceased having a number. It was proposed in 1971 to 'rebuild the portico front in the modern idiom' but this was not followed through.[524] A decade later the bank was refurnished, including the repair of bomb damage from the 1940s.[525]

Formerly 26 Cathedral Yard

From at least 1805 to 1825 the Chave family occupied the eastern tenement (then Number 26) and Mr Prowse was in the western half. In 1805 it was 'Chave's Toy Shop' which acted as the venue to buy tickets for balls at the hotel later known as the Royal Clarence.[526] In 1874 a neighbour recalled that the occupant of the building had in the early 1800s been Miss Lascelles, a straw bonnet maker.[527] Eliza Lascelles was there from 1825 until 1828 when she married C. H. Matthews in St Martin's Church.[528] By 1853 Number 26 referred to the eighteenth-century dwelling house which is set back from the Yard. It was occupied by a series of women who sold millinery, dresses and mantles.[529] Other tenants that followed, with offices, included two chiropodists one of whom cured 'corns, bunions, callosities, nails growing into the flesh, and every disorder of the feet',[530] a lecturer on 'Memory and the Association of Ideas: Illustrated with the History of Exeter'[531] and several dentists[532] including one who had been 'medical officer to the Peruvian establishments on the Upper

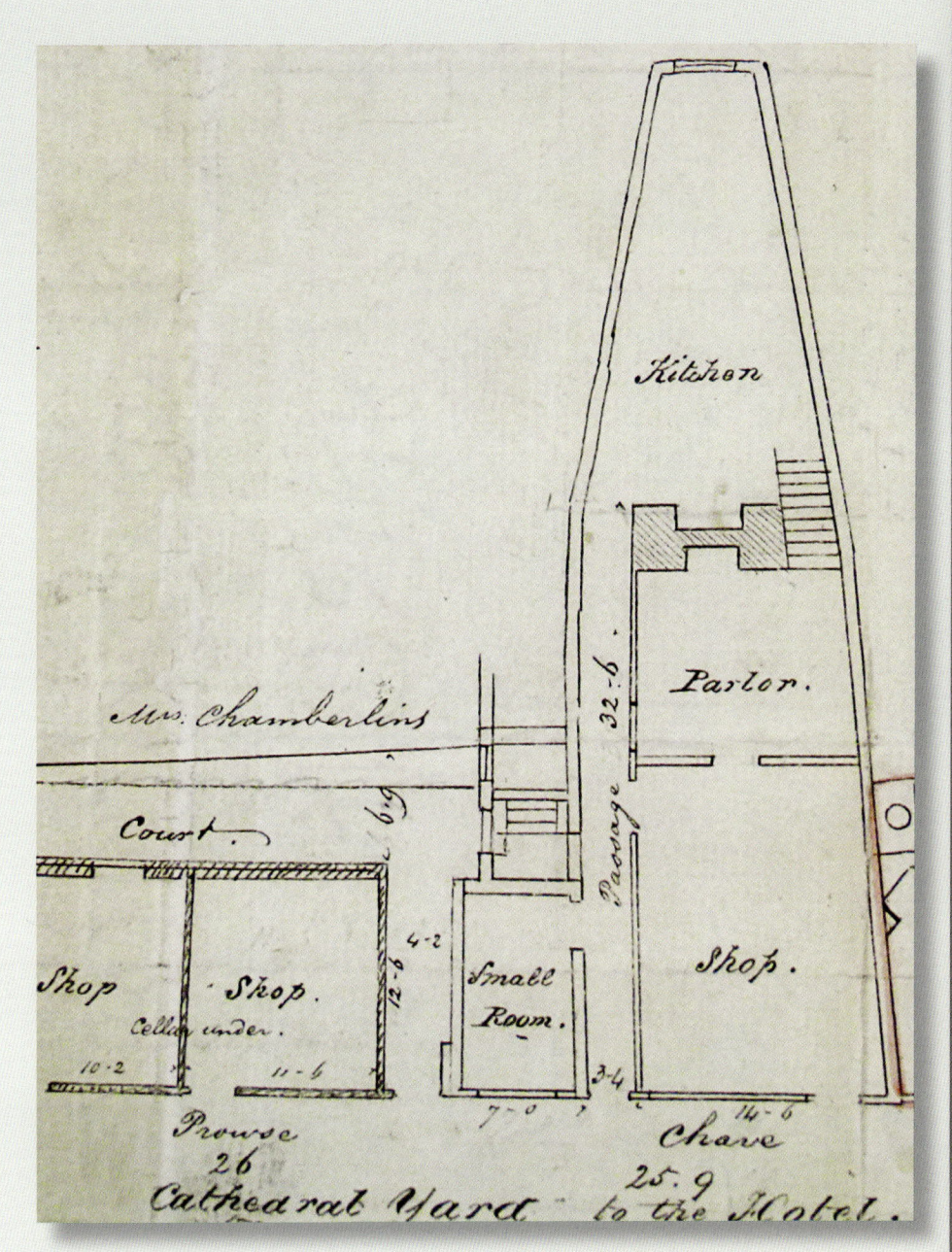

148. Ground plan of the two properties held by Prowse & Chave, 1825.

OCCUPANTS OF THE PROPERTY		
1805 – 1825	Chave's Toy Shop	
1825 – 1828	Eliza Lascelles,	Milliner
1847 – 1851	John Treadwin,	Watchmaker
1853 – 1855	Mrs John Hawkins,	Millinery, Dresses & Mantles
1856 – 1859	Miss Brooks	
1862	Monsieur J. Picard,	Chiropodist
1863	Mr W. F. Wells,	Surgeon Chiropodist
1858 – 1876	Catherine Preston,	Millinery, Mantles & Dresses
1864	William Stokes,	Teacher of Memory
1865 – 1866	J. Howard & Company,	Surgeon Dentists
1867 – 1868	H. Millington Teece,	Dentist
1869 – 1871	Francis Furlong Searle,	Surgeon
1877	James Jerwood,	Barrister
1876 – 1879	Pauline Gibson,	Dress Rooms
1878 – 1879	Confidential Monetary Office	

NUMBER 24 Cathedral Yard

DEVON COUNTY BANK

NUMBER 24 Cathedral Yard

149. Architectural drawing of the building now occupied by National Westminster Bank, by John Hayward & Son, 1879.

Amazon'.[533] Others were James Jerwood, an architect who had a role in the discovery of the planet Neptune, another dress maker[534] and the Confidential Monetary Office.[535] A large front room was for rent in 1877 and later that year 'furnished apartments, sitting room and bedroom'.[536] In 1879 the building was absorbed by the National Provincial Bank with rebuilding under plans by Hayward & Son.[537] Numbers 26 and 27 then ceased as their own numbers.

Formerly 27 Cathedral Yard

The western shop was occupied by James Prowse, a glazier by 1825.[538] In 1846 Mrs Barns and Miss Charlotte Elizabeth Dobbs moved to Number 27. They were referred to as being 'the well known Honiton lace manufacturers of the Cathedral Yard and 304 Regent Street, London'. By at least 1847 Mrs Barn's husband ran the London shop. In 1848 it was noted that 'the shop front of Miss Charlotte Dobbs, in the Cathedral Yard, has been decorated with an elegant display of the Royal Arms, its proprietor having recently been honoured with the appointment of Lacemaker to the Queen'. By January 1849 Dobbs was registering her lace designs with the Patents, Designs and Trade Marks Office in London. A year later she married her neighbour John Treadwin. She had, as Miss Dobbs, advertised herself as conducting business also in Leamington.[539] Elizabeth Smyth, who had been employed by Treadwin, continued the business at 27 Cathedral Yard and renamed it the Honiton Lace Manufactory.[540]

OCCUPANTS OF THE PROPERTY

1825 – 1832	**James W. Prowse**,	*Glazier*
1846 – 1847	**Barns & Dobbs**,	*Honiton Lace Manufacturers*
1848 – 1866	**Charlotte Dobbs** (from 1850 **Treadwin**),	*Honiton Lace Manufacturer*
1867 – 1870	**Elizabeth Smyth** (later **Pollard**)	*Honiton Lace Manufactory*

NUMBER 23

In 2000 the building was listed Grade 2 and noted as 'a good example of a Victorian Gothic commercial front'. The frontage is 50 feet 6 inches.

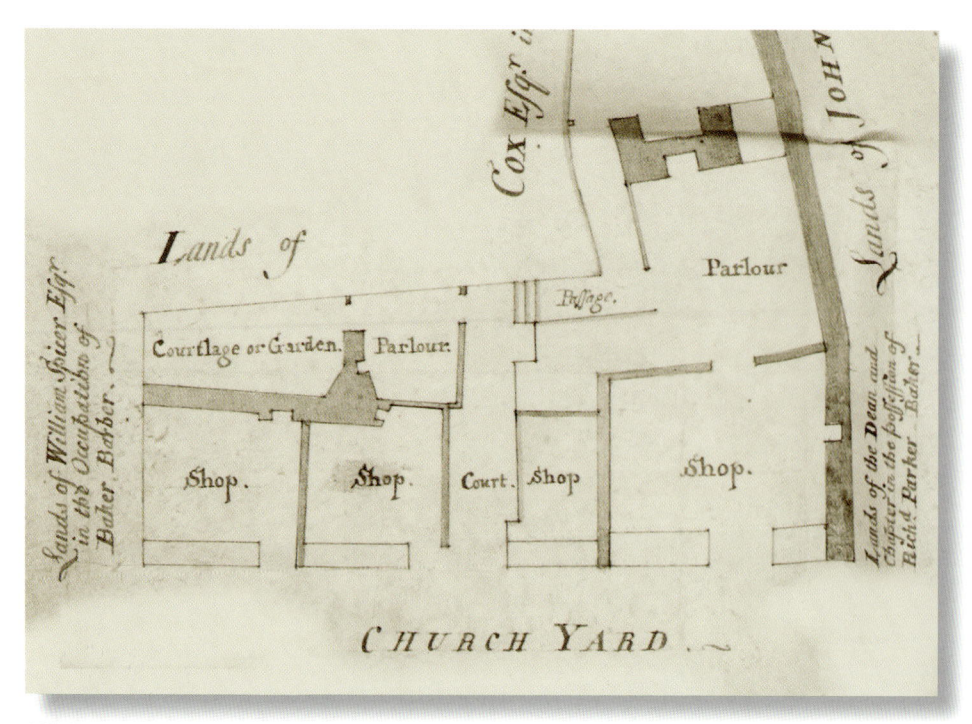

150. Plan by John Tothill, of shops along Cathedral Yard, 1770.

23 Cathedral Yard, a property on land anciently belonging to the Dean & Chapter which had ramshackle structures possibly as late as the eighteenth century. The building was demolished after fire damage in 1881 and replaced with a grand Gothic Revival structure.

A ground floor plan of 1825 shows it was then one room deep with three rooms on the front: a shop on the western side of the building has a single entry onto Cathedral Yard, to its right was the main entry into the building with two parlours and there was a rear kitchen. Two years later it was noted as having shops, a frontage of 50 feet and was 'most eligibly suited for business'. Each of these three rooms had its own address: these were, from 1825 to 1881, 23 to 25 Cathedral Yard. The front shops, dwelling houses and premises were then in the occupation of Messrs. Hutchinson, Angel and Purnell.[541] These properties were damaged by fire in 1881, sold in 1882, pulled down that year and a single building, known from then onwards as 23 Cathedral Yard, was erected on the site in 1883. The use of numbers 24 and 25 ceased because the adjoining building, a bank, was not given a number.[542] The new building was finished in 1884, designed by Best & Commin of Exeter and was noted at the time as being 'a handsome addition' to Cathedral Yard. It was explained that 'the shop on the cathedral side [was] being fitted up for offices and carpet warehouse'.[543] The following year there was an accident on the glass pavement which lit the new building's cellar; a pedestrian slipped, the glass cracked and he plummeted 12 feet into the basement.[544] Wippell occupied the building until 1982. The upper floors are currently being converted for domestic use.

Formerly 23 – 25 Cathedral Yard

The plan of 1825 recorded 'Davis' as the occupier. This was Honor Davis, a lace dealer, who was there possibly as late at 1850[545] by which date William Davis was running her lace business. However, in bankruptcy proceedings that year it was explained that he had previously worked as a cooper, florist, seedsman, mender and lace dealer in Dawlish but had lately been employed a lace dealer and mender in Cathedral Yard as well as a tea dealer and grocer in Smythen Street.[546] There was another occupant sharing the building in 1827.[547] Details of the occupants of the three rooms are incomplete but subsequently become clearer.

Formerly 23 Cathedral Yard

In 1859 Sage & Melhuish, Milliners, Dress and Mantle Makers, opened their shop.[548] Miss Sophia Marriott was an occupant by 1865 to 1877; she and her sister[549] owned the Exeter Plain Worker's Society, a 'self-supporting benevolent institution' which was established in about 1852 and ran in the building from at least 1865 to 1877. It was probably the same Miss Marriot who was the treasurer of the Society of Ladies for the Improvement of the Female Poor in Exeter in 1857. Forty girls, between the ages of 7 and 14, were clothed and instructed in reading, writing, cyphering, knitting and needlework.[550] Mrs E. J. Hutchinson moved from 1 Broadgate in 1877 and sold 'real Honiton lace'. Her husband, a painter and decorator, was the secretary of the Devon & Exeter Fine Art Exhibition but died the next year. In 1880 she placed an advert thanking her husband's friends for their past support and explained future 'orders that they may kindly give in aid of bringing up the family – seven children – will be executed by Mr Edwin Algar'.[551] In 1880 'two good rooms' suitable as an office were offered for letting and the following year she became a furrier and lace manufacturer and ran the Scholastic and Domestic Agency Office for 'ladies requiring servants and servants requiring situations'.[552] Mrs Hutchinson appears to have ceased trading after the great fire of 1881[553] and was succeeded by the Exeter Advance Society which loaned money.[554] The building site, along with that of 54 to 58 High Street, were auctioned and rebuilt.[555]

Formerly 24 Cathedral Yard

In 1852 Alfred Beer opened his shop 'for the convenience of strangers visiting Exeter, where designs and portions of windows in process of execution will

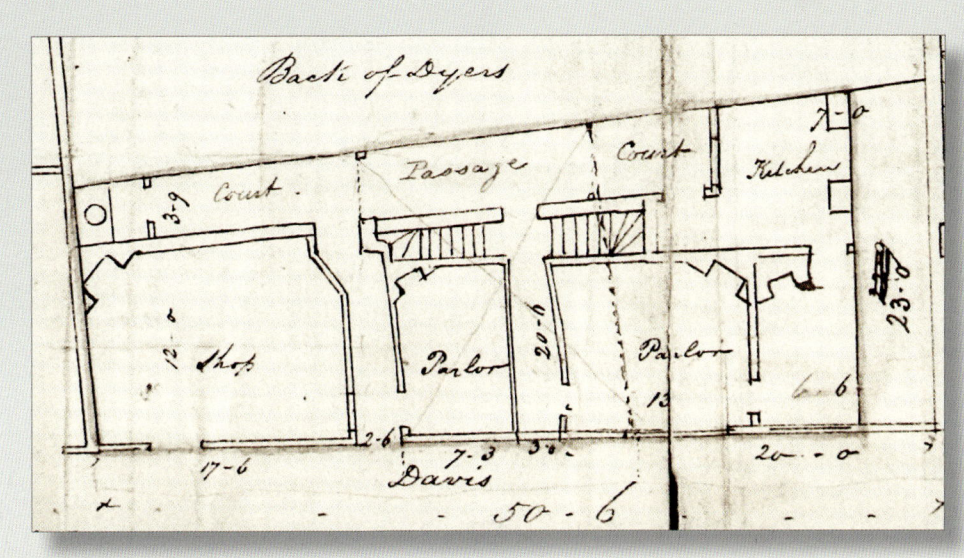

151. 23 Cathedral Yard, as held by Honor Davis in 1825.

152. Map showing building sites of 55–6 High Street and what was then 23–5 Cathedral Yard, 1882.

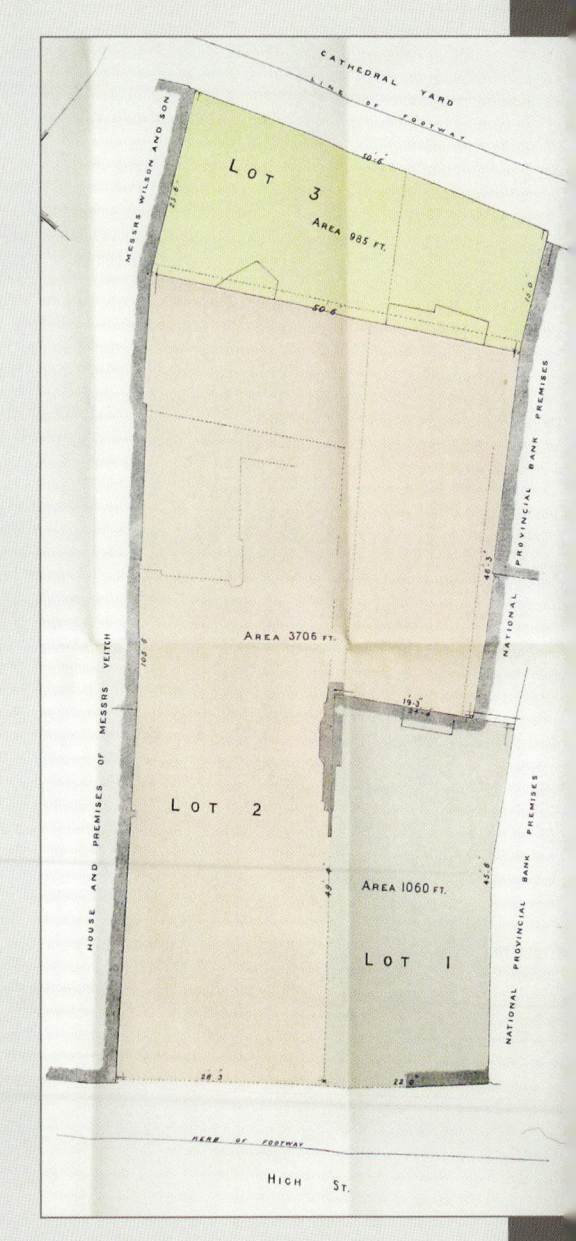

NUMBER 23 Cathedral Yard

153. Front elevation of 23 Cathedral Yard, drawn by Maurice Bingham Adams, 1884.

NUMBER 23 Cathedral Yard

be exhibited'.[556] Beer was the city's premier stained glass craftsman. Two years later he advertised 'he is prepared to make designs and estimates for stained glass works, whether ecclesiastical, or for the decoration of schools, public buildings, private houses etc. in all the different styles from the 12th and 16th centuries and guarantees correctness and purity of design, whether memorial, historical, armorial or simple quarry patterns. Rood screens carefully restored. Wall painting, tablets and all kinds of medieval decorations executed in the best manner by himself and experienced workmen'.[557] In 1855 it became the premises of Albert Angel, engraver and lithographer who moved from Fore Street upon the dissolution of the business Angel & Company. Angel remained there until the fire of 1881 largely destroyed the building.[558]

Formerly 25 Cathedral Yard

In 1849 R. A. Chapple's Hair Dressing and Perfumery Establishment opened in the Yard 'opposite the north tower of the cathedral'.[559] Six years later, in July 1855, Chapple announced he had new premises at 25 Cathedral Yard and boasted his business was based on 'experience in the principal houses of London, New York and Bath, has qualified him to compete with any person in the trade'.[560] In 1860 a watchmaker moved to Exeter from Geneva and continued in the building until 1863[561] when Mrs B. Hill brought her fur business from Broadgate.[562] From 1874 to 1881 the building was the office of several coal merchants.[563]

OCCUPANTS OF THE PROPERTY

1822 – 1850	Honor Davis,	*Lace Dealer* (later **William Davis**)
1827 – 1841	Jane Searle,	*Dressmaker*
1859	Sage & Melhuish,	*Milliners, Dress and Mantle Makers*
1870 – 1877	Miss Sophia Marriott,	*Employment Agency*
1875	Exeter Plain Worker's Society	
1877 – 1881	Mrs Samuel H. Hutchinson,	*Lace Manufacturer & Furrier*
1881 – 1882	Exeter Advance Company	

Formerly 24 Cathedral Yard

1852 – 1854	Alfred Beer,	*Glass Painter & Stainer, Church Decorator*
1855 – 1881	Albert Angel,	*Engraver and Lithographer*

Formerly 25 Cathedral Yard

1849 – 1856	R. A. Chapple,	*hair dressing and perfumery establishment*
1860 – 1863	G. Gulliaume,	*Practical Watchmaker*
1863	Mrs B. Hill,	*Furrier*
1874 – 1881	Thomas B. Purnell,	*Coal Merchant* (later **H. Noble**)
1881	Fire & rebuilding	
1882 – 1982	J. Wippell & Co.,	*Clerical Outfitters and Church Furnishings*
1981	Warham Guild Ltd	
1982 – 1987	Vacant	
1988 – 1989	Antartex	
1990 – 2017	Edinburgh Woollen Mill	

NUMBER 22

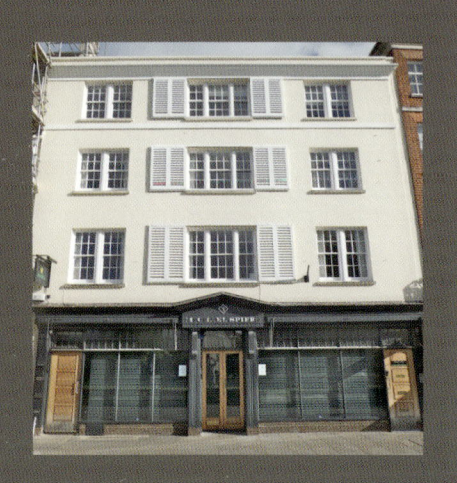

Historic England listed the building Grade 2 and recorded in 1953 'eighteenth-century front, but rebuilt in facsimile. Rendered. 4 storeys, 3 windows, the centre ones are tripartite sashes with glazing bars. Modern shop front and doorway. Cornice, parapet, roof not visible.' Six years earlier a provisional listing had recorded '4 storeys, 3 windows, eighteenth-century front, centre windows, 3 light, 3rd floor windows, blind. Modillion cornice. In spite of the roughcast and applied half-timbering, this remains a well-proportioned Georgian front. Doorway, perhaps original, has pediment and enriched console brackets. Large double-fronted shop with glazing bars. Iron grille over side door'. The frontage is 40 feet.

154. 22 Cathedral Yard, c1954 to 1958, with the timber-framing.

22 Cathedral Yard, a property on land anciently belonging to the Dean & Chapter which had ramshackle structures possibly as late as the eighteenth century and was rebuilt between 1947 and 1953.

The plots of land from 22 Cathedral Yard to Broadgate evolved from being part of the city's Anglo Saxon graveyard to the erection of temporary buildings that gradually became more substantial. 22 Cathedral Yard was a four-storey building, built probably in the eighteenth century. Each of the upper floors had three windows with the central ones slightly larger. In the late 1920s timber-work was placed on the façade.

Two occupiers dominated Number 22 during the last two centuries. The Wilson family held it for more than a century with two main businesses. Under various names the family sold house furnishings, particularly cabinets,[564] and were auctioneers and valuers. This continued, by other firms, through the twentieth century.[565] There were also offices.[566]

Secondly, St Peter's Galleries (or Sellicks) ran from 1928 to 1958. George Sellick was the owner (and also had the Cathedral Lounge at Broadgate and the Cathedral Café at 53 and 54 High Street) until 1932 when he went bankrupt. His architect's plans show the extent of the showrooms.[567] In 1928 the building had 'a bold and commanding elevation recently erected in half timber work. For nearly a century and a quarter it was occupied by a furniture and antique store, with an old established house and estate agency'. It comprised a basement stock room and coal cellar while on the ground floor there was a 'bold shop and showroom, manager's office (estate agency department), two clerks' offices, side entrance, packing yard and store room, Water Closet, etc. back staircase'. The first floor had a 'large and well lit show room, principal's office, secretary's

NUMBER 22 Cathedral Yard

155. Undated aerial view of the view from 20 Cathedral Yard to Broadgate.

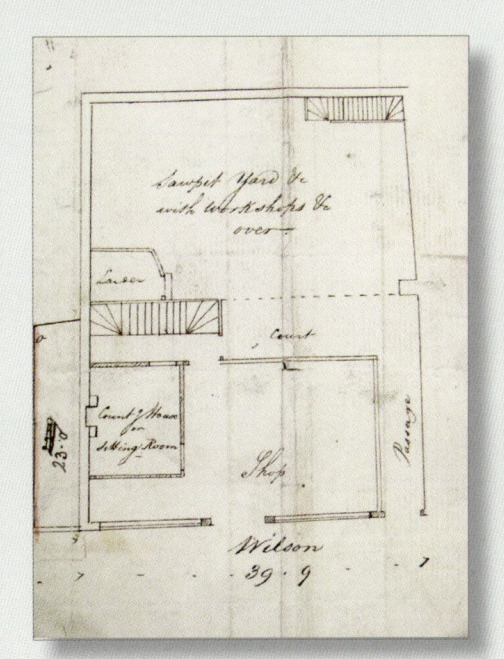

156. Ground plan of 22 Cathedral Yard, 1825.

157. View of 2 Broadgate, then the Cathedral Restaurant, looking along Cathedral Yard to Number 22, c1910.

office'. The second floor was described as having two large connected show rooms, cupboard and store room. Finally, the third floor comprises a 'large front workroom easily converted into good showroom. Two well-lit workrooms, with water laid and Water Closet, hoist to packing yard'. The timber-work on the façade was removed and the building was rebuilt between 1947 and 1953.[568]

OCCUPANTS OF THE PROPERTY

1818 – 1831	T. Wilson & Company,	Furnishings
1829 – 1834	Wilson, Patey & Company,	Surveyors, Auctioneers & Appraisers
1832 – 1858	John Wilson & Company,	Furnishings
1852 – 1855	Thomas W. Gray, Solicitor & Proctor	(upstairs)
1858 – 1928	John Wilson & Son (Thomas),	Cabinet Makers
1928 – 1958	Sellicks	(St Peter's Galleries)
1932 – 1940	Cathedral Café	
1948 – 1952	F J. Chorley, Auctioneer & Valuer	(upstairs)
1957	Fulford & Chorley,	Estate Agents (upstairs)
1959	Possibly vacant	
1960 – 1964	Colsons of Exeter Ltd.,	Furnishings
1965 – 1989	Foster, Fox & Sons,	Chartered Surveyors, etc. (from 1968 Fox & Sons) (upstairs)
1965 – 1976	The Paperback Bookshop (Pitts),	Booksellers
1965	South Western Foresters Ltd.,	Tree Felling Contractors (upstairs)
1965 – 1968	Wyvern Bowls Ltd.	(upstairs)
1965 – 1973	Kalamazoo Ltd.,	Office Equipment (upstairs)
1965 – 1989	Fox Estate Agents	
1969	Dr Barnardo's Homes	(upstairs)
1970 – 1973	Castle Staff Agency (from 1972 Castle Personnel)	(upstairs)
1971 – 1973	Exeter Auctioneers & Estate Agents Association	(upstairs)
1972 – 1973	Peachey & Richards Ltd.,	Finance, Investment & Insurance (upstairs)
1981 – 1983	Burnley Building Society	
1989	G. A. Property Services	(upstairs)
1990	Nationwide Anglia Building Society	
1991	Vacant	
1992 – 1995	Talasio Bridal & Dress Hire	
1996	Vacant	
1997 – 1999	Orvis,	Game Fishing Tackle and Outdoor Clothing
2000 – 2015	Luget,	Bespoke Tailors and Menswear
2015 – 2017	Michael Spiers,	Jewellers
2016 – 2017	Morgan & Pope,	Solicitors (upstairs)

127

NUMBER 21

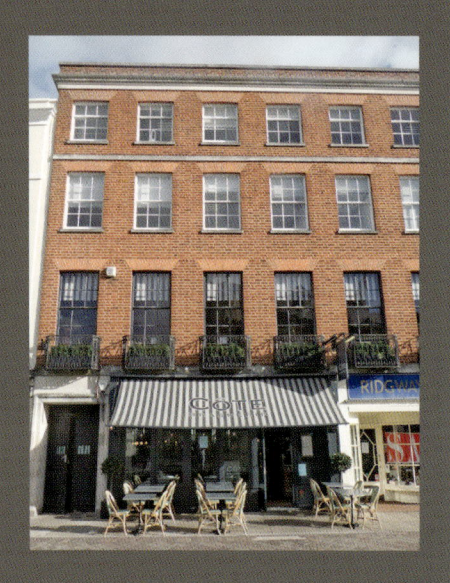

In 1947 the building was provisionally listed Grade 2* and recorded '4 storeys, early nineteenth century, red brick front on older house. Patent stone bands. Unusual rubbed brick window arches. 1st floor cast iron balconies. Slightly recessed round-headed doorways and ground floor windows. Very fine eighteenth-century staircase and panelling to No 21. Double-gabled roof visible at back of building. ("Starred" grading on account of interior). The whole rebuilt in facsimile and No 19 rebuilt in like manner to make a 13 window front, sashes with glazing bars.' The frontage is 27 feet.

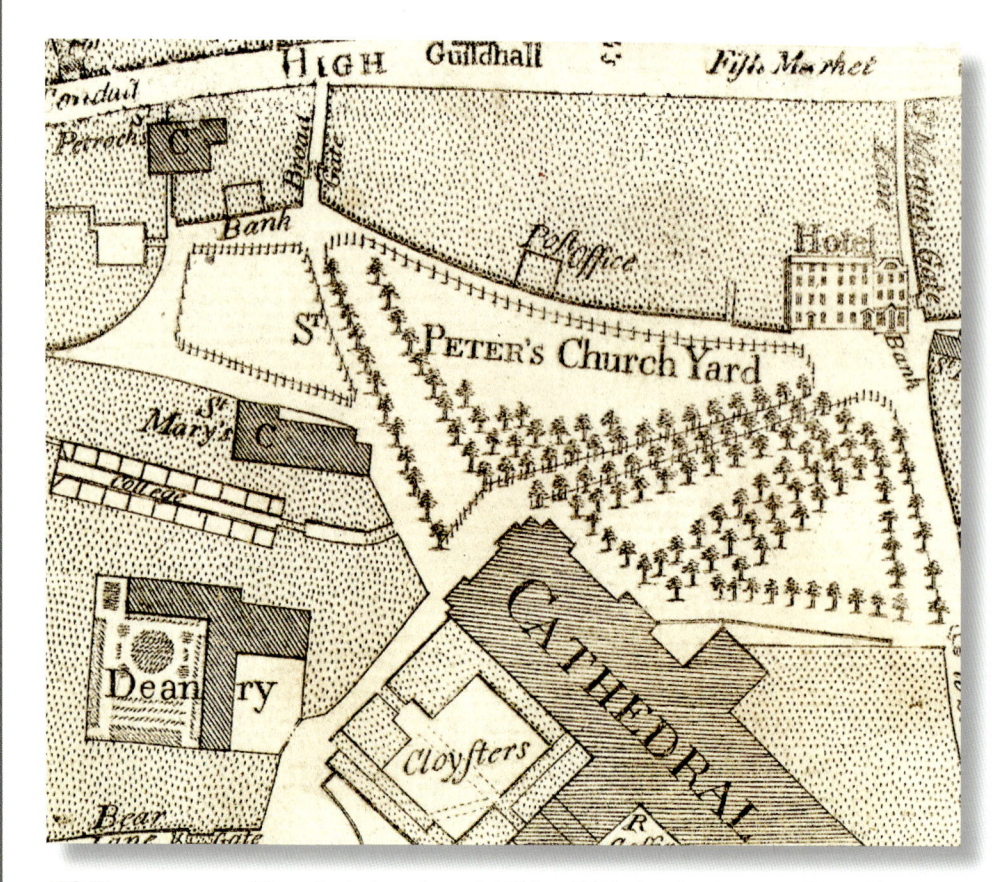

158. Map on reverse of Peter Berlon's trade card, 1768 to 1774, showing the post office at 21 Cathedral Yard.

21 Cathedral Yard, divided into two buildings by 1760, at one time connected with 50 High Street, demolished in 1965 when the current building was erected in its place.

The Little Exchange ran along the eastern side of the building. By 1706 Joseph Quash had converted a shop in 21 Cathedral Yard to use as the city's post office. Several years before, between 1697 and 1698, he employed a considerable number of workmen to rebuild or renovate the premises. Quash purchased 2,835 bricks which presumably were used for a new frontage or could have been used for the chimneys.[569] He required substantial space to house documents because he was also the county's Receiver General of Taxes.[570] Quash was declared bankrupt in 1713 and the building's subsequent use has not been determined.[571] However, in 1760 it was noted as a 'very large, commodious and modern brick-built sashed dwelling house, with large under ground cellars' which had been divided into two residences. The western one, which became 21 Cathedral Yard, was in the possession of Thomas Lavington, a later postmaster. He had been there from at least 1748, if not 1740, and the post office was depicted on Berlon's map of the Yard which was printed between 1766 and 1774.[572] Number 21 may have continued to serve as the post office in these intervening years.[573]

In the early 1800s there was a mix of occupiers including a musical academy.[574] From the early 1830s through to at least 1851 it was the home of a surgeon

NUMBER 21 Cathedral Yard

In 1905 the building was described (see Number 20) as having exceptional mahogany woodwork.[579] The next year the Society for Promoting Christian Knowledge moved into Number 21 and also used the entrance at 50 High Street.[580] In 1965 the interior was stripped, including its staircase and panelling, and the building was destroyed shortly after and a new one erected in its place.[581]

160. Aerial photograph of Exeter with a partial view of Cathedral Yard, 1928.

from Newton St Cyres. His two sons, two daughters and four female servants shared the building.[575] In 1870 the neighbour at Number 18 lived in the building while his home was rebuilt.[576] The following year a Honiton lace manufacturer and dealer in antique lace moved from 27 Cathedral Yard.[577] Her living quarters included a dining room (19 feet by 14 feet), a drawing room (20 feet by 19 feet), a breakfast room, seven bedrooms, a kitchen and cellars.[578]

159. Undated aerial view showing the roof lines of 20 & 21 Cathedral Yard.

OCCUPANTS OF THE PROPERTY

1697 – 1712	Joseph Quash, *Postmaster*
1826	Dr Paget
1827 – 1829	Mr Mudge's Musical Academy
1832 – 1851	John Battishall Parker, *surgeon*
1852 – 1868	Isabella Sanders
1869 – 1870	E. E. Brand, *Dentist*
1871 – 1875	Mrs E. Pollard, *Honiton Lace Manufacturer & Dealer*
1876 – 1880	John Scudder (warehouse & rooms)
1878	Mrs A. E. Alsop
1889 – 1898	William Thomas Munby Snow, *Solicitor*
1898 – 1920	Bromley Sanders, *Auctioneers*
1901 – 1905	H. W. Michelmore, *Solicitor* (& in 1912 at 20 & 21)
1906 – 1953	Church Book Shop *(Society for Promoting Christian Knowledge)*
1918 – 1919	Records *(War Department)* (upstairs)
1923	Fothergill Bros Ltd, *civil engineers* (& 20) (upstairs)
1926 – 1961	Prudential Assurance Co. Ltd (& 20)
1939 – 1955	Charles Lee Wright, *Valuer*, *Surveyor, Land and Estate agent* (upstairs)
1940 – 1943	Orchard & Hamlyn, *Chartered Accountants* (upstairs)
1953 – 1959	Ware, Ward & Co., *Chartered Accountants* (upstairs)
1954 – 1962	Russells, China and Glass
1956	Derek J. Blatchford (upstairs)
1957 – 1964	Tudor Rose Café
1965 – 1967	Demolished & redeveloped
1968	R. Laundon, *Confectioner*
1969 – 1989	Bradford & Bingley Building Society
1979 – 1989	Rendells, Estate Agents, *Auctioneers & Valuers*
1990	Vacant
1991 – 1992	Applewoods Natural Products
1993 – 1997	Old Bears Restaurant
1998 – 2000	Café on the Green
c1998 – 2004	Michelmore, Solicitors (upstairs)
2001 – 2005	Carved Angel Restaurant
2006 – 2011	Cathedral Yard Café
2012 – 2017	Cote Brasserie

129

NUMBER 20

A provisional building listing for Numbers 20 & 21 made in 1947 recorded '4 storeys, early nineteenth century, red brick front on older house. Patent stone bands, unusual rubbed brick window arches. First floor C. I. balconies. Slightly recessed round-headed doorways and ground floor windows. One inserted shop front to Number 21. Double-gabled roof visible at back of building (starred grading on account of interior)'. The frontage is 20 feet 3 inches.

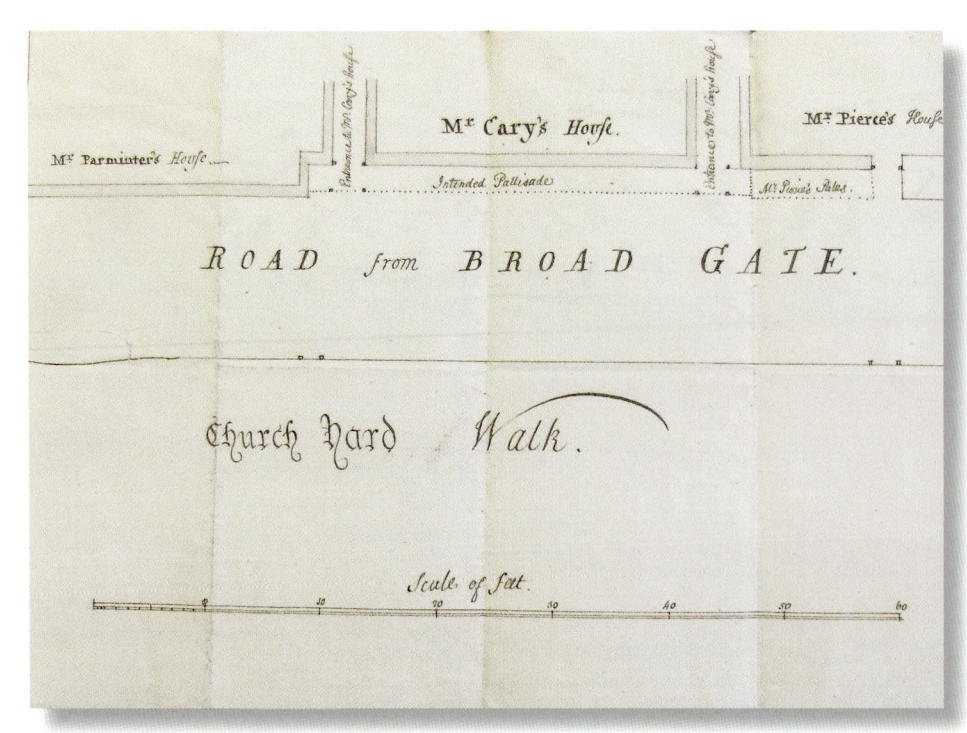

161. Undated plan of Cathedral Yard of Numbers 18 to 20.

20 Cathedral Yard, anciently a Dean & Chapter property, by 1686 had become half of a tenement (the other Number 21), had a brick front erected in 1697, was demolished in 1965 and a new building erected in its place.

The Little Exchange ran along the western side of the building (between it and Number 21) to High Street. Number 20 had been home to a canon and his building may have survived until 1965.[582] By 1686 it had been divided into two residences. The eastern one, which became 20 Cathedral Yard, was then in the occupation of John Vowler, a merchant, and at the rear of his property lay other tenements (see the New Exchange). Joseph Quash (at Number 21) built a brick frontage in 1697 to obscure what was possibly a seventeenth-century (or earlier) building and several generations later, in 1760, Numbers 20 & 21 was noted as a 'very large, commodious and modern brick-built sashed dwelling house, with large under ground cellars'.[583]

The District Registrar of the Exeter Probate Court occupied the building in the early 1800s both as a dwelling house and office.[584] For more than 50 years it was then the home of John Hayward, the celebrated architect. In 1844 he had been one of seven architects practising in Exeter; the others were Robert Brown Best, Richard Brown, Samuel Alxis Greig, Charles Hedgeland, George Julian and David Mackintosh. Hayward also rented 50 High Street and in 1851 lived at Number 20 with his wife, their daughter and three domestic servants.[585]

In 1891 Best, Sanders & Sanders, Architects, Surveyors, Auctioneers, Valuers and House Agents, moved from Queen Street to both 50 High Street and 20 Cathedral Yard. The firm was conducted under the name of William A. Sanders but afterwards called the Central

NUMBER 20 Cathedral Yard

162. Photograph of 16 to 22 Cathedral Yard, taken between 1957 and 1965.

Auction & Estate Office and continued to occupy the building until 1906. It also occupied Number 21.[586] In 1892 it was reported that Sanders had disappeared from Exeter having told his clerk that he would be having a holiday. A deficiency was then found in the Charity Fund he administered.[587] In 1905 the freehold of Numbers 20 & 21 along with 50 High Street was offered for sale. It was noted that 'this property, formerly an old town residence, has a grand mahogany staircase, panelled mahogany staircase and panelled mahogany room, and from its important and central position it has been used as offices, warehouse and show rooms, with small judicious outlay it could be greatly improved in value. The frontage to Cathedral Yard is about 47 feet 3 inches and the total depth from the Cathedral Yard to High Street 150 feet or thereabouts.'[588] The building was demolished in 1965.

OCCUPANTS OF THE PROPERTY

1825 – 1836	Charles H. Turner, *Solicitor*
1839 – 1891	John Hayward, **Architect** (later Hayward & Son)
1891 – 1909	**Best, Sanders & Sanders**, *Architects, Surveyors, Auctioneers, Valuers & House Agents (Central Auction & Estate Office)*
1893 – 1912	H. W. Michelmore, *Solicitor (& 21)*
1923	**Fothergill Bros. Ltd**, *Civil Engineers (& 21)*
1926 – 1961	**Prudential Assurance Co. Ltd** (& 21)
1962 – 1965	Vacant, demolished & redeveloped
1966 – 1985	**Roberts & Andrew**, *Solicitors* (upstairs)
1968 – 1998	**The Regency Shop** *(Fred Keetch Gallery)*
1981 – 1988	SW Trustee Savings Bank Training Centre (upstairs)
1990 – 2004	**Michelmore**, *Solicitors* (upstairs)
1999 – 2011	**Dubarry Cothing**
2011 – 2017	**Ridgways Shoes**

NUMBER 19

The building is not listed. The frontage is approximately 40 feet.

163. Architectural drawing by Edward Robins Cookworthy of the Devon & Cornwall Bank at 19 Cathedral Yard, 1860.

19 Cathedral Yard, anciently a property belonging to the Vicars Choral, rebuilt for the Devon & Cornwall Bank in 1862, connected with 49 High Street in 1912, known as Prudential Buildings or Prudential Chambers in the 1900s, and rebuilt in about 1965.

Number 19 Cathedral Yard was the private home and office of Charles Turner, a solicitor, from 1825 through to 1861 when it was acquired by the Devon & Cornwall Bank. Its frontage was 41 feet and had a depth of 90 feet. Ware & Son of Exeter was the builder and the architects were Kenny & Rogers of London and Bangor. In September 1861 a local commentator noted 'it is supposed that a very magnificent premiated design selected from those of many competitors hangs fire as to its execution upon the site of Mr C. Turner's late house, simply because the modern Italian or Grecian cannot be adapted properly or decently to the hallowed precincts of St Peter's Churchyard'. Not long afterwards a journalist wrote that the architectural features of the building are to be of the style of the Italian period

NUMBER 19 Cathedral Yard

164. Undated view of the eastern end of Cathedral Yard with 19 & 20 Cathedral Yard somewhat obscured by the trees.

generally known as Cinquo Cento. This, as it somewhat combines the feeling of the Gothic and Italian styles, has been adopted to meet the requirements of the locality, with a proper regard for the character of the building; and we have no doubt that when completed will form an ornament to the city'.[589] A gold bodkin and bronze strigil were discovered during the construction and these were given to the museum. The foundation stone was laid on 30 April 1862. The building, designed by Edward Robins Cookworthy, was finished by September 1863 because there were concerns on the need to take down the scaffolding 'in front of the new bank in the Cathedral Yard'. On 9 November the new premises opened. It was one of the two tallest buildings in the island with four storeys and attic. The upper floors had four windows each and the building was made of stone. Forty-three years later, in 1906, Lloyds absorbed the bank and 'soon after secured an entrance to their bank in the Yard from High Street'.[590]

Number 19 was then purchased by the Prudential Assurance Company in 1912 when it intended 'to bring the front of the premises into High Street and for that purpose two of the existing houses fronting the main street will probably be demolished'. Shortly afterwards, and into 1914, a suite of offices in the first and upper floors at Number 19 were offered for renting. These were 'suitable for solicitors, accountants or dentist' but had the potential for use as a private residence and comprised eight bedrooms, two large reception rooms and a bathroom among other rooms.[591] The building was demolished and a replacement was built in about 1965.[592]

OCCUPANTS OF THE PROPERTY

1802 – 1861	Charles H. Turner, *Solicitor*
1861 – 1862	Rebuilding
1863 – 1906	Devon & Cornwall Bank
1906 – 1913	Lloyds Bank (on amalgamation)
1913 – 1965	Prudential Assurance Company
1917	Records Office (upstairs)
1925 – 1939	Royal Automobile Club (upstairs)
1926 – 1934	Exeter & District Safety First Council (upstairs)
1928 – 1940	John Orchard, *Chartered Accountant* (upstairs)
1934	Woolwich Equitable Building Society (upstairs)
1934	Petherick Brothers, *Builders* (upstairs)
1935 – 1955	British Red Cross (upstairs)
1937 – 1941	Come to Devon Association (upstairs)
1939 – 1941	United Development Association Ltd (upstairs)
1965 – 1966	Demolition and redevelopment
1967 – 1989	National & Provincial Building Society
1968 – 1971	Austin Photographic Ltd
1990 – 2004	Michelmore, *Solicitors* (upstairs)
1991 – 2017	Waterstones

NUMBER 18

In 1974 the building was listed Grade 2 and recorded 'house rebuilt circa 1910. Red brick with stucco dressings, pilasters and entablature at each level. 4 storeys and attic, 4 windows, arched sashes. Heavy cornice, slate roof. Front rooms fitted up in an elaborate Louis Quinze style. Staircase with curious double gallery may be genuine C18 woodwork. Turned balusters and inlaid treads. Door cases on 1st floor landing may also be genuine eighteenth-century.' The frontage is 15 feet 6 inches.

165. The interior of 18 Cathedral Yard, 11 August 2017.

18 Cathedral Yard, anciently a Dean & Chapter property, sold in 1870 when the building was rebuilt and renamed The Mansion House. It was gutted by fire in 2016. Lamb Alley runs along the eastern side and follows on its north side.

Lamb Alley runs along the eastern side of the property and in 1757 the occupant, a wine merchant, was given leave to open a door 'through the tenement in Lamb Alley from the churchyard to the Fore [sic] Street, he receiving a key from the chapter and paying one penny a year'.[593] A plan of the building made in 1770 shows it to have been substantial: it has two parlours at the front and three kitchens behind leading to a separate tenement. In 1816 the property was still

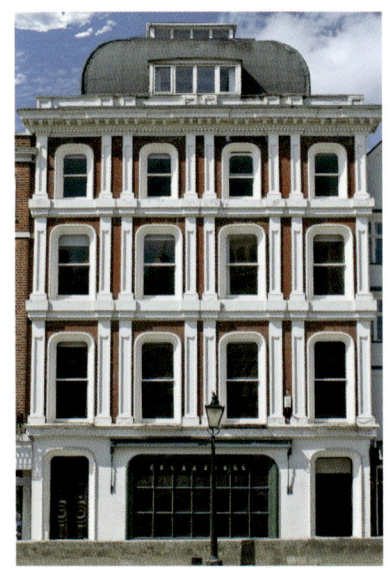

166. The exterior of 18 Cathedral Yard 2006.

NUMBER 18 Cathedral Yard

167. Sketch of 18 Cathedral Yard, 1 February 1870.

being used as two dwelling houses and an advertisement noted that 'the business of a wine and spirit merchant has been carried on in those premises for a great number of years past, for which they are particularly adapted'.[594]

In about 1833 Samuel Kemp, Tailor and Habit Maker, succeeded and his apprentice later took over the business which included supplying clerical and law robes.[595] Sometime between 1822 and 1833 another plan was drawn of the ground floor. It shows central door which led into a passage off of which were once again two parlours behind which were the two kitchens, courts, privies and a larder.[596] The building was drawn in 1870 and showed it had then had three storeys with an attic. On the right can be seen the entrance to Lamb Alley and there are two sets of bay windows on either side of the central entrance.

In 1870 18 Cathedral Yard was demolished by Elihu Edward Brand, a dentist who was well-known as a collector of antiques. He renamed the new building The Mansion House.[597] The following year Pearson B. Hayward, architect son of the distinguished John Hayward, commented at the Devon & Exeter Graphic Society that modern buildings in the Close had not been designed with a sense of harmony. Moreover, he said 'the same may be said of the new house now being built by Mr Brand in what appears to be, as far as one can yet see, a sort of French Chateau style'.[598] In 1914 Number 18 was described as a 'concrete house' which 'for some years past the windows of the house have been noticeable on account of the curios exhibited therein'. It was said that Brand's 'tastes in this direction were almost unlimited. Rare china, old silver, carpets, furniture, in fact anything representative of ancient arts and crafts, captured his fancy'. The house contents included 'Old English, Continental and Oriental porcelain in groups, figures, vases, etc., cut glass, bronze groups and figures, clocks, candelabras, marble and wood mantel pieces, antique carved wood panels'. In 1879 Brand added an extra storey to 18 Cathedral Yard.[599]

The building became multi-occupied with Michelmore, Solicitors, the most notable occupant.[600] In 1920 part of the building was rented. This included the coal cellar, the second floor (two large front rooms, a small inside room, two large back rooms and one lavatory), the third floor (four front rooms, a large filing room at the back and two lavatories) and a large room on the fourth floor. In 1989 was noted that 'a staircase rises through the centre of the building. The first flight is 18th century in style surrounded at first floor level by a gallery. Off this are a number of rooms each entered through dark mahogany doors, framed by Corinthian pilasters, but with the disconcerting addition of mirrored panels. The effect is weirdly surreal. A large room (now divided into two) overlooking the cathedral is equally strange. Beneath a gilded cornice are walls panelled with large mirrors festooned with glass drops and bordered by wallpaper in the

St Martin's Island: An introductory history of forty-two Exeter buildings

168. Undated plan of 18 Cathedral Yard noting D (owned by the bank and rented to Sarah Street and Mr Kemp). c1826–37.

NUMBER 18 Cathedral Yard

169. Mr Brand's decorative interior at 18 Cathedral Yard.

170. Detail of the Mansion House decoration.

Pompeian style. At each end are highly polished black fireplaces supported by stone lions'.[601] The fire in Cathedral Yard began at 18 Cathedral Yard in the early hours of 28 October 2016. Within hours it had gutted the building.

OCCUPANTS OF THE PROPERTY

1790 – 1820	James Pearce, *Peruke Maker*
1821 – 1826	Joseph Congdon, *Hotel Proprietor*
1826 – 1837	Samuel Kemp, *Robe & Habit Maker*
1830 – 1832	Mr Mardon
1835 – 1837	William Denis Moore
1837	James Downe
1838 – 1863	Samuel Davies, *Grocer*
1865 – 1869	Elihu Edward Brand, *Dentist*
1870 – 1871	Demolition & redevelopment
1871 – 1910	Elihu Edward Brand, *Dentist*
1889 – 2004	Michelmore, *Solicitors* (upstairs)
1918 – 1919	Ministry of Labour (upstairs)
1919	Road Transport Board (upstairs)
1920	Devon County Territorial Force Association (upstairs)
1920 – 1928	Devon County Council, Agricultural Committee (upstairs)
1922	Exeter Branch, League of Nations Union (upstairs)
1929 – 1956	Devon County Council, Roads Department (upstairs)
1948 – 1949	Devon County Council, Road Safety Organising Secretary (upstairs)
1948 – 1950	Women's Voluntary Services (upstairs)
1952 – 1956	Devon River Board Engineers' Department (upstairs)
1961 – 1962	Rt Phipps Ltd, *Outfitters*
1961 – 1973	Alan E. Langdon, *Chartered Architect & Surveyor*
1964 – 1987	Jaeger, *Ladies Wear*
1988	Vacant
1989 – 1999	National Trust Shop
2000 – 2004	Orvis, *Game Fishing Tackle and Outdoor Clothing*
2005 – 2009	Vacant
2010 – 2016	Castle Art Gallery
2016	Destroyed by fire

NUMBER 17

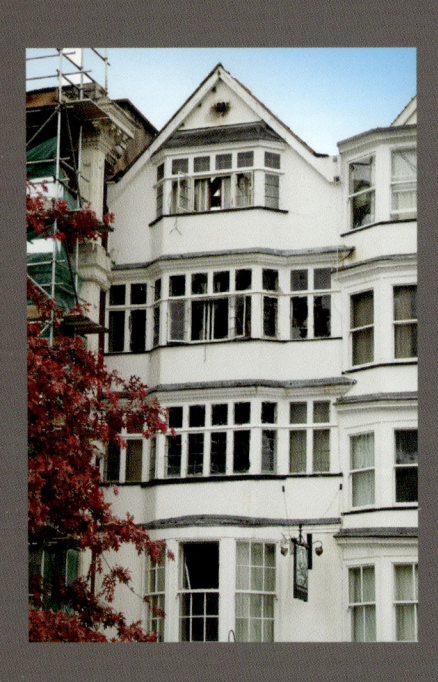

171. 16 & 17 Cathedral Yard as seen within the Cathedral Yard row of buildings. Rogers can be seen at Number 17, 1906–1909.

17 Cathedral Yard (now the western half of the Well House), a tall, narrow property anciently owned by the Vicars Choral, occupied as one building with Number 16 from at least 1887 to 1894.

Number 17, and its companion to the right, have by their appearances little in common with the rest of this part of Cathedral Yard. The fire has revealed that 16 & 17 Cathedral Yard were constructed at different times and not built as a pair. A timber truss has been discovered between the two buildings with a felling date of c1450–60. Number 17 is also a five storey building and the fire exposed decorated woodwork in an upper floor. This was announced in a press release as a peacock ('the peacock matches other examples the hotel group understands have previously been found across Exeter')[602] but has subsequently been shown to be a face, possibly that of an angel.

The most memorable occupant has been Robert Veitch & Sons which in 1930 moved its seed shop from 54 High Street to the ground floor of 17 Cathedral Yard. It continued until 1982.[603] Others that should be better remembered include Robert Medley Fulford, the Exeter architect who had been a pupil of John Hayward. He had an office from at least 1869 until the mid 1880s.[604] In 1870, when he was aged 25, Fulford performed 'Some lady's dropped her chignon' at a church fundraiser at Bow. He was 'dressed up in character' and moved 'people's risible faculties to a fearful extent'. Fulford took holy orders in the early 1890s and died in 1910. Among his buildings was the Art Studios of Harry Hems in Longbrook Street.[605] Fulford practised with J. Emlyn Harvey until 1891 when they admitted Charles James Tait, who until then had worked with John Hayward and his son only a few doors away.[606]

In 1953 Numbers 16 & 17 were listed Grade 2 and recorded 'sixteenth/seventeenth centuries. Timber-framed. 5 storey gabled plaster front. Modern shop front on ground floor, Georgian bow window with glazing bars on 1st floor, splayed oriels with leaded lattice windows above. Parts of the old structure have been exposed internally on the 1st floor. All the listed buildings of Cathedral Yard and Numbers 1 and 2 Deanery Place form a group.' The frontage is 16 feet 9 inches.

NUMBER 17 Cathedral Yard

172. Painted wooden panel of a figure, possibly an Elizabethan angel, discovered post fire in 17 Cathedral Yard.

173. The basement of 16 Cathedral Yard, c.1935–50.

174. View of Cathedral Yard from the Royal Clarence to the Mansion House, c1935-1940.

An employment agency was run from at least 1863 through to 1898. 'Miss Williamson's Registry' was run by Elizabeth Williamson.[607] She also let rooms and was a stationer as well as the 'keeper' of the Devon & Exeter Religious Book & Tract Society from at least 1857. The organisation, which had been started in 1833, remained in the building after her death and continued until 1907.[608] In 1879 Walter Scanes took over the employment registry and advertised it as the oldest in the West Country. He had been Williamson's assistant.[609]

A considerable number of tenants, including the Exeter Homeopathic Dispensary,[610] occupied the building, many for a short term.[611] Rooms were also let: in 1874 one neighbour recalled that in the early 1800s Mr Head was the occupant and offered lodgings.[612] In 1915 17 Cathedral Yard was sold and described in the auction catalogue as being 'on the ground floor [a] double-fronted shop with stock room and small office and yard behind. There are two cellars used as printing rooms in basement. On the first floor are two rooms now let as offices and water closet. On the second floor [a] front sitting room and bedroom. On the third floor [a] bedroom and kitchen with range, dresser and trough. On the fourth floor two attic bedrooms'. It was also noted there was a side entrance 'which could be let off in flats'.[613]

OCCUPANTS OF THE PROPERTY

early 1800s	Mr Head
1824 – 1825	Mr Rickard
1825 – 1827	Mr Arden
1827 – 1843	John Hull Terrell, *Solicitor*
1843 – 1844	Henry Stoneman
1850 – 1851	Charles Wills & Co., *Vesta Lamp & Camphine Dealers*
1852 – 1857	R. W. Wyllie
1858 – 1879	Elizabeth Williamson, *Stationer & Bookseller, Servants' Registry*
1858 – 1907	Devon & Exeter Religious Book & Tract Society
1869 – 1889	Robert Medley Fulford, *Architect*
1883 – 1897	Frank Pince Perkins, *Public Analyst (upstairs)*
1879 – 1898	Walter Scanes, Book Seller & Servants' Registry (& 16 by 1888)
1887 – 1890	Mr Harvey, *Barrister (upstairs)*
1893	John Stephens Carter, *Solicitor*
1893	I. Edward Harvey, *Equity Draftsman*
1898	Gospel Depot & Publishing Office
1899 – 1906	H. E. Marson, *Bookseller*
1900 – 1902	Exeter Homeopathic Dispensary
1906 – 1919	William Charles Rogers, *Stationer & Bookseller*
1929 – 1931	TOCH Club
1930 – 1982	Robert Veitch & Sons, Ltd, *Seedsmen & Nurserymen*
1981 – 1983	Mike Nott, *Bookseller*
1984 – 2017	Well House (& 16)

NUMBER 16

175. 16 Cathedral Yard, late 1880s.

In 1953 the building was listed with Number 17 Grade 2 and recorded 'sixteenth-seventeenth centuries, parts perhaps are earlier. 5 storey timber framed with gabled plaster front with modern ground floor shops and splayed bays above. These have been altered nineteenth- century sash windows being inserted. Slate roof. In 1933 a well, thought to be of Roman [origins], was discovered in the basement.'

16 Cathedral Yard (now the eastern half of the Well House), adjoining the Royal Clarence Hotel, a sixteenth-century building with earlier building fabric, which derives its name from the 'Roman' well (probably a late-medieval garderobe) in the basement, anciently owned by the Vicars Choral, occupied as one building with Number 17 from at least 1887 to 1894 and a part of the hotel since 1984. Current investigation prompted by the recent fire indicates the roof was built c1450–60.

Unlike the neighbours to the east, 16 & 17 Cathedral Yard were not as substantially updated in the 1760s although the windows of 16 Cathedral Yard were already 'sashed in front'.[614] This is a five-storey structure which presents its gable to the Yard, four windows on each of the upper floors and a cellar.

For much of the nineteenth century the building was occupied by two tailors.[615] In 1813 James Ridge was criticised in print by his employer: Mary Howell, of Martin's Lane, accused her foreman of 'very improper conduct' and the 'abuse of her confidence in the transaction of her business'. She dismissed him.[616] Only a few years later, in 1818, his eighteen year old apprentice, Frances Grace, who was five foot and five inches in height, stoutly made, with brown curly hair and dark eyes[617] fled from Ridge and he happened upon her in London four years later, had her arrested and brought to Exeter. The now twenty-two year old paid £20 in compensation rather than serve the

NUMBER 16 Cathedral Yard

176. The rear of 16 & 17 Cathedral Yard, 30 October 2016.

remainder of her service.[618] Ridge, who had been born at Upton Pyne, remained until 1851, by then retired, when he lived in the house with two servants. The year after Ridge died his son John commenced tailoring at 16 Cathedral Yard.[619]

From 1879 16 Cathedral Yard had multi-occupational use which included the Prudential Monetary Office; it charged the poor 50 per cent interest on loans.[620] A notable occupant was Charles Elkin Mathews, a bookseller, whose uncle loaned him £125 to set up in business. Mathews left shortly afterwards, moved to London and established The Bodley Head with John Lane of West Putford in North Devon.[621] Within months Walter Scanes, a bookseller and law stationer, occupied Numbers 16 & 17.[622] In 1889 he discovered a strong smell of gas, lit a match and the subsequent massive explosion caused Scanes to suffer severe burns.[623] There were other occupiers for a short time[624] and in 1909 W. F. Haymes, military boot maker, moved from Bedford Street. During the Great War he advertised a letter from a soldier in France who wrote 'you can tell Haymes that those boots are top hole. I was wandering round the trenches for 3 hours with water over my ankles and sometimes up to my knees and my feet were quite dry at the end of it all'.[625] Gilbert Babbage, a solicitor, was another occupant and at his death in 1935 it was recalled that he 'was prominently identified with the discovery and development as a show place of the ancient St Martin's Well in the Cathedral Yard'.[626] St Martin's Well, in the basement, operated from 1935 to 1950: the previous year an exhibition showed models of the naval ships named after the city. At this time the Mocha Café was on the first floor.[627]

Between the wars the ground floor was used by antique shops[628] and by 1943 James Commins returned the building to selling books. He had acquired the stock of the Guildhall Circulating Library.[629] Other concerns had offices but the most significant change was the acquisition of the building by the Royal Clarence in 1984 with the upper rooms being used for guest accommodation. The bones from a number of individuals make up the skeleton in the basement which has been on show since 1934.[630]

177. The upper floors of 16 & 17 Cathedral Yard, 11 November 2016.

OCCUPANTS OF THE PROPERTY

1817 – 1863	James Ridge, *Tailor Habit and Pellise Maker*
1864 – 1878	John Ridge Junior, *Tailor*
1879	Prudential Monetary Office
1880 – 1882	F. H. Purnell, *Shipping Agent*
1880 – 1882	Thomas B. Purnell, *Colliery Agent*
1884	Preparatory Grammar School for Boys
1884 – 1887	C. Elkin Mathews, *Bookseller*
1887 – 1898	Walter Scanes, *Law Stationer & Servants' Registry (& 17)*
1887 – 1891	H. W. Michelmore, *Solicitor*
1889 – 1890	Exeter Electric Light Company
1897	Charles William Priston, *Tailor*
1897 – 1900	T. Smith & Co., *Financial Agents*
1902	Nelson & Co: *Tea Dealer*, Henry Shooter: *Engraver*
1906	Thomas & Co., *Financial Agents*
1909 – 1917	W. F. Haymes, *Military Bootmaker*
1910 – 1921	Gilbert Babbage & Co., *Solicitors*
1910	Adeline Vavasour, *Teacher of Music*
1920 – 1933	Murray's Antiques (& 17)
1928	Isca Lodge of the Theosophical Society
1928 – 1930	G. & N. Hawkeswell, *Photographers*
1930	J. Pugh
1931	Vacant
1933 – 1941	H. M. Carmichael Antiques
1936 – 1950	St Martin's Well
1936 – 1951	The Mocha Café (upstairs)
1943 – 1962	James G. Commin, *Bookseller*
1952 – 1966	Audrey Clare, *Gowns*
1964 – 1966	Cecil A. James
1964 – 1966	Thomas Sanders & Staff, *Chartered Auctioneers & Estate agents*
1967 – 1983	R. B. Taylor & Sons, *Estate Agents, Auctioneers, Surveyors & Valuers*
1984 – 2016	Well House (& 17)

141

NUMBER 15

178. The Royal Clarence Hotel, 11 December 1942.

15 Cathedral Yard (though the number is not used), a medieval property anciently held by the Dean & Chapter, rebuilt in the 1760s and opened as a hostelry which it has continued to be for some 250 years, repeatedly renovated by succeeding proprietors, destroyed by fire in 2016.

In 1953 the building was listed Grade 2 and recorded it 'said to have been built to provide Assembly Rooms for the City by Wm Mackworth Praed, circa 1768. Original 4 storey, 6 window stucco front has been considerably altered, bays added, glazing bars removed etc. in 1827. Large porte-cochere partly hides Tuscan porch. Dentil cornice'. The frontage is 59 feet 6 inches.

In 1813 this was noted as 'one of the first, if not the very first, hotel and tavern in the west of England' whereas as early as 1836 it had been upgraded to the status of England's first hotel. However, the term had been used in London at least by 1764[631] and may not have been applied to 15 Cathedral Yard until five years later when Peter Berlon advertised his business in a London newspaper as a 'new coffee-house, inn and tavern' but added a corresponding paragraph in French *'Pierre Berlon tenant hotel et caffe sur la place St Pierre à Exeter'*.[632]

The recent fire has revealed the building is earlier than previously thought: thirteenth- or fourteenth-century fabric has been found including a window and a party wall with 14 Cathedral Yard. It was known that in the late sixteenth century 15 Cathedral Yard was still a canon's house and afterwards leased to various high-status men including Sir John Gilbert (whose tomb lies in the cathedral)[633] and Jerome King, a wealthy merchant and father of Peter King, a future Lord Chancellor of England.[634] The property extended to the High Street tenements and by the late 1600s there was a passage through to High Street.[635]

In 1766 15 Cathedral Yard, including the cellar, wall and courtyard, was redeveloped by William Mackworth Praed[636] who spent £400 in adding two storeys.[637] The Dean & Chapter granted use of the churchyard to store timber from the old roof and construct the new frame.[638] Shortly afterwards the premises were 'in the possession and occupation of Peter Berlon, French School Master' and other under-tenants.[639] A few years

179. The demolition of the upper floors of the front of the Royal Clarence Hotel, 5.17 pm, 2 November 2016.

before, in 1763, he had intended to open a French school in South Street; French was to be taught 'in the most polite, easy and intelligible manner, all by grammar rules' but his school does not seem to have been successful.[640] Three months later a public meeting was held to establish an Assembly Room. There had been one in the Close since at least 1748 but in 1763 there was apparently sufficient interest in another to seek private sponsors. A meeting was held to 'determine the proper spot whereon to erect the said building'[641] and architectural plans associated with Robert Adam for an Exeter Assembly Room may have been drawn for this.[642]

Three years later, on 13 June 1766, Berlon announced new plans: he had in construction 'a very handsome and commodious Assembly Room which will be furnished in the neatest and genteelest manner' which would be part of his Coffee House and Tavern situated in his dwelling house. His establishment would, he informed the city's gentlemen, be furnished 'with the most entertaining public papers and the best of wines, and all other liquors, and every thing else that may contribute to their better amusement and accommodation, in the same manner as is done in the coffee houses of London and Bristol'. It opened on the 16th of July. Newspaper advertisements show that in August an Assembly was held to mark the founding of the Royal Devon & Exeter Hospital.[643] Berlon announced the winter season's subscription concerts would begin in October and that he intended to start with a 'specimen concert… the money arising from this specimen concert being to pay Mr Berlon for the use of his room during the ensuing season'. He added that he 'flatters himself those ladies and gentlemen who intend to encourage the undertaking will honour him with their company *that evening*'.[644] The recent fire has revealed the Assembly Room's stone walls; large window openings with arched heads can be seen on the eastern side as well as a smaller circular one. The upper floor was built in the eighteenth century on an earlier wall. The north wall shows signs of an earlier roof which indicates that the Assembly Room was built by remodelling an earlier hall.

By 1768 15 Cathedral Yard was referred to as Berlon's Tavern. In 1774 it was termed in the *Kentish Gazette*

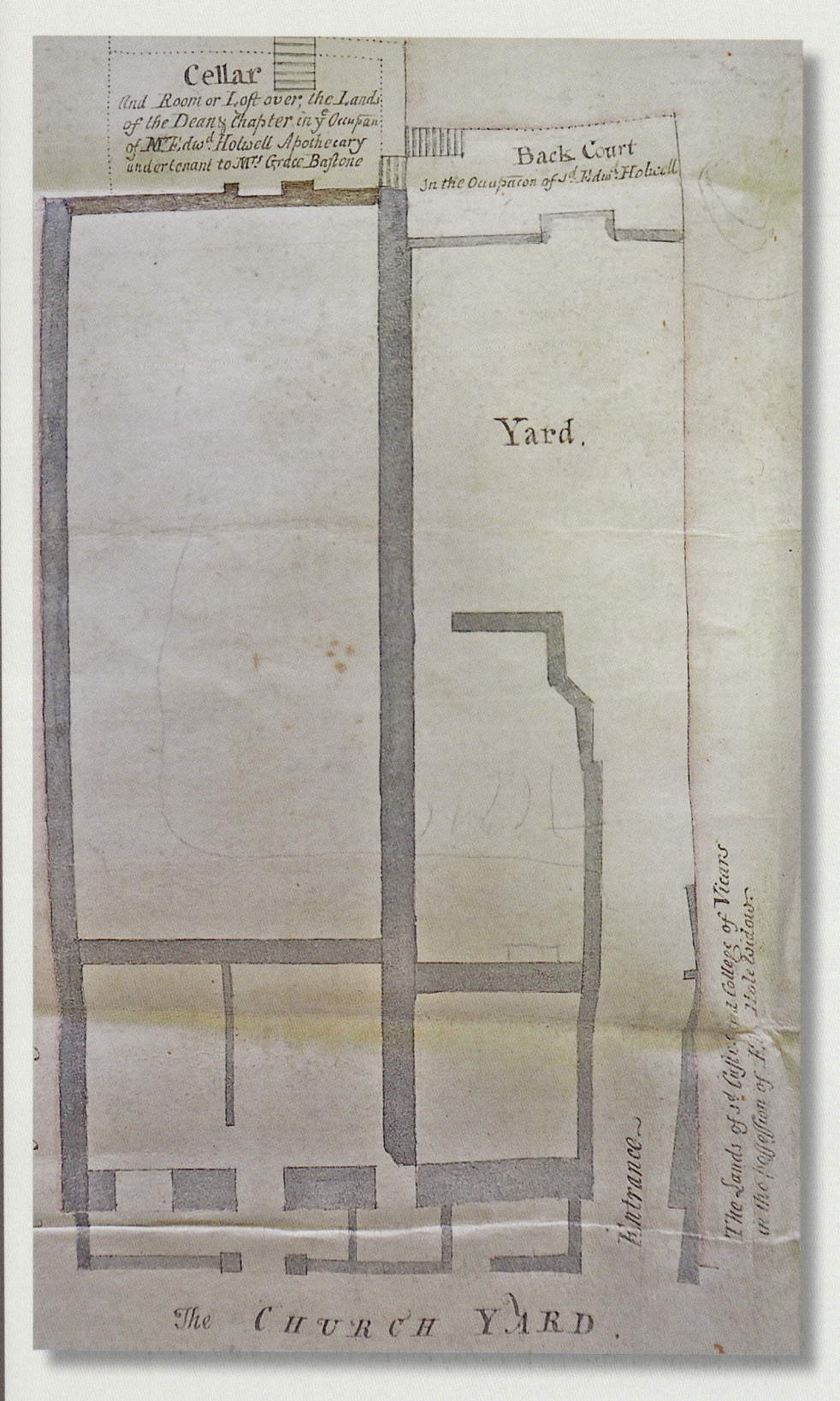

St Martin's Island: An introductory history of forty-two Exeter buildings

180. Ground plan by John Tothill, April 1766.

as 'the house of Peter Berlon called the hotel' but from 1768 to 1774 various English newspapers referred to it as 'the house of Peter Berlon, known by the name of Berlon's Coffee House and Tavern' or simply as 'Berlon's Coffee House'.[645] The names were as erratic as the proprietors would be: Berlon, sometimes described as a vintner and a chapman, was declared bankrupt in 1774 and within a few months, at least by early 1775, the hotel was taken over by Mr Connor who had run the Saracen's Head in London. Berlon's creditors were paid in what was then known as 'Connor's Hotel'.[646] Connor was still there in September but by July 1776 it was taken over by Richard Lloyd[647] who two years later went bankrupt.[648] He was succeeded by Thomas Thompson, thought to be the previous proprietor's waiter. For insurance purposes 15 Cathedral Yard was noted in 1791 as built of brick, brick nogging and stone. In 1798 there was another proprietor (who did not go bankrupt until 1813).[649]

In 1806 Alexander Jenkins wrote 'the only house worthy [of] notice in this parish is the Hotel, a large and commodious Inn, with elegant apartments and accommodation for people of the first quality, with a large assembly room in which are held the assize balls, concerts and winter assemblies of the most distinguished persons of the city and county. In the front is a neat coffee room. The situation of the Hotel is very pleasant, as it opens to the parade, and commands a noble view of the cathedral'.[650] It would shortly afterwards be restyled and a feature of the hotel would be repeated refurbishments undertaken by successive proprietors.

In 1810, and again in 1813, the hotel was for sale. It was noted as an 'elegant structure… built a few years since previously for an Hotel and now in full business'. James Phillips, the proprietor, announced that he had no intention of leaving the business[651] but Samuel Foote, the manager of Plymouth's theatre, moved in during August 1813. He

NUMBER 15 Cathedral Yard

promised the building would 'instantly undergo a complete repair'. Foote alluded to 'obstacles now no longer in existence, which have of late presented themselves owing to the peculiar circumstances under which the business of the hotel has been conducted'. He also announced that the ballroom would be 'in a style of elegance not inferior to any out of London' and that the design 'when completed of its affording such a specimen of the very superior talents of that very eminent artist, Mr De Maria, as cannot fail to ensure universal approbation'. Foote hired James de Maria who had painted the interior of the Plymouth theatre.[652] A journalist enthused the ballroom 'begins to be the subject of general admiration. Those who were acquainted with the mind of Mr De Maria the artist – equally learned and creative – had no conception that so much of grandeur and beauty – of science, taste and execution – could be portrayed on the walls and ceiling of a room which had been hitherto a libel on the county of Devon. It is now an Egyptian temple, which Cleopatra herself might have been proud of'. The 'new city and county assembly room' opened in November.[653] Another commentator wrote 'the eye of folly, indeed, may view the grotesque hieroglyphics which the artist has so happily portrayed, as the forms of childish monstrosity. The learned will contemplate them with reverence'. He concluded 'we consider then this redemption from obscurity of the finest monuments of Egypt, as calculated to give a new stimulus to thought; and, by displaying them in a ball room, to refine our recreations, and give to youth and beauty fresh means of intellectual improvement'.[654] Within weeks Foote held public lectures in the 'New Assembly Room or Egyptian Hall'

but a few years later he was also declared bankrupt.[655]

Foote was the latest in a long list of short-term proprietors but his failure may have been partly due to his treatment of his celebrated daughter. Maria Foote became a leading actress at Covent Garden the year after Foote left Exeter. She was also at the centre of a scandal in 1824 involving two illegitimate children and a broken promise of marriage but it was Samuel Foote who gained a poor reputation. It was said of him 'there is scarcely a family living, or a family dead, that he has not treated with the dirtiest selfishness, whatever were his obligations—spunging till he was insulted, lying till he was discovered, puffing till he was the butt of the town. The people of Plymouth can relate a thousand instances of this description.'[656]

In 1819 Joseph Congdon announced he would reopen the hotel with improvements and repairs particularly to the ball and card rooms. He had run Plymouth's Commercial Hotel and 15 Cathedral Yard became known as 'Congdon's Hotel'. Two years later it was 'in complete repair, every apartment having been newly organised, and is now handsomely fitted up with new and genteel furniture'. Further improvements were made for the coronation of George IV; Congdon employed Mr Lingard and Mr Adams, 'two eminent artists who have been busily employed for some time past and still are in new painting, embellishing and otherwise highly decorating the ball room and orchestra in a superb, fanciful and tasteful style for the occasion and when completed will present a handsome and unique appearance'.[657]

Sarah Street, who had run a Sidmouth hotel, was the next proprietor. 15 Cathedral Yard was initially known as Street's Hotel but this changed with a visit by the Duchess of Clarence, later Queen Adelaide, in 1827. The premises became known as Street's Royal Clarence Hotel and eventually the Royal Clarence

181. Trade card of James Phillips, with an engraving of the hotel front, possibly 1799.

145

St Martin's Island: An introductory history of forty-two Exeter buildings

> NEW COFFEE-HOUSE, INN and TAVERN. Exon, June 13th, 1769.
>
> PETER BERLON begs leave to inform the nobility and gentry, that he has taken and added to his own that handsome and commodious house, (the corner of St. Martin's-gate, in the church-yard) which he has completely and elegantly fitted up for the reception of families, or single travellers. The house is most pleasantly situated, having a command of the cathedral, and all the public walks.
>
> Ladies and gentlemen may be supplied (at the above house) with coaches and post-chaises, able horses with careful drivers.
>
> PIERRE BERLON tenant hotel et caffé sur la place St. Pierre à Exeter, prends la liberté de présenter ses profonds respects à tous les voyageurs, etrangers et autres qui viennent dans ce pays, et comme sa maison est agréablement située, commode et meublée élégamment, il se flatte, par ses soins et son attachment à plaire à ceux qui lui font l'honneur de venir loger chez lui, mériter leur recommendation.
>
> On y a caroffes et chaifes de poftes.

rose pink. Over the doorways on the north side are French imitation statuettes, representing Earth and Water. At the east end appears a handsome vase of flowers, flanked on either side with a Roman statuette holding a lamp. The cornice, which had been plastered over with paper, has been restored, and picked out with colours; the pilasters have been painted in imitation of green Egyptian marble; the lower part of the walls have been sienna-marbled; and the ceiling has been clouded and starred. The apartment is lighted with three burnished brass star chandeliers of neat design, surmounted by large gold stars, supplied by Mr John Vicary. The antique mirror, which frequenters of the room were accustomed to term a relic of Ninevah, has been turned to account by being inserted in plates in the front of the music gallery. At the back of the mirror, on taking it down, were discovered some curiously painted Egyptian figures'. The decorator was Mr Hutchinson (presumably that at Broadgate). Birkett advertised there was a large coffee room,

182. Peter Berlon's advert in *The Middlesex Journal or Chronicle of Liberty*, 17 June 1769.

Hotel. Exeter also then had the Royal Clarence Gardens in Southernhay and there were other Royal Clarence Hotels at Ilfracombe, Seaton, Bridgwater and Bognor.[658] In 1837 it hosted Madame Pasta, the 'unrivalled singer' who was on her farewell tour of England.[659] Street rented an adjoining property in Lamb Alley which had rooms 'attached to the hotel'.[660] In 1851 she lived in the hotel with her two sisters (one was an assistant and the other an annuitant) and six staff all but one of whom were female.

Street was succeeded in 1859 by John Graham[661] but seven years later he was bankrupt and succeeded by William Birkett who had the hotel renovated 'and improved throughout in a most elegant style. The improvements have, of course, extended to the spacious Assembly Room, which has been entirely redecorated. The walls have been panelled with a rich paper of Owen Jones' design, framed with stiles of

183. Undated plan of the eastern end of Cathedral Yard noting A (14 Cathedral Yard – Exeter Bank), B (15 Cathedral Yard – the Royal Clarence Hotel belonging to Sarah Street) and C (property owned by the bank and rented to Sarah Street), c1826–37. Note the hotel extends into 10 Martin's Lane.

NUMBER 15 Cathedral Yard

a ladies' coffee room and a large dining room known as 'The Wellington'.[662] He had been the proprietor of the nearby Globe Hotel.[663]

The Sanders family ran the hotel for more than seventy years. One ('known for his enterprise and energetic talents which will qualify him for the venture which he makes in these days of competition, when the traveller usually expects the style and luxury of high life in the hostel in which he takes temporary sojurn')[664] was the proprietor when, in 1883, T. Raffles Davison wrote 'no one will regret a visit to Exeter, especially if in fine weather they go, and stay at the Clarence Hotel, in the Cathedral Close, one of the most comfortable hotels I have met with'.[665]

In 1919 the hotel was enlarged with the addition of 14 Cathedral Yard.[666] Several fires broke out just before the Great War: in 1913 a large beam of wood caught fire and smouldered for several days before staff discovered it behind a wall in the kitchen[667] and the following year a chimney caught fire but the fire service managed to extinguish the flames as it did a few months later when a back staircase caught fire.[668] In 1937 one commentator wrote that the hotel was 'thoroughly up to date in all modern essentials. Running water and radiators in all rooms, private bathrooms and a lift to all floors leave nothing to be desired in this direction. The cooking is first class in every respect; there is also a Grill Room which is a pleasing amenity for the passing guest. The cellar, as one would expect, is thoroughly representative of the best wines'.[669]

The twenty-first century not only saw the involvement of Michael Caines, the celebrated local chef, with Andrew

184. The rear of the Assembly Room, 11 August 2017.

Brownsword, the current owner, but there were several extensive internal renovations from the mid 1900s onwards.[670] The destruction of 2016, which has only left internal and external walls, is now being followed by a plan of rebuilding with Buttress Architects.

PROPRIETORS OF THE HOTEL

1768 – 1774	Peter Berlon
1775 – 1776	Mr Connor
1776 – 1778	Richard Lloyd
1778 – 1798	Thomas Thompson
1798 – 1813	James Phillips
1813 – 1819	Samuel T. Foote
1819 – 1826	Joseph Congdon
1826 – 1859	Sarah Street
1859 – 1866	John Graham
1866 – 1879	William Birkett
1879 – 1907	John Headon Stanbury
1908 – 1928	John Bailey Rowe Orchard
1928 – 1952	J. G. R. Orchard
1952 – 1959	Empire Hotels
1960 – 1970	Express Hotels
1970 – 1990	Norfolk Capital Hotels
1990 – 1997	Queens Moat Hotels/County Hotels
1997 – 1999	Duke Street
1999 – 2003	Corus & Regal Hotels
2003 – 2017	Andrew Brownsword Hotels

NUMBER 14

185. The Exeter Bank, pre 1906.
186. Stained glass panel, (inset) possibly from Belgium, of Joseph and Potiphar's wife, c.1600.

This structure, gutted by fire in 2016, was listed in 1953 Grade 2 and recorded 'adjoining and now part of the hotel is a 3 storey, 3 window eighteenth-century building, formerly the Exeter Bank. Semi-circular 3-light attic window. The remains of a central porch are still visible, but the front has been altered with late C19 iron balconies etc. Slate roofs.' The frontage is 26 feet 9 inches.

14 Cathedral Yard (though the number has never been used), anciently owned by the Vicars Choral, The Rummer from at least the 1720s, rebuilt about 1766, Exeter Bank until 1906, Deller's Café until 1919 and part of the Royal Clarence since that date.

The origins of this building have been assumed to be medieval and current archaeological work has recently revealed a thirteenth- or fourteenth-century party wall with the Royal Clarence Hotel. This formed part of a canon's house and afterwards was leased to various prominent gentlemen.[671] The building was, until the fire of 2016, largely a structure erected in the mid to late eighteenth century. This had replaced an earlier building constructed by Robert Rous in the 1680s. In 1685 the Dean & Chapter gave him permission to 'have a place in the churchyard to lay and work his timber for his building his house in the churchyard'.[672] Work continued the following year: he was allowed to 'build the west end of the front wall of his house in the Close near St Martin's Gate, a little further out towards the churchyard, to bring the front of the house into square the same being as it was before out of square, he bringing the corner wall of the said house somewhat further back, by which the way at that

NUMBER 14 Cathedral Yard

187. The Rummer Tavern drawn by Jean Rocque, 1744.

corner will be somewhat enlarged and will be easier for carriages to turn there… without prejudice to the house adjoining on the west or to the roadway'.[673] The frontage was approximately 26 feet.[674] It continued in the possession of the Rous family[675] and by 1726, and through to at least 1756, it was the Rummer Tavern.[676] Ten years later the building was advertised for rent and described as 'a house sashed in front, and very pleasantly situated in St Peter's Churchyard, Exeter, adjoining the New Assembly Room'.[677]

William Mackworth Praed rebuilt in the mid 1760s and an engraving shows that his building had two floors above the ground floor and an attic. The first and second floors had three sash windows. It became the Exeter Bank on 9 July 1769 and Praed's partners were Sir John Duntze, Daniel Hamilton and Joseph Sanders. The latter's family held an interest in the bank through to 1901 when it amalgamated with the City Bank and moved four years later.[678] It appears that the bank did not use the upper floors which in 1769 comprised 'two parlours, a large elegant dining room, a good kitchen and ten lodging rooms'. There was also a pantry, cellar and a courtyard. The hotel acquired these rooms.[679]

The bank moved in 1905 and Deller's Café opened on 31 October 1906 when it was reported 'so great were the alterations necessary to allow the scheme of the promoters to be carried out that the old building had to be practically gutted, and the architect, Mr C. Cole of Exeter, was allowed a free hand'. On the ground floor was a café with a balcony for an orchestra at one end. Above the balcony was a skylight fitted in imitation antique glass. White stencil work was used for the walls and curtains.

188. Deller's Café, 1906–1919.

The first floor had a ladies' tea room which had oak furniture and tiled chimney pieces. The second floor had a smoking room, a private room and a kitchen with walls lined with *embecca*, a substance which resembled tiles. The *Western Times* told its readers that no visitor should leave Exeter without visiting the new café. It noted 'the café has been fitted up in a most comfortable and elegant fashion. Everything is bright, attractive and up to date, and anyone wishing to partake of a daintily served luncheon or tea cannot do better than patronise this establishment.' One attraction, the paper noted, was that the firm roasted and ground its coffee on a daily basis. Deller's moved in 1919 and the hotel purchased the building.[680] It may have been at this time that a series of significant stained glass panels were incorporated into the fabric. The premises then comprised a ground floor shop or wareroom (61 feet by 23 feet) with two oak chimney fireplaces. The orchestra gallery had an iron spiral staircase. The first floor had an oak panelled room (31 feet 3 inches by 22 feet 9 inches), a store-room and facilities. The upper floors had five rooms.[681]

189. The Exeter Bank, 1833, with the hotel door to the left, as engraved by W. Deeble after A. Glennie.

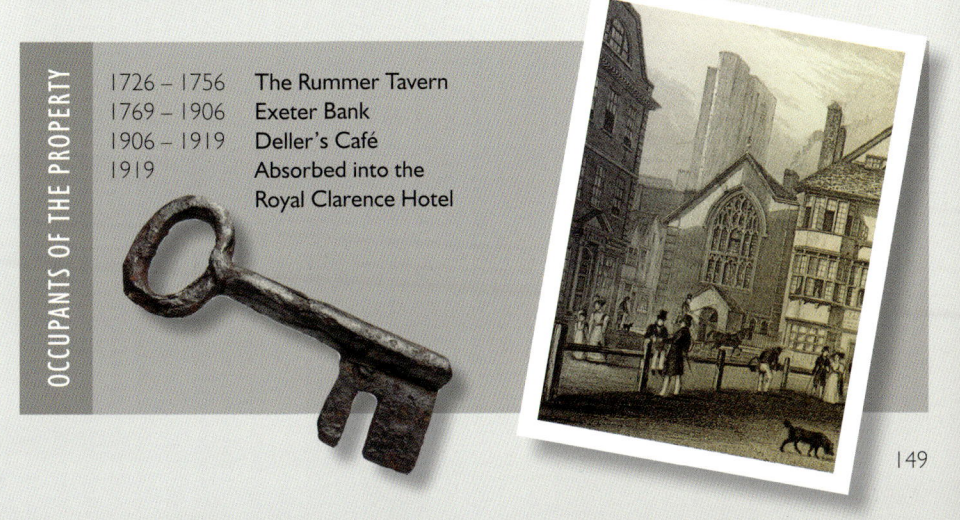

OCCUPANTS OF THE PROPERTY

1726 – 1756	The Rummer Tavern
1769 – 1906	Exeter Bank
1906 – 1919	Deller's Café
1919	Absorbed into the Royal Clarence Hotel

149

190. At the top: St Martin's Church with the gate situated across from it, late 1500s.

4
Martin's Lane

Martin's Lane, also known as St Martin's Lane, Martin's Street and St Martin's Street as well as Canon's Street, Fish Street, Jatoples Lane[682] and Luxury Lane.

This passageway derived its current name from the parish church lying at its southern end and because it forms the eastern boundary of the parish. The thoroughfare became known as Luxury Lane in the late 1800s and first half of the 1900s because of the sale of fish, fowl and fruit. In 1908 one journalist enthused 'never did the title of Luxury Lane more appropriately than now befit the little thoroughfare that connects High Street and the Cathedral Close. It is literally filled to overflowing with the good things of the earth, sea and air'.[683] It had been recorded, in the early 1400s, as being called Fish Street.[684] Nearly four hundred years later fish was being sold in the High Street just outside Martin's Lane. It was one of several places in Exeter where fish was sold.[685]

The longstanding settlement of the lane is indicated by a deed which shows that in 1294 Roger Hanek held the tenement which lay behind 39 High Street.[686] Eight years previously St Martin's Gate had been erected near the southern end of the lane. A stone post, placed on its site when the gate was demolished, can still be seen *in situ*. The gate was built to be wide enough for a cart to pass through. Already by this time the thoroughfare was called St Martin's Lane.[687] The Vicars Choral had rights to the rooms above the gate. By 1803 the proprietor of the Hotel had in his possession the gate's key and presumably he used this to unlock and lock the gate for his guests. Sixteen years later the gate was demolished following a proposal from the Improvement Commissioners. The Dean & Chapter had agreed on condition that the lane was to be 'a flat pavement for foot passengers only' and that the city council would be responsible for future maintenance.[688] Nearly fifty years later the council considered but rejected a proposal to widen St Martin's Lane by removing all existing buildings as well as two others in High Street which faced Queen Street.[689] This scheme was revived by Thomas Mawson in 1914 but also disregarded.

In 1877 there was a complaint in *The Western Times* about sanitation in St Martin's Lane. Another reader responded by writing that 'my experience of this street is all the other way, i.e., when I am not quite well I invariably go there to get better. I usually go there some 15 or 20 times every week; almost every Sunday morning on my way to the cathedral, which is close after the Saturday. I never remember any disagreeable smell, but I frequently find some very agreeable things there, especially Mr Carlile's fruit. I have known it cure my complaint when eminent medical men have failed to give me the desired relief'.[690] The lane was known for the sale of fruit, fish and meat throughout the nineteenth century. The western buildings of Martin's Lane have not had residents since 1968.[691]

191. Map showing properties in Martin's Lane, 1841.

192. Marker erected to note the destruction of Martin's Gate, 1819.

NUMBER 10

The frontage is 26 feet 3 inches.

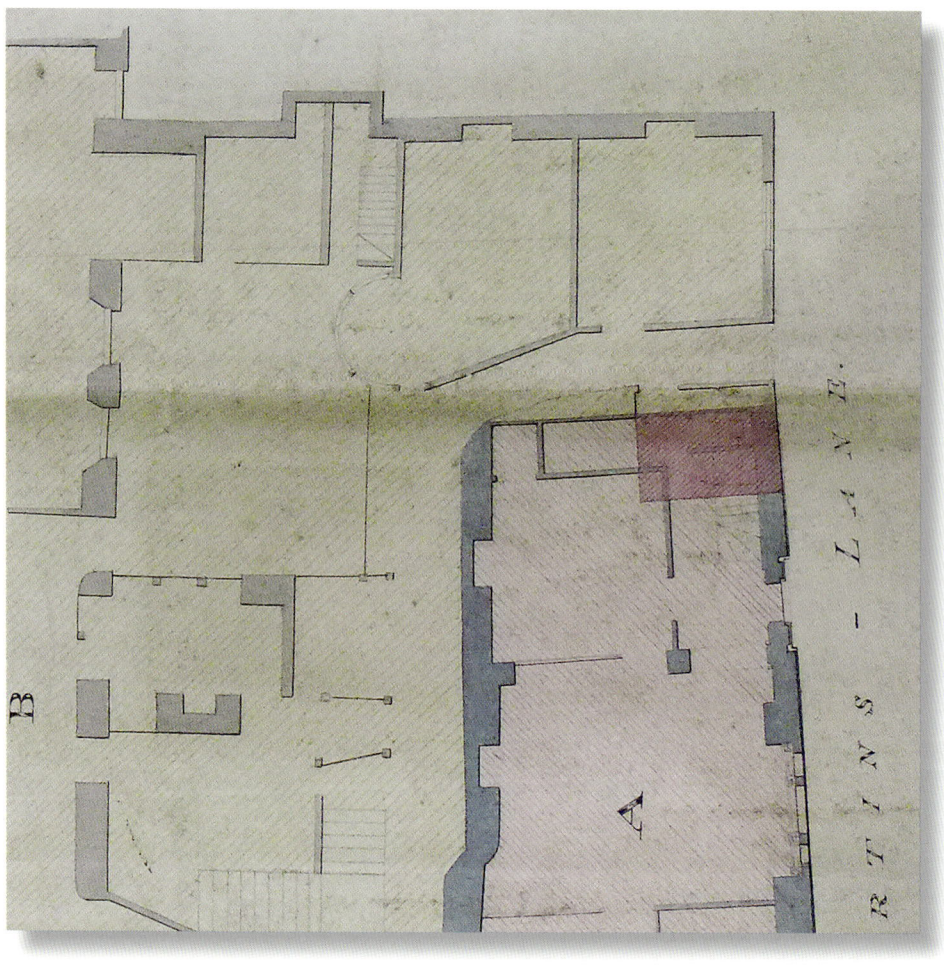

193. Ground plan of 10 Martin's Lane, c1826 – 37, at top right.

10 Martin's Lane, an anonymous three floor building (with an attic) which has been absorbed by the Royal Clarence Hotel.

Number 10 Martin's Lane may date to the eighteenth century and there was an earlier building on the site at least by 1607. The façade is plain, the ground floor comprises a single room with a passage to the yard and the upper floors oversail the ground floor.[692]

The building has been a part of the hotel complex since 1766 and it has been occasionally sublet such as to the Snuff & Tobacco Warehouse (also called the Fancy Snuff & Tobacco Shop). It continued until about 1813 when for a short while the hotel used the building as its booking office. The shop reopened the following year but the owner, William Wescomb, subsequently went bankrupt, reinvented himself as an accountant and used his building as an 'office for the recovery of small debts'. By 1817 he was renting 'a good sitting and two bed rooms' on the upper floors.[693]

Number 10 was subsequently used by various businesses. The immediate successors may have been fruiterers.[694] In 1846 John Rickard, who described himself as a watchmaker and silversmith,

NUMBER 10 Martin's Lane

194. Martin's Lane, possibly 1941.

proprietor of the Ship Inn, moved his Old Curiosity Shop to Number 10[697] but was replaced in 1867 by F. Sprague, a tobacconist who sold cigars, tobacco and snuff as well as Meerschaum, Briar and other pipes. Shortly afterwards he moved 'in consequence of the premises being required for alterations'.[698] Richard Mock, Poulterer & Dealer in Game, then occupied 10 Martin's Lane until 1874.[699] The following year J. Stevens & Son, tailors & drapers, moved into the building and only five years later they left Number 10. The building was then used by the hotel as an off-licence.[700] There was substantial damage caused to the upper floor during the fire of 2016.

195. Martin's Lane depicted in the late 1500s.

announced he was in premises which adjoined the Royal Clarence Hotel in the lane. Rickard manufactured lever and musical watches as well as church, chime, turret, musical, spring and skeleton clocks.[695] He was there until 1859 when, noted as a chronometer, watch and clock maker, his premises were 'required for the enlargement of the Royal Clarence Hotel'.[696] The building was then once again absorbed into the hotel. In 1862 Alfred Tucker,

OCCUPANTS OF THE PROPERTY

1801	William Fryer Tucker,	*tobacconist*
1801 – 1813	Snuff & Tobacco Warehouse (William & H. Wescomb)	
1813	Booking office for what became the Royal Clarence Hotel	
1814 – 1818	William Wescomb, *Snuff Shop*	
1846 – 1859	John Rickard Junior, *Watchmaker & Silversmith*	
1859	Part of the Royal Clarence Hotel	
1862 – 1863	Old Curiosity Shop	
1867 – 1871	F. Sprague, *Tobacconist*	
1871 – 1874	Richard Mock, *Poulterer & Dealer in Game*	
1875 – 1880	J. Stevens & Son, *Tailors & Drapers*	
1881 – 2017	Part of the Royal Clarence Hotel	

NUMBER 11

In 1974 these buildings were listed Grade 2 and collectively recorded 'Eighteenth-century. Timber framed, rendered and painted. Four storeys, two windows, sashes, mostly modern. Modern shop fronts. Slate roof. Included for group value. Nos 11 to 13 (consec) form a group.' The frontage is 16 feet.

196. Side view of 11 Martin's Lane, c1906–1919.

11 Martin's Lane, a fishmongers for more than a century.

For nearly a century the building was used to sell fish. In 1836 Henry Davey, previously a boot and shoe maker, became a fishmonger and opened his shop in the building. He was there until his death six years later and his widow later turned over the business to another fishmonger.[701] John Lear had his 'New & General Fish Shop' in 1854 and Henry Hooper, a fishmonger, was a later occupier. His business was known as the 'Fish & Barrel Oyster Warehouse and Oyster Rooms'. He sold turtle meat, preserved lobsters, grouse soup and Yarmouth bloaters. In 1864 Hooper testified that the Ship Inn, directly across the lane, had become 'the resort of prostitutes and low characters' and that at night he had been wakened in his own house on at least 40 occasions by the women and the men who frequented them.[702] Richard Satchell became Sanders' partner & the firm was known as Sanders & Satchell. It continued until 1891 when Sanders' son Frederick succeeded to the business, and with his partner Walter Gibbons, the firm was known as Frederick Sanders & Company and it ran until 1894 when Mock & Son succeeded to the fish business. In 1903 the building was remodelled; one journalist commented that there had been considerable recent improvements made to Martin's Lane and that one of the most striking was that

NUMBER 11 Martin's Lane

197. The roof of 11 Martin's Lane can be seen on the far left, 30 October 2016.
198. (Inset) Letter head of Henry Davey of 11 Martin's Lane, c1836.

involving Mock's premises. He wrote 'the old fish shop has been completely removed and in its place one finds one of the most up-to-date shops in the city. The walls are tiled throughout and in the centre of the shop is a large slab of solid marble upon which is placed specimens of the finny tribe. The floor is paved with ornamental tiles and at the entrance are massive brass columns. There is an up-to-date oyster bar provided'.[703]

OCCUPANTS OF THE PROPERTY		
1836 – 1842	Henry Davey,	Fishmonger
1842 – 1849	Mary Davey,	Fishmonger
1850	G. L. Tancock,	Fishmonger
1854	John Lear,	Fishmonger
1855 – 1872	Henry Hooper,	Fishmonger
1872 – 1891	Sanders & Satchell,	Fishmongers
1891 – 1894	Frederick Sanders & Company,	Fishmongers
1894 – 1941	Richard Mock & Sons,	Fishmongers
1943 – 1967	Wynne Tighe & Son,	Dispensing & Photographic Chemists
1968 – 2003	Christine Denny,	Ladies' Fashions
2004 – 2006	Friday's Child,	Children's Wear
2007 – 2009	Coco,	Ladies' Wear
2010	Vacant	
2011 – 2017	The Real Cornish Pasty Co.	

155

NUMBER 12

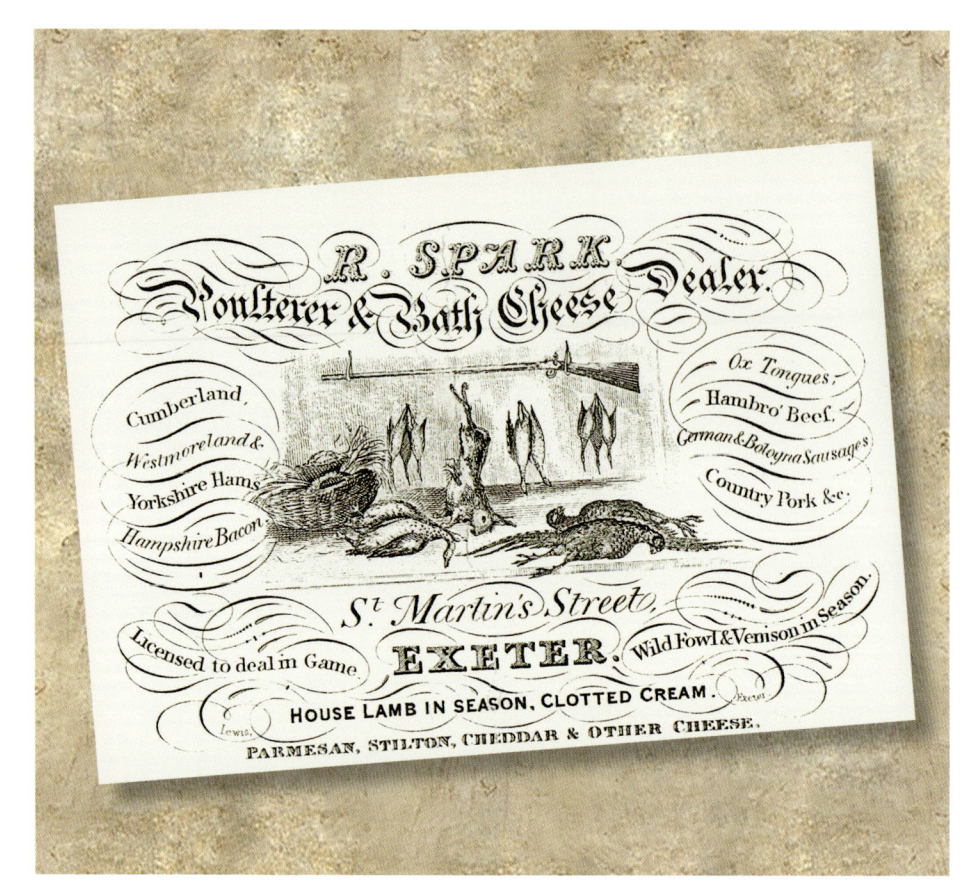

199. Trade card of Robert Spark of 12 Martin's Lane, 1841.

12 Martin's Lane, the building was used by fruiterers for several generations.

Robert Spark occupied the building from the early 1800s until 1853. He sold 'real Dartmoor mutton' and during the Christmas season of 1841 it was said his shop had 'one of the most extraordinary shows of poultry and game ever seen in Devonshire'.[704] He opened a branch in Torquay but in 1850 felt the need to note in the press that he had been established in the lane for 36 years. He asked his customers to remember that his shop was 'the LOWER ONE IN ST MARTIN STREET'. Spark was referring to his rival next door. He was insolvent that year and in his bankruptcy papers was referred to as a poulterer, a bacon factor and a dealer in bacon and cheese.[705]

Charles Collins, a clerical and general tailor who had worked for Wippell, the renowned firm, was another occupant. In 1861 he advertised himself as the originator of the 'Sixteen Shilling Trousers'.[706] Three fruiterers followed: George Carlile[707] was succeeded by Thomas George Dicker whose business was renamed Dicker & Son, Florists and Fruiterers a few years later. He went bankrupt in 1906[708] and R. Mock & Sons took the opportunity to expand their businesses from the two neighbouring premises. Until then the firm called itself fish, game, poultry, ice and oyster merchants but from 1906 also operated as florists. At that time it occupied Numbers 11, 12 & 13 Martin's Lane. It was not until 1933 that the firm left Number 12.[709]

In 1974 these buildings were listed Grade 2 and collectively recorded as 'Eighteenth-century. Timber framed, rendered and painted. Four storeys, two windows, sashes, mostly modern. Modern shop fronts. Slate roof. Included for group value. Nos 11 to 13 (consec) form a group.' The frontage is 15 feet 4 inches.

NUMBER 12 Martin's Lane

200. The rear view of 12 & 13 Martin's Lane, 29 August 2017.

201. County fire mark, 12 Martin's Lane, 30 July 2017.

OCCUPANTS OF THE PROPERTY

1814 – 1851	Robert Spark,	*Poulterer*
1856 – 1866	Charles Collins,	*Tailor & Draper*
1866 – 1888	George Byron Carlile,	*Fruiterer*
1889 – 1906	T. G. Dicker, *Fruiterer* (later **Dicker & Son**) *Florists and Fruiterers*	
1906 – 1933	R. Mock & Sons,	*Florists & Fruiterers*
1933 – 2002	The Red House of Devon,	*Newsagent & Confectioners*
1960 – 1962	Harry Wright (upstairs)	
1981 – 1987	Peachey & Richards Ltd,	*Finance & Insurance Brokers* (upstairs)
1981 – 1987	Business Mortgages Ltd (upstairs)	
2003	Vacant	
2004 – 2017	Polkadot Gallery,	*Artisan Jewelry*
2016 – 2017	Hair@No.12 (upstairs)	

157

NUMBER 13

In 1974 these buildings were listed Grade 2 and collectively recorded as 'Eighteenth-century. Timber framed, rendered and painted. Four storeys, two windows, sashes, mostly modern. Modern shop fronts. Slate roof. Included for group value. Nos 11 to 13 (consec) form a group.' The frontage is 21 feet.

202. The roofline of 39 High Street and 13 Martin's Lane can be glimpsed on the far right, 30 October 2016.

13 Martin's Lane, a poulterer's shop for more than a century.

Number 13 Martin's Lane housed three different types of traders before settling down to a century of selling poultry. From 1833 to 1845 fruiterers were the occupiers; Lamb & Company had a wholesale and retail business in foreign fruit[710] and later it was John Chapple's English & Foreign Fruit Warehouse. Chapple moved in 1845 at which point 13 Martin's Lane and 19 High Street were used for Chapple's other businesses as an auctioneer, carver, gilder, valuer, general broker and commission agent. His new firm was called the 'House Agency & General Commission Office'.[711]

Footwear was sold for a few years from 1844 beginning with John Davey, a boot maker and India rubber galosh manufacturer, who had been in business at 19 High Street and may have swapped buildings with Chapple: in 1848 John Davey Junior, a boot and shoemaker, announced he had bought the entire stock of the 'old established business carried on at 13 Martin's Street' which had been owned by his father. Davey had managed a London business and returned to Exeter not only with his experience but also 'an extensive and well selected stock of every novel and fashionable article in the boot and shoe trade'.[712] A fire that year caused the death of his employee when a bottle of turpentine in his trousers pocket broke,

NUMBER 13 Martin's Lane

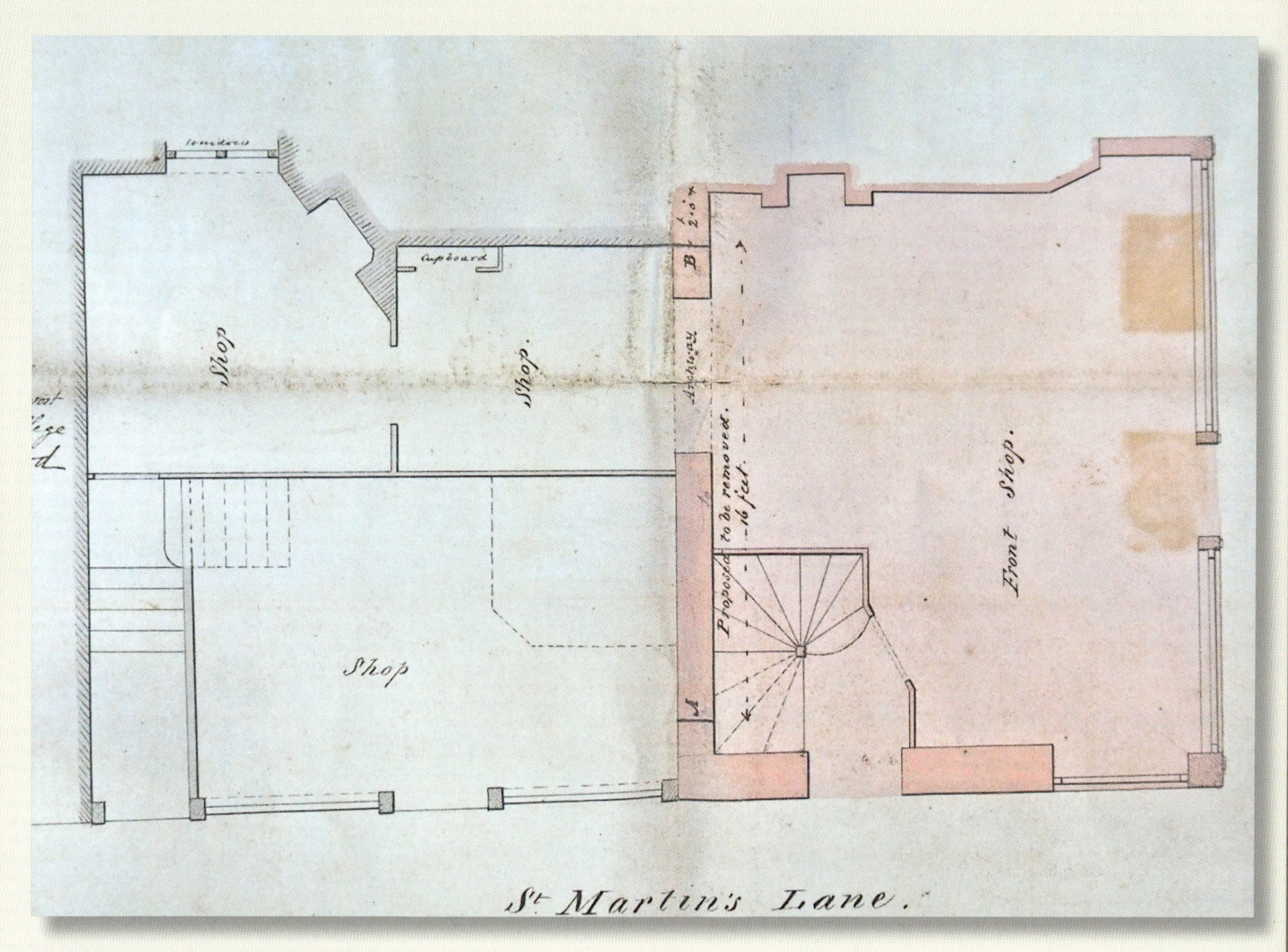

203. Ground plan of 13 Martin's Lane, 1827.

saturated his clothing and he unfortunately came too close to a light.[713]

In 1850 Number 13 comprised a shop, small parlour, kitchen, drawing room, five bedrooms, attic, closets and a cellar under the shop. From this date, and continuing for nearly a century, the building was used to sell poultry. Henry Hooper was the first,[714] his widow Eliza continued after his death and their daughter Mary kept the business.[715] F. Sanders then took over and sold poultry, game and wild fowl as well as clotted cream, butter and cured meats.[716] The last poulterer arrived in 1875: Richard Mock and Sons moved from 10 to 13 Martin's Lane and continued until 1953. Edwardian journalists commented on the impressiveness of the shop at Christmas.[717] Wattys, the delicatessen, was the last occupant; in 1965 13 Martin's Lane combined with 39 High Street to form one retail unit.[718]

1833 – 1837	**Lamb & Company**,	*Foreign Fruit Dealers*
1837 – 1845	**John & Ann Chapple**,	*Foreign Fruit Dealer & Auctioneer*
1846 – 1848	**John Davey**,	*Bootmaker*
1848 – 1850	**John Davey, Junior**,	*Bootmaker*
1850 – 1861	**Henry Hooper**,	*Poulterer & Fishmonger*
1861 – 1870	**Eliza Hooper**,	*Poulterer*
1870 – 1872	**Mary Hooper**,	*Poulterer & Game Dealer*
1873 – 1875	**F. Sanders**,	*Poulterer & Game Dealer*
1875 – 1953	**Richard Mock & Sons**,	*Game & Poultry Dealer*
1954	Vacant	
1955 – 1965	**Watty's Foods Ltd**,	*Delicatessen*
1966 – 1995	**Dorothy Perkins**,	*Ladies' Wear (& 40)*
1968 – 1987	**Tact-Contact**,	*Employment Agency (upstairs)*
1996 – 2015	**Clinton Cards**	
2016	Vacant	
2017	**Skechers**	

OCCUPANTS OF THE PROPERTY

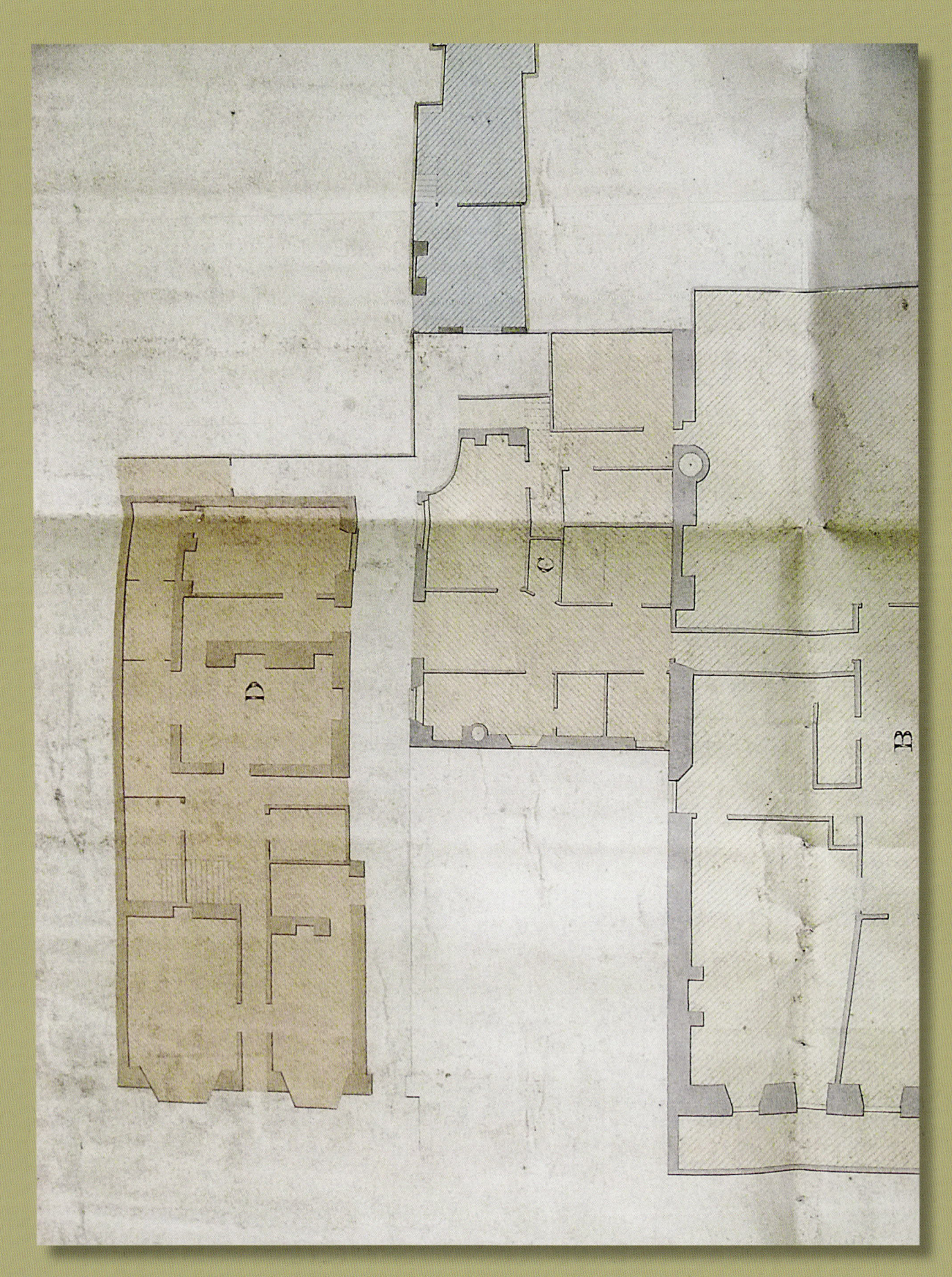

204. Plan of Lamb Alley property marked 'C' owned by Exeter Bank and rented to Sarah Street, c1826–37.

5
Lamb Alley

The name has been in use since at least the early 1600s and may derive from a public house called The Lamb.[719] The lane's southern entrance was between 17 and 18 Cathedral Yard and it ran through to High Street. That entrance is now blocked by 45 High Street which was built in the mid to late sixteenth century. It was later possible to pass into Lamb Alley from various back doors of buildings in High Street. Stretches of Lamb Alley remain. The lane was substantial enough in 1837 for a public call to be made to improve its entrance in Cathedral Yard.[720]

The Hedgeland model of Exeter depicts half a dozen distinct buildings along Lamb Alley but by the early 1800s there were only two listed in the parish rates. These properties, owned by the Vicars Choral, stood between 43 & 44 High Street and 17 & 18 Cathedral Yard. One was described in 1793 as being made of 'plaster' (cob) and had a slate roof.[721] Some indication of its size is given in a partial inventory made in 1622; it then held 'one scriptory standing in the closet, two Russia leather chairs and one table board standing in the upper room and one little and pair of andirons standing in the chimney of the said upper room'.[722] In about 1800 the two tenements were combined and a few years later were described as comprising several cellars, counting houses, curtilages, warerooms, a warehouse, stable and loft. It was claimed the property 'is of very considerable dimension and extends almost to the churchyard'.[723] This was likely to have been the building which was incorporated into the hotel in the first half of the nineteenth century: the hotel had rooms 'attached to the hotel'.[724]

In the late eighteenth century one property was known as Belfields. This was a reference to John Belfield, a former leaseholder, who had taken on the property in 1749 when it was dilapidated.[725] It comprised a kitchen, parlour, four chambers and four closets along with a cellar and curtilage.[726] Charles Pearce, a wine merchant, was a later occupant and in 1790 his son James took over.[727] The family also leased a property in High Street and the elder Pearce had been given leave in 1757 to open a door 'through the tenement in Lamb Alley from the churchyard to the Fore [sic] Street, he receiving a key from the chapter and paying one penny a year'.[728] This may have been the same property referred to as The Three Chambers as early as 1550 and was occasionally known as such through to 1770.[729]

Two properties, with access into Lamb Alley, survive which could be described as service buildings to 45 to 47 High Street. One is situated behind 47 High Street and another is at the rear of 45 & 46 High Street. There appears to have been another situated behind 49 High Street. In 1838 it was noted as being a dwelling house having its entrance from the Cathedral Yard and in the occupation of Elias Butland, a haberdasher and lace-man who occupied 46 High Street.[730]

A much smaller building, owned by the Dean & Chapter, was situated behind 45 & 46 High Street. In 1903 it comprised storerooms on the ground and first floors (both 16 feet by 15 feet) and the top floor had another two storerooms (one 18 feet by 11 feet 3 inches and the other 8 feet by 7 feet). There was also a cupboard at the foot of the stairs.[731]

At the rear of 47 High Street lies a detached stone-built building of two storeys. It has a chimneystack of the sixteenth century. In 1800 this 'dwelling house behind' was sold. Seven years later it was noted that the building had 'lately' been in a chemist's possession and that in it Robert Sowden, a linen draper, was opening a shop.[732] Sixty-two years later it was recorded as comprising four rooms suitable for offices.[733] Another chemist used it as his home in 1873.[734]

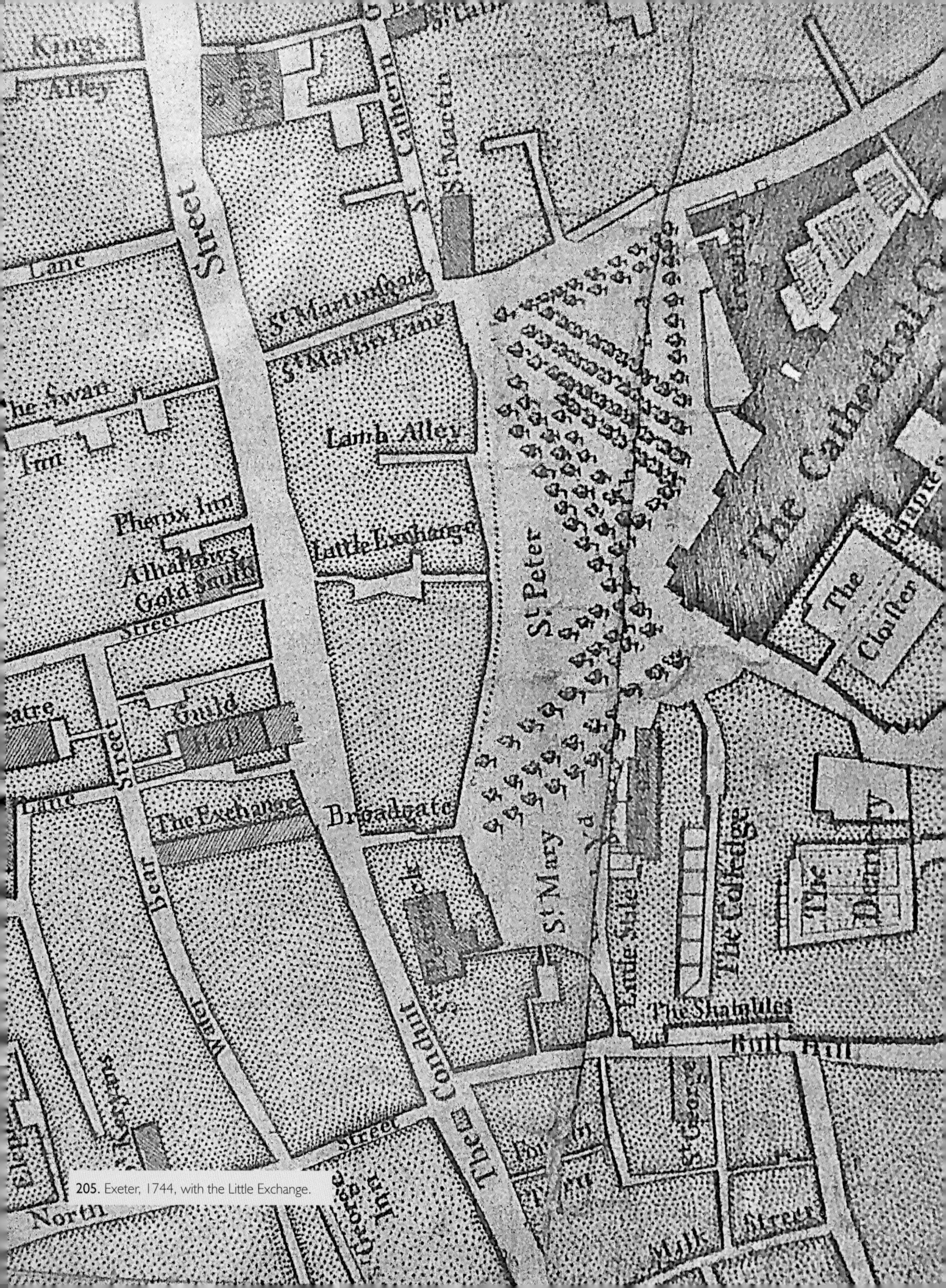

205. Exeter, 1744, with the Little Exchange.

6
The Little or New Exchange

This throughway was created in the first half of the eighteenth century with the northern entrance between 49 & 51 High Street and the southern between 20 & 21 Cathedral Yard. It does not appear to have a fixed name.

Two maps printed in 1756 and 1765 have its course outlined but both failed to provide a name. However, in 1744 John Rocque noted it on his map as the 'Little Exchange'. In contrast, Andrew Brice wrote by 1757 'there has of late been a new passage opened, which had of its owner the name of the New Exchange. It lies midway between Broadgate and St Martin's [Lane], and leads into the High Street'.[737] This term had also been used in 1748 in a letter describing the Close.[738]

The Little or New Exchange was not the same as The Exchange. This was a commercial building situated in High Street to the west of the guildhall. It had been there since at least 1728 and was recorded on Donne's map in 1765 and City Council's map of 1756.[739] There were also three 'plats' or enclosed areas in Cathedral Green called The Change of which it was noted by 1757:
'here, as on a sort of Change, almost daily do gentlemen, merchants and chief traders walking take meridian air, and talk of business or of news, perhaps or laugh at merry tale, till infallible St Peter, with one warning stroke, sends them with whetted appetites to dinner'.[740]
In 1738 the same author had described the Change as being 'the churchyard, where our merchants, etc. assemble to talk of trade and business'.[741]

The city's post office was situated at one corner of the south entrance to the Little or New Exchange. The Post Master was then Thomas Lavington and he rented his premises from John Vowler. The latter held the building with a lease from the Dean & Chapter and it appears the alley had been made illicitly: in 1740 the cathedral authorities issued instructions that the passageway should be closed. However, eight years later Vowler noted in his will there was still a 'free and convenient passage through the court and entries from the church yard to the Fore Street'.[742] The alley continued until 1963: its northern end in High Street was built over when 49 & 51 High Street were rebuilt (currently Burger King). It was later remembered as being 'picturesque, full of interest, and convenient too. One entered it through a doorway adjoining the east side of Number 51 High Street… one went through a narrow covered passage first, before reaching the long, flag-stoned, open court which was between them'.[743] The rebuilding in 1963 was also the cause of the destruction of 50 High Street, a building in the lane which was surrounded by other properties on three sides.

The lane had an irregular shape and continued to do so until 1963. In 1748 there were six tenements, built at least by 1729, at the southern end of the lane. These each ran in a row of three behind Numbers 20 and 21 Cathedral Yard. In 1760 the number of houses had recently been reduced to five.[744] It has not been determined when these properties were demolished.

50 High Street

A property which was anciently held of the Dean & Chapter, and was favoured in the Victorian period by architects, accountants and auctioneers. It was largely hidden from public view and yet located in the heart of the city. It was also often in multi-occupation and known as Central Chambers between 1928 and at least 1955.

The building may have been undistinguished: no details on its architecture have been found.[745] John Wyatt, an accountant, is the first occupier to be identified. He was there in 1828 and may have rented an upstairs office while the ground floor appears to have been used by

St Martin's Island: An introductory history of forty-two Exeter buildings

The Little or New Exchange

Saunders & Son, wholesale linen drapers.[746] Sidney Hayne & Company, Wholesale Linen Drapers, had been there by 1822 and continued until 1838. A neighbour later recalled that 'a snug business used to be done in the woollen drapery down the adjoining passage by Messrs Sanders and Hayne who had large warehouses there'. This firm was the last of its kind to occupy the building.[747]

John Hayward, the illustrious architect, was the occupant from at least 1839 until his death in 1891. He had come to Exeter in about 1835 when the city already had 14 practising architects. In 1891 it was recalled that 'few men were better known or more widely esteemed in the county than Mr Hayward. For many years he has been closely allied with church building and restoration in the city and county'. His lasting legacy in Exeter is the Royal Albert Memorial Museum. In 1876 the firm became Hayward & Son and later Hayward, Son & Tait (with Charles James Tait).[748] By 1845 Hayward had combined the building with 20 Cathedral Yard and advertised himself as being at both addresses.[749] Charles Cole, another architect, took occupancy in 1892, presumably renting an office, and continued there until his death in 1920. Cole, an alderman, was in his last years in partnership with Fred Jerman who carried on after Cole's death until just after the Second World War.[750]

The centrality of the building must have overcome its anonymous nature because there was a long sequence of other occupiers. Some, like the Central Auction & Estate Office used both 50 High Street and 20 Cathedral Yard[751] as did later the Society for Promoting Christian Knowledge.[752] There were also a number of accountants.[753] Peters & Hamlin, Importers, were occupiers from 1914 until 1922 when Walter Henry Hamlin, described as 'one of the best known figures in the city' and also as a wholesale grocer and provision merchant, died of gas poisoning in his office one December day.[754] The building was demolished in 1963 to make way for rebuilding in High Street.

206. This detail of Hedgeland's model of Exeter, shows St Martin's Island and the Cathedral Yard. Hedgeland constructed this model between 1817 and 1824 to record the city as it was during the late 1700s.

OCCUPANTS OF THE PROPERTY

1822 – 1838	**Sidney Hayne & Co.**, *Wholesale Linen Drapers*
1828	**John Wyatt**, *Accountant*
1839 – 1876	**John Hayward**, *Architect*
1876 – 1888	**Hayward & Son**, *Architects*
1888 – 1891	**Hayward, Son & Tait**, *Architects*
1892	**Central Auction & Estate Office**
1892 – 1920	**Charles Cole**, *Architect and Surveyor*
1906 – 1939	**Society for the Promotion of Christian Knowledge**
1909 – 1955	**Ware, Hellyer & Company** (later Ware, Ward & Co), *Accountants*
1914 – 1922	**Peters & Hamlin**, *Importers*
1919 – 1947	**Frederick Jerman**, *Architect & Surveyor*
1923	**William Brand**, *Liquidator*
1923 – 1936	**E. T. Collins**, *Chartered Accountants*
1924 – 1925	**H. E. Cox & Company** *Auctioneers & Estate Agents*
1927	**C. M. S. Depot**
1939 – 1955	**Exeter Municipal Charities**
1963	**Demolition**

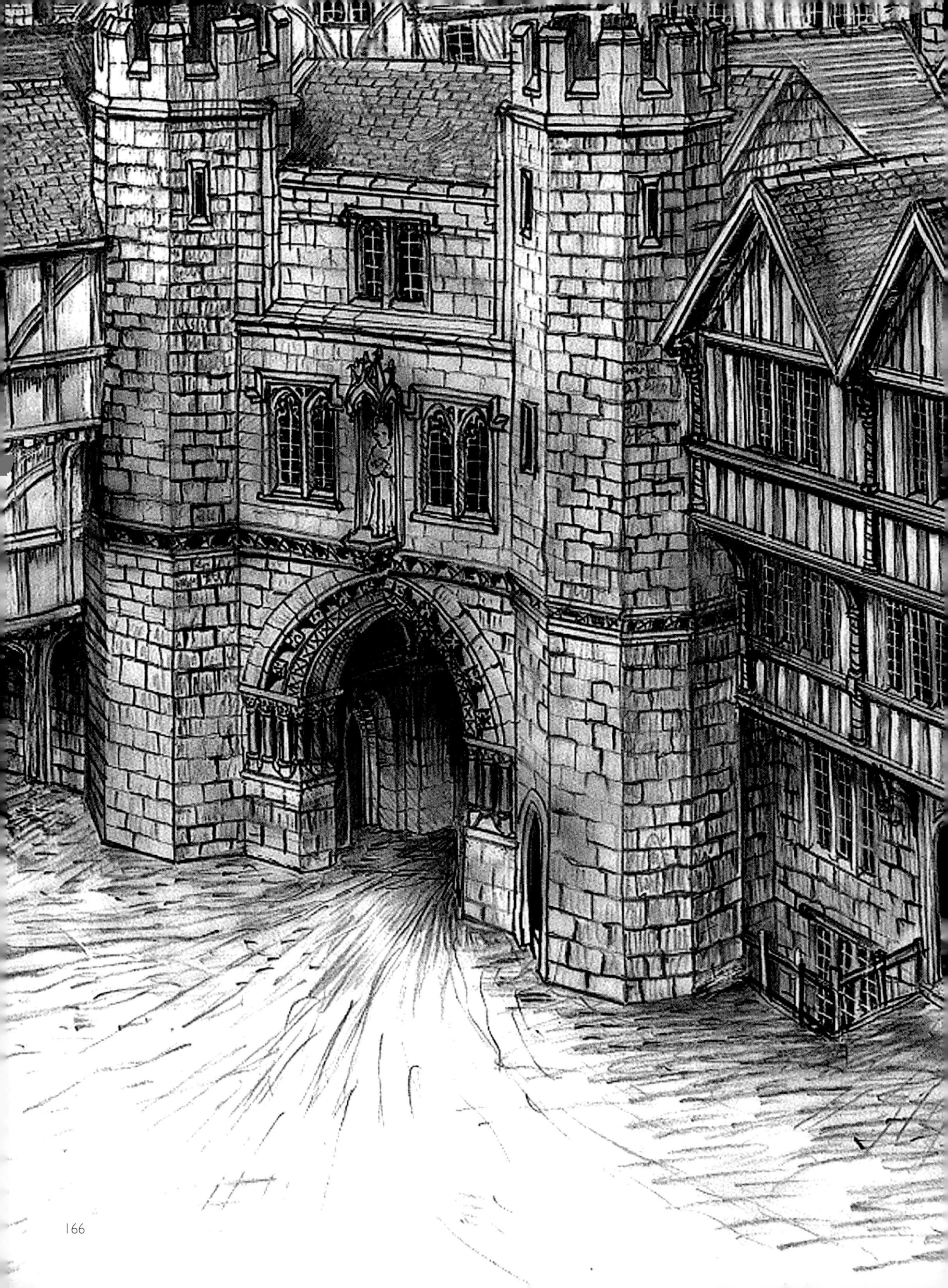

Conclusion

The fire of 28 October 2016 was the single most destructive incident in the centre of Exeter since the Blitz seventy-five years ago. Although there was no loss of life the event was nevertheless disturbing. A year later the scarred landscape is a continual reminder of what has been lost: two buildings were destroyed, another four were substantially damaged and a great number of adjoining properties were harmed.

Exeter's initial reaction was shock and a sense of loss. Almost immediately it was followed by a keen awareness of the fragility of ancient structures with a corresponding increasing interest in, and appreciation of, the city's remaining historic buildings.

This study has examined the development of the buildings in St Martin's Island. It has outlined the ownership role of various religious institutions, in particular the Dean & Chapter and the Vicars Choral, and has shown that after the Reformation buildings were rented in order to raise revenue. Examination of the occupiers has provided social context and revealed that particular trades dominated some buildings. For instance, 59 to 60 High Street and 24 Cathedral Yard have been involved in banking since the 1830s, 15 Cathedral Yard has been an inn (or hotel) for more than 250 years and apothecaries have occupied 41 High Street for some three hundred years. There were streets which were also considered more appropriate for selling particular commodities; Cathedral Yard and Close were preferred for retailing Devon lace than any other part of Exeter. In some instances the occupiers' abandonment of the buildings as dwellings has inadvertently led to the preservation of early fabric. 46 High Street, for example, has not been lived in for nearly 150 years and the last occupiers' Victorian wallpaper remains on the wall of an upstairs' room. Some of these upper floors are also no longer used for commercial purposes and this lack of use presents challenges for their preservation: buildings need to be usefully employed in order to more effectively receive continued maintenance and repair. Curiously, after many generations the movement away from residential use is in one instance being reversed: the upper

207. Drawing by Richard Parker of the Wilford Mansion, c1550.

St Martin's Island: An introductory history of forty-two Exeter buildings

208. A late medieval house in St Mary Arches parish, 1499.

floors of 55 & 56 High Street and 23 Cathedral Yard are currently being converted to domestic use.

Investigation of some Cathedral Yard buildings, such as the Royal Clarence Hotel and 2 Broadgate has chronicled the continual renovation, redevelopment and adaption over seven centuries. The consequence is that it requires specialist knowledge to unravel and decipher not just their complicated medieval origins but also the Roman history lurking beneath all the Island buildings. In contrast, the narrowness of some High Street frontages immediately suggests their building history: these long slender building sites restricted Exeter's early builders who often built structures which were one room in width and with a rear kitchen range separated by a short courtyard. The `irregularity' of this architecture was commended in the sixteenth and seventeenth centuries, dismissed by the Georgians and then applauded by the Victorians. They deserve to be treasured.

Some two thousand years of occupation can be gleaned through these buildings and the diversity of architecture hints at the architects' or owners' intentions at the time they were erected such as 1564 (a towering Elizabethan tradesman's home/shop), 1883 (Victorian Gothic in a nod to the cathedral), 1907 (a national pharmacy referencing Elizabethan architecture and harnessing an Exeter

209. The projected new front of the Royal Clarence Hotel, by Buttress Architects.

Conclusion

historic figure in order to appear local), 1912 (the solid & enduring granite façade of a bank), 1922 (a curious mix of styles including oriel bay windows which echo the city's `Golden Age' buildings) and 1965 (disregarding the past in favour of modernity).

The amount of internal decorative work at 41–42 High Street is a reminder of the keen prosperity of Exeter when it was called the London of the West. It is also a testament to how local workmen were working within a national style but with vernacular results. It suggests many other Island buildings were similarly decorated.

The Island's situation between the civic and ecclesiastical authorities has shaped and influenced the buildings' development. In 1286 Broadgate and Martin's Gate were erected along with a wall which separated the Close from the city. This wall was built behind the High Street properties in St Martin's parish and effectively divided the Island into two halves: for the following four centuries the cathedral authorities maintained this partitioning of the High Street buildings from the rest of the Island. Subsequent notable religious and political change came with the Reformation and the Civil War as secular use became the norm for the Island's buildings. Later the Victorian 5th of November celebrations in support of the Church of England (and against the bishop) gave Cathedral Yard a seasonal character unlike that of any other part of Exeter. Even so, the buildings facing the cathedral had in the rest of the year a quieter if not dignified character than those along the hectic High Street.

Lamb Alley and the New Exchange once offered pedestrians access between Cathedral Yard and High Street and a corresponding feature of some of these buildings has been providing alternative through access. The imminent closure of Waterstones (at 19 Cathedral Yard and 48–9 High Street) will close the last of these throughways.

This study has referred to the relatively small number of historic buildings left in the city centre because of German bombing during the Second World War and the devastation brought by development in the 1960s and 1970s. Even so, the parish of St Martin had no destruction in the Blitz. The twentieth-century losses were nearly all caused by developers; this included several Cathedral Yard buildings that were protected by law but were nevertheless demolished.

This study has also revived the memory of the twentieth-century advocacy role played by the city's foremost historian. In the 1960s Professor W. G. Hoskins was

210. 53 High Street, removed in the 1850s.

169

Conclusion

St Martin's Island: An introductory history of forty-two Exeter buildings

CATHEDRAL N.W. FROM THE AIR.

170

Conclusion

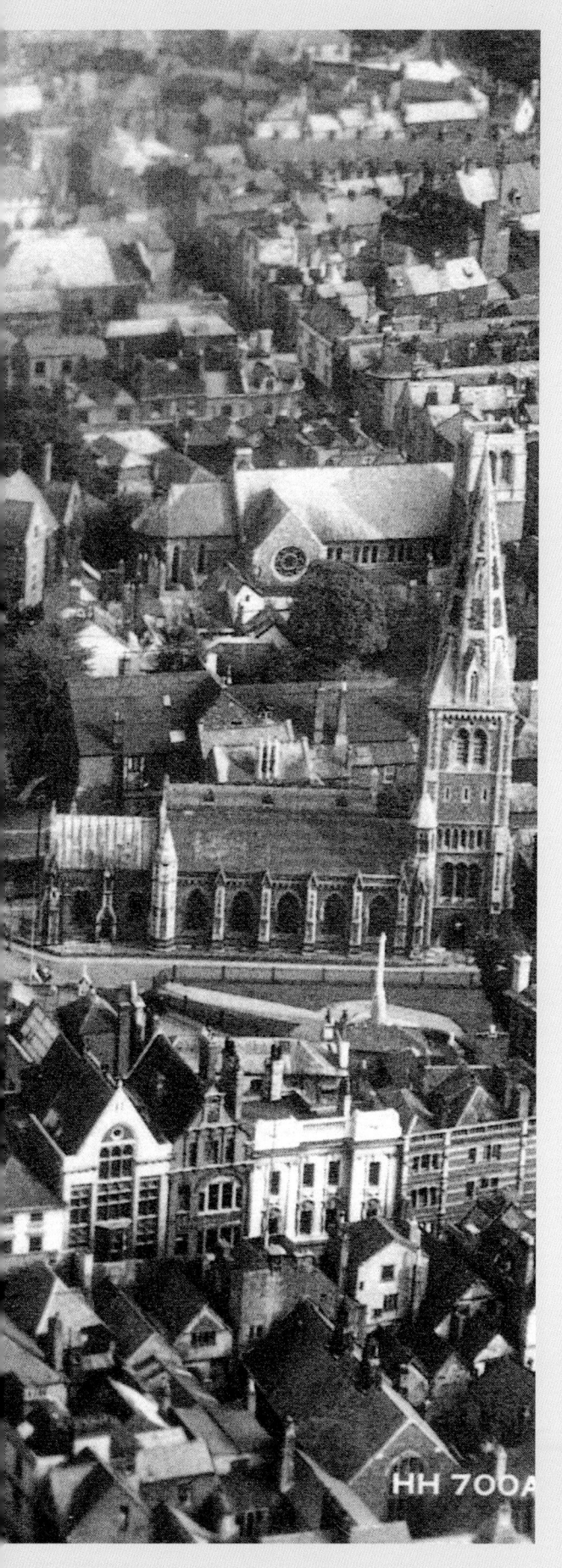

instrumental in highlighting the future of many historic buildings but this history has been unchronicled and increasingly forgotten. He was preceded by Ethel Lega-Weekes, one of Exeter's earliest champions of historic buildings. In the first decades of the new millennium the city faces another challenge in austerity. Exeter has recently seen a loss in the number of librarians, curators and archivists, the transfer of its archives and libraries into trusts, and the closure of the archaeological unit. The result is a diminishing of those employed to facilitate and disseminate research and knowledge to local societies and to the general public.

The most fortunate outcome of the fire was the saving of the High Street buildings immediately behind the hotel complex. Their survival has brought their historic importance to the attention of a wider public but the realisation of their worth has only been recognised because of the earlier painstaking work of a number of building archaeologists. The fire has revealed the lack of detailed work on other buildings of equal importance. Many remain poorly understood.

There is also the continuing need for society, and civic and business leaders in particular, to be mindful that historic buildings perform a key role in the city centre. The diversity of buildings in the main shopping precinct has created an attractive atmosphere that regional rivals cannot match. For instance, the retail centre of Plymouth was virtually cleared of its historic buildings during the Second World War and in the rebuilding afterwards. In contrast, those few parts of Exeter's city centre that have retained historic buildings are a visual delight. Its historic buildings do not impede commercial vitality but are a necessary component in it. They also contribute to creating a city environment that is enjoyable. The row of early High Street buildings are part of a diversity of building types and styles that cry out to be celebrated and recognised for the important part they play in enhancing the lives of Exonians on a daily basis.

The authors hope that readers will look afresh at these buildings if not become aware of them for the first time. Some may merely pause for reflection but others will hopefully view the frontages or even visit those interiors that are open to the public. The introductory histories have revealed in many instances the individual characters of buildings. These can enhance the enjoyment and appreciation of the buildings but the histories also offer a cautionary tale: Exeter has lost many historic buildings for a wide variety of reasons. Some of them were preventable. Hopefully this generation will learn from the mistakes of the 1960s and 1970s when too many historic buildings were needlessly destroyed. We could instead be remembered as the advocates and champions of the rich built heritage that remains across the city and for providing the inspiration for those that will follow us.

211. St Martin's Island, between 1923 and 1942.

Abbreviations

BL	British Library	EPG	*Exeter & Plymouth Gazette*
DAT	*Transactions of the Devonshire Association*	LMA	London Metropolitan Archive
DCNQ	*Devon & Cornwall Notes & Queries*	NDRO	North Devon Record Office
DCRS	Devon & Cornwall Record Society	*PDAS*	*Proceedings of the Devon Archaeological Society*
DEI	Devon & Exeter Institution	PWDRO	Plymouth & West Devon Record Office
DHC	Devon Heritage Centre	SHC	Somerset Heritage Centre
E&E	*Express & Echo*	TNA	The National Archives
ECLA	Exeter Cathedral Library & Archive	*WL*	*Western Luminary*
EFP	*Exeter Flying Post*	*WT*	*Western Times*

References

1. Email communication, 24 September 2017.
2. Email communication, 26 September 2017.
3. Email communication, 24 September 2017.
4. *EPG*, 10 Oct. 1881.
5. Richard Parker pointed out that these buildings nearly form the entirety of St Martin's parish while John Allan noted that they were an island of buildings in the city centre.
6. Richard Parker & John Allan, 'The Transformation of the Building Stock of Exeter, 1450–1700', 56 in John Allan, Nat Alcock and David Dawson (eds), *West Country Households, 1500–1700* (Martlesham, 2015).
7. The register is not fit for production but a transcription is in the DCRS library at the DHC.
8. DHC, 302A-99/PX1-2, church, poor & improvement rates, 1824–58.
9. ECLA, Dean & Chapter Schedule of Deeds and Documents handed over to the Ecclesiastical Commissioners in 1862. For some missing items see DHC, 6631, deeds series 75466-70. The U reference correlates with a map of the Close of 1810: ECLA (D&C4536/2/2).
10. Daniel & Samuel Lysons, *Magna Brittania: Volume 6 Devon* (1822), ccxix; I. FitzRoy Jones, 'Hippisley, Northleigh, Sparkes, Toller and Tothill Families', *DCNQ* (20), 1938-9, 134–5.
11. Joyce Youings (ed.), *Devon Monastic Lands: Calendar of Particulars for Grants, 1536–1558*, DCRS, NS 1 (1955), 55–6; Joyce Youings, 'The City of Exeter and the property of the dissolved monasteries', *DAT*, LXXXIV (1952), 141; Wallace T. MacCaffrey, *Exeter, 1540–1640* (Harvard, 1958), 224.
12. DHC, ECA/Mayor's Court Roll, 21–2 Elizabeth, m.19.
13. SHC, DD/HI/C/520 & 530.
14. Hugh Peskett, *Guide to the Parish and Non-Parochial Registers of Devon and Cornwall, 1538–1837*, DCRS, Extra Series II (1979), 141–7.
15. W. G. Hoskins (ed.), *Exeter In the Seventeenth Century*, DCRS, NS 2 (1957), 123.
16. *EPG*, 14 Oct. 1864.
17. ECLA, D&C3564 pages 186–7; D&C3567, pages 103–4; D&C3570 pages 372–3; D&C4573/2/1.
18. *WT*, 8 July 1864.
19. John Scott, Frank Mack and James Clarke, *Towers & Bells of Devon* (Exeter, 2007), 1, 3.
20. Mark Stoyle, 'Whole Streets converted to ashes: property destruction in Exeter during the English civil war', *Southern History*, 16 (1994), 67–84; Todd Gray, *Lost Exeter* (Exeter, 2002), xxiii.
21. Todd Gray, *Exeter: The Travellers' Tales* (Exeter, 2000), 29.
22. Gray, *Travellers' Tales*, 58.
23. *WT*, 13 May 1854. There is a second translation of this letter in Baretti, *A journey from London to Genoa* (1760), 'It is none of the finest, very ill paved, and very dirty, tho' it is summer. In winter it must be ten times worse. The houses are generally built in such style of architecture that Palladio would have hanged himself for vexation if he had seen them.'
24. Gray, *Travellers' Tales*, 74.
25. Gray, *Travellers' Tales*, 101; John Wood Warter, *Southey's Commonplace Book* (1849), II, 200, & *Southey's Commonplace Book* (1850), IV, 522–3.
26. Alexander Jenkins, *The History and Description of the City of Exeter and its Environs* (Exeter, 1806), v, 213.
27. Robert Newton, *Eighteenth-Century Exeter* (Exeter, 1984), 127–8.
28. Thomas Shapter, *The History of the Cholera in Exeter in 1832* (Exeter, 1849) 10.
29. Gray, *Lost Exeter*, xxvi–xxvii.
30. Shapter, *Cholera*, 223, 216.
31. John Cooke, *A Pamphlet Called Old England Forever* (Exeter, 1819), 28.
32. Gray, *Travellers' Tales*, 129.
33. Charles Knight, *Knight's Excursion Companion, Exeter and the south east of Devon* (c1851), 5 & 8.
34. Thomas H. Mawson & Sons, *Exeter of the Future: A Policy of Improvement within a period of 100 years* (1914), 25–8; *EPG*, 24 March 1914; *WT*, 25 July 1914; *WMN*, 14 March 1914.
35. *EFP*, 3 April 1915.
36. Gray, *Lost Exeter*, xvii; *WT*, 16 July 1914.
37. *EPG*, 31 Dec. 1914; *WT*, 30 Dec. 1914.
38. *EPG*, 8 Feb. 1911; *WT*, 20 Nov. 1913 & 26 Feb. 1915
39. The collection is held by the DHC.
40. Todd Gray, *Exeter Engraved* (Exeter, 2000), 1, 65; Todd Gray, *Lost Exeter* (Exeter, 2003), 94.
41. Gray, *Travellers' Tales*, 172.
42. Gray, *Travellers' Tales*, 183.
43. Todd Gray, *Exeter In the 1940s* (Exeter, 2004), 126.
44. Thomas Sharp, *Exeter Phoenix* (1946), 87–9; John Pendlebury, 'Planning the Historic City: Reconstruction Plans in the United Kingdom in the 1940s', *The Town Planning Review* 74, no. 4 (2003): 382. http://0-www.jstor.org.lib.exeter.ac.uk/stable/40112577.
45. Sharp, *Exeter Phoenix*, 94–6.
46. W. G. Hoskins, *Two Thousand Years in Exeter* (Exeter, 1960), 133.
47. *E&E*, 17 March 1961; Matthew H. Johnson, 'Making a Home: English Culture and English Landscape', 123, in Jonathan Bate, *The Public Value of the Humanities* (2011); Matthew Johnson, *Ideas of Landscape* (Oxford, 2007), 46; Joan Thirsk, 'Hoskins, William George (1908–1992)', *Oxford Dictionary of National Biography*, Oxford, 2004; online edn, Oct 2008 [http://0-www.oxforddnb.com.lib.exeter.ac.uk/view/article/38631, accessed 12 July 2017]
48. We are grateful to Dr Robert Peberdy for sharing his research from his forthcoming biography of W. G. Hoskins.
49. W. G. Hoskins, *Old Devon* (1966), xiii.
50. Roy Millward, 'William George Hoskins, landscape historian (1908–1992)', *Landscape History* (1992), Vol. 14, Issue 1, 65–70.
51. DHC, 4318G, file marked Guildhall Plan.
52. John R. L. Thorp, 'The construction, appearance and regional context of a merchant's town house, c1500–1740: 38 North Street, Exeter', *PDAS* (2012), No. 70, 147.
53. C. G. Henderson, 'The City of Exeter from AD 50 to the early nineteenth century', in Roger Kain & William Ravenhill (eds), *Historical Atlas of South-West England* (Exeter, 1999), 486; J. P. Allan, C. G. Henderson & R. A. Higham, 'Saxon Exeter', in Jeremy Haslam (ed.), *Anglo-Saxon Towns in Southern England* (Chichester, 1984), 385–414; Hoskins, *Two Thousand Years*, 9–10.
54. DHC, ED/M/48.
55. SHC, DD/HI/C/478.
56. *The Gentleman's Magazine*, Vol. 165, March 1839, 330; *NDJ*, 17 Feb. 1839; *EPG*, 1 Oct. 1913; *Exeter Itinerary & General Directory* (Exeter, 1828), 176; DHC, Robert Dymond Scrapbook, letter of Charles Hedgeland to Robert Dymond, 23 Dec. 1872.
57. ECLA, D&C3569, page 409.
58. SHC, DD/HI/C/480.
59. ECLA, D&C 3530.
60. *EPG*, 1 Oct. 1853.
61. ECL&A, VC21656. In 1660 a building plot in Holy Trinity parish was described as a drang: SHC, HI/C/481. Another drang was at Heavitree by Portman Place: *WT*, 7 Jan. 1868.
62. Derek Portman, *Exeter Houses* (Exeter, 1966), 3–22; Todd Gray, *Strumpets & Ninnycocks* (Exeter, 2016), 30.
63. Portman, *Exeter Houses*, 24–9.
64. Margery Rowe (ed.), *Tudor Exeter*, DCRS, NS 22 (1977), 9.
65. *Heritage Statement*, 7.
66. John Cooke, *A Pamphlet Called Old England Forever* (Exeter, 1819), 26–7.
67. *EFP*, 31 Jan. 1805.
68. *EPG*, 26 June & 28 August 1874.
69. ECLA, D&C3564, pages 2–3; City of Westminster Archives, 36/55; William Toone, *The Chronological Historian* (1826), II, 36.
70. Hoskins, *Exeter In the Seventeenth Century*, 123.
71. DHC, CC181A. There were 163 communicants and there would have been the same number of children.
72. *WT*, 20 April 1881.
73. DHC, Voters' Lists, 1972 & 1973. The last residents in parish who were not domiciled at the hotel were the caretaker and his family at Number 60 in the second floor flat.
74. Derived from the census returns for the parish.
75. W. G. Hoskins, *Devon* (Newton Abbot, 1954), 531–2.
76. Derived from the census returns for the parish.
77. *Kelly's Directory of Exeter* (1902); DHC, ECA, Rate Book, 1900; 1901 Census.
78. Judy Egerton, 'Carr, William Holwell (1758–1830)', *Oxford Dictionary of National Biography* (Oxford, 2004) [http://0-www.oxforddnb.com.lib.exeter.ac.uk/view/article/4757, accessed 12 July 2017]
79. *EPG*, 16 March 1877; *EFP*, 24 April 1817; David Lemmings, 'King, Peter, first Baron King (1669–1734)', *Oxford Dictionary of National Biography*, Oxford, 2004; online edn, Jan 2008 [http://0-www.oxforddnb.com.lib.exeter.ac.uk/view/article/15582, accessed 19 July 2017];

John Campbell, *The Lives of the Chancellors and Keepers of the Great Seal of England* (1846), IV, 567; Mark Knights, 'Peter King', D. Hayton, E. Cruckshanks & S. Handley, *The History of Parliament: the House of Commons, 1690–1715* (2002).

80 It is curious that another luminary, Sir Robert Gifford, later first Baron Gifford of St Leonards, is also thought to have been born in this same High Street building. His father, a linen draper and hop merchant, occupied it a century later: *EFP*, 15 May 1817; J. M. Rigg, 'Gifford, Robert, first Baron Gifford (1779–1826)', rev. Hugh Mooney, *Oxford Dictionary of National Biography*, Oxford, 2004 [http://0-www.oxforddnb.com.lib.exeter.ac.uk/view/article/10667, accessed 19 July 2017].; Winifred Stokes & R. G. Thorne, 'Robert Gifford', R. Thorne (ed.), *The History of Parliament: the House of Commons, 1790–1820* (1986).

81 Ian Maxted, 'Brice, Andrew (1692–1773)', *Oxford Dictionary of National Biography*, Oxford, 2004 [http://0-www.oxforddnb.com.lib.exeter.ac.uk/view/article/3379, accessed 20 July 2017].

82 Elizabeth Baigent, 'Veitch family (per. 1768–1929)', *Oxford Dictionary of National Biography*, Oxford, 2004; online edn, May 2010 [http://0-www.oxforddnb.com.lib.exeter.ac.uk/view/article/61986, accessed 20 July 2017].

83 Gray, *Travellers' Tales*, 169.

84 Gray, *Travellers' Tales*, 169.

85 Todd Gray, *The Art of the Devon Garden* (2013), 326–7; S. Heriz-Smith, 'The Veitch Nurseries of Killerton and Exeter, c1780 to 1863: Part I', *Garden History*, 16, No. 1 (Spring, 1988), 41–57.

86 http://demolition-exeter.blogspot.co.uk/2011/07/dellers-cafe-bedford-street.html, accessed 5 July 2017; *WT*, 3 Oct. 1917; *EPG*, 22 Feb. 1932 & 10 Feb. 1933. The business was sold to Cadena Cafes Ltd in 1933 upon Lambhead's death.

87 James G. Nelson, 'Mathews, (Charles) Elkin (1851–1921)', *Oxford Dictionary of National Biography*, Oxford, 2004 [http://0-www.oxforddnb.com.lib.exeter.ac.uk/view/article/53207, accessed 8 July 2017]

88 Jenkins, *Exeter*, 176–7.

89 *EPG*, 3 Sept. 1836.

90 *EPG*, 20 May 1837.

91 *EFP*, 10 & 17 Nov. 1853; *WT*, 12 Nov. 1853.

92 *EPG*, 13 March 1876.

93 *WT*, 10 Oct. 1881.

94 *WT*, 10 May 1882.

95 *EFP*, 27 Feb. 1884.

96 Gray, *Travellers' Tales*, 2, 9, 20, 29, 38, 42, 58, 129.

97 DEI, Tracts 168.13, pages 6–7 & 9.

98 DHC, Voters' Lists.

99 T. J. Joce, 'Exeter Roads and Streets', *DAT*, LXXV (1943), 133; *EFP*, 15 & 22 March 1913.

100 BL, Add. Ch. 55246. See also DHC, DD 50101-5103, copies of documents at King's College, which detail an agreement by the prior of St James with John and Peter Soyth of a grant of 20s from the yearly rent of Number 39; King's College Archive, KCAR/6/18/1/6 & KCAR/3/1/1/8/40. We are grateful to Peter Monteith for examining these records for us.

101 DHC, ECA, Mayor's Court Roll, 45–6 Edward III. m.35.

102 DHC, 50198; W. G. Hoskins, 'Mol's Coffee House', *DCNQ*, Vol. XXI (1941), 25.

103 DHC, DD50233 & DD50169.

104 King's College Archive.

105 LMA, MS11936/358/552645.

106 DHC, DD50171, DD50182, DD50187, DD50190, DD50235, DD50241; TNA, PROB 11/213/340, will of Jane Acland, widow of St Martin's parish, 1650. James was her second son.

107 DHC, DD50294 &DD50296; Chanter, 'Goldsmiths', 766 & 476–8. The guild recorded four of his marks from 1719 to 1722. Mathew Skinner, another warden, acted as the guild's assay master from 1757 to 1773.

108 *EFP*, 13 Nov. 1800 & 19 March 1801. He remained there until 1850: *EFP*, 12 Sept. 1850; Chanter, 'Goldsmiths', 468–70; DHC, 50307.

109 *EFP*, 16 Oct. 1800. He moved from North Street.

110 DHC, DD50278 & DD50258.

111 *EFP*, 17 May 1821.

112 *EFP*, 13 Oct. 1808, 2 May 1822 & 11 Jan. 1827.

113 *EPG*, 21 Feb., 2 May, 16 May & 4 July 1829.

114 *EPG*, 22 May 1830; *WT*, 21 May 1831; *The Alfred*, 16 May 1831.

115 *EPG*, 11 Dec. 1830; *WT*, 29 August, 1829, 15 June 1833 & 2 June 1838.

116 *EPG*, 2 March 1833.

117 Gray, *Lost Exeter*, 60–61; *Exeter Directory for 1835* (Exeter, 1835), 39.

118 *WT*, 21 Feb. 1835 & 4 Feb. 1853; *EFP*, 2 March 1843; TNA, PROB 11/1976/179. Her will titled her a 'spinster bookseller and stationer'.

119 *EFP*, 18 July 1833.

120 *EFP*, 14 Nov. 1860; *EPG*, 4 June 1853 & 23 June 1855; *EPG*, 12 & 26 May 1855; *EFP*, 18 Nov. 1858. James Fitze died at the age of 69 at 28 High Street on 12 August 1861: *EPG*, 16 August 1861.

121 *EPG*, 1 Sept. 1855; *WT*, 17 July 1858; *EPG*, 24 July 1868.

122 *WT*, 6 July 1866 & 16 July 1867.

123 *EFP*, 24 Dec. 1862; *WT*, 2 Jan. 1863, 5 Jan. 1877 & 2 April 1887.

124 *EFP*, 5 April 1890.

125 *EPG*, 29 March & 18 Sept. 1897; *WT*, 24 Dec. 1909.

126 *EPG*, 25 Nov. 1902 & 23 Dec. 1910.

127 *WT*, 16 Nov. 1861; *EPG*, 1 May 1908.

128 *E&E*, 8 March 1939. In 1939 a disagreement over the purchase of the building led to a legal dispute: *E&E*, 20 Jan. 1939.

129 *E&E*, 30 May 1939.

130 *EPG*, 14 Nov. 1918.

131 Portman, *Exeter Houses*, 76.

132 DHC, DD50102-3.

133 DHC, ECA, ED/FC/2. The grant noted King's College owned the property to the east and the City of Exeter on the west.

134 DHC, 74/3/297; He may have taken on Thomas Butter's shop when he married Mrs Butter: http://bookhistory.blogspot.fr/2014/07/devon-book-trades-exeter-b.html, accessed 25 September 2017; TNA, PROB 11/886/179. In his will of 1763 Pring referred to holding 'those two sixth parts or two in six parts of and in two messuages or dwelling houses situate lying and being in the High Street of the said city of Exeter now or lately in the several possessions of Edward Addecot, apothecary, and John Brutton, haberdasher of hats, being other parts of the lands or freehold tenements which I lately purchased of the said Mary Bayley and Gideon Haydon and his mother or of some or one of them'. In his will he called himself a gentleman and an advertisement his address was given as being in a 'handsome new brick built house' in St Peter's Church Yard. This was probably his dwelling house owned by the Dean & Chapter which he noted in his will was in the parish of St Petrock: DHC, FOR/Z/1/1; DHC, 74/3/313a-b.

135 *EFP*, 16 Sept. & 14 Oct. 1802.

136 *EFP*, 17 March 1803; *EPG*, 1 May 1830 & 15 August 1835.

137 *EPG*, 25 Dec. 1841; *EFP*, 29 Sept. 1842.

138 *WT*, 10 August 1844.

139 DHC, 74/3/310-311.

140 *EFP*, 3 Nov. 1859.

141 *WT*, 21 April 1866.

142 James Crocker, *Sketches of Old Exeter with letter press* (Exeter, 1886), Plate XXIII.

143 *E&E*, 3 Dec. 1969.

144 J. B. Bedford & J. P. Salvatore, *Excavations at 41–2 High Street (Star Jeans) Exeter, 1980, Part 1: Roman Military* (Exeter Museums Archaeological Field Unit Report No. 93.07), 2; John R. L. Thorp, 'The Interior Decoration of an Elizabethan Merchant's House: the Evidence from 41–2 High Street, Exeter', in John Allan, Nat Alcock and David Dawson (eds), *West Country Households, 1500–1700* (Martlesham, 2015), 141–53.

145 Thorp, 'Interior Decoration', 141–52.

146 ECLA, D&C 4030 & Chapter Act Book D&C 3562 p.285

147 His widow Jane relinquished the lease the following year to Samuel and Grace Sampson. Sampson had been Hooper's apprentice: ECLA, D&C3562, pages 330–1; A. J. P. S., 'Booksellers and Printers in Devon & Cornwall', *DCNQ* (1918–1919), X, 31.

148 ECLA, D&C 4573/1/7. We are grateful to Tony Collings for sharing his transcription of this document.

149 Sampson died in 1706 and directed in his will that Number 41, as well as other Exeter property, should eventually pass to his son Samuel: TNA, PROB 11/496/16. One of his executors was Daniel Slade, his neighbour at 39 High Street. Grace Sampson was buried on 1 Oct. 1754: DHC, DCRS ts of St Martin parish register. The building continued to be leased by Sampson family members: Sampson was there in 1708 and with a business partner in 1715. ECLA, D&C3565, page 411 & 3566, page 203.

150 DHC, P&D07673. 'Notes by E. L-W. 25 June 1926. At Messrs Hinton Lake's, 41 High Street, Exeter. Remains of old fireplace (?15th cent.) in east wall of first floor, front room. The oak beam forming the lintel of the fireplace has been sawn through and the greater part of the length removed, probably in the 18th century. This room is said to have been re-fitted about 1742. To which period apparently, belongs, the panelling of cupboard-doors reaching up to dado height, each door having a single panel, raised, with chamfered edges. Above dado-height canvas (or sacking-barras) is stretched, on which many layers of papering have been pasted. In a part of this east wall, a finer quality of canvas has been exposed to view, on which there are traces of painting (in oil colours) of floral designs - green leaves and

References

red flowers. The date 1742 agrees with the style of another fireplace, set obliquely across the s.w. corner of the room. rather tall and narrow with very narrow shelf, and with sparse ornament in relief resembling in style the ornamentation of Wedgewood ware. The small cupboard on the right of the older fireplace may be contemporary with it. One can discern (or imagine!) traces of a stopped up round opening (about 5" diam.) on the left side of this cupboard. but there is no mark of any hole or opening in the solid stone side of the fireplace recess. This side of the fireplace is all in one with the moulded jamb. The stone seems to be granite. The foot of the jamb cannot be seen owing to obstructing woodwork. it seems to have reached below the present (raised) floor-level.'

151 Grace Bastone, a widow, had the lease: in 1770 the Chapter granted two leases in 'Late Sampson's and Part of Late King's Tenement'. The latter was part of the rear property previously leased to Jerome King. The fine was 60 guineas but reduced by 10 on condition that Mrs Bastone produced an account to show the value: ECLA, D&C3570, pages 493–4.

152 He died in Exmouth at the age of 66 in 1793: ECLA, D&C3570, pages 372–3; D&C3573, pages 214–215 & 411–412; *The Gentleman's Magazine*, Vol. 63 (1793), 377. In 1780 Holwell had the lease of another tenement previously been possessed by Richard Eastway and John Law. These two were he surrendered in 1780 along with Number 42: ECLA, D&C3572, page 243 & D&C 6007/20/22. In 1773 he was noted as an apothecary: PWDRO, 1302/359.

153 ECLA, D&C3573, page 411.

154 LMA, MS11936/369/571834.

155 ECLA, D&C3573, pages 391–2 & D&C3579, pages 355–6.

156 A. P. Oppe, 'John White Abbot of Exeter (1763–1851)', *The Volume of the Walpole Society*, Vol. 13, (1924–5), 67–9; James Greig (ed.), *The Farington Diary* (1926), VI, 168 & 177.

157 TNA, PROB 11/1705/8.

158 *EFP*, 20 Jan. 1825; *Exeter Itinerary & General Directory* (Exeter, 1828), 128 & 203.

159 *EPG*, 2 Feb. 1833. In 1829 Walter Tucker advertised he had no connection with a bankrupt business with nearly the same name: *EPG*, 27 June 1829. He was listed in the *Exeter Pocket Journal* of 1827 as a boot and shoemaker in High Street.

160 ECLA, D&C 6007/20/24 & D&C 4017. Maunder died in 1837 'at his house in High Street' at the age of 83: *EFP*, 24 August 1837; *Exeter Pocket Journal*, 1830.

161 *WT*, 12 Jan. 1828.

162 *EPG*, 19 July 1828.

163 *Exeter Itinerary & General Directory* (Exeter, 1828), 129–30.

164 *EPG*, 6 & 19 Oct. 1833, 9 May 1835.

165 *WT*, 16 July & 12 Nov. 1836; *Exeter Directory* (1835), 53.

166 *Exeter Directory* (1835), 71; *EPG*, 23 July 1836, 28 Jan. 1837, 11 Nov. 1837.

167 *EFP*, 30 April 1862.

168 *WT*, 29 March 1862 & *EPG*, 20 Nov. 1863, 15 & 29 May 1868.

169 *WT*, 24 July 1868; *EFP*, 15 July 1874.

170 Crocker, *Sketches of Old Exeter with letter press*, Plate XXIII.

171 In 1991 the building, along with Number 42, were sold for two million pounds: *E&E*, 30 Oct. 1991.

172 The entry in the 1676 rental reads 'Mr Philip Hooper for Mr Portbury's house' and this enables the property to be identified in the Hearth Taxes of that decade, in which Edward Portbury paid on five hearths. He was described as a bookseller when he became a freeman in 1669; ECLA, D&C 4573/1/7. Charles Yeo noted in his will of 1707 that he held a moiety in his dwelling house: TNA, PROB 11/496/235.

173 ECLA, D&C 4573/1/7. We are grateful to Tony Collings for providing his transcription.

174 ECLA, 6007/20/24.

175 *EFP*, 26 Nov. 1807.

176 *EFP*, 7 April & 27 Oct. 1814, 25 July & 8 August 1816. His widow continued the business.

177 *EFP*, 8 Dec. 1814, 18 Jan. 1816.

178 *EFP*, 17 Sept. 1818, 4 Feb. 1819 & 17 Feb. 1820. In 1817 she had been at 36 High Street: *EFP*, 15 May 1817.

179 *EFP*, 11 Jan. 1817.

180 *EPG*, 28 March 1840; *EFP*, 25 July 1844.

181 *EPG*, 11 May 1839, 29 Feb. & 11 April 1840; *WT*, 4 July 1840. In 1844 Elizabeth Bailey was listed at 42 High Street in *Pigot's Directory* as a milliner and dressmaker.

182 *WT*, 28 Oct. 1843 & 18 Jan. 1845.

183 *WT*, 22 March & 21 June 1845, 20 June 1840; *EFP*, 13 June 1850.

184 *EPG*, 19 Nov. 1853.

185 *EPG*, 17 Jan. 1852 & 8 Oct. 1853.

186 *WT*, 8 Oct. 1853.

187 *EFP*, 5 Oct. 1854; *WT*, 30 Sept. 1854 & 2 Oct. 1863. She was later in premises at Broadgate and at 25 Cathedral Yard

188 *WT*, 10 Feb. 1855; *EPG*, 11 Oct. 1878.

189 *EPG*, 15 Jan. & 28 Sept. 1886.

190 *WT*, 3 Sept. 1890, 8 Jan. 1891 & 11 Jan. 1898.

191 *WT*, 1 April 1898 & 26 Feb. 1900.

192 *EPG*, 27 April 1900.

193 *WT*, 28 Nov. 1904; *EPG*, 27 June 1908.

194 Allan & Parker, 'Building Stock', 56.

195 *Brice's Weekly Journal*, no. 23, 18 Nov. 1726 & no. 33, 27 Jan. 1727. His stock was sold in Nov. 1726; ECLA, 6007/20/11.

196 *WL*, 7 June 1814; *EFP*, 4 August 1808, 6 April & 4 May 1815. DHC, DCRS Library, ts of St Martin's parish register. Cramp was buried on 6 April 1815. He was 44.

197 *EFP*, 29 Nov. 1838; *WT*, 1 July 1843.

198 *WT*, 12 August 1843.

199 *EFP*, 15 Feb. 1844.

200 *EPG*, 17 August 1844; *WT*, 4 Jan. 1845.

201 *WT*, 22 March 1845, 6 Feb. & 27 Nov. 1847.

202 *EPG*, 19 Feb. 1848; *WT*, 12 May 1855.

203 *EFP*, 12 June 1856; *EPG*, 30 Oct. 1874, 18 Oct. 1904, 12 Dec. 1930, 29 July 1932.

204 *EPG*, 24 Feb., 14 July 1933 & 22 Dec. 1931.

205 Allan & Parker, 'Building Stock', 39–43, 56.

206 ECLA, VC/5/122858; *EPG*, 13 May 1843; *WT*, 6 June 1901.

207 *EFP*, 21 Sept. 1809 & 4 August 1808.

208 *EFP*, 14 Dec. 1809 & 11 Jan. 1810.

209 *EFP*, 9 June & 15 Sept. 1814, 6 April 1815 & 5 Feb. 1818.

210 *EFP*, 20 July 1815. See also 31 Oct. 1816.

211 *EFP*, 24 June & 9 Dec. 1824; *The Alfred*, 23 July & 27 August 1822; In 1822 Chaplin was at 3 Castle Street and advertised himself as an auctioneer and appraiser: *The Alfred*, 12 Feb. 1822.

212 *EFP*, 10 March 1825 & 23 June 1825.

213 *EFP*, 9 Feb. & 2 March 1826; *WT*, 8 Jan. 1831, 21 Dec. 1833 & 9 June 1863; *EPG*, 27 June 1829.

214 *WT*, 20 Sept. 1867.

215 Edwin Lancey, ironmonger, moved from 23 High Street and advertised that his new shop would have 'an entirely new stock of furnishing ironmongery goods'. In 1880 Lancey & Company stopped trading and the building was offered for rent: *WT*, 9 April, 30 April & 18 June 1869 & 8 April 1873; *EPG*, 25 Oct. 1878. See also *WT*, 27 May 1879 & *EPG*, 30 March 1880.

216 In 1881 the building's name was retained by J. T. Cowey when he reopened selling his men's and boys' clothing: *WT*, 8 Nov. 1881 & 30 Oct. 1883. They continued until 1887 when the partnership was dissolved. Their goods were still on sale in 1888: *WT*, 21 Jan. 1887 & 22 June 1888.

217 Frederick William Haydon occupied the property in 1889 but went bankrupt and was out of business in two years: *EFP*, 5 July 1889; *EPG*, 3 Nov. 1891.

218 William Pollard & Company was an occupier on a temporary basis in 1892: *EPG*, 2 April 1892.

219 In Jan. 1893 Miss S. J. Knowling drapery occupied the building. She had moved from 265 High Street and in 1911 moved once more to 17 Dix's Field: *EFP*, 21 Jan. 1893 & 21 Feb. 1911.

220 *EPG*, 22 Dec. 1931.

221 *EPG*, 24 Feb. & 14 July 1933.

222 Portman, *Exeter Houses*, 77–8; Allan & Parker, 'Building Stock', 56.

223 Tony Collings, Aspects of the History of St Martin's Parish, 1660–1850 (University of Exeter certificate in local & regional history dissertation, 1990), 11–12.

224 ECLA, 6007/20/2-6.

225 By Feb. 1854 Frederick Wood sold his whip and fishing tackle at Number 45 but within a year had left. He was declared insolvent and described as a 'journeyman fishing rod and whip maker, and grocer and general shop keeper': *EPG*, 30 June & 4 August 1855.

226 The London Photographic Company occupied from 1857 until 1859 or 1860. In 1861 the Plymouth firm Groom & Company were in the building and later that year J. Frederick Long, artist and photographer, was the next tenant. An individual with the same name, possibly a son, also called an artist and photographer, died in 1864, aged 25, in Torquay. Long's business continued until Sept. 1897 when his business was for sale: *EFP*, 14 May 1857; *WMN*, 6 April 1861; *WT*, 25 May 1861; *EPG*, 26 Feb. 1864 & 10 Sept. 1897. Two examples of his work survive: TNA, COPY 1/8/184 & COPY 1/376/281.

227 In 1806 the building was occupied by J. Jenkins, Draper, who was there until 1813. By April 1814 he had moved to 70 High Street: *EFP*, 5 & 12 June 1806, 7 Oct. 1813, 21 April 1814.

228 By May 1814 F. & E. Snell were selling millinery at 45 High Street and in 1819 they advertised their move to No. 220: *WL*, 24 May 1814; *EFP*, 1 Dec. 1814 & 18 March 1819.

229 *EFP*, 30 Sept. 1819. J. D. Sheppard was the occupier by July 1821 although in 1822 he announced he was selling off his 'elegant and

175

fashionable stock of haberdashery, drapery, etc…' for ready money': *EFP*, 12 July 1821 & 2 May 1822. He was at 183 High Street in 1819: *EFP*, 29 July 1819.

230 In July 1829 Elias Butland, who sold haberdashery, moved from 45 to 46 High Street. His reason was 'many of his friends from the country are at a loss to find him, the original shop having been so long closed': *EPG*, 25 July 1829; By Oct. 1829 D. Westaway & Son relocated from premises in St Thomas. The firm was there until Michaelmas 1834 when it moved to Mr Kemp's house in Cathedral Yard: *EPG*, 24 Oct. 1829 & 6 Sept. 1834.

231 R. Hillier took over Sheppard's business and opened The Silk Mercery, Urling, Thread Lace & Glove Warehouse in spring 1823 but by 1825 had moved to 244 High Street: *EFP*, 24 April 1823 & 24 Nov. 1825.

232 In 1834 Mrs Eliza Mayne sold her London Straw Hat Warehouse at 189 Fore Street and moved to 45 High Street with her 'millinery, dress and straw hat' business along with her husband Robert, an accountant. Mrs Mayne continued through to 1850. The family was still there in Oct. when their eldest son died at the age of 21. Days later a second son died: *EPG*, 17 May & 9 Oct. 1834, 5 March 1836 & 27 July 1850; *WT*, 27 Dec. 1845; *EFP*, 17 Oct. 1850; *EPG*, 19 Oct. 1850; LMA, MS 11936/549/1219430.

233 In July 1850 George Haines, haberdasher, advertised his millinery goods were for sale at the Millinery Rooms. Unfortunately only two years later, in July 1852, he was no longer in business and the building was let once again: *EPG*, 10 July 1852, *WT*, 11 Oct. 1851; Within two months Samuel B. Watts, Hat & Cap Manufacturer, was the occupier. He also sold other clothing: *EPG*, 25 Sept. & 30 Oct. 1852.

234 He was there from 1855 to 1856. By 1857 he had moved to 186 Fore Street: *EPG*, 29 Dec. 1855; *EFP*, 9 Feb. 1854 & 5 Feb. 1857; *EPG*, 8 March & 8 Nov. 1856.

235 Robert Henry Baker sold hats, shirts and ties at Number 45 from 1899 until 1909 when he closed his business. *EPG*, 17 June 1909; *EFP*, 27 May 1899; *WT*, 18 Feb. 1919.

236 *WT*, 30 August 1946.

237 *WMN*, 5 August 2004; ECA/21/5, 4 June 1946.

238 Alison Arnold and Robert Howard, *46 High Street, Exeter, Devon; Tree-Ring Analysis of Timbers* (English Heritage Research Department Report Series no.71-2009), ii.

239 G. M. Young, 'Archaeological recording during repair works to 46 High Street, Exeter', Exeter Archaeology, Report No. 09.127, project no. 6770, November 2009; Allan & Parker, 'Building Stock', 56.

240 DHC, 54/13/1/9.

241 DHC, 54/13/1/9.

242 *EFP*, 16 Jan. 1800. He married Miss Boutcher in 1802 and moved to her brother's old shop near St Stephen's church in August 1804. He died the following year: *EFP*, 21 Jan. 1802, 2 August 1804, 3 Oct. 1805.

243 *EFP*, 22 May 1806, 17 August & 26 Oct. 1809.

244 *EFP*, 5 August 1819 & 18 May 1820.

245 *EPG*, 21 March 1829 & 27 March 1830.

246 On 25 Feb. 1811 William Coplestone, a linen draper, opened his shop at 46 & 47 High Street: *EFP*, 7 Feb. 1811; In 1813 M. Comerford resold books and prints he had bought in London. He was at 51 High Street in 1820 but moved in 1821: *WL*, 17 August 1813; *EFP*, 3 August 1820; *The Alfred*, 27 Feb. 1821; By May 1814 William Maunder, junior, a woollen draper and mercer, was the occupant of 46 High Street. Amongst the goods he sold were bombazets and bombazeens. In Nov. 1818 Maunder advertised that he was selling his stock of clothing and that his building would be subsequently either sold or offered for rent. By April 1819 he had sold out to John Madgwick Wilcocks of 216 High Street: *EFP*, 19 May 1814, 5 & 19 Nov. 1818; *WL*, 17 May 1814; *EFP*, 15 April 1819. In 1830 Butland announced his removal from 45 High Street, which shop had been 'so long closed', to No. 46. He had also purchased the stock of the Misses Tapley. In 1838 an auction notice advertised the sale of Mr Butland's premises at 47 High Street. In March 1840 he moved to 212 High Street: *EPG*, 25 July 1829; *WT*, 9 June 1838; *Exeter Pocket Journal* (1841), page 51. Butland died in 1858: *EFP*, 3 June 1858. By Feb. 1840 he had purchased the lease of 212 High Street: *WT*, 22 Feb. 1840; Butland's place was taken in 1840 by John Burgess, a boot and shoemaker: *EPG*, 25 July 1840; In 1842 George Elworthy moved into the building. He was a woollen draper, hatter and tailor and remained until 1853. The 1851 census recorded that Elworthy was aged 38 and that he, his wife and their seven children and a niece, all of whom lived in the building, were Exeter born: *EFP*, 12 May 1842; *WT*, 19 March 1853. *Pigot's Directory* recorded George Elworthy, a tailor, as the occupant in 1844; Charles Benjamin Presswell, ladies' habit maker and tailor, occupied the building from at least March 1854 until his death in 1869: *EFP*, 16 March 1854 & *WT*, 16 Feb. 1869. In 1862 Presswell, noted as a tailor and draper, signed a fourteen-year lease and after his death Presswell's stock was auctioned: DHC, 54/13/1/10; *EFP*, 17 Feb. 1869; Samuel Colin Sleep & Company took over by 1870 and although Sleep died in April 1877 the family announced that it would continue in business: *WT*, 210 Oct. 1870 & 5 April 1877; *EFP*, 9 May 1877. The firm is noted in the *Exeter Pocket Journal* of 1871.

247 *WT*, 6 June 1877.

248 *EPG*, 15 Dec. 1925 & 4 Jan. 1926. See also DHC, 54/13/1/11-12, for ownership in 1881 & 1892.

249 *EG*, 13 Feb. 1926.

250 *EPG*, 22 April 1932.

251 In 1800 the lease was for sale of the 'messuage or dwelling house and shop, situate in the centre of the High Street, now in the possession of Mr Hill, druggist'. In April 1807 the building had 'lately' been in his possession and Robert Sowden, Linen Draper, was opening a shop: *EFP*, 16 Jan. 1800, 15 Jan. 1801, 23 April 1807 & 14 May 1807; *EPG*, 28 Jan. 1802. The *Exeter Pocket Journal* of 1796 notes a John Hill, druggist, in business on the High Street; Sowden was still there in 1808 when he announced he was about to take on a partner. Sowdon & Children was in business at Number 47 through to July 1809: *EFP*, 31 March, 1 Dec. 1808, 16 March & 6 July 1809; On 25 Feb. 1811 William Coplestone, a linen draper, opened his shop at Numbers 46 & 47 High Street. He was there through to at least 1813 when he was declared bankrupt: *EFP*, 21 Feb. 1811, 25 March & 7 Oct. 1813. Copplestone was noted in the *Exeter Pocket Journal* of 1816 as being a linen draper in business in the High Street.

252 By March 1820 S. Cornish ran his India Tea House in the building. In 1817 he had taken over the business from W. J. P. Wilkinson who was then at 223 High Street. In 1824, by which time Cornish was at Goldsmith Street, his goods were sold including his household furniture and stock: *EFP*, 22 May 1817 & 2 March 1820. He was still at 223 High Street in 1819: *EFP*, 7 Jan. 1819, *EFP*, 29 Jan. 1824.

253 Beedle & Salter were the occupiers from 1822 to 1826. The families were related through the marriage of John Salter, chemist, to Anna Maria Beedle in 1824: *EFP*, 2 July 1824; John Fegan, also a chemist and an apprentice of Knapman's, was the occupier until his death at 31 in Dec. 1879. In Jan. 1880 David Jones advertised that he was carrying on Fegan's business but in April Walter Wright announced that he was Fegan's successor: *WT*, 28 July 1871; *EFP*, 31 Dec. 1879 & 15 July 1874; *EPG*, 9 Jan. & 21 April 1880; Three years later, in 1883, Wright advertised that he had sold the business to Eric Lemmon whose business had been established in 1822: *EPG*, 19 Oct. 1883; DHC, Kevin White's Scrapbooks, Vol. I; By March 1827 T. G. Beedle had his own Exeter Genuine Drug Establishment in the building. Six years later, in 1833, Beedle relinquished his business to John Croome, another chemist, who had been apprenticed in Bristol: *EPG*, 3 March 1827; *WT*, 27 Oct. 1827 & 6 April 1833; The 1851 census recorded that John Croome was born in Wiltshire, was aged 44 and lived with his sister, their niece and two servants. Croome was there until 1853 when he sold his business to John Knapman, another dispensing chemist, who remained until 1874. He called his business the 'Pharmaceutical Hall'. In 1873 Knapman signed a lease with Croome along with the tenement situated behind in Lamb Alley: *EFP*, 26 May 1853; DHC, 6631M; Harold Densem, another chemist who had been working with Lemmon, operated in the building from at least 1920 and continued, under W. Hosegood Clarke, through to 1932: *WT*, 5 August 1921; In 1932 the business was acquired by Hinton Lake & Son, Ltd who were established at 41 High Street: *EPG*, 12 Feb. 1932.

254 *EFP*, 15 July 1874.

255 *WT*, 24 Feb. 1903; DHC, 547B/P/73/ii, sale particulars for 47 High Street, 1903.

256 *EPG*, 17 April 1913; *WT*, 8 Feb. 1916.

257 *WT*, 7 March 1921; *EPG*, 21 Sept. 1922 & 16 Feb. 1923.

258 *EPG*, 8 June & 21 Sept. 1923.

259 He had already sold his business to John Somers Gard of 53 High Street: *EFP*, 7 April 1803, 14 Oct. 1813 & 15 July 1874; *EPG*, 8 & 22 Dec. 1827, 4 March 1837; *WT*, 16 Dec. 1837; *WL*, 6 March 1837; *Exeter Directory* (1835), 49–50.

260 *EPG*, 25 Nov. 1837; *EFP*, 21 August 1845.

261 *WT*, 28 March & 13 June 1846; *EPG*, 27 June 1846.

262 *WT*, 24 Oct. 1846, 13 May 1848.

263 *WT*, 8 May 1847.

264 *EFP*, 16 July 1857.

265 *EPG*, 7 Nov. & 25 Nov. 1872.

References

266 *WT*, 16 Sept. 1872; *EPG*, 30 May 1873.
267 *EFP*, 13 August 1879.
268 *EPG*, 9 May 1878 & 8 May 1879.
269 In 1879 there were also premises at 156 Fore Street: *EFP*, 17 Dec. 1879.
270 *EPG*, 18 Dec. 1889.
271 *EFP*, 22 Dec. 1894.
272 DHC, 6631.
273 DHC, ECA/Book 58, Map 13.
274 Roger Rowe, a linen draper, occupied the building from the 1760s until Dec. 1803 when he was declared bankrupt. His stock was sold at auction as was his lease of which had begun in 1799. In 1804 it was stated that he had occupied the building 'for many years last past': *EFP*, 22 Dec. 1803 & 12 Jan. 1804. He may have been the individual of the same name of St Martin's parish who in 1773 had Ann Sharland as his apprentice: DHC, 1633A/PO/579. He was listed in the *Exeter Pocket Journal* in 1796 as a linen draper in business in High Street.
275 Robert Cross, Junior, a mercer and woollen draper, then became the occupier from the spring of 1804 until 1812: *EFP*, 15 March 1804, 28 Nov. 1805, 2 March 1809 & 26 March 1812.
276 In 1800 Hugh Veysey advertised that he had moved from 'opposite the guildhall to a very commodious house nine doors higher up opposite Goldsmith Street'. He died eight years later: *Sherborne Mercury*, 24 Nov. & 8 Dec. 1800; *EFP*, 15 Dec. 1808; His widow Ann was bankrupt by 1812 and that year a lease of 2,850 years was offered for sale of the 'messuage, tenement of dwelling house in the high street' lately in the occupation of Mrs Ann Veysey, hosier and haberdasher. It was advertised that 'the premises are nearly central between Broadgate and Martin's Lane, are large and commodious and form altogether one of the most eligible and desirable situations in this city': *EFP*, 22 Oct. 1812; *Stamford Mercury*, 11 Sept. 1812. See also DHC, 337B/10/11a. See DHC, 337B/10/11a. The following year she 'recommenced her business in the house [Number 49] adjoining her late residence [Number 48]'. Four years later, in 1817, she opened a branch store in Tiverton. In 1819 Veysey advertised her business as the 'hat, hosiery, glove and ladies boot and shoe warehouse'. In 1821 her eldest son, William, who had been in the business for the last eight years, was her partner: *WL*, 9 Nov. 1813; *EFP*, 11 Nov. 1813, 16 Oct. 1817, 29 July 1819 & 15 Nov. 1821; Six years later he gave up the hat trade in favour of his brother Francis who moved to Number 51. He continued selling hosiery, gloves and shoes and in 1833 acquired the stock of his mother-in-law, Grace Phillips. In 1845 he discontinued selling hosiery and gloves and intended to rent the building: *WT*, 4 March 1837; *EFP*, 28 August 1845.
277 ECLA, 6010/15/6.
278 *EFP*, 20 May 1813.
279 *EPG*, 9 Nov. 1839.
280 In 1847 Veysey sold all of his stock 'for ready money' and died in 1854. His business continued until the spring of 1856: *EPG*, 4 Sept. 1847; *WT*, 27 Sept. 1856; *EFP*, 21 Dec. 1854 & 26 June 1856; *WT*, 13 Oct. 1860.
281 *EFP*, 22 May 1861.
282 *WT*, 28 August 1863 & 7 May 1878.
283 *WT*, 1 Oct. 1870 & 1 Oct. 1872.
284 *EPG*, 24 Oct. 1873 & 5 Jan. 1874.
285 *WT*, 21 Feb. 1873.
286 *WT*, 24 March 1877.
287 *WT*, 13 May 1880.
288 PWDRO, 457/1106.
289 He occupied part of the building until 1907 and his goods were eventually sold in the building in April 1910: *WT*, 14 June 190; *E&E*, 8 April 1910.
290 He moved from Guildhall Chambers (59½ High Street) to 49 High Street. At his death in 1945 he was described as the 'father' of Exeter City Council: *EPG*, 7 Feb. 1912 & 9 March 1945.
291 *EPG*, 16 Oct. 1913.
292 *EPG*, 31 Jan. 1852.
293 ECLA, D&C6004/8/13-18.
294 ECLA, 6000/1/10, 6000/11/9-12, 6007/4/1-3. In 1734 Numbers 51–2 were in the possession of Thomas Bale and Sarah Ford: ECLA, 3566/pages 306–307.
295 Exeter's council noted in 1756 that the property was leased to 'the Dean and Chapter, lands on each side the passage opposite Goldsmith Street, out of which lands a chief rent of 2s 6d a year is paid to the Mayor, Burgesses & Chamber': DHC, ECA/Book 58, Map 13.
296 ECLA, 6004/13/34.
297 *EFP*, 2 July 1801, 11 Feb. 1802, & 11 July 1805. Luke had signed a new lease in 1797: ECLA, D&C3574, pages 541–2.
298 In 1805 the buildings were once again offered for sale and were in the occupation of William & John Mildrum, two brothers who were linen drapers, and Mr Philips, glover: *EFP*, 2 July 1801, 9 August 1804, 11 Feb. 1805 & 22 August 1805. Luke was bankrupt by spring 1810: *EFP*, 28 April 1810. John Mildrum, linen draper, married on 8 April 1803: DHC, DEX/7/b/1/1803/136. Thomas Luke was listed in the *Exeter Pocket Journal* of 1796 as a grocer in High Street. The Mildrum brothers dissolved their partnership in 1808 and William Mildrum moved to Totnes where he was declared bankrupt in 1811. John Mildrum continued with a new partner, Mr Proctor, and died in 1809 only nine months after having opened a second shop in Tiverton: *EFP*, 10 July 1806, 1 June 1809 & 4 April 1811; *WT*, 13 April 1883; Richard Burn, *The Justice of the Peace and Parish Officer* (1837), IV, 551. Copp, Alford & Copp (comprising William Copp, Henry Alford and Anthony Copp, linen drapers) was dissolved in 1817. William & Anthony Copp continued trading but two years later they moved to 208–9 High Street. They dissolved their partnership in 1820: *EFP*, 12 Feb. 1818, 4 Feb. 1819 & 20 July 1820.
299 *EFP*, 27 July & 19 Oct. 1820; *WL*, 17 August 1813.
300 By 1821 H. & J. Veysey were occupants and renamed the building 'Union House'. Two years later the executors of H. H. Veysey sold his linen drapery, silk mercery and lace goods and in 1827 the family business altered. William Veysey gave the hat trade to his brother Francis who moved to 51 High Street. William Veysey continued at 49 High Street: *EFP*, 26 April 1821 & 10 April 1823; *EPG*, 19 May 1827; *WT*, 25 March 1837. In 1827 E. Veysey, milliner and dress maker, opened her own business at 51 High Street: *EPG*, 7 July 1827. In 1834 the partnership between I. and Francis Veysey, brothers, was dissolved. The latter continued at 51 High Street: *EFP*, 26 April 1821; *EPG*, 27 Dec. 1834.
301 In 1843 Mrs Sarah Lendon moved her Ready-Made and Baby Linen Warehouse from 243 High Street to 51 High Street 'over Mr [James] Blunden's artificial flower warehouse'. He was also a straw hat maker. There was then one other artificial flower warehouse in Exeter: *WT*, 7 Jan. 1843; *EPG*, 4 May 1844; *Pigot's Directory* (1844), 51. In 1845 Bond & Jones sold Mr Blunden's stock: *EFP*, 27 March 1845. William Bond, with his Flower & Feather Warehouse, was the successor to Blunden in 1845. Bond was noted as head of the household in 1851. He was then aged 44, had been born in Chulmleigh and lived with his wife and one daughter. There were also seven female servants all of whom were aged between 15 and 28: *WT*, 6 Sept. 1845. In 1854 Mrs Haycock opened her Millinery & Fancy Show Room but in 1856 the shop fittings were for sale: *WT*, 6 May & 11 Nov. 1854, *EPG*, 20 Dec. 1856.
302 In 1857 Mr G. B. Luke had his wooden trap door, in front of the shop, replaced by a metal one: *EPG*, 17 Jan. 1857. In 1857 Charles Bisney opened Bisney's New Hat & Cap Warehouse from Number 51. He was there until 1876. A few years earlier a neighbour referred to him as a 'respectable citizen, the architect of his own fortune'. When Bisney died in 1887 he was referred to as 'an old and esteemed citizen of Exeter': *WT*, 24 Jan. 1857 & 3 Jan. 1887; *EPG*, 10 Nov. 1876 & 7 August 1878; *EFP*, 15 July 1874. In 1876 the contents were sold and the upper part of the house, with its own entrance at the front, was to be let: *WT*, 1 Dec. 1876. Mrs S. A. Brailey, a milliner, moved in during 1878 and retired by Christmas: *EPG*, 8 March & 8 Nov. 1878. In 1879 W. H. Seaton began selling boots and shoes but two year later, in 1881, he moved to the arcade: *WT*, 17 Jan. 1879 & 28 Dec. 1881.
303 *EPG*, 21 Sept. 1882 & 27 Oct. 1881.
304 Eduardo Hoyos-Saavedra, *Discovering Exeter II: Twentieth-Century Architecture* (Exeter, 2001), 21–2; *E&E*, 27 July 1963.
305 *E&E*, 1 July 1981.
306 ECLA, D&C6004/8/13-18.
307 ECLA, 6000/1/10, 6000/11/9-12, 6007/4/1-3. In 1734 Numbers 51–2 were in the possession of Thomas Bale and Sarah Ford: ECLA, 3566/pages 306–307.
308 In 1805 it had a lease of 31 years granted by the Dean & Chapter: *EFP*, 2 & 11 Feb. 1805 & 22 August 1805.
309 *EFP*, 18 April 1833; *EPG*, 22 Nov. 1834 & 26 March 1836.
310 *EPG*, 12 Nov. 1836.
311 From 1837 to 1838 the lease was offered at auction: *EPG*, 22 April 1837; *WT*, 30 Dec. 1837.
312 In 1838 Miss F. C. Holmes had her millinery show rooms in the building and continued through to May 1841 but in April she married James H. Hooper at the cathedral. She sold hats and he sold stationery. In Jan. 1842 Mrs Hooper gave birth to a baby daughter at Number 52: *EPG*, 17 Nov. 1838, 11 May & 9 Nov. 1839, 2 May & 14 Nov. 1840, 1 May 1841; *WT*, 17 April, 18 Dec. 1841, 29 Jan. 1842.
313 *WT*, 9 July 1842. In March 1844 he sold his entire stock and advertised the house and shop for rent: *EFP*, 14 March 1844.

314 John Raddon, a Laceman, Mercer, Hosier & Glover, occupied from 1845 to 1847 but went bankrupt by 1848: *EFP*, 10 July 1845 & 27 April 1848; *WT*, 6 May 1848.

315 In spring 1849 George Heseltine Plowman and Henry Lewis Brewster, dress and upholstery trimming manufacturers, opened their business. Brewster was recorded as living in the building in 1851. He was 31 years old, had been born in Hertfordshire and lived with his wife Mary, one daughter and a female servant. Brewster and Plowman dissolved their partnership three years later in 1852 and Plowman continued on his own until 1860 when he relinquished his business to his nephew, John Scudder: *EFP*, 7 April 1849; *WT*, 6 & 27 March 1852; *EPG*, 25 Feb. 1860. Scudder retired in 1883 and blamed it on having to relinquish part of his premises: *EFP*, 3 & 10 Jan. 1883

316 His business was taken over by John Bailey, his neighbour in Number 53. Bailey had renamed Number 53 High Street as 'Victoria House' and absorbed Number 52 in this new name: *WT*, 17 Sept. 1906.

317 W. H. Trelease, Hosier, was the occupier in 1893 and continued until the Second World War: *EFP*, 16 Sept. 1893.

318 *EPG*, 13 Dec. 1902. The new windows were praised: *WT*, 18 Dec. 1902.

319 SHC, DD/HC/C/483.

320 *WL*, 18 May 1813. He was listed in the *Exeter Pocket Journal* as a bookseller in High Street.

321 *EFP*, 12 June 1817 & 29 July 1819.

322 *EFP*, 7 Oct. 1819.

323 *EFP*, 23 Nov. 1820, 30 Oct. & 27 Nov. 1823 & 12 August 1824. Hedgeland was still in business in 1825 and 1827: *EFP*, 17 March 1825 & *EPG*, 14 April 1827.

324 John Somers Gard moved in during 1827 and ten years later took over the ironmongery business of Thomas R. Baker of 48 High Street. Gard opened at Number 53 in summer 1827 and remained until 1854: *WT*, 11 March 1837; *WL*, 6 March 1837; *EFP*, 28 Sept. 1854. Hedgeland had moved to 197 High Street by 1829: *EPG*, 19 Sept. 1829. The census of 1851 recorded that Gard was aged 64 and had been born in North Tawton. His wife and three sons also lived in the building along with two female servants who were also born in North Tawton.

325 In 1855 Mr & Mrs Charles Adams opened their millinery businesses: she had her Millinery & Mantle Show Rooms while he ran his Millinery, Bonnet & Fancy Drapery Warehouse: *EPG*, 31 March 1855; Mrs Adams died in 1861 and seven years later her husband Charles relinquished his business to Stanbury & Company which continued in the building until 1875: *EPG*, 16 August 1861; *WT*, 6 March 1868 & 5 Feb. 1875.

326 *WT*, 6 March 1863. There was also damage to the rear of the building in 1881: *WT*, 10 Oct. 1881.

327 T. G. Wheeler was the next occupant in 1874 and left three years later. James Bailey then occupied the building; his motto in business was 'high class goods at moderate prices'. In 1879 he renamed Numbers 52 & 53 'Victoria House' and he was there until 1896 when Stuart Hunt took over. Ten years later, in 1906, Hunt gave up his business. The shop front was improved in 1902: *EPG*, 26 Oct. 1874 & 13 Dec. 1902; *WT*, 14 March 1879 & 7 Sept. 1906.

328 DHC, ECA, Streets Committee 1898–1906, 458; Walgreens Boots Alliance Heritage Archive, WBA/BT/16/8/43/9 & WBA/BT/4/15/1/2; Sally Dugan, 'The Boots Book-Lovers' Library', 158, in Nicolas Louise Wilson (ed.), *The Book World* (Boston, 2016); *EFP*, 9 Feb. 1907.

329 The shop fittings were sold in 1929: *WT*, 2 Nov. 1928; *EPG*, 19 July 1929.

330 He went bankrupt the following year. There was a dispute over the disposal of the fittings in 1932: *WT*, 1 July 1932; *EPG*, 28 Oct. 1932.

331 SHC, DD/HI/C/481 & 534, unnumbered leases of 1/58, 1762 and 1765; LMA, MS11936/331/508185; Harbottle Reed, 'Demolition of ancient buildings of Exeter during the last half century', *DAT*, LXIII, (1931), 280.

332 DHC, FOR/Z/1/1, *Brice and Thorn's Old Exeter Journal or the Weekly Advertiser*, 8 August 1766, No. 1.

333 DHC, FOR/Z/1/1, *Brice and Thorn's Old Exeter Journal or the Weekly Advertiser*, 8 Jan. 1768, No. LXXIV.

334 T. N. Brushfield, *The Life and Bibliography of Andrew Brice, Author and Journalist* (privately printed, 1888), 40–42. Barnabas' father was also a bookseller and had lived in a house in Cathedral Yard. Barnabas Thorn was buried on 1 March 1785 and Richard Thorn on 13 Sept. 1787: DHC, DCRS Library, transcript of St Martin's parish register. In 1780 Thorn had been accused of obstructing High Street by placing his goods in front of his shop: Jeroen Salman, *Pedlars and the Popular Press* (Leiden, 2013), 130. Six years later his stock was valued as being worth £500, equivalent to £34,000 today: LMA, MS11936/331/508185.

335 In 1789 Benjamin Mardon, Mercer and Woollen Draper, announced he was moving his business premises to a building 'immediately opposite' the guildhall. He noted that the building had been recently occupied by Mr Thorn, a bookseller: *New Exeter Journal*, 21 May 1789. Mardon died in Oct. 1814 but his widow, Elizabeth Mardon, appears to have continued to occupy the building: *The Alfred*, 22 May 1822. She died in 1832: *EPG*, 15 Sept. 1832; Copp & Tory were in business from May 1822 when they offered 'unparalleled bargains in linen drapery, silk mercery, hosiery'. The firm occupied the rooms previously used by Mrs Mardon. In 1829 George Pelly Tory, Linen Draper, Dealer & Chapman, continued the business on his own and remained in the building until 1836. There may have been a tenant upstairs: 'Mrs Mardon' was listed as an occupant in a directory in 1828 but no further details were given. She died in 1832 and was then 'advanced in years': *The Alfred*, 21 & 28 May 1822; Pigot, *Directory* (1822); *EPG*, 21 March 1829, 17 Sept. 1836, 28 Oct. 1837, 13 Oct. 1838; In Sept. 1836 John Bending sold Tory's stock and he became the occupier: *The WL*, 16 Jan. & 3 April 1837; *WT*, 15 Sept. 1832 & 22 Sept. 1838; *Exeter Itinerary & General Directory* (Exeter, 1828), 188

336 *EFP*, 8 Nov. 1838; *Exeter Directory* (1835), 51.

337 *EPG*, 2 May 1840.

338 *EPG*, 27 Feb. 1841. *Pigot's Directory* listed Marianne Welch, a milliner and corset maker, at 54 High Street in 1844.

339 *WT*, 2 Sept. 1864; *EFP*, 15 July 1874.

340 *WT*, 28 March 1857. See *EFP*, 12 June 1856 for Thomas Veitch & Company's advert in which their business was termed the 'Western Counties Seed Depot'.

341 *WT*, 21 March 1930; *The Exeter Itinerary & General Directory* (Exeter, 1828), 160.

342 *WT*, 1 July 1932.

343 Ethel Lega-Weekes, 'An Account of the Hospitium de le Egle, Exeter, with Ancient Chapels in the Close and some Persons connected therewith', *DAT*, XLIV (1912), 480–511; Crocker, *Sketches of Old Exeter with letter press*, Plate VI.

344 *EFP*, 22 July 1802, 1 March 1804, 4 Dec. 1806 & 19 March 1807; *WT*, 27 July 1839; *EFP*, 15 Jan. 1801; *WT*, 30 August 1845; *Exeter Directory* (1835), 48. Richard Dunsford the younger had been at 12 South Street in 1836: *EPG*, 27 August 1836.

345 *WT*, 12 July 1834.

346 In Oct. 1850 the Exeter Chess Club was advertised. W. Balle announced *The Western Times* 'to the gentlemen of Exeter and its vicinity, particularly to the lovers of chess, that in accordance with a request which has been expressed by several amateurs of that scientific game, he will be prepared to open a room with the required furniture, etc., for the accommodation of an Exeter Chess Club': *WT*, 12 Oct. 1850.

347 In 1852 William H. Warren took over his father's business at 14 North Street and moved it to his new premises at 55 High Street. This new firm were tailors, drapers and habit makers: *WT*, 8 May 1852; Twenty years later, in May 1872, Warren announced he was leaving Exeter and that his business was being taken over by Mr J. J. Norris junior: *WT*, 21 May 1872; John J. Norris, who had been a cutter with Lewis Sons & Parker of London, subsequently explained that he was continuing the high standards set by Mr Warren and his father for more than 50 years: *WT*, 1 June 1872; Not long afterwards, in 1874, Mrs Norris gave birth to a daughter at Number 55: *WT*, 17 April 1874; In the spring of 1877 Norris moved his business to Number 23 and Number 55 was let: *EPG*, 11 April 1877.

348 *EPG*, 18 Sept. 1877.

349 *EPG*, 10 Oct. 1881.

350 *WT*, 1 Nov. 1881.

351 DHC, FOR/B/6/1/39.

352 *EPG*, 15 & 29 March, 21 August 1883; *The Builder*, 25 August 1883, 243; DHC, ECA/9/6, pages 228–30, 247, 254–5, 278.

353 *EFP*, 27 Feb. 1884.

354 *EFP*, 15 July 1874.

355 *WT*, 31 Jan. 1829; *EPG*, 11 Oct. 1881; *WT*, 11 Oct. 1881.

356 *EFP*, 26 Oct. 1820; Thomas Frognall Dibdin, *Bibliomania* (1842), 470.

357 *EPG*, 19 Dec. 1829.

358 *EFP*, 15 July 1874 & *EPG*, 11 Oct. 1881.

359 *WL*, 2 Nov. 1813; *The Alfred*, 27 March 1821.

360 *EPG*, 19 Jan. 1839, 25 July 1840 & 31 July 1841; *WT*, 31 Jan. 1829, 6 Oct. 1837, 14 August 1841.

361 Five months later Nash & Company, which sold woollen cloths, hats, linen drapery, silk hosiery, haberdashery and lace, opened at Christmas. They had moved from 70–1 South Street: *WT*,

6 Nov. 1841; The firm was subsequently known as Nash & Gardiner and went bankrupt three years later in 1844: *WT*, 1 June 1844; The next occupier was Henry Farrant, who was also a Woollen and Linen Draper. He opened in May 1845 but went out of business in Dec. 1847: *WT*, 26 April 1845; *EPG*, 25 Dec. 1847.

362 *EFP*, 3 May 1849. The shop fittings were sold a year later: *WT*, 2 March 1850.

363 *WT*, 6 April & 21 Sept. 1850, 14 April, 28 April & 21 July 1855; *EPG*, 27 April 1850; *The Exeter Journal and Almanack for 1855* (Exeter, 1855), 60.

364 John Evans, Bookseller and Stationer, took over Balle's bookselling and stationery business in Jan. 1853 but Evans continued his printing business, the Public Select Library and the Exeter Reading Room in Number 56: *WT*, 15 Jan. 1853. Henry Hodge lasted longer. His bookbinding and stationery firm occupied the building from 1855 until 1870: *WT*, 14 April 1855 & 26 March 1870.

365 *EPG*, 29 Jan. & 26 Feb. 1869.

366 *EPG*, 10 Oct. 1881.

367 *EPG*, 11 Oct. 1881.

368 *WT*, 27 Feb. 1882; DHC, FOR/B/6/1/39.

369 *Andrew Brice's Old Exeter Journal*, 12 Dec. 1766; Mary R. Ravenhill & Margery M. Rowe (eds), *Devon Maps and Map-Makers, Volume II*, DCRS, NS 45 (2002), 390.

370 LMA, MS11936/358/551723; By 1800 Hitchcock, Linen Draper & Haberdasher, was in the building 'opposite the guildhall, High Street'. That year he had a one-year lease of the fore-room over the shop and the passage in front. The rest was in the occupation of Edward Wills, 'china-man', but formerly held by Grace Floyd. Hitchcock died in 1812. That year Mrs Elizabeth Dinneford, Haberdasher, became the occupant and advertised herself as Hitchcock's succesor, but she kept her existing millinery business at New Bridge where it had been since at least 1808. Dinneford occupied Number 57 until she retired in 1834. Upon her death in 1847 the building was sold: DHC, 74/3/313a-b; *EFP*, 26 June 1800, 13 August & 5 Nov. 1812, 13 August 1808; *EPG*, 29 Nov. 1828, 5 July 1834 & 20 March 1847. For her will see DHC, 1078/IRW/D/400. John Hitchcock was listed in the *Exeter Pocket Journal* of 1796 as being a linen draper in business in High Street. By 1823 she occupied Number 58 and her business was called the 'General Haberdashery Warehouse': *EFP*, 4 Dec. 1823. From at least 1827 Mesdames Gilbert & Pickard also ran their millinery business at Number 57. In 1829 Miss M. A. Gilbert continued the business without her partner, Miss C. Pickard. She married in 1830: *EPG*, 5 May 1827, 14 Nov. 1829 & 13 March 1830. Mrs Dinneford retired and sold her business to Robert Nightingale in 1834 and he remained there until 1840. At that time the building served as a dwelling and a shop: *EPG*, 5 July 1834, 21 March 1835 & 23 Jan. 1841; DHC, 302A-99/PX1, rate of 1836. In 1841 Abraham Cleeve, a linen draper, opened his business in the building and remained until 1847: *EFP*, 11 March 1841; *WT*, 20 March 1847. In 1843 he offered 'a chance that will never again [be] offer[ed]' with a thirty per cent reduction in his stock's prices. This was caused by the need to put in a new shop front and 'make other alterations'. In 1845, at the age of 27, he testified regarding his watch having been stolen by Adelaide Harrison, a resident of what was described as being 'a house of bad character' in North Street. It may have been as a result of this trial that Trew's stock was sold in its entirety 1846 and 1847: *WT*, 30 Dec. 1843, 13 June 1846 & 27 Nov. 1847.

371 In 1847 and 1848 Number 57 was offered for sale or letting. It comprised 'a shop, over which are sitting rooms, sleep and domestic apartments, with cellar in the basement'. There were two leases: one was for 2,000 years (which had begun in 1814) and another for 31 years (of which 16 were unexpired): *WT*, 6 May 1848. The census recorded in 1851 that Mrs Jane Cole, a widow aged 47, had four children living with her and one domestic servant. All were born in Exeter except for Mrs Cole who came from Clyst Honiton. Cole ran a corset business and hosiery and haberdashery shop in the building and continued until 1861: *WT*, 25 Sept. 1852 & 7 Oct. 1854; *EPG*, 2 August 1861. Mr & Mrs R. R. Chubb were the next occupants and were there from 1862 until 1863: *WT*, 20 Sept. 1862 & 28 March 1863. That year S. Pyne & Son, Brush Merchants, extended their business from 146 Fore Street to Number 57. The firm continued until the autumn of 1866: *WT*, 11 Dec. 1863 & 25 Sept. 1866. By Christmas the building was occupied by Albert Sully, 'the people's draper', but he left in 1868: *WT*, 5 Dec. 1866. In 1867 he shared the building with Charles Cambridge: DHC, 74/2/4.

372 Henry Whitton, a draper, ran his business in the building from 1869 until 1877: *EPG*, 25 Nov. 1869, 15 July 1874 & 26 Oct. 1877. The building sites of Numbers 55 to 58, along with those of 23 to 25 Cathedral Yard, were sold in 1882: DHC, FOR/B/6/1/39.

373 *The Builder*, 25 August 1883.

374 *EPG*, 21 August 1883; *The Builder*, 8 Sept. 1883.

375 *WT*, 29 Dec. 1884.

376 *EPG*, 3 Jan. 1936 & 10 July 1942; *E&E*, 23 Dec. 1940.

377 In 1574 John Parr signed a new lease for the building; his parents had also lived in the premises: SHC, DD/HI/C/484; In 1608 his son Robert, a merchant, gave the lease of both of his tenements in St Martin's parish, held under Henry Tothill, to his wife Sabine during her lifetime: TNA, PROB 11/111/520; His son John was granted leases in 1638 and 1673. In his will of 1650 John gave the remainder of his tenancy to his wife Sibley: TNA, PROB 11/211/699.

378 ECLA, 6007/17/2-7 & 6007/9/1-3. There was a dispute between the executors of Mrs Parr and Mr Northleigh regarding the house and curtilage in 1688: ECLA, D&C3562, pages 114–115. Her son, another John, became the chief occupier in 1673; Stanley D. Chapman (ed.), The *Devon Cloth Industry in the Eighteenth Century*, DCRS, NS 23 (1978), 68.

379 ECLA, D&C3560, pages 322–323. Upon John's death his widow Elizabeth took out a further lease in 1683.

380 The next lessee was Richard Croker, a fuller, in 1725 and the occupants were Samuel Stephens, an apothecary, Richard Greenfield and 'others'. Stephens continued in the building until at least 1753 by which time he had been joined by William Kittoe. In 1759 the occupants were Sarah and Mary Spry, milliners, and in 1759 Thomas Wigginton, a mercer, along with other identified individuals shared the building with Mary Spry. Wigginton was noted in an advertisement as being a woollen draper and mercer in 1765 who was situated 'opposite the guildhall': ECLA, D&C3565, pages 36–7, 6007/20/23 & 6006/10/1-6; DHC, FOR/Z/1/1, *Andrew Brice's Old Exeter Journal or the Weekly Advertiser*, 6 Dec. 1765, No. 428; In 1780 there were new occupants: these were Deborah Cornish, a widow, [blank] Broadmead, a milliner, Henry Gard, a watchmaker, and yet more unidentified 'others'. In 1809 it was noted that Enoch Francis, minister of the South Street Baptists, had been the occupant as had Mrs Francis, formerly Broadmead, a milliner: DHC, Z9/Box28/8/5b; Alan Brockett, *Nonconformity in Exeter* (Manchester, 1962), 161.

381 By Oct. 1813 Thomas Sparkes Junior had opened his general haberdashery business at Number 58. He advertised that it was his 'design to establish a shop similar to that kept by the late John Hitchcock, he has engaged the young woman who was in that shop'. Mrs Dinneford claimed in another advert that she was Hitchcock's successor at Number 57: *WL*, 2 Nov. 1813; *EFP*, 28 Oct. 1813; It may be that Hitchcock had occupied both 57 & 58. In 1823 Mrs Dinneford advertised that her business was being run from both buildings. She continued until 1834: *EFP*, 27 Nov. 1823. Dinneford sold her business to R. Nightingale in 1834 and he remained until his move in 1840 to Queen Street: *EPG*, 21 March 1835 & 23 Jan. 1841.

382 *EPG*, 10 Feb. 1838.

383 In March 1853 Charles Adams, a laceman and glover, began and mainly sold millinery and with Mrs Adams, a milliner, remained until at least 1857: *WT*, 26 March 1853; *The Exeter Journal and Almanack* (Exeter, 1857), 64. In 1855 Charles Cambridge began selling boots and shoes in the building and retired in May 1868: *EPG*, 14 April 1855, *WT*, 29 May 1868.

384 *WT*, 3 August 1850. That year it appears that James Madgwick Wilcocks surrendered the lease: DHC, Z9/Box 28/8/8a-b.

385 *EPG*, 10 Oct. 1881.

386 *WT*, 29 Dec. 1884.

387 *EPG*, 8 June 1934; *E&E*, 23 Dec. 1940.

388 His widow, Elizabeth, continued his business at 59 High Street. A year later she brought one of her sons and James Pittman into the business: *EFP*, 5 & 26 Feb. 1807, 24 March 1808; In 1812 the partnership between Elizabeth Chamberlain, Richard Hart Chamberlain and James Chamberlain (which had operated as E. Chamberlain, Son & Pittman) was dissolved. A new firm, under the partnership of Elizabeth Chamberlain and James Pittman, Linen Drapers, began and five years later, in 1817, it too was dissolved. However, Pittman continued in the 'long-established and extensive concern' until 1826: *EFP*, 26 March 1812 & 6 Nov. 1817.

389 *EPG*, 11 August 1827.

390 *EFP*, 26 July 1827. The partnership was dissolved in May 1828 with Pinwill & Please continuing in business: *WT*, 7 & 14 June 1828. By March 1829 the firm had moved to Number 223: *EFP*, 12 March 1829.

391 While the firm was at Number 59 they shared its

179

entrance with Mesdames Snell & Darke who sold French and English millinery. In 1826 the ladies advertised that the 'principal entrance is through the shop of Messrs Snell, Pinwill & Please'. There was a second entrance via Cathedral Yard: *EFP*, 18 May 1826; In Oct. 1827 Mrs A. S. Twose joined the firm and it changed its name to Snell & Company: *EPG*, 13 Oct. & 17 Nov. 1827; Mrs Twose was joined by Mrs Baker at 59 in spring 1830 following the vacating by Pinwill & Please: *WT*, 1 May & 27 Nov. 1830; In May 1828 the 'neat and modern' furniture of Mr Clarke, behind the shop of Snell, Pinwill and Please, had been sold at auction: *EPG*, 17 May 1828.

392 *EPG*, 13 March 1830, 20 August 1836. By 1838 Pilbrow had moved to Number 254. He died in 1845 and was noted as a professor of music who was 'universally respected'. Pilbrow shared the building with E. & J. Nash, who sold clothing, from 1832 to 1834: *EPG*, 10 Nov. 1832 & 5 April 1845; *EFP*, 8 May 1834.

393 DHC, 1926B/NP/E9/2. It was a branch office of the United Motor and General Insurance Company in 1921; *EPG*, 20 May 1921.

394 From 1840 to 1841 the building was the office of William Dennis Moore, secretary to the Norwich Union Office. Moore, who had moved from 18 Cathedral Close, became the city's town clerk and 59 became the Town Clerk's Office. Norwich Union was at Number 59 until rebuilding in 1911: *EPG*, 12 May 1838; *WT*, 13 June 1840, 30 Oct. 1841, 28 August 1874; William Norris, a surveyor, was there in 1840 and possibly as early as 1839 when he surveyed the tithe maps of Pinhoe and Woodland parishes. He held the second and third floors as well as the basement: *EPG*, 24 April 1841; TNA, IR 30/9/457; DHC, DEX/4/a/TM/Woodland & 1360A/PB/4/a/1; A. P. Prowse, public accountant, had his office there in 1842: *EPG*, 21 May 1842.

395 *WT*, 25 July 1846 & 26 Jan. 1894; *EPG*, 19 Oct. 1844, 19 July 1845 & 30 Sept. 1848; *EFP*, 27 Jan. 1894; *Pigot's Directory* (1844), 51.

396 *Pigot's Directory of Exeter* (1844), 45.

397 *EFP*, 14 Feb. 1883.

398 *WT*, 10 Oct. 1881.

399 *EFP*, 25 Nov. 1911.

400 *EFP*, 20 April 1912.

401 *EFP*, 7 Jan. 1893.

402 *EFP*, 30 April 1807, 2 Feb. & 11 May 1815.

403 *EFP*, 3 April 1817, 9 Feb. 1826; *EPG*, 20 May 1843.

404 From 1826 and into May 1828 Lee & Wescombe sold their millinery and dresses but by Oct. Thomas and Mrs Neale were selling fancy goods and 'ladies' costume': *EFP*, 14 Sept. 1826; *EPG*, 10 May & 11 Oct. 1828, 16 May 1829. In 1832 the household furniture belonging to Mr I. W. Snell was sold at auction: *EPG*, 17 March 1832.

405 John Risdon, bookseller, was the occupant in 1831 & 1832. He may have been at Number 60 as early as in 1828 when he advertised for a business partner: *The Exeter Independent*, 30 August 1831; *EPG*, 13 Sept. 1828, 27 August 1831, 6 Oct. 1832 & 19 Jan. 1833. He was noted in the 1832 list of voters as a stationer: DEI, Tracts, 168.13.

406 *WT*, 4 & 25 May 1833 & 28 August 1834.

407 *WT*, 15 August 1835 & 9 April 1836; *EPG*, 16 April 1836.

408 *EPG*, 16 July 1836; *WT*, 29 Oct. 1836.

409 Holden was born in Bristol and lived in the building with his wife, their two daughters and four children. He was also the agent for Australian, Colonial and General Life Insurance: *EFP*, 15 June 1843; *EPG*, 31 May 1856; *Slater's Royal National and Commercial Directory and Topography* (1852–3), 68; *EPG*, 16 May 1857. William Drayton died in 1879: *WT*, 30 Dec. 1879.

410 In 1858 Myers Solomon, an optician, became the occupier. He remained until his move to London in 1874: *EFP*, 8 July 1858; *WT*, 21 August 1874.

411 *EFP*, 23 Sept. 1874; *WT*, 12 April 1875. Luget Brothers were at 242 High Street by 1882: *EPG*, 4 July 1882. Wood's wife gave birth to a son in 1878 at Number 65: *EPG*, 1 Nov. 1878.

412 Fulford & Caseley opened their hat firm in 1880. It closed in 1892 and the building was offered to let by the end of 1893 with an auction of fittings early in 1894: *WT*, 15 Oct., 10 Dec. & 24 Dec. 1880; *EPG*, 29 Sept. 1892 & 31 Jan. 1894; *WT*, 22 Dec. 1893.

413 *EPG*, 11 August 1898.

414 DHC, 1926B/NP/E9/2; *EPG*, 19 Feb. 1904; *WT*, 26 April 1907.

415 *WT*, 10 Oct. 1881.

416 *EPG*, 21 Nov. 1912; *EFP*, 30 Nov. 1912.

417 Thomas Smith rebuilt in about 1700 and the property may have been in his family before 1528: DHC, ECA/ED/M/1011; DHC, ECA, D7/47/1-18. The two occupiers were Robert Mudge and Edward Score.

418 In 1815 George Strong began his ironmongery business at Number 61 but continued only two years: in 1817 he went bankrupt. The building was offered for letting July: *EFP*, 16 Feb. 1815 & 10, 17 & 24 July 1817. He died in 1831 at Bristol and was then noted in Exeter as 'formerly of this city, and many years past traveller for the house of Messrs. Nott & Son, iron merchants, Bristol': *EPG*, 23 April 1831. From 1822 to at least 1826 Joseph Trist, silversmith and jeweller, was the occupant and retired from business at 5 High Street in 1827: *EPG*, 17 March 1827.

419 By 1830 the building was the premises of Edwin & Anna Dunn, cheesemongers: *EPG*, 6 March 1830; *WT*, 23 Jan. & 24 April, 1830; *EFP*, 4 March 1830.

420 *WT*, 2 Nov. 1833; *EFP*, 4 May 1826, 19 June 1834 & *EPG*, 18 March, 1 April & 19 August 1837.

421 *EPG*, 3 Dec. 1836.

422 *WT*, 22 April & 12 August 1837 & 13 Oct. 1838; *EPG*, 1 June 1838.

423 *EPG*, 18 April 1846 & 28 March 1857; *WT*, 3 April 1846 & 9 May 1857.

424 By Dec. 1857 Mr Abel Uglow, watch and clock maker of South Street, had become the occupant. He announced his retirement in 1860 and dissolved his partnership with John Hall in Sept. 1861: *EFP*, 24 Dec. 1857 & 20 Sept. 1861; *WT*, 4 August 1860. The business closed in Oct.: *EPG*, 27 Sept. 1861. John Mortimore, Brush, Mop & Clog Maker, then occupied the building from 1862 but was bankrupt shortly afterwards: *EFP*, 28 May 1862 & 23 March 1864.

425 The building was again offered for sale: *WT*, 8 Nov. 1862. The following year, 1863, Henry Welsford, Wholesale & Retail Stationer & Account Book Manufacturer, became the new occupant and continued in that business until 1881: *WT*, 6 March 1863 & 23 April 1881. Early in 1876 he began a new occupation which he continued for five years: *WT*, 4 Jan. 1876.

426 *EPG*, 17 Nov. 1884 & 8 Feb. & 21 August 1905; *WT*, 7 Feb. 1887.

427 *WT*, 25 Jan. 1905.

428 DHC, FOR/B/6/1/326; *EPG*, 7 July 1905.

429 *WT*, 20 July 1910.

430 LMA, 4460/01/10/010.

431 NA, PROB 11/307/583. 'that messuage or tenement with the appurtenances wherein I now inhabit and dwell situate within the parish of St Martin within the said city of Exeter near unto the Broadgate there which I lately purchased to me and my heirs of and from Dr Bridgeman late Bishop of Chester and Sir Orlando Bridgeman his son'. Bridgeman was the son-in-law of William Hellyar, Exeter Canon and Archdeacon of Barnstaple; *Report of the Commissioners*, 36, 471.

432 DHC, ECA/Book 58, Map 13.

433 *EPG*, 23 April 1831 & 17 March 1832.

434 *WT*, 9 March 1833 & 12 Oct. 1833.

435 *EFP*, 10 & 3 Oct. 1833.

436 *WT*, 28 June 1834.

437 *Exeter Directory* (Exeter, 1835), 49; *EPG*, 21 June 1834; *EFP*, 5 March 1835.

438 *EFP*, 14 Jan. 1836.

439 In 1845 James Windeat's business was taken over by Edger & Harris who ran the Fur, Cloak, Shawl and Family Linen Warehouse in both 62 & 63. It remained until 1852 when E. W. Harris moved across the street to Number 194: *EFP*, 13 March 1845; *WT*, 24 April 1852.

440 James Windeat & John Taylor moved into the building in 1853 and continued trading until the partnership was dissolved in Oct. 1855 because of Taylor's ill health: *EPG*, 15 Dec. 1855; *WT*, 25 August 1855. Windeat continued trading in both buildings from 1855 and continued until he retired in Nov. 1864: *EFP*, 4 Oct. 1855; *WT*, 8 Nov. 1864.

441 *EPG*, 28 Feb. 1857. This appears to be different from the Broadgate House which adjoined the City Bank: *Devonshire Chronicle & Exeter News*, 11 June 1836. In 1857 Mrs Hake, at Broadgate House, was the agent for J. H. Mintorm, modeller to the queen, and she was based, presumably upstairs, at Broadgate House. She was there until 1862: *EPG*, 28 Feb. 1857; *EFP*, 4 June 1862.

442 Brewer Howell (who was a partner in his father Robert's firm of Howell, Knapman and Howell) took over on Windeat's retirement. He continued until spring 1867: *WT*, 4 Oct. 1862; *EPG*, 12 April & 8 Nov. 1867, 10 July 1868, 8 August 1873. In 1873 drapery fixtures were sold at auction; In 1874 C. Wood, Hatter, moved from the corner of Broadgate to 62 High Street: *EFP*, 14 Jan. 1874.

443 *EPG*, 2 Nov. 1874.

444 *EPG*, 9 June 1876 & 2 Nov. 1877. The firm was the successor to J. Kingdon & Sons. In 1880 the upper part of Number 62 was offered for letting and four years later it was again let along with the 'upper part' of Number 63: *EPG*, 25 June 1880 & 14 June 1884. In 1891 Miss Chastey, Dressmaker, moved from Broadgate House to Number 63 or possibly Number 65: *EFP*, 3 Oct. 1891 & 25 Oct. 1892.

445 *WT*, 25 Jan. 1905.

446 *EPG*, 7 July 1905; DHC, FOR/B/6/1/326.

References

447 *EPG*, 21 Oct. 1910.
448 *WT*, 14 March 1913.
449 *EPG*, 2 Nov. 1928.
450 *The Report of the Commissioners*, 132–4; DHC, ECA/Book 58, Map 13; *EFP*, 5 April 1804; DHC, ECA/1264.
451 DHC, ECA, Exeter City Map Book.
452 W. T. P. Short, *The Gentleman's Magazine* (1837), 156; W. T. P. Shortt, *Sylva Antiqua Iscana* (Exeter, 1841), 45.
453 J. Milles, 'Account of some Roman Antiquities discovered at Exeter', *Archaeologia*, Volume 6, Jan. 1782, pages 1–5; *EFP*, 14 Dec. 1848.
454 T. J. Pettigrew, 'On Roman *Penates* discovered at Exeter', *The Journal of the British Archaeological Association* (1865), 217–221.
455 In 1820 Mrs Clark moved her millinery business to Number 63 and continued until 1828 when she was succeeded by two firms run by members of the Snell family. Mr J. W. Snell, Draper & Tailor moved by Feb. of that year from 2 Martin's Lane to Number 63 and in 1828 was listed in a directory as J. W. Snell & Company, tailors and habit makers: *EFP*, 23 Nov. 1820; *EPG*, 23 Feb. & 15 March 1828; *Exeter Itinerary & General Directory* (Exeter, 1828), 208. In Oct. 1828 'Mrs Clark, widow' died: *EPG*, 25 Oct. 1828.
456 *EFP*, 11 May 1820; *WT*, 16 May 1829. Upon her retirement the business was taken up by Snell & Company.
457 The business was taken over in 1832 by Thomas Hourston, a former foreman: *EFP*, 4 Feb. 1832 & *EFP*, 10 Oct. 1833.
458 *WT*, 28 June 1834.
459 *WT*, 19 Sept. 1835 & 13 May 1837; *EPG*, 4 May 1839; Windeat & Taylor were in business until 1855: *WT*, 25 August 1855; In May 1867 the building was offered to let and in Nov. R. B. Ling & Company took occupancy of 62 & 63. However, by Sept. 1868 Ling had to sell its drapery and haberdashery fixtures in the two buildings: *WT*, 13 Dec. 1864 & 3 May 1867; *EPG*, 8 Nov. 1867 & 11 Sept. 1868.
460 William Opie & William Dymond, wine and brandy importers, moved from 27 Dix's Field to Number 63: *WT*, 1 Jan. 1869; In 1871 their partnership was dissolved but Dymond continued trading in the building: *EPG*, 11 August 1871; *WT*, 1873; Frederick Townsend, Wholesale Wine & Spirit Merchant, occupied the building from at least 1884: *WT*, 14 Feb. 1884. In 1896 the firm, which was later run by Townsend's widow, was taken over by Southwood Brothers. It continued until 1902: *EFP*, 4 April 1896. Early in 1902 Lloyd Jones opened 'Ye Olde Broadgate Wine & Spirit Stores' but ill health caused him to sell the business in June. In 1903 it was said in a licensing committee meeting that at Number 63 'Mr Lloyd Jones did a big business up to the time he sold the premises to Messrs. Carr & Quick': *WT*, 10 June 1902; *EPG*, 11 Feb. 1903.
461 Eighteen months later, in June that year and in 1876, W. Dymond, wine merchant, again offered the upper part of Number 63, comprising eight rooms, for let: *WT*, 16 Oct. 1874, 21 Jan. 1875, 14 Dec. 1875 & 9 June 1876.
462 *EPG*, 16 March 1877.
463 *EPG*, 22 Sept. 1885.
464 *EPG*, 8 Nov. 1902.
465 *EPG*, 7 July 1905; *DHC*, FOR/B/6/1/326.

466 *WT*, 8 Dec. 1905; *EPG*, 20 Feb. 1925.
467 *WT*, 29 June 1928; *EPG*, 24 June 1929.
468 DEG, 13 April 1934; *WT*, 4 May 1934.
469 *Exeter Weekly News*, 20 Jan. 1978; *E&E*, 25 Sept. 1976 & 17 Nov. 1979; Trailfinders opened in Sept. 2010: information supplied by Mark West, Property Director, Trailfinders.
470 *WT*, 15 March 1828; *White's Directory* (1879), 372: Miss C. B. Cossins, Honiton Lace Manufacturer, was listed at Broad Street; *Exeter Directories* (Exeter, 1835), 96 and (Exeter, 1850), 70.
471 Lega-Weekes, 'Studies', 19–22. Several years before Karl Cherry also wrote about the wall: *E&E*, 28 Oct. 1911.
472 Gray, *Lost Exeter*, 48; *EFP*, 30 Dec. 1824.
473 Jenkins, *Exeter*, 312.
474 *EPG*, 3 August 1881.
475 *WT*, 20 May 1921.
476 Stuart A. Moore (ed.), *Letters and Papers of John Shillingford, Mayor of Exeter, 1447–50*, 90.
477 Muriel E. Curtis, *Some disputes between the city and the cathedral authorities of Exeter* (Manchester, 1932), 44–7; ECLA, D&C3530, pages 57–60.
478 Stoyle, *From Deliverance to Destruction*, 38–42; Gray, *Strumpets & Ninnycocks*, 106; ECLA, D&C3557, page 311.
479 Gray, *Lost Exeter*, 48–50; *EFP*, 11 July 1822.
480 ECLA, D&C7076/186.
481 DHC, 76/20/3, 257.
482 ECLA, D&C3579, pages 269–70 & 444–7.
483 *EFP*, 15 July 1874.
484 ECLA, D&C3577, 430–1 & 526–30.
485 ECLA, D&C3560, pages 322–3.
486 ECLA, D&C3579, pages 251–4.
487 *EFP*, 6 Jan. 1825.
488 *Archaeological Recording at No. 2 Broadgate, Exeter* by R. W. Parker with a contribution by A. G. Collings (Exeter Archaeology Report No. 97.73, Oct. 1997); Richard Parker & Anthony G. Collings, 'The historic buildings and tenural history of No. 2 Broadgate, Exeter', 267–72; LMA, MS11936/358/553058.
489 *WT*, 29 March & 3 May 1867.
490 She moved to 23 Cathedral Yard in 1877 whereas her husband was at 60 North Street by 1872: *EPG*, 13 & 27 Sept. 1867, 27 July 1877, 25 June 1872.
491 Miss C. B. Cossins, designer and manufacturer of Honiton lace, succeeded Mr Pollard of 21 Cathedral Yard in 1875 and was based at Broadgate: *EFP*, 28 April 1875.
492 *EPG*, 26 Dec. 1902; *WT*, 12 Feb. 1903 & 4 May 1903. P. T. Bidwell, *The Legionary Bath-house and Basilica and Forum at Exeter*, Exeter Archaeological Report 1 (Exeter, 1979), 120–1.
493 *EPG*, 29 Sept. 1904.
494 *WT*, 20 July 1910.
495 DHC, FOR/B/6/1/326.
496 *EPG*, 27 Jan. 1917.
497 Parker & Collings, 'historic buildings', 270–2.
498 DHC, ECA, Book 58/Map 13.
499 Clive N. Ponsford, *Time in Exeter* (Exeter, 1978), 96. Richard Upjohn ran the shop from 1778 with his brother Peter's son William Brown as the foreman: John Leopold and Roger Smith, *The Life and Travels of James Upjohn* (2016), 6–7; LMA, MS11936/358/553058.
500 *EFP*, 23 August 1810. In 1824 Miss Eliza Smale, who described herself as a pastry book and confectioner, moved from what was noted as her old-established shop at Broadgate to new premises near Mol's Coffee House: *EFP*, 23 Sept. 1824. Miss Smale had occupied the Broadgate building by 1823 and her leasehold was offered for sale in 1827: *EPG*, 23 August 1823 & 14 July 1827. Smale died at the age of 54 in 1840 at Moretonhampstead 'where she had gone for the change of air': *Sherborne Mercury*, 6 April 1840; *EPG*, 4 April 1840. See DHC, 1078/IRW/S/814; DHC, III, 257.
501 In 1828 Sarah Mardon was listed as a confectioner at Broadgate Place Exeter Itinerary & General Directory (Exeter, 1828), 188; *Royal Cornwall Gazette*, 1 March 1828. In May 1827 an auction was held of a messuage or dwelling house at Broadgate which had been occupied by Mrs Mary Parnell but was currently held by one Mrs [M]Arden, near Broadgate. It was held under a lease from the Dean & Chapter and included 'two good cellars one of which is occupied by Miss Mardon as tenant at will'. This was probably the same Mrs Parnell who died aged 87 the year before. She was the widow of a lay vicar of the cathedral: *EFP*, 19 April 1827 & 25 May 1826.
502 *WT*, 11 May 1833; *EPG*, 31 August 1833; *Exeter Directory* (Exeter, 1835), 96; *EPG*, 13 August 1836 & 8 March 1856; *WT*, 20 Oct. 1849; *Sherborne Mercury*, 8 Oct 1838. Mrs Murch died at the age of 81 in 1877: *EPG*, 12 Jan. 1877.
503 *EPG*, 29 May 1868; *WT*, 22 Sept. 1873. James Murch had married Miss Ann Setten of Exmouth in 1868: *EPG*, 20 March 1868. For his will see DHC, 159B/2/39.
504 *EPG*, 31 Jan. 1876.
505 *WT*, 30 March 1894. See also *EPG*, 31 Jan. 1887. Mrs Ann Goff died in Dec. 1916 at her home at Cathedral Yard: *WT*, 19 Dec. 1916.
506 *EPG*, 21 Dec. 1916, 26 Oct. 1917, 8 Jan. 1920 & 13 June 1924; *WT*, 12 Jan. 1877, 19 July 1873 & 28 June 1920.
507 *EPG*, 13 Nov., 3 Dec. 1924 & 25 April 1929.
508 *EPG*, 29 Oct. 1924.
509 *EPG*, 28 Nov. 1924.
510 DHC, ECA/Planning Committee Minute Book, 476: plan no. 513/65.
511 George Oliver, *The History of Exeter* (Exeter, 1821), 137.
512 Gray, *Travelllers' Tales*, 20.
513 Gray, *Travellers' Tales*, 29.
514 Gray, *Travellers' Tales*, 32.
515 *EFP*, 8 Nov. 1849; *WT*, 10 Nov. 1849; Gray, *Travellers' Tales*, 158.
516 ECLA, D&C7076/195; *EPG*, 14 Oct. 1826.
517 *WT*, 7 Nov. 1846; *EPG*, 7 Nov. 1846. In 1851 the census recorded that Samuel Davies was aged 48 and lived with his two daughters, a sister-in-law, three assistant grocers and two domestic servants. In 1863 he left Exeter and his furniture was auctioned in May: *EPG*, 15 May 1863.
518 *WT*, 12 Nov. 1879.
519 LMA, 4460/01/10/010.
520 DHC, Voters Lists, 1968.
521 *EFP*, 21 July 1836.
522 *EPG*, 19. Nov. & 10 Dec. 1836.
523 ECA/9/5, page 148; *WT*, 7 May 1879.
524 LMA, 4460/01/10/010.
525 *E&E*, 20 July 1982.
526 *EFP*, 7 Nov. 1805 & 9 June 1808.
527 *EFP*, 29 Oct. 1873.

528 *WT*, 5 Jan. 1828.
529 *WT*, 12 Nov. 1853; *EFP*, 25 Dec. 1856; *EPG*, 22 Jan. 1859 & 13 Nov. 1863; *WT*, 18 Nov. 1864. See also *EPG*, 15 May 1863.
530 *EFP*, 19 Feb. 1862 & 22 April 1863.
531 *WT*, 20 Sept. 1864.
532 *EPG*, 31 March 1865; *WT*, 12 March 1867.
533 *EPG*, 11 March 1869; *WT*, 18 July 1871; *EFP*, 6 Dec. 1871.
534 *WT*, 4 Jan. 1877 & 9 May 1879; *EFP*, 24 Jan. 1877.
535 *EPG*, 12 Nov. 1878; *WT*, 30 Jan. 1879.
536 *WT*, 29 August & 11 Oct. 1877.
537 ECA/9/5, page 148; *WT*, 7 May 1879.
538 *EFP*, 29 Oct. 1873.
539 *WT*, 21 March 1846, 8 July 1848, 31 Oct. 1846; *EPG*, 10 Feb. 1844; *EFP*, 31 Jan. 1851; *Morning Post*, 6 April 1847; *EPG*, 19 Oct. 1866; *Leamington Advertiser*, 28 Nov. 1850; TNA, BT 44/31/57250; Mrs Treadwin was noted as having been at 27 Cathedral Yard in a document dated 1868: TNA, BT 43/417/224947.
540 *WT*, 17 May 1867 & 27 Jan. 1870; *EFP*, 27 April 1870.
541 *EFP*, 12 March 1879; *WT*, 1 April 1879.
542 *WT*, 10 May 1882.
543 *WT*, 25 Feb. 1884; *EFP*, 27 Feb. 1884.
544 *EPG*, 19 Nov. 1885.
545 *EFP*, 29 Oct. 1873; *EPG*, 16 March 1833; *The Exeter Journal & Almanack for 1850* (Exeter, 1850), 60.
546 *EPG*, 30 June 1827 & 26 Jan. 1850; *WT*, 19 Jan. 1850.
547 William Loveless Searle signed leases in 1827 & 1838: *EFP*, 29 Oct. 1873. Davis is listed in the Besley's *Exeter Directory* in 1828; DHC, ECA/Misc. Roll 23, m.74b & Z9/Box28/9/1.
548 *WT*, 2 April 1859.
549 *EFP*, 25 Oct. 1865; *WT*, 4 June 1909.
550 *WT*, 13 Oct. 1875; *EFP*, 20 Oct. 1875 & 27 June 1877. It then moved to 18 High Street; *The Exeter Pocket Journal and Almanack* (Exeter, 1857), 180.
551 *EPG*, 28 July 1877. In 1876 she had been at 42 North Street and Broadgate: *EPG*, 6 Jan. & 25 Nov. 1876; *WT*, 24 Sept. 1878 & 6 May 1879; *EPG*, 3 June 1880.
552 *EPG*, 19 March 1880 & 10 May 1881.
553 *WT*, 10 Oct. 1881.
554 *EPG*, 29 Oct. 1881; *WT*, 18 Nov. 1882.
555 DHC, FOR/B/6/1/39.
556 *EPG*, 15 May 1852.
557 *EFP*, 19 Jan. 1854.
558 *WT*, 10 Nov. 1855; *EPG*, 4 Oct. 1882. Angel died in 1915 at the age of 82: *WT*, 26 Feb. 1915.
559 *EFP*, 11 Oct. 1849.
560 *WT*, 28 July 1855 & 18 Oct. 1856.
561 *WT*, 21 March & 7 July 1860 & 18 Sept. 1863.
562 *WT*, 2 Oct. 1863 & 23 May 1865.
563 *WT*, 29 Oct. 1875; *EPG*, 20 August 1881.
564 By 1818 Thomas Wilson & Company had their Fashionable Upholstery, Chair & Cabinet Ware-Rooms, later known as its Cabinet & Upholstery Warehouse, in the building. Wilson was a cabinet maker and in 1817 he had premises in North Street. In 1822 the firm offered Brussells carpetings, Moreens and London Paper Hangings. In 1832 his firm was succeeded by John Wilson & Company and then in 1858 it was renamed John Wilson & Son: *EFP*, 30 Jan. 1817 & 16 April 1818; *The Alfred*, 19 March 1822; *EPG*, 4 August 1832; *WT*, 24 July 1858.
565 In 1829 Wilson, Patey & Company, Surveyors, Auctioneers & Appraisers, established an office at 22 Cathedral Yard. After Andrew Patey's death in 1834 Wilson continued as both upholsterer and house agent. Patey was an architect who was described at his death as having superior abilities. He designed the West of England Fire Office building as well as the Exeter Bank in Cathedral Yard. Of him it was written that his 'habits were those of persevering industry, joined to an ardent love of his profession such as placed him high in the walk he had chosen': *EFP*, 21 Feb. 1839 & 18 Sept. 1834; *The Times*, 30 March 1836.
566 The census of 1851 noted Wilson was a cabinet maker, that he was born in London, was aged 45 and lived in the building with his wife, their three children and one servant. From at least 1852 until 1856 Mr Gray, a solicitor and proctor, also had an office: *EFP*, 16 Dec. 1852 & 28 June 1856.
567 *WT*, 1 July 1932; DHC, 4139B/P/92–95.
568 There were planning applications in 1956 for rebuilding a portion of the building and changes to the staircase and accommodation: Exeter City Council, planning department index cards.
569 TNA, C106/202.
570 D. Hayton, E. Cruickshanks and S. Handley (eds), *The History of Parliament: the House of Commons, 1690–1715* (2002).
571 Duncan Campbell-Smith, *Masters of the Post* (2011).
572 DHC, FOR/Z/1/1, *Andrew Brice's Old Exeter Journal or the Weekly Advertiser*, 22 August 1760, No. 164; TNA, PROB11/763/16. Lavington had been Exeter's postmaster by 1740: TNA, SP36/51/369.
573 A bookseller was there in 1715 but this may not have prohibited the building's use as a post office: Thomas Nadauld Brushfield, *The Life and Bibliography of Andrew Brice* (privately printed, 1888), 7.
574 *EFP*, 8 June 1826; *EPG*, 27 Jan. & 3 Feb. 1827.
575 He was at Dix's Field by 1857: *Exeter Directory* (Exeter, 1857), 173.
576 *EPG*, 15 Sept. 1870. In 1870 that 'large and convenient dwelling house and offices' of Number 21 were offered for letting. The city's rate book shows that E. Brand was the occupier.
577 *WT*, 17 April 1871.
578 *EFP*, 27 Jan. 1875. W. T. M. Snow was the occupier in 1889 and continued through to the late 1890s: *WT*, 13 Nov. 1889. The Sanders family partly occupied the building from 1898 until 1920: *EPG*, 22 July 1920.
579 *EPG*, 26 May 1905; *WT*, 2 June 1905.
580 *EPG*, 20 Oct. 1906.
581 *WMN*, 17 August 1965; *E&E*, 12 August 1965.
582 Collings, Aspects, 8–9.
583 TNA, PROB11/763/16; ECLA, 6000/8/1-5.
584 DHC, 302A-99/PX1-2, 1836 rate; *EPG*, 5 May 1832.
585 *Pigot's Directory* (1844), 51.
586 *WT*, 4 & 11 Dec. 1891; *EPG*, 24 Dec. 1891; *WT*, 29 June 1894.
587 *EFP*, 26 March 1892.
588 *EPG*, 26 May 1905; *WT*, 2 June 1905.
589 *Exeter Itinerary & General Directory* (Exeter, 1828), 217; *EPG*, 6 Sept. & 1 Nov. 1861; *EFP*, 7 May 1862; *The Building News*, Volume 6, March 1860, page 222.
590 *EPG*, 18 Sept., 9 Oct. 1863 & 22 April 1914; *WT*, 11 June 1912 & 22 Sept. 1913. The bank opened new premises in the high street near Bedford Street in 1913.
591 *WT*, 11 June 1912; *EPG*, 30 Sept. & 29 Dec. 1913. From at least 1925 the upstairs rooms appear to have been known as Prudential Chambers. In 1925 Mr J. Pemberton Stubbs acted as the local manager for the Royal Automobile Club and the premises comprised 'a pleasantly arranged reading and writing room for the convenience of associated members'. In 1935 it was the administrative centre of the county's branch of the British Record Cross. It continued through to at least 1955: *WT*, 29 May 1925; *EPG*, 14 June 1940; *E&E*, 20 Nov. 1940. From 1928 to 1931 Stubbs also used the address for the Exeter & District Safety First Council: *EPG*, 22 Feb. 1929 & 30 July 1931.
592 DHC, ECA/1960 Planning Committee Minute Book, meeting of 28 January. The council required that the mansard roof was set back an approved distance.
593 ECLA, D&C3575, page 234, 236–7 & 253; D&C3569, pages 262–3.
594 *EFP*, 17 Oct. 1816 & 27 Feb. 1817.
595 *EFP*, 7 April 1808; *EPG*, 28 Jan. 1837.
596 DHC, 6631M, a collection of uncatalogued papers.
597 In May 1870 the building was discussed by the council's Street Committee when it approved the plans except for the distance with the property at the rear. Mr Croom, who owned 47 High Street, argued the new building would damage the light into his premises. A few days later Brand placed an advert in the *Western Times*. It read 'my name having been brought before the local board in reference to the building in the Cathedral Yard, I beg to leave to say that everything that I have done has been in strict accordance with the law. The plans have been passed by the Local Board. I trust, therefore, that the public will suspend their judgment and not be misled by any solicitor in the case': *EPG*, 27 May 1870; *WT*, 28 May 1870. Brand continued to be the occupier until shortly before his death in 1914: *WT*, 5 Oct. 1870 & 17 Nov. 1914. As early as 1861 Brand had a reputation for showing curiosities: *EPG*, 30 August 1861.
598 *EPG*, 10 Feb. 1870.
599 *EPG*, 14 Nov. 1914; *WT*, 20 April & 23 Nov. 1915; ECA, Book 514/9/5, 16 August 1879.
600 *EPG*, 16 Nov. 1918.
601 DHC, 2380C/L131; Hugh Meller, *Exeter Architecture* (Chichester, 1989), 23.
602 Press release issued by Thomasons, 21 Feb. 2017.
603 *WT*, 21 March 1930.
604 *WT*, 25 May 1874, 28 July 1874.
605 *WT*, 14 Oct. 1870 & 20 Sept. 1910.
606 *WT*, 21 Jan. 1891.
607 *EPG*, 29 May 1863.
608 In 1863 Miss Williamson had 'two good first floor rooms' and in 1869 'large and convenient offices' to let: *WT*, 23 Oct. 1863, 19 March 1869, 25 April 1879, 1 July 1902; *EPG*, 21 August 1863 & 8 Oct. 1907. In 1854 it was located at 20 Bedford Circus but moved to Cathedral Yard by 1857: *EFP*, 29 June 1854 & *WT*, 14 March 1857 & 30 Jan. 1858.

References

609 He moved the agency to Gandy Street in 1898: *WT*, 16 May 1879 & 27 May 1881; *EPG*, 6 March 1883, 28 Oct. 1884, 19 August 1898, 4 April 1878. There had also been a servants' registry kept at Goldsmith Street in 1857: *Exeter Directory* (Exeter, 1857), 199.

610 *EPG*, 30 May 1889 & 4 & 22 June 1909.

611 In April 1827 the lease of a dwelling house occupied by Mrs Arden was offered for sale: *EPG*, 28 April 1827. By May John Terrell, Solicitor, was the occupier and he remained until his death: *EPG*, 12 May 1827 & 12 August 1843. Charles Veasey Wills & John Richard Treble were in partnership as C. Wills & Company in their capacity as Vesta Lamp & Camphine Dealers until Jan. 1851. Wills continued as a sole trader and had in Jan. 1850 only recently moved from 45 Magdalene Street. He went out of business by autumn 1851. He was still listed on the census that year. He was Exeter-born, aged 30 and lived in the building with his wife, two daughters and two servants: *EPG*, 19 Jan. 1851; *EFP*, 3 Jan. 1850 & 9 Oct. 1851; *WT*, 7 April 1860

612 *EFP*, 29 Ocotber 1873.

613 DHC, FOR/B/6/1/422.

614 DHC, FOR/Z/1/1, *Andrew Brice's Old Exeter Journal or the Weekly Advertiser*, 1 August 1766, No. 461.

615 In 1806 a lease renewal was obtained by James Phillips, the proprietor of the hotel. By 1815 the occupier was James Ridge, who described himself as a tailor and habit maker. In 1817 he obtained a renewal of his lease: *EFP*, 18 May 1815 & DHC, DD 22286.

616 *EFP*, 15 July 1813.

617 *EFP*, 13 May 1819.

618 *EFP*, 21 Nov. 1822.

619 *WT*, 26 April 1864 & 8 Feb. 1877. He moved from London where he had trained and disputed legacies his father had made.

620 *WT*, 26 March 1879. Frederick Horatio Purnell, Shipping Agent, was an occupier from 1880 to 1882 as was T. B. Purnell, Colliery Agent: *EFP*, 28 April 1880 & 8 March 1882; *WT*, 12 Nov. 1880 & 18 Nov. 1882. In 1884 the Preparatory Grammar School for Boys, based in Topsham, used 16 Cathedral Yard for its 'class for little boys': *WT*, 16 Sept. 1884.

621 *EPG*, 14 July 1885 & 12 March 1886; *WT*, 3 Sept. 1887; *EPG*, 1 Dec. 1883; James G. Nelson, 'Mathews, (Charles) Elkin (1851–1921)', *Oxford Dictionary of National Biography*, Oxford, 2004 [http://0-www.oxforddnb.com.lib.exeter.ac.uk/view/article/53207, accessed 8 July 2017]. Mathews had been in Exeter since at least Dec. 1883.

622 *WT*, 12 Nov. 1887.

623 *WT*, 26 July 1890; *EPG*, 19 August 1898. The Gospel Depot & Publishing Office moved from 42 High Street: *WT*, 11 Jan. 1898.

624 By 1888 Henry William Michelmore, solicitor, had an office and remained there until 1891: *WT*, 9 March 1888; *EPG*, 23 Jan. 1891. It was probably through Michelmore that the Electric Light Company had its headquarters at 16 Cathedral Yard from 1889 to 1890: *EPG*, 24 July 1889; *WT*, 2 Jan. & 30 Oct. 1890.

625 *EPG*, 27 August 1909, 24 March 1911, 4 Oct. 1912 & 27 August 1915.

626 *DEG*, 27 Sept. 1935.

627 *EPG*, 23 Feb. 1934 & 27 Sept. 1935.

628 *EPG*, 10 Sept. 1920; *WT*, 15 June 1921. Gertrude Alice Carmichael signed a lease for most of 16 & 17 Cathedral Close in 1935: DHC, 8483, uncatalogued papers.

629 *EPG*, 14 August 1931; *WMN*, 11 Sept. 1942.

630 In 1928 G. and N. Hawkswell opened their 'high class photographic portrait studio' in the building: *EPG*, 8 May 1928. In 1929 two shops, with basements and rooms over which were situated adjoining the hotel were offered for letting: *EPG*, 12 Nov. 1929. In 1940 a flat was rented out to Alan Woodward who was fined 10s for a blackout offence: *E&E*, 12 August 1940; *EPG*, 23 Feb. 1934.

631 *EFP*, 13 May 1813; *EPG*, 2 July 1836. There are two primary works on the history of the site: *An Archaeo-Historical Assessment of the Royal Clarence Hotel, Exeter* (Exeter Archaeology, Jan. 1998), Report No. 98.03, and Darren Marsh, *Exeter's Royal Clarence Hotel* (Exeter, 2017). The latter relies heavily on the archaeological report for the pre-1766 period. Current investigation of the site, in the aftermath of the fire, is revealing further information on the fabric of the building. A letter was printed in *The Guardian* at the time of the fire that the Gentleman's Hotel had been named in 1764 in London: *The Guardian*, 30 Oct. 2016. See *London Evening Post*, 1 Dec. 1764.

632 *The Middlesex Journal or Chronicle of Liberty*, 17 June 1769.

633 ECLA, 6003/1/2 & 6000/b. Edward Carey of Bradford held the lease in 1621 and it continued in his family's possession until 1661 when Robert Warren, a barber, took it on: ECLA, 6001/5/1, 6003/1/53, 6004/1/8 & 6004/11/12.

634 ECLA, 6001/5/5-7 & D&C3563, page 402.

635 ECLA, 6001/6/2. See also D&C 3560, pages 63 & 360–1.

636 ECLA, 6004/12/16, 6004/11/19, 6003/7/1-2 & 6002/12/18.

637 ECLA, 6004/15/11

638 ECLA, 3570, pages 244–5.

639 ECLA, D&C 6003/7/1

640 DHC, FOR/Z/1/1, *Andrew Brice's Old Exeter Journal or the Weekly Advertiser*, 3 June 1763, No. 303.

641 DHC, FOR/Z/1/1, *Andrew Brice's Old Exeter Journal or the Weekly Advertiser*, 5 August 1763, No. 311 & 2 Sept. 1763, No. 315; ECLA, D&C7076/69 & D&C4709.

642 Marsh, *Royal Clarence*, 18–24.

643 DHC, FOR/Z/1/1, *Andrew Brice's Old Exeter Journal or the Weekly Advertiser*, 13 June 1766, No. 454 & 11 July 1766, No. 458, 29 August 1766, No. IV, 29 July 1768, No. CIII.

644 DHC, FOR/Z/1/1, *Brice and Thorn's Old Exeter Journal or the Weekly Advertiser*, 2 Sept. 1768, No. CVIII.

645 DHC, FOR/Z/1/1, *Brice and Thorn's Old Exeter Journal or the Weekly Advertiser*, 5 August 1768, No. CIV; *St James Chronicle*, 2 June 1768; *Kentish Gazette*, 3 August 1774. For instance, see *Manchester Mercury*, 14 August 1770 or *Derby Mercury*, 1 July 1774; Marsh, *Exeter's Royal Clarence*, 27.

646 *Ipswich Journal*, 26 Nov. 1774; *Bath Chronicle & Weekly Gazette*, 16 Feb. 1775; *Chester Chronicle*, 17 July 1775. He was noted as an innkeeper and victualler in a lease of 1770: PWDRO, 69/M/4/512.

647 *Kentish Gazette*, 13 Sept. 1775 & 10 July 1776.

648 *Kentish Gazette*, 2 Sept. 1778; *Manchester Mercury*, 20 Oct. 1778.

649 *Kentish Gazette*, 25 Nov. 1778; *Manchester Mercury*, 11 Dec. 1781 & 21 Jan. 1794; *Bath Chronicle & Weekly Gazette*, 9 Oct. 1788; *Staffordshire Advertiser*, 21 Nov. 1795 & 29 Sept. 1798; *EFP*, 27 Sept. & 25 Oct. 1798; *Kentish Weekly Post*, 12 March 1799; *Kentish Gazette*, 31 Dec. 1813; *WL*, 13 July 1813; LMA, MS 11936/375/580398.

650 Jenkins, *Exeter*, 312.

651 *EFP*, 30 August & 4 Oct. 1810, 13 May 1813; *WL*, 27 April 1813.

652 Eric Shane, *The Young Mr Turner* (New Haven, 2016), 428–9. We are grateful to Dr Richard Stephens for this reference.

653 R. Dymond, 'The Old Inns and Taverns of Exeter', *DAT*, XII (1880), 414–415; *WL*, 17 August, 12 & 26 Oct., 9 Nov. 1813; *EFP*, 25 Nov. 1813.

654 *WL*, 23 Nov. 1813.

655 *WL*, 21 Dec. 1813; *EFP*, 16 Dec., 8 April 1819 & 27 Feb. 1823.

656 Sabine Baring Gould, *Devonshire Characters and Strange Events* (1908), 21–34.

657 *EFP*, 1 July 1819; *The Alfred*, 31 March & 26 June 1821.

658 *EFP*, 27 April 1826 & 22 June 1826; *EPG*, 22 Dec. 1827 & 17 Nov. 1827; *WT*, 23 March 1866.

659 *WL*, 21 August 1837.

660 DHC, 302A-99/PX1, rate for 1836.

661 *EFP*, 17 Feb. 1859.

662 DHC, ECA/9/1/156; *EPG*, 6 August 1859, 4 & 11 May 1866.

663 *EPG*, 14 Sept. 1889.

664 *WT*, 11 July 1879.

665 *The British Architect*, 19.11, 16 March 1811, page 130. In 1896 'a great improvement' was noted to the entrance and front: 'the contractors had to cope with some very substantial walls which in some places were over six feet thick. The superstructure is now carried on steel girders and massive iron piers': *WT*, 14 July 1896 & 27 March 1899; *EPG*, 21 May 1907. In 1908 John B. R. Orchard, who had married Miss Stanbury, daughter of a previous owner, became the owner of the hotel. He purchased the freehold the following year.

666 *WT*, 22 March 1909; *EPG*, 13 Dec. 1928 & 1 July 1929.

667 *EPG*, 31 March 1913.

668 *WT*, 31 Jan. 1914; *EPG*, 4 May 1914.

669 Ashley Courtenay, 'Some discoveries in the hotel world', *The Illustrated Sporting and Dramatic News*, 4 Nov. 1937, 278.

670 Marsh, *Royal Clarence*, 98–155.

671 ECLA, VC21652, VC21661, VC21696; DHC, 103M/T/22.

672 ECLA, D&C3562, pages 36–7.

673 ECLA, D&C3562, pages 40–1.

674 ECLA, VC21696.

675 ECLA, VC21679.

676 *Brice's Weekly Journal*, Number 59, 28 July 1727; ECLA, D&C3567, pages 173–4; DHC, FOR/Z/1/1, *Andrew Brice's Old Exeter Journal or the Weekly Advertiser*, 16 Jan. 1756, No. 325.

677 DHC, FOR/Z/1/1, *Andrew Brice's Old Exeter*

678 John Ryton, *Banks and Banknotes of Exeter* (Exeter, 1983), 23–9.
679 *Archaeo-Historical Assessment*, 4; Marsh, *Royal Clarence*, 26.
680 *EPG*, 31 Oct. 1906; *WT*, 8 Dec. 1906; *EPG*, 29 Nov. 1919.
681 David Cook, 'Continental Painted Glass Panels at the Royal Clarence Hotel, Exeter', *The Journal of Stained Glass*, XXXIII (2009), 26–49; *EPG*, 27 June 1919; *WT*, 18 July 1919.
682 DHC, MCR 10–11, Edward II, m.36.
683 *WT*, 19 August 1880 & 23 Dec. 1908.
684 Curtis, *Some disputes*, 39.
685 DHC, ECA/Misc. Papers/Byelaws.
686 DHC, DD50102-3.
687 ECLA, D&C2118–9 & ED/M/149.
688 ECLA, VC1677B; D&C3578, pages 227–8; D&C3577, pages 50–1.
689 *EPG*, 28 August 1874.
690 *WT*, 26 July 1877.
691 DHC, Voters' Lists. Number 11 last had a resident in 1960, Number 12 in 1967 and Number 13 in 1964.
692 *Heritage Statement*, 9.
693 Marsh, *Royal Clarence*, 5–7; *EFP*, 3 Dec. 1801, 27 May & 30 Dec. 1802, 21 March 1805, *EFP*, 21 July 1814, *WL*, 8 March 1814; *EFP*, 12 June 1817, *WT*, 2 August 1814, *EFP*, 13 March 1817, *EFP*, 28 May 1818, *EFP*, 15 March & 30 August 1821; *EFP*, 15 July 1874.
694 Joseph Vinnicombe was in Martin's Lane from 1835 to 1837: *EFP*, 30 April 1835 & *EPG*, 29 July 1837. He also sold tobacco.; Eliza Rench was also a fruiterer in the lane in 1837 and 1838: *WT*, 15 April 1837 & *EFP*, 27 Oct. 1836 & 7 Dec. 1839.
695 *EPG*, 5 Dec. 1846; *EPG*, 17 Dec. 1846 & 4 Feb. 1847.
696 *EFP*, 3 Feb. 1859. He had been John Skinner's apprentice and upon his death went into business on his own. In 1856 the shop was sold: *EFP*, 17 April 1856.
697 *WT*, 22 Feb. 1862; *EFP*, 19 March & 13 August 1862; *WT*, 14 April 1863; *EPG*, 9 April 1895. By 1872 he had moved to High Street.
698 *WT*, 26 Feb. 1867 & 27 June 1870.
699 *EPG*, 15 Dec. 1871; *EFP*, 23 Dec. 1874.
700 *EFP*, 20 Oct. 1875; *WT*, 10 August 1880; Marsh, *Royal Clarence Hotel*, 60.
701 *EPG*, 16 July 1836; *WT*, 8 April 1837, *EPG*, 16 July & 1 Dec. 1836; *WT*, 1 Oct. 1842; *EFP*, 18 August 1849; *EPG*, 18 August 1849 & 12 Jan. 1850. It is possible that Mrs W. H. Brown Hill, a furrier, was the next occupant. She moved from an unidentified building in the lane in 1853 and had been resident there since 1850: *WT*, 8 Oct. 1853 & 10 August 1850.
702 *EFP*, 23 March 1854; *WT*, 21 April 1855 & 14 June 1856; *Exeter Directory* (1857), 200; *EFP*, 15 Dec. 1859; *WT*, 3 Nov. 1860 & 16 Sept. 1864.
703 *EFP*, 15 Dec. 1859; *WT*, 18 Oct. 1872, 21 April 1888, 10 Sept. 1891, 27 March 1903; *EFP*, 15 August & 19 Sept. 1891; *EPG*, 24 July 1894.
704 *The Alfred*, 17 July 1821 & 5 Feb. 1822; *EFP*, 25 March 1824, 21 Dec. 1826; *EPG*, 25 Dec. 1841 & 21 Dec. 1850; *WT*, 24 June 1848. Spark's father was John Spark, a well-known poulterer of Milk Street: *EFP*, 1 March 1838.
705 *EFP*, 24 August 1848; *EPG*, 7 Dec. 1850; *WT*, 17 August 1850. He was there in 1853: *Slater's Royal National and Commercial Directory and Topography (1852–3)*, 57; *EPG*, 14 Nov. 1840.
706 *EPG*, 8 June 1839; *WT*, 13 May 1843; *EPG*, 12 July 1856; *WT*, 15 June 1839 & 3 August 1866; *EFP*, 3 April 1861.
707 *EFP*, 3 Jan. 1866 & 18 Sept. 1863; *WT*, 5 April 1887.
708 *WT*, 12 Dec. 1896; *EPG*, 25 July 1906.
709 *EPG*, 21 Sept., 20 Dec. 1906, 15 Dec. 1933.
710 *EFP*, 19 Dec. 1833; *EPG*, 21 Dec. 1833.
711 *EPG*, 25 July 1840, 13 & 18 Nov. 1843, 18 & 25 Oct. 1845; *WT*, 9 Sept. 1837, 15 June 1839, 14 Oct. 1843 & 10 June 1848; *Pigot's Directory* (1844), 51, 54. Ann Chapple was listed as the fruiterer in business at 13 Martin's Street.
712 *EFP*, 5 Oct. 1848; *WT*, 27 Oct. 1849; *EPG*, 10 Nov. 1849; *Pigot's Directory* (1844), 38.
713 *EPG*, 16 Sept. & 7 Oct. 1848.
714 *WT*, 7 Sept. 1850 & 23 August 1861.
715 *EPG*, 26 Oct. 1850, 2 Dec. & 8 April 1870; *WT*, 16 Sept. 1864, 29 April 1870, 19 Jan. 1872.
716 *EFP*, 11 Dec. 1872; *EPG*, 26 Dec. 1873.
717 *EFP*, 30 June 1875; *WT*, 27 March 1903 & 20 Dec. 1901.
718 DHC, ECA/1965 Planning Committee Minute Book, 665/65.
719 TNA, C11/890/12. This public house was in existence in 1718.
720 *EFP*, 17 August 1837.
721 LMA, MS11936/391/608859.
722 ECLA, VC21653-4.
723 ECLA, VC12853-7; *EFP*, 8 & 22 June 1815.
724 DHC, 302A-99/PX1-2, rate for 1836; Marsh, *Royal Clarence*, 49–50.
725 ECLA, D&C3568, pages 271–2.
726 WAC, 36/55, (FB/0036/2/5/1).
727 ECLA, 6002/5/8 & 10–11, 6003/1/56-7, 6002/5/12, 6000/2/3a-b, 6000/2/6a-b, VC21680, 6002/12/11, 6002/12/12a-b, D&C 3565, pages 86–7, 6001/6/10, 6001/3/16, 6002/13/30.
728 ECLA, D&C3575, page 234, 236–7 & 253; D&C3569, pages 262–3.
729 In 1550 John Southcote, along with his sons Thomas and George and Oliver Maynwarren, signed a lease for Three Chambers adjacent to one another in the Close for 80 years. Thirty-four years later, in 1584, George's two sons, Thomas and Humphrey, signed another lease: ECLA, 6003/1/67-8. They were followed by Mary Smith, a widow, in 1634 and John Lavers, a goldsmith, in 1640. Edward Mitchell was the occupier and his son William was granted a new lease in 1662: ECLA, 6004/1/4; D&C3556, page 104; 6000/e; D&C3557, page 180; D&C3567, pages 22–3. His widow Susanna leased the building until 1697 when her daughter Susanna Mitchell of Alphington, took over. She was there until at least 1701. In 1718 another leasee, Edward Cook, an Exeter gentleman, continued his interest in the building until 1742 when a tailor took over. Charles Pearce remained until 1790 when his son James became the possessor. James Pearce remained until at least 1801: ECLA, 6002/5/8 & 10-11, 6003/1/56-7, 6002/5/12, 6000/2/3a-b, 6000/2/6a-b, VC21680, 6002/12/11, 6002/12/12a-b, D&C 3565, pages 86–7, 6001/6/10, 6001/3/16, 6002/13/30.
730 *EFP*, 14 June 1838; *WT*, 9 June 1838.
731 *WT*, 24 Feb. 1903; *EPG*, 13 Feb. 1903; DHC, 547B/P/73ii.
732 *EFP*, 16 Jan. 1800, 15 Jan. 1801, 23 April & 14 May 1807. *The Exeter Pocket Journal* of 1796 noted John Hill, druggist, in High Street.
733 *WT*, 5 & 12 Nov. 1869.
734 *EFP*, 26 May 1873; DHC, 6631M; *WT*, 26 Sept. 1873.
735 *EPG*, 27 Jan. 1927 & 26 Nov. 1930.
736 *EPG*, 22 May 1909 & 24 March 1921.
737 *EPG*, 5 April 1869; Andrew Brice, *The Grand Gazetteer* (Exeter, 1759), 543.
738 ECL&A, D&C7076/69.
739 *Brice's Weekly Journal*, Number 86, 2 Feb. 1728.
740 Andrew Brice, *The Grand Gazetteer or Topographical Dictionary* (Exeter, 1759), 544.
741 Andrew Brice, *The Mobiad or Battle of the Voice* (Exeter, 1770), 20.
742 ECLA, D&C3567, pages 38–9; TNA, PROB 11/736/16.
743 Peter Thomas & Jacqueline Warren, *Aspects of Exeter* (Exeter, 1981 edn), 331.
744 TNA, PROB 11/736/16. These were rented out to Jane Furse, John Marks, Elizabeth Russell, Mary Luckraft, Thomas Glanville and Elizabeth Spriggs; *Andrew Brice's Old Exeter Journal or the Weekly Advertiser*, 23 August 1760.
745 DHC, ECA, Exeter City Map Book.
746 *Exeter Itinerary & General Directory* (Exeter, 1828), 224 & 204.
747 *EFP*, 15 July 1874.
748 Pigot, *Directory* (1822); *EFP*, 9 May 1839 & 15 July 1874; *WT*, 13 Oct. 1888, 21 Jan. 1891, 8 May 1891; *EPG*, 31 March 1892; *Exeter Directory* (1835), 45.
749 *EPG*, 19 April 1845.
750 *EFP*, 16 Jan. 1892; *EPG*, 20 March 1913, 14 April & 22 Dec. 1920.
751 *EPG*, 9 & 29 Jan. 1892.
752 *EPG*, 16 Nov. 1906.
753 *EPG*, 1 March 1909.
754 *EPG*, 17 Sept. 1914 & 22 Dec. 1922.

Index

A

Abbott, John White 31, 47–8, 53

accountants A. P. Prowse 91; Bishop, Fleming & Co. 93; E. T. Collins 165; Fleming & Co. 93; Godfrey & Brand 101; Institute of Chartered Accountants 105; John Orchard 133; John Wyatt 165; Neville, Hovey, Smith & Co. 101; Neville, Hovey, Smith & Co. 105; Orchard & Hamlyn 129; Portley & Lethbridge, 93; Ware, Hellyer & Company 165; Ware, Ward & Co. 129Abraham, Benjamin 93

Acland, James 34; Jane 170; Joan 34; Thomas 81

Adam, Robert 143

Adams, Charles **34**, 79, 89, 174, 175; John 43; Maurice Bingham **83**, **124**; Mr 145

Addecot, Edward 170

Adelaide, Queen 147

Alford, Henry 173

Alfred 24

Algar, Edwin 123

Allen, Ernest **30**

Alsop, A. E. 129

Angel, Albert 121, 125

animals, cat 83; camels 107; hawk 46; horse 107

Anstice, Frederick William 61

Aplin, Weston 95

architects, Robert Brown Best 130; Best & Commin 29, 83, 122; J. H. Brewerton 95; Richard Brown, 130; Buttress 147; Robert Medley Fulford 138–9; Samuel Alexis Greig 130; J. Emlyn Harvey 138; Hayward & Son 119, 129–30, 121, 138, 165; Charles Hedgeland 130; George Julian 130; Kenny & Rogers 132; J. Archibald Lucas 68, 73, 93, 97; David McIntosh 130; J. Henry Pitt 68; Charles James Tait 87, 138, 165; Michael Vyne Treleaven 79; Hugh Wilson 105; W. H. Woodroffe & Son 69

Arden, Mr 139; Mrs 179

Ash, John 61

Aviolet, Samuel Anthony 43

B

Babbage, Gilbert 141

Bailey, Elizabeth 52–3, 171; James 79; John 77, 174

Baker, J. H. 91; Joseph 77; Mrs 176; Robert Henry 61, 172; Thomas Russell 71

Bale, Thomas 77, 173

Ball, Henry Melville 93

Balle, William 85, 174

Barns, Mrs 121

Barons, John 73

Bartlett, W. H. **95**

Bastone, Grace 171

Beedell, John 61

Beedle, Anna Maria 172; Thomas George 67, 172

Beer, Alfred 105, 123–5; J. R. 65

Belfield, John 161

Bending, John 81, 174

Bennett, James 55

Berlon, Peter **15**, 128, 142–4, 147

Birkett, William 147

Bisney, Charles 97, 173

Blackall, Offspring 47

Blackamore, Mathew 87

Blake, Thomas 71

Blatchford, Derek 129

Blunden, Ann 48–9; James 77, 173

Bodley, Sir Thomas 34

Bond, William 173

Bondon, Ms 109

Boutcher, Miss 172

Bowchers, Madame 43

Bradford, Robert 55

Bradley, R. 53

Brailey, S.A. 75, 173

Brand, Elihu Edward 129, 135–7, 179; William 165

Braund, Lewis 87

Brewster, Henry Lewis 174

Brice, Andrew **32**, 80, 163

Bridgeman, Orlando 176

Broadmead 175

Brockedon, William 108

Brookman, James 97

Brooks, Charles 20; Miss 119

Brown, Mrs 180; Peter 177; William 177

Browning, J. Bodley 73

Brownsword, Andrew 147

Bruford, William 55

Brutton, John 170

buildings 12–37; Allhallows Goldsmith Church 72; Alliance House 86; Bedford Chambers 29; Bedford Circus 37; Belfields 29; 1 Broadgate 97, **106**–**111**, 123; 2 Broadgate 29, 33, 98, 112–113, **127**, **167**, 168, 169; Broadgate House 98, 99, 176; Castle Chambers 29; 14 Cathedral Yard **148**–**9**; 15 Cathedral Yard see Royal Clarence Hotel; 16 Cathedral Yard 8, **138**–**9**, **140**–**1**, 167, **168**; 17 Cathedral Yard 8, 27, 32, 39, **138**–**9**, 141, 161, 178; 18 Cathedral Yard 8, **26**, 29, 39, 64, **134**–**7**, 161; 19 Cathedral Yard 8, 29, 34, **132**–**3**; 20 Cathedral Yard 27, 29, 39, 127, **130**–**1**, 163, 165; 21 Cathedral Yard 23, 27, 29, 39, **128**–**9**, 163, 177; 22 Cathedral Yard 23, 29, **126**–**7**, 179; 23 Cathedral Yard **19**, 32, 83, **122**–**5**, 168, 177; 24 Cathedral Yard 83, **118**–**121**, 123, 125; 25 Cathedral Yard 83, 123, 125, 171; 26 Cathedral Yard 34, 119–21; 27 Cathedral Yard 121, 180; Central Chambers 29, 163; Chapel of St Peter the Less 82; Cheviot House 54; City Chambers 29; Colleton Crescent 37; Commercial Chambers 29; Corn Exchange 11; Custom House Chambers 29; Dispensary 37; East Gate 20, 23, 24, 37, 39; Eastern Market 37; Fish & Potato Market 39, 43; gates 24, 107–109, 169; Great Conduit 37; Guildhall 11, **19**, 39, **51**, 80, **94**–**5**, **98**, **102**–**103**; Guildhall Chambers 29, 86; Guildhall Shopping Centre 11, 24; Harlequin's Shopping Centre 18, 24; Henri Fashions 83; Higher Market 18, 39; 39 High Street 11, 25, 31, 34, 40, **42**–**3**, **47**, **159**; 40 High Street **25**, 43, **44**–**5**, **54**; 41 High Street **25**, **31**, 34, **40**, **44**, **46**–**52**, 77, 167, 169; 42 High Street 32, **44**, **46**–**53**, 169; 43 High Street **11**, **25**, 31, 34, **45**, **49**, **50**, 53, **54**–**5**, 59, 60, 61; 44 High Street **11**, **25**, 27, 31, 36, **56**–**9**, **61**; 45 High Street **11**, 24, 39, **56**, **58**, **60**–**1**, 73, 161; 46 High Street **11**, **14**, **16**–**17**, 27, **30**, **56**, **58**, **60**, **61**, **62**–**6**, 67, 75, 161, 172; 47 High Street **11**, 25, 29, 30, 34, **40**, **55**, **56**, **58**, **61**–**3**, 65, **66**–**7**, 161, 179; 48 High Street 27, 29, 33, 34, 35, 49, **68**–**71**, **72**–**3**, 173; 49 High Street 27, 29, 35, 39, 49, 68–9, 72–3; 50 High Street 23, 31, **68**–**9**, **74**–**5**, 77; 51 High Street 27, 39, **68**–**9**, 72, **74**–**5**, **76**–**7**, 97; 52 High Street 23, 29, 31, **68**–**9**, **76**–**7**, 78–9; 53 High Street 12, 18, 29, **34**, **76**–**9**, 80–1; 54 High Street 12, 31, 32, 79, **80**–**1**; 55 High Street 31, 32, 36–7, **82**–**3**, 84–5, 87, 123, 168; 56 High Street **19**, 31, 32, 36–7, **82**–**7**, 168; 57 High Street 12, **19**, 31, 34, 36–7, **86**–**9**; 58 High Street 11, 12, **19**, 31, 34, 36–7, **88**–**9**; 59 High Street 12, 29, 31, 34–5, 90–3, 95, 97; 60 High Street 29, 34, 40, 90–5; 61 High Street 11, 29, 34, 40, 96–8, **100**–**101**, 105, 113; 62 High Street 11, 29, 34, 40, **96**–**7**, 98–101, 102, 105, 110, 113; 63 High Street 11, 29, 34, 40, **96**–**7**, 98, **100**, 101, **102**–**5**, 110, 113; Hospital of St Mary Magdalene 29; House that moved 24; Longbrook Street 138; Mansion House 29, **134**–**7**, 139; Marks & Spencer 52; 10 Martin's Lane **152**–**3**; 11 Martin's Lane **154**–**5**, 156; 12 Martin's Lane **156**–**7**; 13 Martin's Lane 156, **157**–**9**; North Gate 37; Nottingham House 76; Plympton Priory 29; Polsloe Priory 15, 29; Post Office Chambers 29; Princesshay 11; Prudential Chambers 29, 132, 179; Rose & Crown 20; Rougemont Castle 12, 119; Smythen Street 123; South Gate 15; St James Priory 29, 42; St John's Hospital 11, **35**, 80; St Mary Major Church 24; St Nicholas Priory 15; St Stephen's Church 24; Three Chambers 29, 161, 180; Three Gables 11; Victoria

Index

St Martin's Island: An introductory history of forty-two Exeter buildings

House 29, 76, 77–9, 81, **169**, 174; Well House 138–41; West Gate 36, 39; Western Market 37

Burden, John 42–3

Burgess, John 65, 172

Burrington, George 89

Burrow, Robert 65

businesses, A. H. Shooter Ltd 81; ABC Tobacconists 97; Ann Summers 12; Antartex 125; Applewoods Natural Products 129; Ashley Courtenay 93; Audrey Clare 71, 73, 141; Austin Photographic Ltd 133; Bambers 77; Bambridge Moyse & Co. 71; Beavis Tavern 107; Beer & Driffield 105; Berlin Wool Warehouse 97; BOCM Silcock Ltd 71, 73; Boots **18**, 79; Boyds of Bond Street 87; Broadgate Mart 113; Brock & Co. 69; Bromley Sanders 129; Brooking & Son 97; Brown's 77; Bruford 55; Burger King 11, 23, 36, 77, 163; Business Mortgages Ltd 157; C. M. S. Depot 165; Card Factory 83; Castle Art Gallery 137; Castle Staff Agency 127; Cathedral Café **76**, 81, 126; Cathedral Lounge 126; Cathedral Restaurant & Café 113, 127, **212**; Cathedral Yard Café 129; Central Auction & Estate Office 131, 165; Chalk's Stores 101; Charles Ltd 87; Chiro Podia 71; Christine Denny 155; Clinton Cards 43, 45, 159; Coco 155; Collingwood 71, 73; Colsons 127; Connect 65; Cornish & Co. 110–111; Corus & Regal Hotels 147; Costa Coffee 55, 61, 79; Cote Brasserie 129; Daniel Maher & Co. 43; David Greig 87; Deller's Café **33**, **68–71**, 73, 148–9; Dolcis 77, 79; Dorothy Perkins 43, 45, 159; Drive Yourself Cars 93; Dubarry Clothing 131; Duke Street 147; Dunn & Co. 97, 101; Edinburgh Woollen Mill 36, 125; Electric Light Company 141, 178; Electronic Boutique Computer Games 97, 101, 105; Empire Hotels 147; Etam Ltd 65; Exeter Auctioneers 127; Express Hotels 147; First Sports 55, 61; Focus 81; Forestry Commission 93; Foster, Fox & Sons 127; Fothergill Bros. Ltd 129, 131; Fox & Sons 81, 127; Freeth's Tofferies 65; French Stix 113; Friday's Child 155; Fulford & Chorley 127; G. A. Property Services 127; Game Computer Games 97, 101, 105; Gerardo 71, 73; Glebelands 113; Goff & Gully 101; Golden Egg 81; Granada 67; Guildhall Art Studios 101; Guildhall Circulating Library 141; H. M. Carmichael Antiques 141; Hair@No.12 157; Haroll Chorley & Irlam 93; Harry Hems & Sons 78, 138; Hill, Palmer & Edwards 43; Hinton Lake **38**, **44**, **46–9**, **50**, **54**; Hoskins & Son 43; House of Bewlay 65; J. Howard & Co. 119; J. L. Tannar Ltd 101; Jaeger 87, 89, 137; Jigsaw 12; John Farmer Ltd 81; John Lewis 23; Kalamazoo Ltd 127; Kate Karneys 81; King & Kearey Ltd 93; L'Occitaine 67; Laura Ashley 36, 49, 53; Lillywhites 11, **77**; Luget 34, 127, 176; Lush 89; Marcina School of Dancing 81; Martin's Café 43; May, Dunn & Co. 105; Maypole Diary Co. 97; Mazawattee Tea Co. 101; Melvilles 105; Michael Spiers 127; Michelmores 10, 129, 131, 135–7, 141, 178; Mocha Café 141; Mol's Coffee House 42; Montague Burton 87; Morgan & Pope 127; Murray's Antiques 141; National Trust Shop 137; Nelson & Co. 141; Norfolk Capital Hotels 147; Old Bears Restaurant 129; Old Curiosity Shop 153; Orange Shop 67; Orchard & Hamlyn 129; Original Levis Store 97, 101, 105; Orvis 127, 137; Overdrive Ltd 71, 73; Peachey & Richards Ltd 127; Peter Robinson 77; Petherick Brothers 133; Picture Zone Computer Games 101, 105; Pinder & Tuckwell 34, **38**, **55**, 61; Pitts 127; Pizza Express 29, 113; Polkadot Gallery 157; Poppins 81; Principles 55, 61; Property Seekers Ltd 71, 73; Public Benefit Boot Co. 101; Queens Moat Hotels 147; R. B. Taylor 141; Real Cornish Pasty Co. 153; Red House of Devon 157; Regency Shop 131; Reginald Howard Publications 101; Rendells 129; Ricky 71, 73; Ridgways Shoes 131; Road Haulage Association 93; Robin Hills 71, 73; Rowland's Fabrics & Fashions 81; Royal Automobile Club 133, 179; Royal Clarence Hotel 7–10, 142–53; Rt Phipps Ltd 137; Russells 129; Salisbury, 66–7, 71, 73; Scholastic & Domestic Agency Office 123; Sellicks 126–7; Sherratt & Hughes 71, 73; Ship Inn 153, 154; Skechers 43, 45, 159; Skirt Shop 61; Smith & Marshall 93; Songbird Tattoo 89; Songhurst & Richard 93; South Western Foresters Ltd 127; St Martin's Café 43; St Martin's Well 141; Star Jeans 49, 53; T. Smith & Co. 141; Tact-Contact 159, 43; Talasio Bridal & Dress Hire 127; Teffont 71; Telefusion 63, 65; The Rummer 148–9; Thomas & Co. 141; Thomas Sanders & Staff 141; Thorntons 65; Timothy White 105; Tinleys Café 29, 33–4, 112–**113**; Trailfinders 11, 40, 97–101, 105; Tudor Rose Café 129; United Development Assoc. Ltd 133; Veitch 32, **33**, 81, 138–9; Visionhire 67; Ware, Ward & Co. 129; Warham Guild Ltd 125; Warren & Son 83; Watches of Switzerland 65; Waterstones 36, 69, 71, 73; Watty's 159; Webber **72**, 97; Well House 7; Wilson & Co. 127; Wimpy 77; Wippell & Co., **18**, 32, 37, 82–5, 122–125, 156; Wyvern Bowls Ltd 127

Butland, Elias 61, **62**, 65, 161, 172

Butter, Thomas 170

C

Caines, Michael 147

Cambridge, Charles 89, 175

Carey, Bishop 109; Edward 178

Carlile, George Byron 151, 156–7

Carmichael, Gertrude Alice 178

Carr, William Holwell 31

Carter, George 49; John Stephens 139

Caseley, 176

Chamberlain, Charlotte 53; Elizabeth 91, 175; Grace 91; James 175; Richard 90, 91, 175

Chaplin, John 36, 55, 171

Chapple, Ann 159, 180; John 158–9; R. A. 125

Chastey, Miss 101, 177

Chave, family 119

cholera 16

Chorley, F. J. 127

Chubb, R. R. 87, 175

Chute, Mr 49

Clare, Audrey 141

Clark, Mrs 104–105, 177

Clarke 175; W. Hosegood 172

Cleeve, Abraham 87, 175

cloth 12–14

Coffin, Mr 20; Richard 78–9

Coker, Richard 81; William 81

Cole, Charles 149, 165; Jane 87, 175; William Henry 55

Collibear, Thomas 67

Collins, Charles 156–7; E.T. 165

Comerford, M. 65, 172

Commin, James G. 141; Richard 109

Congdon, Joseph 137, 145, 147

Connor, Mr 144, 147

Cook, Edward 180

Cooke, John 16, 29

Cookworthy, Edward Robins 132

Copleston, Joseph 97; William 65, 67, 172

Copp, Anthony 75, 173; William 75, 173

Cornish, Deborah 175; Robert 73; S. 67, 172

Cossins, C. B. 111, 177

Couch, William 55

Courtall, Lewis 43

Cowey, J. T. 55, 171

Coxwell, Caroline A. 97

Cramp, Benjamin 55, 55, 171

Crocker, James **45**, **82**

Croker, Richard 175

Croome, John 67, 172, 179

Cross, Robert 73, 173

Cummings, R. H. 53

D

Darke, family 176

Davey, Henry 154–5; John 43, 158–9; Mary 153

Davies, Samuel 55, 177; W. G. 36

Davis, Honor 123, 125; Mr 36; William 123, 125

Davison, T. Raffles 147

Davy, John 65

De Maria, Mr 145

Deller, Edwin 33

Densem, Harold 67, 172

Densham, W. 97

Devon & Exeter Fine Art Exhibition 123

Devon & Exeter Institution 36

Devon 11, 15; Alphington 180; Bow 138; Bradford 178; Broadclyst 45; Chulmleigh 173; Clyst Honiton 175; Crediton 87; Dartmoor 154; Dawlish 123; Devonport 15; Exminster 11; Exmouth 15, 177; Honiton 113; Ilfracombe 146; Newton St Cyres 129; North Tawton 174; Paignton 33; Peamore 11, 79; Plymouth 15, 29, 145, 171; Seaton 146; Sidmouth 15;

186

Index

Teignmouth 15; Tiverton 173; Topsham 178; Torquay 15, 154, 171; Upton Pyne 141; West Putford 36, 141

Dicker, T. G. 156–7

Dinneford, Elizabeth 87, 89, 175

Dobbs, Charlotte 121

Donn, Robert 77

Donne, Benjamin 162–3

Downe, James 137

Drayton, S. 95

Drew, Thomas 42–3

Drewe, John 113

Dunn, Anna 176; Edwin 97, 176

Dunsford, Richard 82–3; Richard the Younger 82–3, 174

Duntze, John 149

Dyer, Gilbert 31

Dymond, William 101, 105, 177

Dyson, Miss 113

educational institutions, Exeter College 23; Exeter University 23; Preparatory Grammar School for Boys 141

E

Edward I 107

Elworthy, E. **17**; George 65, 172

England, Bath 125; Bristol 176; Cambridge 42; Cornwall 15, 43, 96, 115; East Anglia 39; Herefordshire 174; Leicester 24; London 11, 12, 15, 29, 32, 36, 43, 61, 64, 94, 115, 125, 132, 142, 144, 158, 169, 171; Oxford 24, 36, 104; Salisbury 116–117; Somerset, 12, 87, 95; Tewkesbury 73

Evans, John 65, 85, 175

Exeter City Library 91

Exeter Homeopathic Dispensary 139

Exeter, parishes 12; Heavitree 15, 102, 118; St David 15; St Leonard 15; St Mary Arches 168; St Pancras 12; St Petrock 12, 16; St Sidwell 15, 96; St Thomas 15

F

Farington, Joseph 47

Farrant, Henry 85

Fegan, John 67, 172

financial institutions, Abbey National Building Society 79, 81; African Life Assurance Society Ltd 93; Alliance & Leicester Building Society 34, 83, 89; Anglian Insurance Co. Ltd 93; Australian, Colonial & General Life Insurance Co. 176; Bradford & Bingley 129; Burnley Building Society 127; Caledonian Insurance Co. 93; Car & General Insurance Corp. 105; Charing Cross Bank 34, 101; City Bank 111, 149; Clerical, Medical & General Life Assurance Society 93; Confidential Monetary Office 119, 121; Devon & Cornwall Bank 34, 132–3; Devon County Bank 34, 118; Devon Insurance Committee 93; Employers Liability Assurance Corporation Ltd 93; Exeter Advance Co. 125; Exeter Bank 34, 148–9, 179; Fowler & Co. Bank 34, 87; Fox Brothers Bank 34, 87, 89; Friends' Provident & Century Insurance 101; Guardian Assurance Co. Ltd 93; Leicester Permanent Building Society 83; Life Association of Scotland Ltd 89; Lloyds Bank 34, 87, 133; National Provident Bank 87; National Provincial Bank 34, 94–5, 119, 121; National Westminster Bank 34, 36, 95, 118–119; Nationwide Anglia Building Society 127; Norwich Union Fire Insurance 91, 93, 95, 176; Portman Building Society 55, 61; Provident Accident & White Cross Insurance Company 93; Prudential Assurance Co. 68–9, 73, 129, 131, 133; Prudential Monetary Office 141; Royal Exchange Assurance Corp. 105; Santander 79, 81, 83; South West Trustee Savings Bank Training Centre 131; Sun Life Assurance Society 87, 89; West of England Fire Office 179; West of England and South Wales District Bank 34, 94–5; Woolwich Equitable Building Society 133

fires 7–10, 17, 36–7, 43, 65, 83, 86–7, 93, 96–7, 101, 122, 137, 138, 142, 147, 167

Fitze, Ellen 43; James 43; Maria 43

Floyde, Grace 175; William 61

Foote, Maria 145; Samuel T. 145

Ford, Sarah 173

foreign countries, Egypt 55, 145–6; France 47, 53, 135, 142–3; Paris 25, 52, 71; Germany 55; Holland 115; India 55; Italy 39, 44–5, 55, 103–**105**, 115, 132–3; Peru 121; Portugal 15; Russia 161; United States of America 125

Fouraker, Thomas 93

Fox, Aileen 97; George William 61

Francis, Enoch 89, 175; Mrs 89

Furse, Jane 180

G

Gadd, Henry 101

Galen, bust of **17**, 66

Gandy, Abraham 55

Gard, Henry 175; John Somers 79, 172, 174

Gardner, W.A. 97

Garland, Theodore 93

Gascoyne, Alexander 79

Gatrill, Mrs 97; Walter 97

Gendall, John 106

Gibbons, Maria Susannah 36

Gibson, Pauline 119

Gifford, Robert 170

Gilbert, M.A. 87, 175; John 142

Girle, Miss 15

Glanville, Thomas 180

Goff, Ann 113, 177; J. C. 113

Gollop, R. N. 69, 70

Gould, Charles Spry **45**; George Goodwin 45; Miss 101; Sarah 45; William 45

Gove, Madame 43

Graham, John 146–7

Gray, Mr 179

Greenfield, Richard 175

Grey, Henry 11; Jane 11

Gulliaume, G. 125

H

Hagedott, Margaret 87

Haines, George 61, 172

Haiusselin, Henry 93

Hake, Mrs 101

Hall, Simon 11

Ham, Charles 49

Hamilton, Daniel 149

Hamlin Walter Henry 165

Hancock, George 45

Hanek, Roger 151

Harbottle, Mr 111

Harris, John 111

Harrison, Adelaide 175

Harvey, I. Edward 139; Mr 139

Havill, Frederick 93

Hawkeswell, G. 141, 178; N. 178

Hawkins, Mrs John 119

Haycock, Mrs 75, 173

Haydon, F. W. 55, 171

Haymes, W. F. 141

Hayne, Sidney 163

Head, Mr 139

Hedgeland, Caleb 24–5, 40, 42; Philip 79, 174; Samuel 79, 174

Hellyar, William 176

Hems, Harry 79

Herbert, George 87, 89; Harriet 89

Herman, Ralph 98

Heywood, G. 53

Higgs, Mrs 52–3

Hill, B. Mrs 125; John 66–7, 172; Thomas 65; W. H. Brown 53

Hillier, R. 61

187

Index

Hippisley-Coxe family 12; John 12

Hitchcock, John 87, 175

Hodge, Henry 85 , 175

Holden, Adam 94–5, 176

Holmes, F. C. 77, 173

Hooke, Joseph 73

Hooker, John 67

Hooper, Eliza 159; F. C. 173; Henry 155, 159; J. H. 77; James H. 173; Jane 49, 170; Mary 159; Philip **31**, 47, 53, 170, 171

Hopekirk, Robert Craigee 53

Horswell, James 65

Hoskins, J. P. 43; W. G. 23–4, 169–70

Houlditch, Edward H.

Hourston, Thomas 105, 177

Howard, John H. 71

Howell, Brewer 101, 105, 111, 176; Edward 49, 53; Mary 140–1

Huckvale, William 71

Hunt, Stuart 79, 174

Hussey, William 55

Hutchings, Zoe 101

Hutchinson, E. J. 111, 123; Samuel H. 110–111, 121, 125, 147

Hutton, J. V. 81

Huxham, William 113

I

improvement **96**–101; Commissioners 16

J

James, Cecil A. 141

Jeanes, Edwin 85

Jeffery, Emmanuel 101

Jenkins, Alexander 15–16, 79, 107, 144; J. 61, 171

Jennings, Michael 61

Jerman, Frederick 165; James 60

Jerwood, James 119

Jones, David 67, 172; Pitman 109; William Lloyd 105, 177

K

Kemp, Samuel 135, **136**, 137

Kennaway, I. J.

Kernick, Miss 68

King, Jerome 32, 142, 170; Peter 31–2, 142

Kingdon, J. 176–7

Kittoe, William 175

Knapman, John 67, 172

Knight, Charles 16–17

Knott, Thomas **49**, 52–3

Knowling, S. J. 55, 171

L

Lake, A. H. 53; Bessie 53; Henry 55; J. C. 71; John Ellett 49, **52**, **55**; John Hinton 46–9; Miss 49; Mrs 71

Lamb, Mr 158

Lambeth, Denis 81

Lambshead, William 33

Lancey, Edwin 55, 171

Lane, John 141

Langford, Douglas C. 93

Lascelles, Eliza 119

Laundon, R. 129

Lavers, John 180

Lavington Thomas 163, 179

Lawrence, Richard 10

Leakey, James 93

Lear, John 154–5

Leland, John 39

Lemmon, Eric 67, 172

Lendon, Sarah 173

Leofric 78

LePetit, Mr 95

Lethbridge, R. J. G. 93

Ling, R. B. 101, 105, 177

Lingard, Mr 145

Linwood, Ernest 71

Lloyd, Richard 147

Long, James Frederick 61, 171

Lucas, J. Archibald 93, 97

Luckraft, Mary 180

Luget, Samuel F. 95

Luke, G. B.173; Thomas 75

Luxmoore, William 55

M

Maddock, Agnes 61

Maher, Daniel 43

March, John 54–5

Mardon, Benjamin 81, 174; Elizabeth 81, 174; Mr 137; Sarah 112–113, 177

Marks, John 180

Marriott, Sophia 123, 125

Marshall, Hamish 7–9

Marson, H. E. 139

Mathews, Charles Elkin 32, 34–6, **140**, 141

Matthews, C. H. 119

Maunder, Samuel 49; William 53, 65; William Jr 53, 172

Mawson, Thomas 17–19, 151

Mayne, Eliza **17**, 61, 73, 172; Robert 61, 172

Maynwarren, George 180; Humphrey 180; Oliver 180; Thomas 180

media, BBC 7–10; ITV 10

Melhuish, J. W. 71

Michelmore, H. W. 178

Michie, James 43

Mildrum, John 75, 173; William 75, 173

Mitchell, Edward 180; Susanna 180

Mock, Richard 153–9

Molle, Thomas 42

Monkhouse, William 101

Moore, William 55; William Denis 137, 175

Mortimore, John 97, 176

Moss, Henry Stafford 71

Mudge, Mr 129; Robert 61

Mugford, Annie 71

Murch, James 112–113, 177; Sarah 34, 112–113

museums, Ashmolean 104; Chaplin's 36, 55; Royal Albert Memorial Museum 46, 91, 165

N

Nash, E. 91,176; F. 112; J. 91, 176

Neale, Mrs 176; Thomas 95

Newman, J. H. 71, 73

Nightingale, Robert 87, 89, 175

Noble, Henry 125

Norris, John J. 83, 174; William 91, 176

Northleigh, Margaret 12; Mr 175

Nott, Mike 139

O

Occupy Exeter 10

Oliver, George 115

188

Opie, William 105, 177

Orchard, J. G. R. 147; John Bailey Rowe 147

P

Paget, Dr 129

Painter, Edward 65

Parker, John Battishall 129

Parnell, Mary 113, 177

Parr, Elizabeth 89; John 89, 175; Judith 89; Robert 89, 175; Sabine 89, 175; Sarah 89; Sibley 89, 175

Passmore, G. E. 111

Pasta, Madame 146

Paul, Richard 94, 95

Payne, Mr 95

Pearce, Charles 161, 180; James 55, 137, 161, 180

Perkins, Frank Pince 139

Phillips, James 145, 147, 178; John 77; W. H.

Philpot, Mr 55

Picard, J. 119

Pickard, C. 87 175

Pilbrow, Tycho 91, 119, 175

Pim, William 93

Pinwill, Mrs 43, 175–6

Pittman, James 91, 175

Plowman, George Heseltine 174

Pocknell, Edward **72**

Pollard 177; E. 129; William 55, 171

Ponsford, W. L. 52–3

population 30–1

Portbury, Edward 53, 61, 171

Potter, Beatrix 115

Praed, William Mackworth 15–16, 142–9

Presswell, Charles Benjamin 65, 172

Preston, Miss 119

Prince, Henry 71

Pring, Daniel 44–5

Priston, Charles William 141

Proctor, Mr 75, 173

Prowse, A.P. 91, 175; James W. 119–121

public agencies and government, British Red Cross 87, 133, 179; Devon County Agricultural Committee 137; Devon County Council 137; Devon County Council 93; Devon County Territorial Force Assoc. 137; Devon River Board 137; Dr Barnado's Homes 127; Exeter & District Safety First Council 133; Exeter Municipal Charities 165; Manpower Employment Agency 71; Ministry of Agriculture & Fisheries 93; Ministry of Labour 137; National Society for Handicapped Children, 93; Road Transport Board 137; Territorial Force Assoc. 87; Women's Land Army 93; Women's Voluntary Services 137

Pugh, N. 141

Purnell, Frederick Horatio 141, 178; Thomas B. 125, 141

Pyne, S. 87, 175

Q

Quantrell, Miss 52–3

Quash, Joseph 128–30

R

Raddon, John 77, 174

Reynolds, Robert 77

Richard, Edmund 87, 89

Rickard, James 53; John 152–3; Mr 139

Ridge, James 140–1, 178; John 141

Risdon, John 95, 176

Robinson, David 71

Rogers, Henry 73; William Charles 139

Ross, James 77

Rous, Robert 148–9

Rovedino, Maria 48

Rowe, Joseph 45; Roger 173

Royal Devon & Exeter Hospital 143

Rudall, S. & E. 53

Russell, Elizabeth 180

S

Salaman, S. 54–5

Salter, John 172

Sampson, Grace 170; Samuel 49, 53, 170

Sanders, family 179; Frederick 154–5; Isabella 129; Joseph 149, 159; William A. 130–1

Saunders, John 55; M.A. 101

Scanes, Walter 139, 141

Score, Edward 97

Scotland 53

Scudder, Anna 53; Emma 53; John 77, 129, 174

Searle, Francis Furlong 119, 179; Jane 125

Seaton, W. H. 75, 173

Sellick, Frederick William 79, 81

Setten, Ann 177

Shapley, Frederick **33**, 71, 73

Shapter, Thomas 91

Sharland, John 53, 55

Sharp, Thomas 20–23

Shephard, J. D. 61, 171

Shortt, W. P. S. 118

Skinner, Matthew 43, 170

Slade, Daniel 45, 170; William 45

Sleep, Colin 65, 172

Smale, Eliza 113, 177; John 113

Smallridge, W. 55

Smith, Mary 180; Sidney Albert 73; Thomas 176

Smyth, Elizabeth 121

Snell, 105, 176; E. 61, 171; F. 61, 171; I. W. 176

Snow, William Thomas Munby 129, 179

societies, Devon & Exeter Architectural Society 19; Devon & Exeter Religious Book & Tract Society 139; Exeter Chess Club 83, 174; Exeter Civic Society 23, 24, 97; Exeter Pictorial Record Society 20; Exeter Plain Workers' Society 123, 125; Society for Promoting Christian Knowledge 129, 165; Society for the Protection of Ancient Buildings 116

Solomon, Myers 95, 176

Southcote, John 180

Southey, Robert 15

Southwood 177; Richard 105

Sowden, Robert 67, 161, 172

Spark, John 180; Robert 156–7

Sparkes, Thomas 89, 175

Spoure, Edmund 15

Sprague, F. 153

Spreat, William 93

Spriggs, Elizabeth 180

Spry, Mary 89, 90, 175; Nathaniel 91; Sarah 89, 90, 175

St. John O'Neill, B. H. 20

Stamp, A. 64–5; E. 64–5

Stanbury, John 79, 174; John Headon 147

Stephens, Samuel 89, 175

Stevens, J. 153

Stocker, Henry **16**, 65

Stockham, Sarah 75

Stokes, William 119

Stoneman, Henry 139

Street, Sarah 115–116, **136**

streets 27–9; Bampfylde Street 29; Bartholomew Street 12, 19–20, 25; Bedford Circus 33, 178; Bedford Street 141, 179; Black Boy Road 31; Broad

189

St Martin's Island: An introductory history of forty-two Exeter buildings

Street 101, 107; Broadgate 10, 11, 24, 27, 29, 31, 33, **35**, 37, **94**, **97**, **99**, **100**, **102**–**104**, 105, **106**–113, **117**, **118**, 126, 147; Broadgate Place 107; Castle Street 29; Cathedral Close 115; Cathedral Yard 7–37, 39, 46, 68–9, 75, 85, 107, 110, 112, 114–49, 161, 163–5, 170–80; College Road 61; Dix's Field 179; Fishfoldsgate 107; Fore Street 11, 20, 29, 39, 80; Gandy Street 29, 36, 179; George Street 37; Goldsmith Street **23**, 29, **70**, **72**, 179; Grosvenor Place 31; Haldon Road 31; High Street 7–37; King Street 20; Lamb Alley 25, 27, 29, 39, 54, 55, 61, 60, 63, **67**, 134–5, 160–1, 169; Luxury Lane 151; Lyndhurst Road 31; Magdalen Road 31; Magdalene Street 179; Market Street 43; Martin's Lane 7–11, **19**, 24, 27, 29, 30, 33, **35**, 36–7, 53, 55, 150–9; New (or Little) Exchange 23, 27, 39, 128, 130, 162–3, 169; New North Road 31; North Street 175; Old Tiverton Road 31; Paris Street 20; Paul Street 20; Pennsylvania Park 31, 37; Pennsylvania Road 31; Powderham Crescent 31; Preston Street 20; Prospect Park 31; Queen Street 18, 19, 27, 29, 39, 49, 151; Sidwell Street 20; South Street 11, 20, 175; Southernhay 15, 37

Strong, George 97, 176; William 61

Stubbs, J. Pemberton 179

Suffolk, Duke of, see Grey

Sully, Albert 87, 101, 175

surveyors Alan E. Langdon 137; Bambridge, Moyse & Co. 71; Best, Sanders & Sanders 131; Charles Cole 165; Charles Lee Wright 129; Foster Fox & Sons 127; Frederick Jerman 165; John Archibald Lucas 93; Matthew Blackamore 87; Property Seekers Ltd. 71, 73; R. B. Taylor & Sons 141; Smith & Marshall 93; Songhurst & Richard 93; William Norris 91; Wilson, Patey & Company 127

Swain, Mrs 98, 101

T

Tancock, G. L. 155

Tapley, Charlotte 64–5; Elizabeth 64–5

Taylor, John 101, 105, 176

Teece, H. Millington 119

Terrell, John Hull 139, 179

Thompson, Thomas 144, 147

Thomson, David 55

Thorn, Barnabas 70–1, 174; Richard 70–1, 174

Thornley, Charles 97

Tighe, Wynne 155

Toms, John 54–5

Tory, George 81, 179

Tothill, family 79, 80, 89; Geoffrey 11; Henry 175; John 25, **64**, **88**, **122**; William 11

Townsend, Frederick 105, 177; George 20, 91

Tozer, Aaron 55, 60; Samuel 65

Traies, William 93

Treadwin, Charlotte 121, 180; John 119

Treble, John Richard 179

Trehane, Christopher 55; Mary 55

Trelease, Arthur 77; W. H. 77, 174

Trew, W. H. 71

Tripe, Anthony 71; Jane 71; Nicholas 71

Trist, Joseph 97, 176

Trotter, Charles 77

Trump, Miss 71

Tucker, Alfred 153; Edward 93; Richard 65; Walter 49, 171; William Fryer

Tuckfield, Joan 102

Turner, Charles H. 131, 132–3

Twose, A. S. 176

U

Uglow, Abel 97, 176

Upham, Charles 98, 101, 102–104; Edward 104; John 101

Upjohn, James 113; Richard 112, 113; Robert 43

V

Vavasour, Adeline 141

Veitch, James 32, 81; John 32; Robert 32, 81, 138; Thomas 81, 174

Veysey Ann 73, 173; E. 173; Francis 75, 173; Hugh 173; I. 173; William 71, 73, 173

Vicary, John 146

Vinnicombe, Joseph 101, 180

Visitors 15–16, 20, 32, 39, 82, 115–116; Italian 15, 115

Vowler, John 130, 163

W

Wales 132

Walker, William

war, Civil 15; First World 20, 141; Second World 11, 20, 21, 24, 87, 169

Warren, Robert 178; W. H. 83, 174

Watts, Samuel B. 61, 172

Wayborn, Mrs 71

Webber, John 83

Weekes, Ethel Lega **frontispiece**, 47, 82, 107, 171

Welch, Marianne 81, 174

Wells, W. F. 119

Welsford, Henry 97, 101, 176

Welsh, Miss 36

Wescomb, William 152–3; William Frederick 43

West Quarter 16, 19

Westaway, D. 61, 172

Wheeler, T. G. 79, 174

Whitton, Henry J. 87, 175

Whitty, Thomas 55

Wigginton, Thomas 89, 175

Wilcocks, Henry 91; John Magdwick 172, 175

Wilford, 112; Robert 82

Williamson, Elizabeth 139, 178–9

Wills, Charles 139; Charles Veasey 179; Edward 87, 175

Wilson, John 127, 179; Thomas 95, 127

Windeat, James 101, 105, 111, 176

Wippell, Joseph 52–3

Wish, Lucretia 79; Richard 79

Wood, Benjamin 55; Charles 43, 95, 101, 176; Frederick 61, 171

Woodley, R. J. 55

Woodward, Alan 178

Wrenn, W. A. 43

Wright, Charles Lee 129; Harry 157; Walter 67, 172

Wyatt, John 163–5

Wylie, R. W. 139

XYZ

Yelland, Joseph C. 95

Yeo, Charles, 47, 53, 171

Sources of Illustrations

Illustrations have been reproduced with the kind permission of the Royal Albert Memorial Museum & Art Gallery, Exeter City Council (cover illustration & **206**. Hedgeland model; **117**. 743/1997/2; **144**. 147/2004;) Dean & Chapter of Exeter Cathedral (**frontispiece**. ED109; **27**. D&C6010/15/3; **39**. 7065/8; **40**. 4536/2/2; **91**. 6010/15/6; **92**. 6004/13/34; **110**. 6010/15/3; **141, 145, 148, 151** & **156**. 7065/7; **150**. 6007/20/23; **161**. 6010/15/8; **167**. P&D06460; **180**. D&C6010/15/1; **191**. 7065/8; **195**. D&C3530, f59–60); London Metropolitan Archives (**7**. CLC/B/227/MS09803); Devon Archives & Local Studies Service (**8**. 62/2/3; **11**. p&d06938; **28–9** & **86**. 6631M; **41, 44–5**. no reference numbers; **49**. Kevin White Collection, Vol. 1; **55**. p&d06457; **59**. p&d09981; **74**. p&d48202; **76**. 54/13/1/9; **95**. p&d43665; **108**. p&d06455; **115**. p&d07283; **120** & **122**. FOR/B/6/1/326; **123–4**. Edward Pocknell Collection of Exeter & Devon Photographs; **125**. no reference; **134**. p&d06912; **135**. p&d07107; **136**. D2/363; **137**. Z19/2/4; **138**. ECA/City Map Book; **143**. 68/28; **149**, SC1008; **152**. FOR/B/6/1/39; **168, 183, 193** & **204**. 69/1; **190**. ECA/Book 56; **198**. Kevin White Collection, Vol. 5; **199**. 7065/8; **208**. ECA/ED/M/933); Trustees of the British Museum (**9.** & **158**. D,2.2966; **181**. D,2.2958); Private Collectors (**10, 34–7, 42, 48, 52, 56–8, 65–7, 79, 82, 85, 87–90, 94, 105, 107, 111, 116, 118, 126–9, 131, 139, 142, 146, 147, 153–4, 155, 157, 159, 162, 164, 171, 173, 174, 186, 188, 189, 196, 210, 211, 212**); Historic England (**22**. EAW005854; **160**. EPW024105; **178**. OWS01_17_109); Tony Collings (**30**.); Trustees of the Devon & Exeter Institution (**38, 71, 175** & **185**. Stone Scrapbook, Volume 15; **133**. SC899; Exeter City Council (**43, 54, 68, 70, 75, 77, 140, 187, 207**); King's College, Cambridge (**46–7** & **203**. KCE-882-21); Express & Echo (**50, 93, 96–7** & **194**: issues 3 December 1969, 2 September 1941, 29 July 1963 & undated); John Thorp (**62**.); Derek Portman (**69** & **72**.); The Walgreens Boots Alliance Archive (**98**. WBA-BT-16-8-43-9 Exeter); The Royal Bank of Scotland Group plc (**106**. D3739; **109, 114** & **121**. D4008); Library of Congress (**122**. Lot 13415 no. 385); Yale Center for British Art (**132**. B1977.14.1490 (23)); Royal Institute of British Architects (**163**. 37849); Stuart Blaylock (**166, 169–70**); Andrew Brownsword Hotels (**172**.); Richard Parker (**207**.); Buttress (**209**.)

Photographs copyright Todd Gray (**frontispiece, opp. title page, 1–8, 11–21, 23–9, 31–3, 37–42, 44–5, 48–53, 55–61, 63–7, 71, 73–4, 76, 78–84, 86, 90–7, 99–105, 100–108, 110–113, 115–116, 118–19, 121, 123–5, 127–8, 131, 133–9, 141, 143, 145–8, 150–3, 156, 159, 161, 165–8, 175–7, 179–80, 182–4, 187–93, 195, 197–205, 208, 210**.), John Thorp (**62**.), Stuart Blaylock (**169–70**). Sources of other images comprise **12**, William Cotton, *An Elizabethan Guild of the City of Exeter* (Exeter, 1873), 44; **18–20**, Thomas H. Mawson, *Exeter of the Future* (1914), opp. 25, 27 & 29; **21, 23–4**, Thomas Sharp, *Exeter Phoenix* (Exeter, 1946), 42, opp. 98, foll. 94; Somerset Heritage Centre: **26**. DD/HI/CC478; **100–103** & **112–113**; DD/HI/CC483; **51, 81, 104**, James Crocker, *Sketches of Old Exeter* (Exeter, 1886), plates 23, 1 & 6; **205**. Benjamin Donn's map of Exeter; **130**. *Archaeologia* Vol. VI (1782), plate 1.

212. Murch's Cathedral Restaurant and Cafe, c.1900, later Tinley's Cafe.